FIXING ACCESS ANNOYANCES™

FIXING ACCESS ANNOYANCES ™

How to Fix the Most Annoying Things
About Your Favorite Database

Phil Mitchell and Evan Callahan

Beijing · Cambridge · Farnham · Köln · Paris · Sebastopol · Taipei · Tokyo

Fixing Access Annoyances™
How to Fix the Most Annoying Things About Your Favorite Database

by Phil Mitchell and Evan Callahan

Published by O'Reilly Media, Inc., 1005 Gravenstein Highway North, Sebastopol, CA 95472.

O'Reilly books may be purchased for educational, business, or sales promotional use. Online editions are also available for most titles (*safari.oreilly.com*). For more information, contact our corporate/institutional sales department: 800-998-9938 or *corporate@oreilly.com*.

Print History:

February 2006:   First Edition.

Editors: Michael Oliver-Goodwin and Robert Luhn

Production Editor: Genevieve d'Entremont

Copyeditor: Rachel Wheeler

Proofreader: Jeffrey Liggett

Indexer: Julie Hawks

Interior Designer: David Futato

Illustrators: Robert Romano, Jessamyn Read, and Lesley Borash

0-596-00852-X

[C]

◆ ◆ ◆

Dedicated to all those working toward an
ecologically sustainable and just future.

◆ ◆ ◆

Contents

5. FORMS 185

7. EXPRESSIONS, MACROS, CODE MODULES, AND CUSTOM CONTROLS — 277

Introduction

> "I have been at this for two months already. So far nothing seems to work."
>
> —*Seen in an Access newsgroup*

The first time I used Access, I tore my hair out. I'd volunteered to help one of my favorite nonprofits (*http://www.earthdance.net*) fix their database, figuring that it would be a piece of cake for a "seasoned" pro like me. Instead, it was a nightmare. Every time I tried something that I knew *should* work, it didn't *quite* work.

Since that first wrestling bout, I've used Access many times in my job as a software developer. Once you know its pathways and tricks, it's almost indispensable—but it's as frustrating as it is useful. In fact, at one point when I was talking to O'Reilly Executive Editor Robert Luhn about doing such a book, he asked if Access had enough "annoyances." I shot back, "How many volumes did you have in mind?"

Access is a goulash of pitfalls and idiosyncrasies. Sometimes its user interface seems well designed and easy to use, and sometimes it seems to be a maze of narrow, twisty paths that dead-end. Some things in Access "just work," while others require a secret handshake. (Don't get me started on the Help system.)

For this book, I have been really fortunate to collaborate with Microsoft veteran Evan Callahan, who's been working with Access since Version 1.0. We've drawn on our own experience as developers and teachers, and we've scoured newsgroups, user groups, and online communities to identify the Access features, practices, and glitches that cause the most confusion, exasperation, and desperate calls to that Access guy your cousin Sharlene knows.

This book covers a wide range of annoyances, some so basic that even new Microsoft Office users will appreciate them, and some so advanced that only hard-core Access programmers will be able to follow the code. So before we start, let's talk about how you can get the most out of this book.

For openers, check out the Glossary at the back of the book. As you work your way through the various chapters, if you encounter a term or a concept that confuses you, check the Glossary. Hopefully you'll find a definition that helps.

For an overview of fundamental Access operations, see our cleverly titled "Chapter 0," *Access Basics*. For the inside scoop from Microsoft, see the section entitled "MSKB 123456" on how to mine the company's Knowledge Base articles. Finally, if you need more technical reference material (such as a list of Visual Basic functions or macro actions), check the Appendix at the back of the book.

How to Use This Book

This book starts out with general annoyances, and then targets specific areas such as queries and reports. Each chapter is organized (more or less) with simpler annoyances toward the front and more advanced material toward the back. If you open to one of the chapter-closers and find yourself neck-deep in complicated code, don't panic; the easy stuff is just a few pages toward the front. Also, we've tried to include enough background so that newbies can fix things they didn't even know were broken. If you're still working your way up the Access learning curve, there's a lot you can learn here.

There are two different kinds of annoyances in Access. One kind, such as those listed in "Errors with Imported Data" in Chapter 3, pops up and hits you over the head. You'll come to this book looking for help with these issues, because you can't get the @#$@%# features to work at all. The other kind of annoyance has to do with making Access work better (rather than just work at all). For example, you can use Access for months and never think of changing the default option that leaves Name AutoCorrect turned on (see "Access's Bad Defaults" in Chapter 1). Maybe no one ever told you that this is a hidden bomb that can cause database corruption and poor performance. When you start browsing through this book, pay special attention to the topics that offer preventive medicine (for instance, "Keeping Access Running Smoothly" in Chapter 2).

> **NOTE**
>
> *Don't worry about typing in the long Visual Basic Applications (VBA) code samples you'll find in this book. They're available for download at http:// www.oreilly.com/catalog/accessannoy/index.html.*

Access Versions

Most of the material in this book is valid for most versions of Access, but when we need to be specific about commands or options, we usually refer to Access 2002 and 2003. We'll let you know if something is substantially different in Access 2000. We don't cover versions prior to Access 2000, but here and there we may drop hints for dealing with Access 97 hassles.

MSKB 123456

Throughout this book you'll see references that look like this: MSKB 209132. This is our shorthand for referring to Microsoft Knowledge Base articles by ID number. The main Knowledge Base is found at *http://support. microsoft.com/default.aspx?pr=kbhowto*, but to look up an article by its number you'll want to browse to Microsoft's advanced search page (*http:// support.microsoft.com/search/?adv=1*) and set the Search Type drop-down menu to Article ID. In the For box above the Search Type drop-down menu, type in the number and hit Enter. You can also just do a plain search on the ID number, but you may have to wade through multiple hits.

If you're using a browser that supports keyword substitution in URLs (such as Mozilla or Firefox), bookmark *http://support.microsoft.com/default. aspx?kbid=%s* and set the keyword to "mskb". Then you'll be able to jump directly to any Knowledge Base article by entering "mskb" followed by the article ID in the browser's address box. (The browser substitutes the ID for the *%s* in the bookmark.) If, for some incomprehensible reason, you're still using Internet Explorer, there's a software patch that lets it do the same thing. See "A Shorter Path to Microsoft's Knowledge" in Steve Bass's *PC Annoyances*, Second Edition (O'Reilly) for details, and download PowerToys for Windows XP from *http://www.oreilly.com/catalog/pcannoy2/ index.html*.

There's a wealth of useful information in the Knowledge Base, but the search interface has some maddening blind spots. If you're getting no hits on a specific phrase (and you really, truly spelled it correctly), chances are you set your search to use "The exact phrase entered." That may seem like a reasonable option, but it doesn't work very well. Instead, select "All of the words entered," and you should get the hits you're looking for. (Incidentally, Google crawls the Knowledge Base, so you can bypass Microsoft's search interface entirely by doing an advanced Google search and limiting your results to the *support.microsoft.com* domain.)

Most of the Knowledge Base's search interface is self-explanatory, but there are a couple of places where you need to be careful. First, you'll probably want to click the "Specify a product or version" link to limit your search to materials related to Access. We recommend searching for information on *all* versions of Access—you'll miss too many useful articles if you limit your search to a specific version. To specify all versions of Access, go to the advanced search page noted above, pop open the Search Product drop-down, and select "More Products." Scroll down and click the "Office Access" item that has no version number.

The "Show results for" drop-down on the advanced search page is just as confusing. By default it's set to "This product only," which means that it ignores articles that aren't associated with the specific product you've selected (i.e., Access). This is usually fine, but if you're not getting any hits you should try "This product first," which will scour the whole Knowledge Base and use your product preference to weight hits accordingly.

Conventions Used in This Book

The following typographic conventions are used in this book:

- *Italic* is used for filenames, pathnames, URLs, email addresses, new terms where they are defined, and emphasis.

- Constant width is used for code excerpts, commands, method names, and function names.

- **Constant width bold** is used for items that should be typed verbatim by the user.

- ***Constant width italic*** is used for text that should be replaced with user-supplied values.

- Menu sequences are separated by arrows, such as Data→List→Create List. Tabs, radio buttons, checkboxes, and the like are identified by name, such as "click the Options tab and check the 'Always show full menus' box."

Using Code Examples

This book is here to help you get your job done. In general, you may use the code in this book in your programs and documentation. You do not need to contact us for permission unless you're reproducing a significant portion of the code. For example, writing a program that uses several chunks of code from this book does not require permission. Selling or distributing a CD-ROM of examples from O'Reilly books *does* require permission. Answering a question by citing this book and quoting example code does not require permission. Incorporating a significant amount of example code from this book into your product's documentation *does* require permission.

We appreciate, but do not require, attribution. An attribution usually includes the title, author, publisher, and ISBN. For example: "*Fixing Access Annoyances* by Phil Mitchell and Evan Callahan. Copyright 2006 O'Reilly Media, Inc., 0-596-00852-X."

If you feel your use of code examples falls outside fair use or the permission given here, feel free to contact us at *permissions@oreilly.com*.

I Did Exactly What You Said, and It Still Doesn't Work!

This book is full of advice, and all of it has been tested. So how come some fix doesn't work for you? Well...there *could* be something about your setup or Access version that's causing problems. It's even possible that one of our pinpoint instructions somehow eluded your unflinching eye. Or maybe, just maybe, we screwed up. In any case, let us know! We want to hear from you. Send email to *annoyances@oreilly.com*.

Safari® Enabled

When you see a Safari® Enabled icon on the cover of your favorite technology book, that means it's available online through the O'Reilly Network Safari Bookshelf.

Safari offers a solution that's better than e-books: it's a virtual library that lets you easily search thousands of top tech books, cut and paste code samples, download chapters, and find quick answers when you need the most accurate, current information. Try it for free at *http://safari.oreilly.com*.

Acknowledgments

First, we'd like to acknowledge the Access MVPs, and everyone who contributes to Access newsgroups; this is where so many of the "gotchas" in Access are brought to light, and these discussions were a great source of ideas for this book. Access MVP Lynn Trapp made an exceptional contribution to the early chapters of this book, and MVP Joan Wild kindly commented on an early outline. The Microsoft Support professionals who write the articles in the Knowledge Base also deserve our thanks for the expertise they share with the Access community.

Thanks to "Uncle Bob" (a.k.a. Robert Luhn, Executive Editor at O'Reilly), specifically for his prank phone calls pretending to be a foreign speaker with little English seeking Access help, and, in general, for shepherding this project through its highs and lows with unflappability.

Thanks also to Michael Oliver-Goodwin, editor extraordinaire, for his steamrolling patience and meticulous desire to make the book better. He didn't even lose his cool when we got cranky....

O'Reilly Would Like to Hear from You

Please address comments and questions concerning this book to the publisher:

O'Reilly Media, Inc.
1005 Gravenstein Highway North
Sebastopol, CA 95472
(800) 998-9938 (in the United States or Canada)
(707) 829-0515 (international or local)
(707) 829-0104 (fax)

There is a web page for this book, where you'll find links to the code and utilities mentioned in the book. You'll also find errata and additional information. You can access this page via:

http://annoyances.oreilly.com

To comment or ask technical questions about this book, send email to:

annoyances@oreilly.com

For more information about books, conferences, Resource Centers, and the O'Reilly Network, go to:

http://www.oreilly.com

Access Basics

If you're already an Access ace, you can skip this chapter and move right into the meat of the book. But if you're still clawing your way up the learning curve, here's a brief overview of some basic Access concepts and procedures.

The Database Window

When you start Access and create a new database (File→New), you'll find yourself in the *Database window*. This is home base when working in Access. A list of the object types in your database appears on the left side of the window. You can click an object name to show objects of that type (of course, there won't be any until you create some). The key types of objects are:

Tables

Tables are where data gets stored. A table in Access is roughly analogous to a table in Word or a worksheet in Excel—column headings (a.k.a. *fields*) and rows (a.k.a. *records*) are the main structural elements. The difference is that in a database, you must define these structures much more precisely. This is the foundation on which everything else rests. (See "Table Design 101" in Chapter 3 for more info.)

Queries

Queries which are based on Structured Query Language (SQL) typically retrieve selected data from tables. They can also be used to modify or delete existing data, add new data, and create new tables. Of course, you could view all of your data just by looking at the table, but the power of a database is that it lets you create alternate views of your data to answer specific questions. For example, your boss may say, "I need a list of all our products with sales over $10,000 per month that come from a single supplier." You'd go nuts trying to extract this information by looking at the raw data in a table, but you can easily find it with a query. (See "Query Basics" in Chapter 4 for more information.)

Forms

As a general rule, you don't want users entering data directly into tables; there's too much potential for error and data damage. The safest and easiest way for users to enter data is via forms. You can use forms to provide clear, user-friendly data entry templates, and with a bit of Visual Basic (VB) code you can add an additional layer of error-checking to prevent erroneous or improperly formatted entries. Forms are also a useful way to browse a database and look up information. If you've ever filled out a web form, you're already familiar with the basic concept behind Access forms: text boxes, checkboxes, and other widgets provide ways for users to input data in a structured way. Access has a Form Wizard that makes it easy to create a basic form for any table. (For more on forms, see Chapter 5.)

Reports

Reports, which are actually based on queries, let you present, summarize, and print your data in various elegant ways. The key to a good report is basing it on a query that selects all the data the report needs from the underlying tables. Access's Report Wizard makes it easy to group, order, and summarize the data from the query. (We provide lots more information on reports in Chapter 6.)

Pages

Data Access Pages use Microsoft technology designed to let users view *and* edit Access data on the Web. Unfortunately, the technology doesn't work very well. At best, the feature is useful for intranets, but we recommend you look into other solutions first. (For more information, see "Putting Data on the Web" in Chapter 3.)

Macros

Much like macros in Word and Excel, Access macros can be used to automate certain tasks. For example, if you import the same worksheet data into a database every week, you can set up a macro that does the job with the click of a button. Unlike Word or Excel macros, however, you *cannot* create Access macros by recording a series of keystrokes and button clicks. Instead, you must construct a macro explicitly from a list of predefined actions, using the Macro Designer.

Modules

One of the most powerful aspects of Access is that you can write Visual Basic code to do everything you can do with macros, plus a whole lot more. Modules are where you store that Visual Basic code. If you're not a programmer, don't worry—you can accomplish a lot in Access without writing any code. But as you become more familiar with Access, you'll find that even a line or two of VB code can make life a lot easier.

We've provided helpful code samples in various chapters, along with an overview titled "How to Create an Event Procedure" that you'll find later in this chapter.

Wizards

If there's one secret to becoming instantly productive with Access, it's the wizards. These step-by-step dialog boxes walk you through many key tasks. Even advanced developers use them, simply because it saves time; the Form, Report, and Mailing Label Wizards are especially useful.

Here's a list of the main wizards. Unless otherwise noted, these wizards can be activated in the Database window by first selecting the specific type of object you want to create and then clicking the New button:

Form Wizard

> This wizard creates a basic, no-frills data entry form for any table. It's very useful. Power users will probably want to open the resulting form in Design View and tweak it (see Chapter 5), but the wizard gives you a good starting point.

Control wizards

> Forms, queries, and reports are based on *controls*—text boxes, labels, and so on. Access provides several wizards that make it easy to customize these controls and apply the kinds of tweaks that were once the preserve of power users. Here's where you can make a big improvement in the usability of your forms with surprisingly little effort (see "Activating the Wizards" in Chapter 5).

> For example, instead of using a text box in a form where users must enter country names, you could deploy the Combo Box Wizard to create a combo box control, providing a drop-down menu that lets users pick standardized country names from a list stored in a table. This prevents spelling errors and ensures that every user enters the same version of each name. Some other controls that have useful wizards include:

Command buttons

> The wizard makes it easy to put a button on your form that can trigger various actions, such as opening another form, running a macro, or saving the current record.

List boxes

> List boxes are similar to combo boxes, but instead of seeing a drop-down menu, users see a list of all the items at once.

Option groups

> Option groups present a fixed choice ("Yes," "No," "Maybe") as a set of mutually exclusive radio buttons.

Report Wizard

This wizard creates a basic, no-frills report based on a table or query. It's a good starting point, but you'll definitely need to go in afterwards and tweak the design. (For details, see Chapter 6.) Since reports are usually based on queries, designing a good report means building the right query first—many headaches in report design are due to so-so queries. Chapter 4 will put you on the path to understanding how to build the query you need.

Mailing Label Wizard

The Mailing Label Wizard has built-in knowledge of the sizes and specifications of many commercial labels and is an indispensable tool for creating mailing labels. Though there are some gotchas (see "Mailing Labels" in Chapter 6), it makes creating labels pretty easy. You can even create custom specifications for odd-sized labels. Since mailing labels are technically a kind of report, you invoke the Mailing Label Wizard from the New Report dialog (click Insert→Report from the Database window).

Chart Wizard

Building an Access chart from scratch can be painful, because there's no integrated graphical editor; every time you make a change, you must switch views to see the results. Though it's pretty basic, the Chart Wizard will at least get you started. For solutions to common problems, see "Charts and Graphs" in Chapter 6.

Table Wizard

This wizard gives you some sample prefab tables that you can customize. It's worth a look, but it's not especially useful. In most cases you'll want to build tables by hand. (See Chapter 3 for tips on designing your tables.)

Query wizards

The Simple Query Wizard enables you to build (what else?) a very simple query. This may be useful for absolute beginners, but it won't help much with most real-life queries. The other query wizards are more useful, but mainly for very specialized needs, such as crosstabs and duplicates queries. You'll need to design most queries yourself (see Chapter 4).

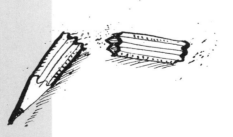

Design View and User Views

Wizards only take you so far. If you spend much time developing Access databases, most of the time you'll probably be working in *Design View*. Every type of object (table, query, report, and so on) has its own Design View. For example, in Table Design View you can define field names and determine what type of data is allowed to go into each field. In form and report Design Views, you'll tweak the behavior and layout of your controls. Queries have two different Design Views: the Query Builder provides a graphical user interface, while the SQL View lets you write queries in the SQL programming language. You'll find much more information about these different views in subsequent chapters.

Any view that *isn't* a Design View is a *user view*: user views show your objects as they will appear to users who are entering or viewing data. (Neither macros nor modules have user views—they're just code that works behind the scenes.) Table 0-1 lists the user views associated with some of the objects you'll be working with.

Table 0-1. Main user views

Object	Most common user views
Table	Datasheet
Query	Datasheet
Form	Single, Continuous, Datasheet
Report	Print Preview, Layout Preview

Here's an overview of the main user views:

Datasheet View

When you look directly at the data in a table, Access presents it in Datasheet View, a column and row layout that looks a lot like an Excel worksheet. The columns are the fields, and each row is a record. By default, you get the same view when you look at the results of a query, since a query is basically a recipe for creating a "virtual" (temporary) table (see "Query Basics" in Chapter 4). A form can also be presented in Datasheet View—this is mostly useful for certain kinds of subforms (i.e., forms nested inside other forms). See Chapter 5 for more on subforms.

Single Form View

When you want your form to present one record at a time, use Single Form View; it's the default.

Continuous Forms View

> When you want users to view a full page of records at the same time (this is sort of like looking at search engine results on the Web; you wouldn't want them presented one hit at a time), use either this view or Datasheet View. Continuous Forms View works best when each record is relatively small, so that many records can fit on one page. To turn it on in Design View, set Default View on the Format tab in the form's properties sheet to "Continuous Forms."

Print Preview and Layout Preview

> To see a report as it will appear in print, use Print Preview. For long reports, this may take some time to view. You can view the layout of a sample of records by using Layout Preview instead.

Setting Properties

In many places throughout this book, we'll tell you to look at, or set, this or that *property* of an object. Nearly all Access objects (tables, fields, queries, joins, forms, reports, sections, controls, and pages) have properties that define the way they look and work. For example, a form's Caption property determines the text that appears in the titlebar of that form's window.

In general, you will enter and change property settings in the object's properties sheet. However, the properties sheet isn't always found in the same way, and sometimes it's hard to find, period. Here are the steps for setting a property:

1. Open a table, query, form, or report in Design View.

2. Open the properties sheet for the object (for some of these objects, you can just press F4):

   Table

   > Click View→Properties.

   Query

   > Click the background of the upper pane of the query window, then click View→Properties.

   Table field

   > Click on the field; its properties sheet will appear in the bottom half of the window.

   Query field

   > Click the field in the query grid and click View→Properties.

   Query join

   > Double-click the join line between field lists.

Form or report

Double-click the form or report selector box at the top-left intersection of the rulers.

Control or section

Double-click the control or section bar.

Data Access Page

Open the page in Design View, select View→Properties, and then select Edit→Select Page.

3. If the properties sheet organizes properties on tabs, click the tab that contains the property you want, or click the All tab to see all the properties in a single, scrollable list (see Figure 0-1).

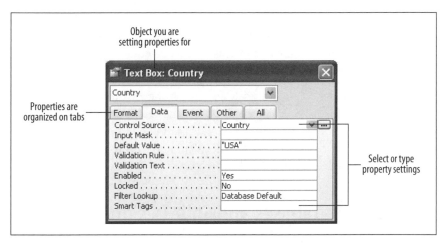

Figure 0-1. The properties sheet for a text box control.

4. Click the properties field you want to change and type in a setting. If there's a drop-down arrow, click it to select a property setting from the list. If a Build (...) button appears, click it to display an appropriate builder for the property.

Bound Versus Unbound Objects

You hear Access programmers make this distinction all the time, because it's fundamental to the way forms and controls work. An object is *bound* when it's linked directly to a data source (a table, say) and *unbound* when it isn't. The simplest example is a text box control on a form. Let's say you have a customers data entry form, with a text box where the user can type in the company name. The text box's Control Source property (on the Data tab of its properties sheet) is set to the companyName field in the customers table. This ensures that when data is typed into the text box and saved, it goes directly into that field on that table; the text box is *bound* to that field.

On the other hand, you might have a data display form with two text boxes in which users type start and end dates, so the form will select and display a set of orders matching that date range. (Essentially, the text boxes allow the user to enter query parameters.) The Control Source properties of the two text boxes are blank, because the dates that get entered into them won't be stored permanently in the database; they are simply used to limit the range of the query. These text boxes are *unbound*.

There's actually a third case, too. Sometimes a text box has its Control Source property set to an expression—for instance, the total value of a customer's orders. This is called a *calculated* field, and it is neither bound nor unbound. Because the value of this field is calculated, you can't edit it or save it into the database. It's for display only.

In addition to controls, a form itself can be bound or unbound. A form is *bound* when its Record Source property (on the Data tab) is set to a table or query. If its Record Source is left blank, it is *unbound*. Generally, bound forms are used to display bound and calculated controls, and unbound forms are used to display unbound controls.

Multi-User Databases and Split Design

A *single-user database* lives on a single PC and is used by only one person at a time. This might be a personal contacts database, or an orders database that's used by several people who share the same computer. Obviously, sharing a single PC can be inconvenient, and that's why you can also use Access to design and manage multi-user databases.

A *multi-user database* can be accessed over a network by multiple users, from multiple PCs, at the same time. Access databases are often deployed this way, but it's important to do it correctly. Deploying Access across a network increases the risk of database corruption (see "That Darn Corruption" in Chapter 1), but if you do it right, the risk is manageable and the gain is substantial.

To create a multi-user database, it's standard to adopt a *split* design. *Splitting* involves separating your database into two different Access database (MDB) files: a backend that contains only your data (i.e., your tables) and a frontend that contains all of your user interface paraphernalia (queries, forms, reports, and so on). This is easier to do than it sounds, because Access has a Database Splitter tool that makes it easy to split an MDB file into a backend and a frontend: it moves your tables into the backend and creates links to them from the frontend.

Once you've split your database, it's important to deploy it correctly. Because all users will share a single copy of the backend, it must be put in a network-accessible location—ideally, on a server. That way, all users can access the same data at all times. On the other hand, every user gets her own copy of the frontend, installed on her own PC.

It's a bad idea to attempt to use a split design over a wide area network (WAN) or the Internet; the reliability of the network connection is simply not good enough to prevent database corruption. One option is replication, which enables each user to have his own copy of the database, which is then synchronized periodically with the master copy. (See the sidebar "What Is Replication?" in Chapter 2 for more information.) However, we recommend against replication, because it's very difficult to implement correctly. An option we *do* recommend is to web-enable your database. (See "Putting Data on the Web" in Chapter 3 for a full discussion.)

How to Create an Event Procedure

We've already mentioned using the properties sheet to define the way controls look or work. That's just the beginning. Access has thousands of places where one or two lines of code added to an "event procedure" can fix a problem or dramatically improve an application. Throughout this book, we'll say things like: "Add this line of code to the Before Update event," or "Use the Click event of the command button to make this happen." Here's how it works.

At certain points in the program flow (when the user enters data, for instance, or runs a query), Access checks to see whether a developer has added any custom code. For example, every time a report is opened, Access sees if any code has been added to that report's Open event. If code *has* been added, Access runs it before it opens the report. This is powerful!

To cite a very simple example, you can automatically maximize a report window (see "Report Preview Is Too Small" in Chapter 6 for the full story) by dropping a single line of code in the report's Open event, such as:

```
DoCmd.Maximize
```

Here's how:

1. Open the report in Design View, and then open its properties sheet (View→Properties).

2. On the Event tab (see Figure 0-2), click in the On Open field, and then click the Build (...) button that appears. If you get a Choose Builder dialog, select "Code Builder" and then click OK. The Visual Basic Editor will open and create the appropriate empty event procedure for you. The empty procedure will look something like this:

```
Private Sub Report_Open(Cancel As Integer)

End Sub
```

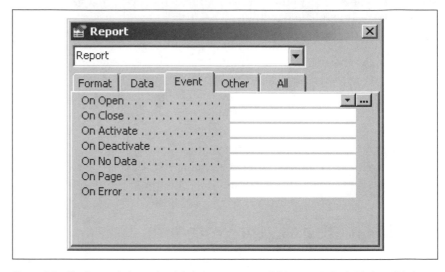

Figure 0-2. The Event tab shows the global report events—click in a particular field, then click the Build (...) button on the right to create an event procedure.

3. The procedure starts executing at the top and continues line-by-line until it gets to the bottom. Simply add your code on the blank line in between the top and bottom lines, so it looks like this:

```
Private Sub Report_Open(Cancel As Integer)
    DoCmd.Maximize
End Sub
```

Indentation and blank lines have no effect on what your code does, but they do help to make code more readable.

That's all there is to it. Of course, the more you learn Visual Basic, the better you'll be able to take advantage of these event hooks. See the Appendix for a list of all Access events organized by category, and see "Tame the Visual Basic Editor" in Chapter 7 for help on using the VB Editor.

How to Add Code to Your Application

Adding a few lines of code to an event procedure on a properties sheet is easy. But suppose you want to add a *lot* of code?

There are numerous annoyances in this book where we say something like, "Fortunately you won't have to write this code yourself, because so-and-so has already written it. And here it is." But in order to take advantage of that free code, you must know how to add it to your application, and then how to run it.

The first part—adding the code—is easy, and that's what we'll cover here. The second part—running it—depends on the code. In some cases, you can run it immediately simply by typing the name of the new procedure in Visual Basic's Immediate window and pressing Enter; in others, you'll need to add at least a line or two of additional code yourself—often in an event procedure.

For now, let's talk about adding code to your database. For example, in Chapter 7 (see "Use Excel Functions") we show you how to call functions that are available only in Excel. Suppose you decide that the xlCeiling function is just what you need for your query. Here's what you'd do:

1. **Create a new model.** In the Database window, select Insert→Module. The Visual Basic Editor opens and puts the cursor into the new module.

2. **Add the code.** Copy the code in question (such as one of the samples we list on the *Fixing Access Annoyances* page at *http://www.oreilly.com/catalog/accessannoy/index.html*) and paste it into the new module. If you prefer, you can even type it in, but if you do this you are more likely to introduce typos.

3. **Save the module.** Ctrl-S saves the new module and lets you give it a name; something like **basWhatever** is good. ("bas" is the standard prefix for code modules—it stands for "basic," as in Visual Basic; **Whatever** is the memorable name you supply.)

That's all there is to it. Now you can use the xlCeiling function in expressions, just like any other Visual Basic function. For example, suppose your query showed grade averages, and you wanted to round them using the Excel CEILING function with a "significance" of 5. In the properties sheet of the Field line, instead of avgGrade, you could now write xlCeiling([avgGrade], 5).

DAO Versus ADO

OK, you're ready to write some VB code. Prior to Access 2000, there was a single code library for working with data via recordsets, bookmarks, and so forth: the Data Access Objects (DAO) library. With Access 2000, however, Microsoft introduced a new code library: ActiveX Data Objects (ADO). Whereas DAO was designed specifically for Access's Jet database engine—and may actually offer some performance advantages with data in

MDB files—ADO is intended to work with a wider variety of data sources, including any Object Linking and Embedding (OLE) DB sources.

Does this mean that you can now forget about DAO and just work with ADO? Unfortunately, no. For example, the default recordsets that Access uses for bound forms are DAO objects. If you want to work with them, you must use DAO. In general, when you're working strictly inside MDB files (as opposed to using Access as a frontend to another Database Management System [DBMS], such as SQL Server), you may want to use DAO exclusively to avoid confusion. If you need to use a mix of DAO and ADO code, remember to be explicit about which library you are using. When you declare objects such as recordsets or connections, you must be sure to specify which type you mean, like this:

```
Dim rst1 As DAO.Recordset
Dim rst2 As ADODB.Recordset
```

Whichever library or libraries you use, make sure your database has references to them. In the VB Editor, click Tools→References and make sure Microsoft DAO Object Library and/or Microsoft ActiveX Data Objects Library are checked—use the latest versions. If you plan to use DAO or ADO only, uncheck the reference to the library you won't use to avoid confusion. Note that new databases created in Access 2003 include references to both libraries, while those created in Access 2002 and 2000 include only an ADO reference.

General Annoyances

It's fitting to start this book with a chapter on "General" Access annoyances, since no other military rank (Private? Major?) suggests how aggravating—or impressive—Access can be. Truly, Access is the supreme commander of all annoyances. And yet, when it works, it rules.

General annoyances aren't just annoyances we couldn't fit in anywhere else. They're global annoyances, such as the ridiculously bad default settings that affect everything you do in Access, mysterious #Name? errors that can crop up almost anywhere (in queries, forms, reports, and so on), and data corruption that can turn your database into digital mush. In this chapter we'll show you how to make the most of Access's user interface, demystify its obscure error messages, and take preventive measures against its worst booby traps.

CUSTOMIZING ACCESS

Access's Bad Defaults

THE ANNOYANCE: My database was running like a dog until I found out that Name AutoCorrect was turned on by default—and it's a known cause of corruption, too! Are there any other disasters hiding in Access's default settings?

THE FIX: You bet. Access has hundreds of default settings, and they range from quite sensible to pretty troublesome. Let's take a look at some of the worst offenders, along with some of our favorite tweaks. You can set the global defaults by clicking Tools→Options; the specific defaults that follow can be set inside individual forms or reports.

Global Defaults

Changing these global defaults will vastly improve Access's performance:

Turn off Name AutoCorrect.
> When you change the name of a table (and many other things), Access is set by default to look for all the references to that table name and update them automatically. Although this can be convenient, it also causes a real performance hit. Worse yet, the feature has been known to cause database corruption. Just say no: select Tools→Options, click the General tab, uncheck the "Track name AutoCorrect info" box, and you're good to go (see Figure 1-1).

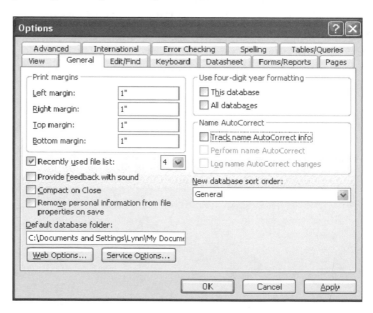

Figure 1-1. Turn off Name AutoCorrect by unchecking the "Track name AutoCorrect info" box.

> **NOTE**
>
> *Don't check the "Compact on Close" box. In this case, the (unchecked) default is right. It may sound like a good idea to have Access automatically compact your database every time you close it, but there's just one little problem: this feature can cause database corruption. Leave it unchecked.*

Turn off spelling AutoCorrect.

You type in ACN (for the Association of Computing Nerds), and Access silently changes it to CAN, thinking it's correcting your typing. To avoid unexpected alterations to your data, turn off Office's spelling AutoCorrect. You can do this easily using Tools→AutoCorrect Options; see "Access Changes My Data," later in this chapter, for the details.

Reject AutoJoin.

A *join* is a temporary merging of two tables into a single virtual table. With AutoJoin on, Access looks for fields with the same name and automatically adds joins for those fields in the Query Designer. Depending on how you name your fields, this may be helpful, or it may produce lots of joins you don't want. In any case, it's easy enough to add them by hand. Also, if you create relationships between your tables, Access will add joins for them in the Query Designer automatically. So...turn off this automatic feature. Choose Tools→Options, click the Tables/Queries tab, and uncheck the "Enable AutoJoin" box.

Refine record locking.

If you're the only person using your database, you can skip this tip. But if multiple users are accessing the same MDB file at the same time, some form of record locking is essential to keep users from overwriting each other's data. The choices are found by selecting Tools→Options, clicking the Advanced tab, and looking in the "Default record locking" section. Access defaults to no locks, which means that records don't get locked until the moment they're saved. This can leave one user unable to save her edits if another user saves his changes first. A better choice is "Edited record," which locks the record at the moment it's opened for editing; multiple users are unable to edit the same record at the same time. Make sure you leave the "Open databases using record-level locking" box checked. Otherwise, page-level locking will be used, and users may be unnecessarily locked out of records that are *not* being edited by anyone. (In versions prior to Access 2000, you couldn't lock an individual record—you had to lock a 2-KB "page" containing the record in question, which meant locking neighboring records, too. Now that record-level locking is available, use it. It's a better choice.)

Stop unnecessary indexing.

Indexing is a technique Access uses to make search (and sort) operations faster; it relies on maintaining a pre-sorted copy of your data. (For more information, see "Speed Up Slow Queries" in Chapter 4.) With AutoIndex on, Access automatically creates indexes for fields whose names match a stored list ("id," "code," and so on). However, most of these indexes aren't really necessary; they slow Access's update performance, and they may cause you to exceed Access's 32-indexes-per-table limit. Access automatically indexes the primary key and unique fields anyway, and any other indexes you need can be added by hand. Click

Tools→Options, click the Tables/Queries tab, and clear the list of field names in the "AutoIndex on Import/Create" box.

Clean up your taskbar.

Tired of having every single database object you open show up in your Windows Taskbar? Turn off this annoying option by choosing Tools→ Options, clicking the View tab, and unchecking the "Windows in Taskbar" box. Then multiple windows will be displayed as a drop-down list inside one single Taskbar item. (See "A Better Alt-Tab," later in this chapter, for alternatives.)

Specific Defaults

Here are some defaults you can set inside forms, reports, or tables to further improve performance:

Keep the Tab cycle inside one record.

By default, the Tab key moves the insertion point from field to field on a form; when it hits the end of the form, it moves on to the next record. This is great for expert data entry clerks, but confusing for inexperienced users. To change this behavior, open your form in Design View, open its properties sheet (View→Properties), select the Other tab, and set Cycle to "Current Record."

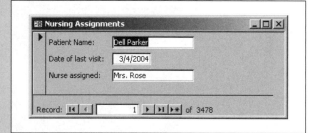

Figure 1-2. The record selector (bold black arrow) is not useful when your Form View shows only one record at a time.

Turn off record selectors.

Record selectors are the black arrows that Access puts to the left of a record, indicating that it's currently selected or being edited. They're useful in Continuous Forms or Datasheet View, where multiple records are displayed. However, if most of your forms display only a single record at a time (see Figure 1-2), you may want to turn these off. Open your form in Design View, open its properties sheet, go to the Format tab, and set Record Selectors to "No."

Disable design changes during data entry.

By default, design changes can be made to forms while they're open in Form View. This can be confusing to users, particularly if a properties sheet appears because it was left open in Design View. In most cases, you're better off restricting design changes to Design View. To do so, open your form in Design View, open its properties sheet (View→ Properties), select the Other tab, and set Allow Design Changes to "Design View Only."

Allow users to save form layouts.

By default, no matter how you resize or lay out form windows, Access will not save your settings. This is more than a tad annoying, so open your form in Design View, open its properties sheet (View→Properties) and on the Format tab set Auto Resize and Auto Center to "No." See "Save Custom Form Placement," later in this chapter, for more details on saving form layouts.

Prevent shrunken reports.

By default, Access shrinks every report to fit the whole page on the screen, giving most users a single, unreadable window. To change this behavior, open the report in Design View, open its properties sheet (View→Properties), click the Format tab, and set Auto Resize to "No."

Disable the Subdatasheet Name property.

If you have any one-to-many relationships in your database (e.g., customers-to-orders, where there is exactly one customer for each order but there can be many orders for a given customer). Access considerately adds subdatasheets to the tables on the "one" side of the relationship. (If "one-to-many" is an unfamiliar concept, see "Relationship Angst" in Chapter 3 for an explanation.) When you open your customers table in Datasheet View, you'll see a little plus sign next to each record; click to open the related records from the "many" side of the relationship.

This may sound helpful, but to provide this service Access must constantly check to see if these relationships exist, which drags down overall performance. To prevent this from happening, open your table in Design View, open its properties sheet (View→Properties), and set Subdatasheet Name to "[None]." (If you don't want to do this for every table, see "Defaults for Tables, Queries, and Datasheets," later in this chapter.) For tables where you *do* want a subdatasheet, it's perfectly fine to set the Subdatasheet Name property to the specific name of a related table; just don't set it to "Auto."

Default Values for Numeric Fields

Unlike all the other data types, which by default have no values (i.e., are null), Access automatically sets the Number data type to default to zero. This is dumb. Although zero can be a useful default value, it shouldn't be assigned automatically—that's what null is for. Unfortunately, there's no way to clear this setting globally. Whenever you use the Number data type you'll have to clear its Default Value property manually.

Alt-Tab Clutter

THE ANNOYANCE: I like to use Alt-Tab to switch between open applications, but when I use Access, every single database object drops its own icon into the Windows Taskbar, so Alt-Tabbing means swimming through Access objects. Whose idea was this? Is there no end to this clutter?!

THE FIX: I guess it seemed like a good idea at the time. Fortunately, there's a simple fix: in Access, select Tools→Options, click the View tab, and uncheck the "Windows in Taskbar" box. This will give you a clutter-free Alt-Tab experience. To flip through Access objects and databases within Access, press Ctrl-F6.

A Better Alt-Tab

THE ANNOYANCE: Personally, I don't mind Alt-Tabbing among Access objects—in fact, I kind of like it that Windows puts everything in the Taskbar. What peeves me is that it's hard to tell which Access object is which.

THE FIX: The Alt-Tab window does have a little text field at the bottom that lets you identify exactly what you want to switch to, but you're hardly alone in dreaming of a more perfect Alt-Tab. In fact, there's a veritable cottage industry in Alt-Tab replacements. Start with Microsoft's own (unsupported) Power Toys app, available at *http://www.microsoft.com/windowsxp/downloads/powertoys/xppowertoys.mspx*, which adds a page preview to Alt-Tab. (You can also just download the Alt-Tab replacement, *Taskswitch.exe*, from this page.)

There are also several inexpensive shareware programs that likewise add functionality to Alt-Tab, with all-at-once views, hotkeys, and more. Check out WinGlance (*http://www.download.com/3000-2340-10280681.html*) and Exposer for Windows (*http://www.onlinetoolsteam.com/WindowsExposer*), which go for about $7 each.

The Recently Used File List

THE ANNOYANCE: The File menu in Access lists the last four MDB files that I've opened. Can't it list more than four files?

THE FIX: It can. Go to Tools→Options, click the General tab, check the "Recently used file list" box, and select as many as nine from the drop-down menu.

Grayed-Out Menu Items

THE ANNOYANCE: This drives me crazy: I finally figure out which menu command I need to use, only to discover it's grayed out. There ought to be a law that menu items can't be disabled without having a tool tip that explains why. Aaargh!

THE FIX: Gray-outs typically occur because Access thinks a command isn't relevant to the task at hand. Sometimes Access is right: you can't paste if you haven't copied first. At other times, though, you may wonder what the heck it's thinking. For instance, why can't you File→Save As a whole database? Sometimes the quickest way to find a solution is to run a Google Groups search on the particular command. On the other hand, you might be running into a more general permissions or versioning problem.

Sometimes a slight change in context is all that's needed. Run through this list of possibilities first when things go gray:

- The command is not supported for this version of your database file. You may have to convert your MDB file to a more recent version.

- The command requires permissions that you don't have. Are you trying to modify the design of an object you don't have rights to?

- The database has been opened in read-only mode. Another user may have an exclusive lock on the database, or the MDB file itself may have its read-only flag set. Right-click the file in Windows Explorer and check its properties.

- The menu has been customized to disable the command. Check with your system administrator.

That said, let's take a look at some of the most commonly grayed-out commands, and what to do about them.

Import Spreadsheet Wizard: Data Type box

For reasons that are not entirely clear, Access won't allow data types to be specified for an imported spreadsheet. Instead, it prefers to guess the data types (see "Errors with Imported Data" in Chapter 3). One workaround is to save the worksheet as a tab- or comma-separated text file. The Import Text Wizard *does* allow data types to be specified on a field-by-field basis when you import a text file.

Import Spreadsheet Wizard: "In an Existing Table" option

If you want to import data into an existing Access table, the first row of your spreadsheet must have column headings that match the table fields exactly, and you must leave "First Row Contains Column Headings" checked.

Tools→Database Utilities: Linked Table Manager, Convert Database, and Upsizing Wizard

You must convert your MDB file to Access 2000 format or later to use these features.

New Record (*) Button on a Form, or Insert→New Record for a Table

There are several possible reasons why these features may be grayed out. You may not have permission to write to the table or modify the query, someone else may have opened the database, or you may have opened the database in read-only mode. If it's not a permissions problem, the form is probably based on a query that's not updatable (see the sidebar "Updatable Queries" in Chapter 4).

Tools→Database Utilities→Convert Database→To Access 2000 File Format

One of the Convert Database choices is always grayed out, because the file is already in that format. You can't convert a file to a format that it's already in. Since Access 2000 format is the default format for Access 2002 and 2003, that's the one that's usually grayed out.

Edit Relationships Dialog (Tools→Relationships): Enforce Referential Integrity

You may be trying to define relationships on linked tables—that is, tables that are stored not in the current MDB file, but in some remote data source. You must define the relationship in the database where the tables actually live. (New to relationships? See "Relationship Angst" in Chapter 3.)

Format→Conditional Formatting (Design View for a form)

Access lets you change the formatting of text boxes and combo boxes in a form based on conditions, just as Excel lets you apply conditional formatting to cells. For instance, you can tell Access to boldface the total revenue text box *if* the amount is greater than your target revenue. However, for some reason Access does not support conditional formatting for any other type of control, such as labels or list boxes. For these, you must write VB code to set the conditional formatting.

Query→Parameters

This is not available in SQL View; switch to Design View.

Tools→Database Utilities→Make MDE File or Make ADE File

You can only make an MDE or ADE file if your MDB file is compiled without errors *and* your version of Access matches the version of the MDB file that you're working with. For instance, if you're working with an Access 2000 file in Access 2002, you'll have to convert it to Access 2002 format before making an MDE file.

Change Owner Button in Tools→Security→User and Group Permissions

This button is usually grayed out when you try to change ownership of the database itself and you don't have permission to do so. Try logging into your secured Access database as a member with "administrative privileges."

Define Your Own Defaults for Forms, Reports, and Controls

THE ANNOYANCE: Access's built-in defaults are fine for setting up a quick-and-dirty table or form, but for anything serious I start customizing right away—I change the fonts, resize the text boxes, and so on. But going through the same steps over and over again is a drag. Isn't there some way to customize the defaults?

THE FIX: There is, but it's not obvious. Access lets you set defaults either on a per-form (or per-report) basis, or for an entire database. The following explanation focuses on creating reports, where custom defaults are especially useful, but it applies just as well to forms.

To set control defaults for a preexisting report, open it in Design View, select a control (let's say, Label) in the toolbox, and press F4 to bring up its default properties sheet. (See Figure 1-3.) Notice that "Default" shows up in the titlebar. Set the properties the way you want them. From now on, any labels you add to this report will have those same settings. Alternatively, if you've already created a label that you want to use as your default, just open the form in Design View, select the label, and then select Format→Set Control Defaults from the main menu. Some controls, such as text boxes, have default properties that can only be set here; for instance, Auto Label specifies whether text boxes have attached labels, and Add Colon lets you remove colons in labels.

To set defaults that will apply to every report you create, you must create a *report template*. Open a new report in Design View, and name it anything you want. (I think "Report_Template" has a nice ring to it.) Now change the desired properties and the properties of any controls that you care about. Save your changes, and then go to Tools→Options, click the Forms/Reports tab, and type the template's name in the "Report template" field. (If you ever need to restore Access's defaults, just change the name in this field back to "Normal.")

Once you've defined your custom look and feel, you can add it as an autoformat style that shows up in the Form and Report Wizards. Open the template in Design View and choose Format→Autoformat. You'll see a dialog box where you can add, remove, and customize any of the autoformat styles. (Prior to Access 2002, you couldn't remove built-ins.) Click the Customize button and select "Create a new AutoFormat based on the Report *reportname*," where *reportname* is the name of the report you've customized. Be aware that changes you make to autoformat styles will affect all of your Access databases, not just the one you're working on. In other words, if you delete the corporate template, it's gone.

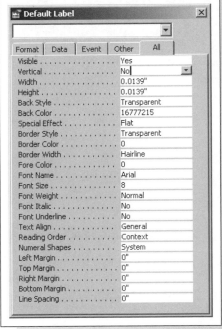

Figure 1-3. The properties sheet for a default label.

> **NOTE**
>
> *If you set a default size for a control, be sure you don't drag your mouse when you add it to a report or form; that will override the default. Just click once, and it'll spring into existence sized the way you want it.*

Defaults for Tables, Queries, and Datasheets

THE ANNOYANCE: Every time I create a new table, I have to open its properties sheet and disable Subdatasheet Name (see "Access's Bad Defaults," earlier in this chapter). Then I add an AutoNumber ID field as its first field. Why can't I make this my default table, and avoid having to repeat these steps *ad nauseam*?

THE FIX: Unlike forms and reports, Access doesn't have templates for tables, queries, or datasheets. If you want to set defaults for these objects, start with the built-in options. Open Tools→Options, and look on the Tables/Queries and Datasheet tabs. There are quite a few options you can set for datasheets; there aren't quite as many for tables and queries.

An easy workaround is to create your own template, in the form of a blank table, query, or datasheet. For instance, set up a table just the way you want it, and save it as Table_Blank. Whenever you want to create a new table, just make a copy of Table_Blank and rename it. Pretty easy, eh? (The only limitation is that subdatasheets won't be carried along in the copy—but that's rarely an issue.)

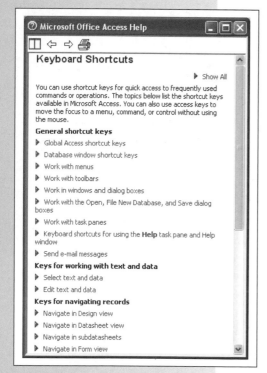

Figure 1-4. The big list of keyboard shortcuts, in Help under Microsoft Access Accessibility.

Hidden (but Indispensable) Keyboard Shortcuts

THE ANNOYANCE: Four mouse clicks is just too many when I have to get to the same command over and over again. Can't I create a single keystroke to execute the most common tasks?

THE FIX: To be fair, Access has quite a few built-in keyboard shortcuts, but only a few of them appear in menus and tooltips. If you don't see any, go to Tools→Customize and click the Options tab. Check the "Show ScreenTips on toolbars" and "Show shortcut keys in ScreenTips" boxes. This will reveal them in Access and all your other Office apps. Why Microsoft doesn't make them easier to find, or put more of them on menus and in tool tips, is a mystery. You can find the full list in Help. Select Help→Microsoft Access Help, click the Contents tab, then open Microsoft Access Accessibility. Click "Using the Keyboard," then "Keyboard Shortcuts" (see Figure 1-4).

One overall time-saver is typing directly into drop-down menus. For instance, to turn off record selectors in a form's properties sheet, you can just type **n** (for "No") into that properties field, rather than opening the menu and mousing down to make a choice. The same trick works in the Database window, jumping you to an object when you type the first letter of its name. (Of course, if more than one item in the drop-down menu starts with the same letter, you may need to navigate further to reach the actual item you need.)

To make your life easier, we've assembled the truly indispensable shortcuts in two tables: Table 1-1 lists shortcuts for designing a database, and Table 1-2 lists shortcuts for data entry.

Table 1-1. Design View keyboard shortcuts

Task	Shortcut
Open the properties sheet for a control.[1]	F4
Open the zoom box for a text field.	Shift-F2
Move a control on a form or report.	\<arrow\> keys, Ctrl-\<arrow\>[2]
Resize controls.	Shift-\<arrow\>, Ctrl-Shift-\<arrow\>
Open the Field List for a form or report.[1]	F8
Bring the Database window to the front.	F11
Switch between different kinds of objects in the Database window.	Ctrl-Tab
Create a new object in the Database window.	Alt-N
Jump to a specific (visible) object in the Database window.	Type its name
Open an object in Design View.	Ctrl-Enter
Switch to and from the VB code window from a form or report.[1]	F7, Shift-F7
Switch to the VB Immediate window.	Ctrl-G
Undo.[1] (To revert to last saved version, use File→Revert.)	Ctrl-Z
Open context-sensitive help.	F1

1. Not available in Access 2000 or earlier versions.
2. For Access 2000, use Ctrl-\<arrow\> and Shift-\<arrow\>.

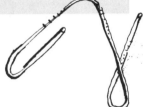

Table 1-2. Data entry keyboard shortcuts

Task	Shortcut
Insert the same value as that in the previous record.	Ctrl-<apostrophe>
Insert the default value.	Ctrl-Alt-Spacebar
Add a new record.	Ctrl-<plus sign>
Delete the current record.	Ctrl-<minus sign>
Save changes to the current record.	Shift-Enter
Toggle checkbox or option group.	Spacebar
Insert a new line in a memo field.	Ctrl-Enter
Insert the current date.	Ctrl-<semicolon>
Insert the current time.	Ctrl-Shift-<colon>
Refresh a form or query.	F9
Requery.	Shift-F9
Undo.[1]	Esc or Ctrl-Z

1. The first undo undoes the current field; the second one undoes the entire record. Only changes that have not been saved can be undone.

Create Keyboard Shortcuts

THE ANNOYANCE: I followed the Help instructions on how to create my own keyboard shortcuts, but they don't work. I press the keys, and nothing happens.

THE FIX: Access's Help supplies convoluted instructions that, in the end, only let you create awkward Alt-key shortcuts, such as Alt-E-A for Select All. What you really want to do is create simple shortcuts, such as Ctrl-C for copy.

In Access, you *can* create simple two-key shortcuts by using *AutoKeys macros*. This works fine, except that when you close your database and open another one, the macro won't work. You must copy the macro into any database where you want it to be available. Still, it's better than nothing. We'll walk through creating a simple macro here.

Start by creating a new macro (Tools→Macros) and saving it with the name "AutoKeys." (This special name tells Access that you're using it to define keyboard shortcuts; all your shortcuts will go into this one macro.) In the Macro Name column, define the keystroke you want, using the examples in Table 1-3 as a guide. (If you can't see the Macro Name column, choose View→Macro Names. If you can't see the Condition column, choose View→ Condition.)

Table 1-3. Syntax examples for AutoKeys macros

Macro name	Keyboard shortcut
^Q	Ctrl-Q[1]
+Q	Shift-Q
^+Q	Ctrl-Shift-Q
{F4}	F4 function key
^{F4}	Ctrl-F4
{INSERT}	Insert key
{DELETE}	Delete key (Insert and Delete are the only two named keys that are available)

1. Letters are not case-sensitive.

In the Action column, choose the action you want, and as with any macro, set any arguments it needs (see Figure 1-5). This will work fine if your keyboard shortcut corresponds to a single macro action, such as opening a form or importing a spreadsheet. To assign multiple actions (such as import, then append, then delete) to a shortcut, first create a separate macro (say, mcrImportProducts) that has all the actions you want. Then, in AutoKeys, add your keyboard shortcut and use the RunMacro action to run the multi-action macro.

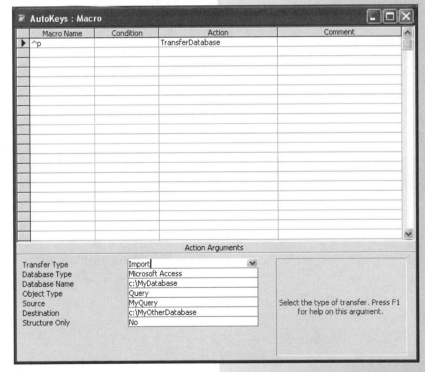

Figure 1-5. This AutoKeys macro assigns the Ctrl-P keystroke to the TransferDatabase action, in this case importing a query from one database to another.

Toggle Between Design View and Object View

THE ANNOYANCE: When I'm developing in Access, I constantly go back and forth between Design View and Form View, Design View and report Layout View, or Design View and query Datasheet View. Why isn't there a toggle button—or better yet, a single keystroke—that makes the leap?

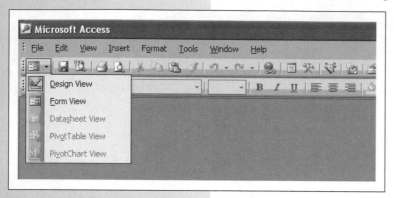

Figure 1-6. The built-in toggle button/ drop-down list for form design.

THE FIX: The good news is that there *is* a toggle button, tucked away in the upper-left corner on the Form Design toolbar (see Figure 1-6). Click it to jump back and forth between Design and Form Views. To get to other views quickly, click the down arrow to the right of the button and select the view you want from the drop-down menu. The bad news? There's no keyboard shortcut, and no easy way to make one.

Type Looooong Lines in Small Places

THE ANNOYANCE: I need to type a long expression into a tiny text box. Access displays a Build (...) button when it thinks I want to build an expression, but at other times it just displays that pathetic little text box. It's like trying to watch a movie with three linebackers sitting in front of you. How can I keep track of what I'm typing when I can only see two words at a time?

THE FIX: One of Access's handiest features is the *zoom box* (see Figure 1-7). Hit Shift-F2, and Access opens a big, empty text area for editing a long line of text. You can use this trick just about anywhere you see a text box: in the query design grid, in properties sheets, or in a Table Design window or datasheet (but not in text box controls in Design View—pet peeve!). It works in form fields as well. Incidentally, you'll notice that the zoom box closes when you hit Enter. If you need a line break in what you're typing, press Ctrl-Enter instead.

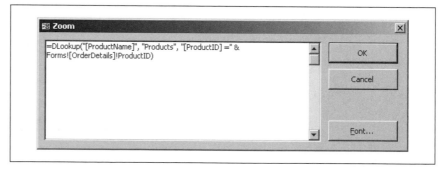

Figure 1-7. Shift-F2 opens the zoom box, which is very handy for seeing the whole expression as you type.

Access Changes My Data

THE ANNOYANCE: Whenever I enter "TEH" Access changes it to "THE." It doesn't even ask! I don't mean "THE," I mean "TEH," short for Tetrahedral Elevator Handles. (I use lots of acronyms in my database.) This is driving me crazy. Make it stop!

THE FIX: From a database designer's standpoint, this is one of the most ridiculous things that Access does. Databases shouldn't tamper with what a user enters, but Access does, applying the same AutoCorrect settings Word uses. Dumb!

Fortunately, this is easily fixed—sort of. Go to Tools→AutoCorrect Options (see Figure 1-8), and uncheck any of the choices that apply. The only problem? These options will affect every Office application. If you don't want to turn off AutoCorrect entirely, you have two choices. To turn it off for a specific form control, open that control's properties (click the control, then click View→Properties), click the Other tab, and set Allow AutoCorrect to "No." Alternatively, you can delete the particular corrections that are causing problems in the global AutoCorrect Options dialog. Click Tools→ AutoCorrect Options, and look through the list of corrections and the Exceptions list.

> **NOTE**
>
> *AutoCorrect can be a data entry time-saver. If you have long text strings that you frequently enter in fields where it's not convenient to set up a lookup table, create an AutoCorrect abbreviation that fills them in automatically. One dog's poison is another dog's bone, I guess.*

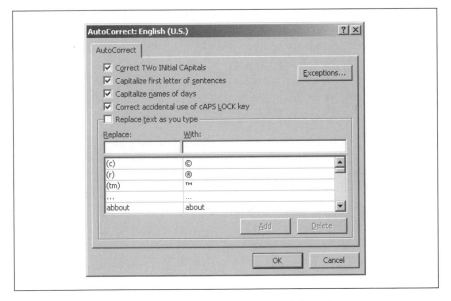

Figure 1-8. Tools→AutoCorrect Options gives you control over Office AutoCorrect.

Help That Isn't/Is Helpful

THE ANNOYANCE: Was Access's Help system written by Martians? The table of contents is jumbled, the selection of topics is haphazard, the indexes often don't work at all, and when I do finally locate a topic it often doesn't tell me anything useful. Help!!!

THE FIX: Look at it from our standpoint: if Access had a decent Help system, you wouldn't have bought this book. (Kidding!) But yes, the Access Help system is a swamp of bad organization, mumbo-jumbo, redundancy, and missing information. And just to torment us, Microsoft throws in a lot of useful info, too, hidden amongst the 'gators.

There *are* alternatives, but for starters, maximize what you've got. Your first avenue into Access's pathetic context-sensitive Help system is to press F1 wherever you are. It's especially useful when you're writing code, or (to take just one example) in properties sheets. For example, pressing F1 with the cursor in the Input Mask property for a field in a table will bring up some useful info...although, if you need help with the syntax, doing a search on "input mask" will bring up a more useful page. With Access Help, you've got to try multiple approaches and hope that one works.

Sometimes when you search for and find a relevant topic, it's useful to browse the Contents tab for neighboring topics. Normally, the Contents tab won't give you a clue as to where your current Help article is located in the Help system, but sometimes you can coax it into doing so. The trick is to open the folders on the Contents tab by clicking the plus sign next to Microsoft Access Help. Now, when you're on the Answer Wizard tab and you click a topic, the table of contents will open to that topic too. It doesn't always work, but it's worth a try.

A significant gotcha in Access Help is that some very common functions, such as DLookup() and FormatCurrency(), can't be found there at all. Why not? Because technically, they're Visual Basic functions. And even though VB Help is listed in Access Help's table of contents, search (maddeningly) doesn't find them. You can, however, get good help on these functions by switching to the VB Editor (Ctrl-G) first, and *then* opening Help. (A cool trick: type the name of the function in the Immediate window of the VB Editor and press F1.) Another gotcha is that the Help search engine ignores common words. For example, "Like" gets no hits, even though there is help available on the Like operator. You'll have to search for "Like operator" to find it.

The bottom line is that Access Help is a mixed bag. If you really want to wring everything out of it, it's all stored in CHM (compiled HTML) files, so you can try using something like Zilverline (*http://www.zilverline.org*) to index and search it.

When you grow weary of beating your head against the wall of Access Help, try the following alternate sources.

Newsgroups

There are more than 20 highly active newsgroups devoted to different aspects of Access, such as forms, reports, and security. (See the Appendix for a full list.) If you have a question, chances are it has already been answered in one of the newsgroups. Learn to use Google's advanced groups search screen (*http://groups.google.com/advanced_group_search*), and you'll be able to find answers to most questions without even having to post a message (see Figure 1-9). Just put **comp.databases.ms-access, microsoft.public.access.*** in the newsgroup field, and type in some keywords or a key phrase. You may want to change the starting date to something more recent than 1981. You'll almost always find useful results, but if nothing helpful shows up, there are many *very* knowledgeable people reading the newsgroups and answering questions, and they can handle just about anything.

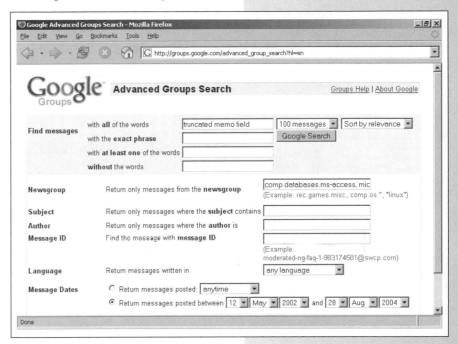

Figure 1-9. Google's advanced groups search page lets you target your search of Access newsgroups.

Post a clear, concise question, and you'll almost certainly get an answer; see the sidebar "How to Ask a Question in a Newsgroup (and Get an Answer)." Google does have one major limitation: it ignores special characters, so a search for "#Error!" is no more precise than a search for "error." There's a Google hack (see Hack #31, "Search for Special Characters," in *Google Hacks*, Second Edition, also from O'Reilly) that addresses this, but it requires a CGI script.

Utter Access

Utter Access (*http://www.utteraccess.com*) is a lot like the newsgroups, but with more of a community feel. People get to know each other, and the help that you get is sometimes more sustained than in the newsgroups. If you're just starting a project and need some ongoing guidance, start here.

Expert Sites

If you're looking for code, or for tips on how to do everything from numbering entries in a report to simulating a clock on your form, these sites are your dream come true. Some of the best known are:

- The Access Web (*http://www.mvps.org/access/*)
- Tony Toews's Main Microsoft Access Page (*http://www.granite.ab.ca/accsmstr.htm*)
- Stephen Lebans's Access Page (*http://www.lebans.com*)

OK, so these sites aren't especially stylish. Don't be misled by appearances—good hackers are always a little quirky. These sites are the mother lode of sophisticated Access techniques.

The Microsoft Knowledge Base

If you're running into strange or flaky behavior, you're getting weird error messages, or Access suddenly starts doing something that it wasn't doing before, your first stop should probably be the Knowledge Base. This is

---

How to Ask a Question in a Newsgroup (and Get an Answer)

The vast majority of people answering questions in news-groups are not paid to do so; they just do it because they like to. If you really want your question answered, ask it in a way that respects their time and intelligence. Here are a few simple tips that will make a big difference in the response you get:

Choose the right group.
> (See "Newsgroups" in the Appendix.) You'd be surprised how often people post questions about Windows in an Access group, or about security in the forms coding group.

Search before you post.
> Although it's amazing how patient most newsgroup-ies are, they do get ticked off when someone asks a question that could easily be answered with a quick Google search. If you don't get any search results, try searching again *after* you've written your problem description. Often, writing down a problem will help you come up with better search terms to use, so you can save the trouble of posting.

Write a clear, concise description of your problem.
> Don't tell people where you were born and how you got into database design in the first place. Get to the point, and be as specific as possible. Don't say, "It won't print!!! Urgent help needed!!!" Tell them what won't print (my report) what happens instead (Access hangs), and provide any related info that might be important (I just installed a new printer). If your problem is a really long, complicated one, chances are you haven't yet broken it down enough to post a question. Try to isolate which part of the whole puzzle is actually causing the problem (i.e., the query, the report that's based on it, or the tables). At least half the time when I start to write down a newsgroup question, I think of something else I should try—which often ends up solving my problem before I ever post.

Tell them how you tried to fix it.
> This helps the experts narrow down your problem, and it also shows them that you're not just another lazy worm hoping for help with your homework assignment!

Tell them what version of Access and Windows you're using.
> Many problems are tied to specific versions. Always include this info.

Microsoft's own repository of bugs and tips, which tries to address the myriad problems that users run into. Learn to use its advanced search screen, located at *http://support.microsoft.com/search/?adv=1* (which works best with—surprise!—Internet Explorer). If you're tracking down an error message, include the key words from the error. For more on mining the Knowledge Base, see "MSKB 123456" in the Introduction.

Microsoft Developer Network (MSDN)

When you need hard-core nitty-gritty straight from the horse's mouth, look into this repository of Microsoft white papers and other technical information aimed at developers. You can also sometimes find archived Help files from earlier Access versions. The Access section of MSDN starts here: *http://msdn.microsoft.com/office/understanding/access/*.

Give Me Full Menus!

THE ANNOYANCE: I hate it when Access abbreviates my menus with that ⊻ sign. Just give me full menus!

THE FIX: Some versions of Access default to hiding the less frequently used menu options and showing only the ones you've used recently (see Figure 1-10). This means the menu options are constantly shifting, which violates a basic rule of good interface design. To eliminate this behavior, go to Tools→Customize, click the Options tab, and check the "Always show full menus" box. Be aware that this is a global Office setting. (In Access 2000, *uncheck* the box that says, "Menus show recently used commands first." Yeah, that's real clear!)

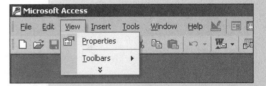

Figure 1-10. Access abbreviates menus to keep things simple, but this can quickly become annoying—especially when menu items keep changing.

Missing or Mangled Toolbars and Menus

THE ANNOYANCE: Damn! What happened to my toolbars!? They were fine yesterday, and then our new intern got on my computer....

THE FIX: Like any good Office app, Access makes it easy to customize its toolbars—too easy, sometimes, where interns (and other "helpful" people) are concerned. There are a few different ways to mess with toolbars and menus, so depending on what the problem is, here are the things to check.

Toolbar/Menu Is Missing

Open the Customize dialog (View→Toolbars→Customize), then click the Toolbars tab and make sure there's a checkmark next to the desired toolbar/ menu bar (see the sidebar "Customize to Your Heart's Content" for more on the Customize dialog). If Access won't let you check a box, click the Properties button and check the "Allow Showing/Hiding" box.

Toolbar/Menu Has Been Altered

What you do here depends on whether or not you customized the toolbar or menu before it was altered. If you just want the default toolbar back, click View→Toolbars→Customize, select the desired toolbar (or menu bar), and hit the Reset button. If you want a customized version back, you'll have to restore it from a backup or recreate it by hand. (To restore from a backup, choose File→Get External Data→Import, choose a backup MDB file that includes your custom menus and toolbars, and click the Import button. Then, in the Import Objects dialog, click the Options button and check the "Menus and Toolbars" box.)

Toolbar/Menu Has Been Moved or Merged into Another One

Someone may have simply dragged your toolbar and merged it with another one. Look for an extra toolbar "handle" (the faint gray raised vertical bar) somewhere in the middle of a toolbar, as seen in Figure 1-11, just to the left of the New icon. Place the mouse pointer on a handle, and it will turn into a four-headed arrow that lets you drag the toolbar wherever you want.

Figure 1-11. A toolbar typically has just one faint gray vertical handle at its far left. If you see two handles in a single row—as you do here—it means that two toolbars have been merged onto the same line.

Toolbar Is Disabled at Startup

If your menus and/or toolbars are reduced almost to nothing—for instance, if your File menu only lists Close, Search, and Exit—someone has probably changed your startup options. Close Access, then reopen it by pressing the Shift key and double-clicking the MDB file. This tells Access to bypass non-standard startup options. Then go into Tools→Startup and check "Allow Full Menus" and "Allow Built-in Toolbars."

> **NOTE**
>
> *It is possible to disable the Shift key. If the developer of your database has intentionally done so, this bypass will not work.*

Missing Objects (Forms, Reports, Queries…)

THE ANNOYANCE: It took me three weeks to design a year-end report, but now when I open my database, that report is nowhere to be found. If Access ate this one, I'm resorting to the three-story drop-kick technique. I never liked this computer, anyway….

THE FIX: Back away from that ledge! If the Database window doesn't show an object you know should be there, there are two possibilities. Perhaps (as in Figure 1-12) you simply need to maximize the Database window, or scroll through it to reveal all the objects. Still can't find your report? Go into Tools→Options, click the View tab, and make sure that the "Hidden objects" box is checked. If your report was inadvertently set to "hidden," this'll reveal it. Then right-click the report, choose "Properties," and uncheck the hidden attribute.

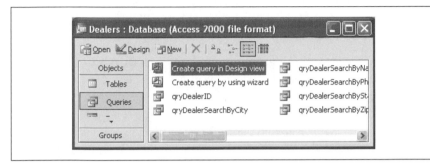

Figure 1-12. The most common cause of "missing objects" is that you just can't see them. Resize the Database window and/or scroll over to see more.

Still can't find it? Well, the object could have been deleted by accident, or by another user. In that case, you'll have to restore from a backup. Unfortunately, Access's Undo command works only on deletes of queries and tables, not on reports and other database objects.

Scroll Wheel Confusion

THE ANNOYANCE: Some of my users have wheels on their mice, which are supposed to help them scroll down the current page. Instead, if you even touch the thing Access shoots through every record in the database. Can I turn this thing off?

THE FIX: Unfortunately, there's no easy fix; this odd behavior is hard-coded into Access. The Microsoft Knowledge Base has an article on this problem, appropriately titled "How to Detect and Prevent the Mouse Wheel from Scrolling Through Records in a Form" (MSKB 278379), but Microsoft's technique requires writing your own ActiveX Dynamic Link Library (DLL). Yeah, umm, I'll do that right after I write my own Visual Basic compiler, and all before breakfast, hi ho!

But not to worry—Access guru Stephen Lebans comes to the rescue. You'll find his (free) fix at *http://www.lebans.com/mousewheelonoff.htm*. To use it, you'll need to copy the code module into a code module in your database, add his DLL to your system, and call it from the Immediate window to set it as the global option. Use the MouseHook version (rather than MouseWheel) to avoid the headaches of DLL registration.

Customize to Your Heart's Content

If you're not familiar with toolbar customization, it's worth learning. Putting frequently used buttons and commands close at hand and hiding the ones that you never use can save you lots of time and reduce clutter.

The basic process is simple. Access toolbars and menus are just groups of buttons, and you can add or remove those buttons as you wish. It all happens in the Customize dialog. To open it, right-click any toolbar and select "Customize" from the pop-up menu.

The Toolbars tab lets you show/hide toolbars (just click the appropriate checkbox), create new ones, and set properties for each one via the Properties button.

The Commands tab groups all the menu buttons by category. To add a button to a toolbar, find the command you want on the tab, drag it to the toolbar, and drop it where you want it. Easy, huh? To remove a button, drag it from the toolbar and drop it back on the Commands tab. Use exactly the same technique to drag commands on and off menus. The only tricky part here is that commands are not always categorized the way you'd expect—SQL View, for instance, is not in Views, but in Query Design.

Finally, don't forget the "four allows." If Access won't let you customize a menu or toolbar, check its properties: move, show/hide, customize, and resize can all be enabled/disabled.

Turn Off Dire Hyperlink Warnings

THE ANNOYANCE: My company uses Access to manage about 10,000 Microsoft Word documents. A hyperlink field on a form lets users open any document from within the Access database. The link works fine, except that every time you click it, you get a dire warning about viruses: "You are about to activate an embedded object that may contain viruses or be otherwise harmful to your computer. It is important to be certain that it is from a trustworthy source. Do you want to continue?" All our docs are created in-house; there's no need for these warnings. I set Office's macro security to low, but it still won't shut up.

THE FIX: Alas, the hyperlink warning is unrelated to macro security and won't be affected by those settings. Meet another great new feature of Office 2003! Unfortunately, the only way to disable these warnings is by editing the Windows Registry directly (see Figure 1-13). You'll need to set a couple of security keys to "DisableHyperlinkWarning." How convenient! MSKB 829072 gives detailed instructions. Be sure to back up your Registry before making any edits (see MSKB 322756).

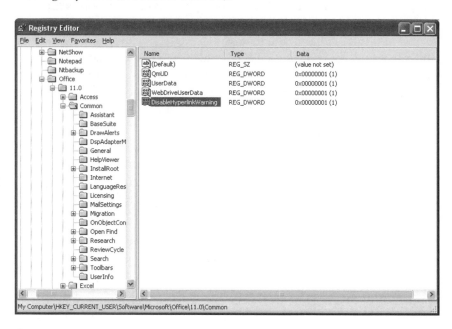

Figure 1-13. You can use the Registry Editor to disable hyperlink warnings.

Find/Replace for Database Objects

THE ANNOYANCE: I have a database that contains about 150 queries. Recently, I decided to change some table and field names. However, since you recommended that I turn off Name AutoCorrect, I now have to edit all my queries by hand—and the reports that reference those fields. Grrr....

THE FIX: I don't know why Access doesn't have a built-in Find/Replace function for database objects. (And you're right to keep Name AutoCorrect off; it's not reliable.) Your best bet is to use a third-party solution. There are plenty of choices, ranging from free (V-Tools, MDBSearch) to cheap (Fisher Find and Replace, ReplaceWiz) to the $199 Speed Ferret. Try before you buy—they all have different capabilities and user interfaces. Here's a list of the tools and where you can find them:

- V-Tools (*http://www.skrol29.com/dev/en_vtools.htm*)

- MDBSearch (*http://www3.bc.sympatico.ca/starthere/findandreplace/*)

- Fisher Find and Replace (*http://www.rickworld.com/products.html*)

- ReplaceWiz (*http://www.softwareaddins.com/Products.htm*)

- Speed Ferret (*http://www.moshannon.com/speedferret.html*)

If you're comfortable with Visual Basic, you might want to create your own Find/Replace function, using Chas Dillon's Visual Basic code. It's available at *http://allenbrowne.com/ser-41.html*.

Save Custom Form Placement

THE ANNOYANCE: I use Access 2002 for data entry, and every day I arrange my forms so they fit my window just the way I want. But no matter what I do, the next time I open Access, my careful arrangement is forgotten. How can I cure Access's amnesia?

THE FIX: Access doesn't let you save layouts for multiple windows (like Photoshop does), but it does allow you to save the layout of each form. The stupid part (yes, there's always a stupid part) is that you'll have to modify the default settings. Open the form in Design View, select View→Properties, click the Format tab, and set Auto Resize and Auto Center to "No" (see Figure 1-14). Now, set up the form the way you want it, and choose File→Save. The next time you open it, it'll be just where you left it.

Data Entry Without Access

THE ANNOYANCE: There are dozens of people at my company who need to enter data into our Access 2002 database, but we're a small company and can't afford to put a copy of Access on everyone's desktop. Is there some way to just give these people a data entry form?

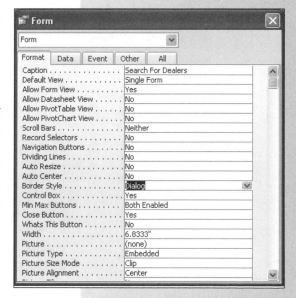

Figure 1-14. To enable saved form layouts, set Auto Resize and Auto Center to "No."

THE FIX: Yes, there is a free runtime version of Access that's intended for just this purpose. It doesn't have any "developer" features, but it gives users the ability to run a frontend of your design for data entry. (For more information on frontends and backends, see "Multi-User Databases and Split Design" in Chapter 0.) To distribute the Access runtime, you must have a copy of Office Developer Edition (or Visual Studio Tools for Office 2003). Use the Packaging Wizard in the Developer's Toolkit to bundle your MDB file together with the runtime app to create a self-executing install file. You can test your application in the runtime environment without actually installing it; just open your database using the /runtime command-line switch.

Be aware that the runtime version is not very user-friendly when it comes to error handling; untrapped errors will shut down Access without any warning or error message. Therefore, if you're writing VB code (to do data validation, for instance), it's essential to include error handling. If you use macros in your frontend (and remember, you can't trap errors in macros), convert them to VB code (Tools→Macro→Convert Macros to Visual Basic) and add error handling. See "Better Error Handling" in Chapter 7 for more on handling errors, and see MSKB 247530 for more on deploying runtime applications.

The Packaging Wizard works fine for simple installations where no full version of Access is present on the target system. It does not, however, recognize Jet service pack updates, even if they are installed on the system where the packaging is done. This means that even if you've upgraded to the latest Jet service pack (see the "Installation Checklist" section in the Appendix), the Packaging Wizard will use the old version. Your users will have to do the service pack upgrades themselves.

Getting Lost in Datasheet View

THE ANNOYANCE: I like using datasheets, because they provide a familiar, spreadsheet-like view of the data in a table or query, and because I often consult other records while I'm entering data. The only problem is that if I scroll too far to the right it's easy to lose track of exactly which record I'm editing.

THE FIX: Datasheets are useful, but like spreadsheets, when there are a lot of columns, it's hard to keep all your data in view. Fortunately, Access has an Excel-like fix: select the columns you want to keep in view, and choose Format→Freeze Columns. Now when you scroll to the right, those columns will stay in view. You can only select contiguous columns—if the ones you want aren't contiguous, rearrange them temporarily so that they're all together, then select and freeze them. And don't worry, this won't affect other views of your data. To move a column, click the column heading once, then click again and drag it right or left. To unfreeze your columns, choose Format→Unfreeze All Columns.

ACCESS RUNS AMOK

Access Is Buggy and Unstable

THE ANNOYANCE: Access hasn't behaved right since day one. It hangs, it's unpredictable, things that worked yesterday don't work today, and I get all sorts of weird error messages. This morning it gave me a key violation error, telling me that I'm entering a duplicate value in an AutoNumber field—but my form lets Access enter data in that field itself! Am I cursed?

THE FIX: We hope not, because it's a curse we'd rather not catch. A few things could explain such painfully flaky behavior.

First, some versions of Access are more stable than others. Access 97, for instance, is generally regarded as the most rock-solid. Access 95 was pretty bad, and some regard Access 2000 as a disaster—especially with respect to corruption problems. Access 2002 and 2003 seem to be quite a bit better. So, if you're using Access 2000, your best bet is to upgrade. In addition, make sure that the version of Windows you're running is compatible with your version of Access. The same fix applies if you're sharing Access over a network. (See "Access/Windows Compatibility Issues" in Chapter 2 for more information.)

If you're stuck with a lemon, you'll have to be sure to treat it right—that means installing service packs, Jet upgrades, and so on (see the "Installation Checklist" section in the Appendix).

But what if you've done all the right things, and Access still can't walk straight? Here are some other things to check:

Bad install
> It's possible that your Windows Registry is corrupted, your DLLs are improperly registered, or some other aspect of your Access (or Windows) installation is not right. See "Agonies of a Sick Installation," later in this chapter.

Network issues
> Access is known to be unstable on some networks, and network dropouts are one of the chief causes of database corruption. See "That Darn Corruption," later in this chapter.

Corruption
> If your database is corrupted, all bets are off. Until it's fixed, you may as well give your data to a drunken sailor on a leaky ship. (See the next Annoyance, "Flaky or Corrupted Database.")

Bad application design
> If you're running a custom database that was poorly designed, this can also be a source of instability. For example, if your design requires you to keep adding fields to your tables, Access may misbehave long before you

hit the 255-field limit. As a general rule, you should add rows, not fields, to accommodate new data. If the application uses VB code you added yourself, be aware that errors in the code can also lead to instability.

Flaky or Corrupted Database

THE ANNOYANCE: My company stores vital sales records in an Access database. We've been using this system for over a year without a hiccup, and suddenly today I got an "Unrecognized database format" error. How is that possible? It's the same *^#!!%$ format we've been using all along! Also, our sales rep noticed some of the records show #Deleted, but we never delete records. If we lose this data, we are really up a creek!

THE FIX: Sounds like your database is corrupted. But don't panic—remember, you can restore data from a backup. (You do back up your data, right? See "Automating Maintenance Chores" in Chapter 2.) And in a *really* worst-case scenario (your backups are also corrupt, or you can't find them), you can hire a data recovery specialist...but we'll get to that later.

Database corruption in Access is a significant but manageable problem. The root of the problem is that an Access database is one big file—or, if you've split it, two big files. No matter how many users you have, or how you set it up, all your data, form objects, report objects, and so on live inside that file. For the most part, this works fine. But every once in a while, something—often a network dropout, or a system crash—causes a write operation to fail at just the wrong moment, and some part of the file gets corrupted. Since it's one big file, if any part fails, the whole thing appears broken—though it's usually not. Here are some of the common symptoms of corruption:

- The database won't open, generates an error, or nothing happens.

- Specific forms/reports won't open.

- You get the "The database <database name> needs to be repaired or isn't a Microsoft Access database file" error.

- You get the "Unrecognized database format" error.

- You get the "The Microsoft Jet database engine stopped the process because you and another user are attempting to change the same data at the same time" error.

- You get the "The Microsoft Jet engine cannot open this file" error.

- You get a permissions failure, when permissions are set up correctly.

- You get a password prompt when no password was set on the database.

- You get the "<database name> isn't an Index in This Table" error.

- #Deleted appears in the data.

Why Enterprise DBMSes Are More Reliable

Enterprise DBMSes do many things to ensure reliability that Access, by design, does not do. That's why Access should not be used in situations where data reliability is paramount—it's just not robust enough.

One of the most important features of enterprise DBMSes is *transactional logging*. The idea is that since you can't prevent all failures, you *must* have a system that detects and corrects them. After all, just like Access, enterprise DBMSes have to live on operating systems that experience unexpected errors.

With transactional logging, each data entry transaction is written to a log file *before* the database is ever touched. Only when the transaction is logged is it sent to the database. Then, if any part of the write operation fails, the log is used to recover the database file and redo the transaction (or at least undo any partial changes). In this way, transactions are essentially guaranteed to succeed or fail absolutely.

If you're experiencing any of these symptoms, take the steps outlined in the following sections to recover your data and application objects. (See MSKB 283849 for more information.)

Preparation

Before you get started, do the following:

1. Make a backup of your corrupted file.

2. Make sure that your database is not being used while you're attempting to repair it.

3. Check for an LDB file in the directory where your MDB file is stored. (Figure 1-15 shows what the icon looks like.) This is a lock file, and there should *not* be one when your database is closed. If there is, it indicates that someone else is using the file, or that the database was shut down improperly. In the latter case, delete this file (or move it—it can be used to identify who was using the database at the time of corruption). See MSKB 208778 and 198755 for more information.

4. Defragment your hard drive.

5. Make sure that your hard drive has plenty of free space on it—at least double the size of your MDB file. (If you've nearly filled your hard drive, this alone can cause corruption.)

6. Install all the latest service packs and releases, especially for Jet. (See the "Installation Checklist" section in the Appendix.) These upgrades can enable a repair that would otherwise fail.

Figure 1-15. Note the difference between a regular database icon (.mdb) and the icon for a lock file (.ldb).

Use the Built-in Compact/Repair Utility

Access has a built-in Compact/Repair utility that you can deploy by clicking Tools→Database Utilities→Compact and Repair Database. After it compacts your database (see the sidebar "What Is Compacting?"), it attempts to repair corrupted tables, queries, and indexes. It won't repair objects such as forms or reports. Of course, if you can't even *open* your database, you won't be able to run this utility on it. Instead, run the JETCOMP utility (Figure 1-16), which will perform the same process without requiring your database file to be open. You can download the JETCOMP utility at *http://support.microsoft.com/default.aspx?scid=kb;en-us;273956.*

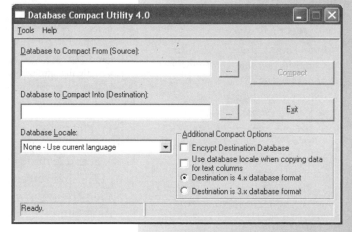

Figure 1-16. JETCOMP can compact and repair without opening the database.

What Is Compacting?

Compacting your database is analogous to defragmenting your hard drive. Because of the way Access stores tables and indexes in an MDB file, both can become fragmented. Compacting fixes this problem; it also recovers unused space, resets AutoNumbers to the next usable value, and regenerates table statistics for better query optimization. It can't be beat.

NOTE

If your system tables are visible (they have names like MSysQueries and MSysObjects), make sure you don't import them. That would defeat the purpose of the import. System tables (which are normally hidden) are used by Access to store its own descriptions of your user tables and objects.

NOTE

Importing is pretty quick, and it preserves table relationships (unless you uncheck that option). But on large databases, be prepared for some tedious work recreating the layout of your relationships window, which cannot be imported. Thankfully, Michael Kaplan's free TSI SysRel Copy Utility (http://www.trigeminal.com/lang/1033/utility.asp?ItemID=12#12) makes that a breeze.

After you run the Compact/Repair utility, open your database and see how it looks. Even if it appears to be fixed, we recommend you export it to a new database. You should also see if the MsysCompactErrors system table exists, by selecting Tools→Options, clicking the View tab, and checking the "System objects" box. MsysCompactErrors will only show up if there were errors during the compact process.

Export to a New Database

Compact/Repair won't fix all corruption problems, particularly those in system tables. You can force Access to rebuild the system tables from scratch by importing all your objects into a blank database. You may be able to do this even if you can't open the database. First, create a blank database by choosing File→New and clicking "Blank Database" in the Task Pane on the right. Then choose File→Get External Data→Import and select the MDB file that you're trying to repair. Select all your objects, and import them (see Figure 1-17).

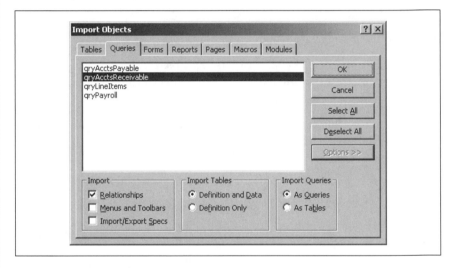

Figure 1-17. You can import one or many objects from one database into another. To repair damaged objects, the defaults in this dialog are fine. Just select the objects you need, or press Select All. You'll need to do the same on each tab that contains objects.

Now you can give your new (and presumably repaired) database a full road test. If the import does not fix the problem, you can try importing objects one at a time into another new database. If an object is corrupted the import will fail, and you can then attempt to recreate it or restore it from a previous backup. Be aware that you must import related tables at the same time if you wish to preserve relationships.

Problem-Specific Suggestions

Depending on what you think the problem is, there are several things you can try:

Data

Export the table as a text file (choose File→Export, save as type Text, then accept the defaults in the export dialog), then open the exported data in a text editor and look for bad data. If you find any, fix or remove it. Then delete the table. (If it has relationships, you'll have to delete them first: click Tools→Relationships and delete them in the Relationships window.) Next, compact the database, and recreate the table and its relationships. Import the repaired text file into the new table (File→Get External Data→Import and choose the text file), and accept the Import Wizard's defaults.

Code

If a code module is corrupted, export the module as a text file and check for non-ASCII characters (they'll show up as garbage if you open the file in Notepad). Delete any spurious characters, repair the code if necessary, and copy the module back into your application. You can also try decompiling your code. First, compact the database and close it. Then reopen it using the undocumented command-line switch /decompile. (Select Start→Run, and in the Open box, type the paths to the Access executable file and the database, such as **"C:\Program Files\ Microsoft Office\Office\msaccess.exe" "C:\databases\mydatabase.mdd /decompile"**. Hold down the Shift key before you press OK. This decompiles the database's code. Now compact the database again.)

Indexes

If your indexes become corrupted, create a new table with an identical structure and restore the data to it, either with an append query (add the original table to a new query, drag * to the query grid, then choose Query→Append Query and select the new table in the Table Name box) or by importing a text file holding the suspect table. Recreate the indexes on the new table (see "Speed Up Slow Queries" in Chapter 4).

Opening the database

You may be able to open your MDB file with a newer version of Access, and then repair it and convert it back to the older version if you wish. Alternatively, you may be able to get your data out without opening the database at all, by using Open Database Connectivity (ODBC), a Windows standard that enables data to be exchanged between different

applications, systems, and databases. You can try ODBC by setting up a Data Source Name (DSN) that points to the original database (see "Avoiding Manual DSN Setup for ODBC" in Chapter 2), then linking to it from a new MDB file and using File→Get External Data→Link Tables. You can also try importing the data into Excel: from Excel 2002/2003, select Data→Import External Data→Import Data; from Excel 2000, select Data→Get External Data→Import Text file. (See "Give Up and Try Excel Instead" in Chapter 6 for help with this command, and see MSKB 304561 for doing this from Excel using MS Query.)

Professional Help

If you're still stuck, or don't have time to go through all of the above steps, turn to a data recovery service—these companies have pretty good success rates. Access MVP Tony Toews has a list at *http://www.granite.ab.ca/access/ corruptmdbs.htm*, or you can just Google "Microsoft Access data repair."

That Darn Corruption

THE ANNOYANCE: OK, fine. You've told us how to fix corruption. But what the heck is causing it? An ounce of prevention...

THE FIX: ...is worth a pound of Annoyances. OK, you ask, I'll tell. The most common cause of corruption in Access is an interrupted write operation. In a best-case scenario, the only harm done is that the flag Access sets when it starts the write operation never gets cleared. The next time Access starts up, it sees the uncleared flag and sends you a warning that the database needs to be repaired. Compact/Repair can fix this kind of "corruption" easily. However, depending on what Access was doing when it was interrupted, your database may be in a far less stable state, with critical data in a partially written condition.

Other causes of database corruption include file corruption at the system level, bugs in Access, bugs in your VB code, and user error. Let's look at some common causes of corruption, and how to prevent them.

Network Problems

Running Access on a network greatly increases the risk of corruption. In addition to dropped connections, problems with *opportunistic locking* (oplocks)—a Windows file-sharing protocol that allows multiple clients to share locks (i.e., the exclusive privilege to write to a single file)—are a major cause of corruption. To minimize this risk, it is important to optimize the network, avoid flaky hardware, and make sure that your server has enough horsepower for the demands you're placing on it. (See "Best Practices for Access on Networks" in Chapter 2.)

System Crashes

If your database application, or the system it's on, is prone to crashes, your database is almost guaranteed to develop corruption. Therefore, it's essential to be proactive in addressing the causes of fatal errors. Fatal errors can be caused by:

Bugs in Microsoft Access
> Apply all relevant Windows, Office, and Access service packs. (See the "Installation Checklist" section in the Appendix.)

A corrupted or fragmented database
> Yes, it's circular. Address mild corruption right away, or it *will* get worse.

Incorrect Registry settings, mismatched DLLs, and other system installation issues
> See "Agonies of a Sick Installation," later in this chapter.

Bad hard drive management
> Defragment regularly, make sure there's plenty of empty space, clean out your Temp folder from time to time, and so on.

Improper computer shutdown
> Don't push the power off button in a fit of pique; it isn't really helpful. Bad user!

Unexpected power loss or surge
> Hook up your PC to an uninterruptible power supply (UPS).

Killing Access from the Task Manager, or shutting down the whole system from the Start menu while Access is running
> Big no-nos—always shut down from within Access.

Access Bugs

Complex software always has bugs, and some of these bugs can cause corruption. Most of them get fixed, eventually, which is why it's important to apply all available service packs and relevant patches.

Application Bugs

Bugs in your own code can be just as damaging as bugs in Access. Here are some basic guidelines to avoid corrupting your own database:

Don't use reserved words for names of objects, fields, or variables.
> The obvious ones are fields such as 'name' and 'date', but there are lots of others, such as 'document', 'currency', and 'report'. See MSKB 286335 for a detailed list.

Don't edit code while it's running.
> Yes, isn't it cool that Visual Basic lets you do it? Avoid the temptation!

On subforms, include a (hidden) text box for each field used in the Link Child Fields property.

Strictly speaking, it's not necessary, but Access guru Allen Browne says that this simple trick will prevent a lot of headaches. We believe him. (If this form-related stuff confuses you, see "Building the Right Form" in Chapter 5.)

Close all DAOs and ADOs that you open (when you're done with them, of course).

If you're writing Visual Basic code, explicitly close any objects (such as recordsets) that you open. Yes, Visual Basic will do it for you (that's what the garbage collector is for), but it's safer if you do it as soon as the object is no longer needed. (DAO and ADO are code libraries Access programmers use with databases. For more information, see "DAO Versus ADO" in Chapter 0.)

User Error

Users occasionally make errors that can corrupt your database (in addition to the improper shutdown techniques mentioned above). Here are a few possible culprits:

Sharing the same copy of the frontend across a network.

People like to do this, but it's a bad idea. It causes your network traffic to increase by about a zillionfold, which increases your risk of corruption. Make sure each user has his own copy of the frontend on his own system.

Opening and saving the MDB file in another program.

Does anyone open their databases—and save them—in Word? According to Microsoft, they do—and it's a very bad idea, because Word stupidly lets you overwrite the MDB! (Something Excel, for example, won't do.)

Missing Wizards or Import/Export/Link Options

THE ANNOYANCE: We just upgraded to Access 2002, and now when I try to use the Get External Data→Import command it doesn't show Excel (*.xls*) as a file type! Where'd it go?

THE FIX: Losing import file types seems to happen a lot, usually due to a missing Indexed Sequential Access Method (ISAM) driver. Remember that certain Access features (such as wizards) depend on external files. If these files didn't get installed, were improperly installed, were accidentally deleted (Clean Sweep *swore* it wouldn't do anything bad...), or have become corrupted, the features may be unavailable, disappear, or quit working. Since a number of external files can be involved, it may take some trial and error to solve the problem. (We'll assume that you've already checked for menu customizations that might be hiding the command; see "Missing or Mangled Toolbars and Menus," earlier in this chapter.) Here are some things you should check.

Missing or Broken Wizards

If you run across wizards that are either missing or not working properly, check out the following suggestions:

- See if the wizard you're trying to use is actually installed. If you chose "Typical" when you installed Access, some wizards will not have been copied to your hard drive. To find out which were, go to *http://office. microsoft.com* and search for "installing wizards." The page you want is titled "Which wizards are installed in Access 2003."

- Make sure your Jet service pack is up-to-date. (See the "Installation Checklist" section in the Appendix, and MSKB 835415.)

- Use *Regsvr32.exe* to re-register the following DLL files: *Dao360. dll*, *Msado15.dll*, and *Accwiz.dll* (see Figure 1-18). For instructions, see the "Installation Checklist" section in the Appendix.

- There are three MDE files that contain the wizards—*Acwzmain. mde*, *Acwztool.mde*, and *Acwzlib.mde*—and they may be corrupted. To repair them, first locate these files on your system (typically under *Program Files\\Microsoft Office*), rename them just to be on the safe side, then use Help→Detect and Repair and follow the onscreen instructions. (See also the next annoyance, "Agonies of a Sick Installation.")

- If you get a "Data cannot be retrieved" error, you may have a problem with your Microsoft Data Access Components (MDAC) files. To reinstall them, go to MSDN and download the latest version: *http://msdn.microsoft.com/data/downloads/updates/default. aspx#MDACDownloads*.

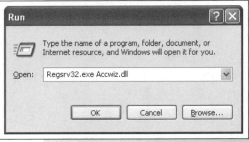

Figure 1-18. Running the Regsrv32 utility to re-register a DLL.

Missing Import/Export/Link Options

ISAM is a method for managing how your computer accesses *records* and *files*. If Access can't find the ISAM driver it needs to interact with a particular type of file, it leaves that type off the import/export list. The most common ISAM drivers are *Msexcl40.dll* for Excel and *Mstext40.dll* for text files. (See MSKB 209805 for a full list of the others.) The solution is to re-register the driver you need using *Regsvr32.exe* (see the "Installation Checklist" section in the Appendix). If this remedy fails, you'll need to fully uninstall and reinstall the ISAM driver via the Windows Add/Remove Programs applet. See MSKB 171955 for more detailed instructions.

Agonies of a Sick Installation

THE ANNOYANCE: I'm trying to run Access XP on Windows XP Pro, but every time I double-click an MDB file, the Office Installer starts up and tries to install something. It won't tell me what it's trying to install, and afterwards Access still doesn't work! This is driving me crazy.

THE FIX: A "Preparing to install" message is a sure sign there's a problem with your Access installation. Other signs of a sickly installation include fatal errors (such as "Access needs to close"), missing wizards, and errors that are just plain strange, such as "No object in this control." Sometimes Access won't even start. This fix will clean up your installation and get Access back on track.

If Access detects an incorrect Registry setting or a problem with one of its components when it starts up, it tries to be helpful by calling the Installer and repairing the problem. What's maddening is that, if it can't fix it, it's not smart enough to log the problem—it just quits, and does exactly the same thing the next time around.

The first fix is to run Office's repair utility. If you can start Access, simply click Help→Detect and Repair and follow the onscreen instructions. If you can't open Access, try opening it in Office Safe mode, via the command line. Here's how:

1. Open the Start menu and select Run.

2. Type the path of the Access executable, such as **C:\Program Files\ Microsoft Office\Office\msaccess.exe /safe**.

3. Press Enter.

If you can't run Detect and Repair from Access in safe mode, you can run it from any other Office XP application.

If the Office Detect and Repair utility fails, try using the Add or Remove Programs control panel to uninstall and reinstall Access. Alas, just repairing or reinstalling Access doesn't always fix the problem. Configuration information and settings left over from previous installations can confuse the installer. Use Microsoft's Windows Installer CleanUp utility to zap the config info (see MSKB 290301). Be sure to uninstall Access *before* you run the CleanUp utility. Once done, do a complete reinstall. At that point, follow the installation checklist in the Appendix to make sure your installation is up-to-date.

> **NOTE**
>
> *To determine whether the problem is with your MDB file or Access, try opening your database on another computer. If it runs fine on a different system, your Access installation is probably the culprit. Also try opening Access without loading any database; if it runs fine, that suggests the problem is with your MDB file.*

> **NOTE**
>
> *If you have multiple versions of Access on your system, this fix will succeed only if you target the version of Access that runs when you double-click an MDB file. See "Running Different Versions of Access on the Same PC" in Chapter 2.*

ERROR MESSAGES

#Name? and #Error?

THE ANNOYANCE: Our travel expenses form has a calculated field that computes each employee's travel budget using information found in a separate budgets table. I'm sure the calculation is correct, but all I see in the form is a #Name? error message where the employee's total budget calculation should be. I built this expression using the Builder; it should work!

THE FIX: It is maddening that Access's Expression Builder lets you spend hours building all sorts of expressions that you can't test until you close the Builder and go back to your form or query. In your case (see Figure 1-19), you're getting a #Name? error because you can't directly reference information in a separate table. (And yes, this is an Access "feature," not a bug.)

In general, #Name? and #Error? are just crude indicators that something is wrong with the source for a field or control source. (Never heard of a "control source?" See "Bound Versus Unbound Objects" in Chapter 0.) Let's take a look at some of the most common causes for these errors. See also "Debugging Expressions" in Chapter 7.

Misspelled or Nonexistent Name

If a field, table, or function name you are using is misspelled, or just plain missing, obviously Access won't be able to find it.

Missing Equals Sign

If the control source for a text box on a form is an expression, you must precede the expression with an equals sign. Check the Control Source property on the Data tab of the text box's properties sheet.

Name Is Out of Scope

For expressions on a form (or report), you can only use names that appear in the record source for the form. For instance, if your form is based on a table, you can use the names of the fields in that table, but not the names of fields in other tables. If you need to reach outside your form's record source, use the DLookup() (domain lookup) function. In the example above, you might have used =DLookup("[travelBudget]", "tblBudgets", "[employeeId]=" & Forms!TravelExpenses!employeeId). This expression tells Access to look up the field called "travelBudget" from the table "tblBudgets," using the criterion that tblBudgets.employeeId matches the employeeId of the current record on the TravelExpenses form.

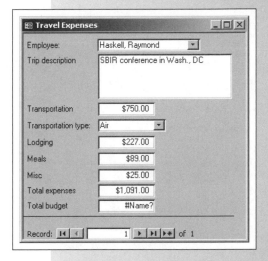

Figure 1-19. The dreaded #Name? error—shown here, in the "Total budget" text box—can be caused by a wide variety of conditions. It's a sure sign that something is wrong!

Incorrect Expression Syntax

If you use a VB function in your expression and you don't get the syntax *exactly* right, you'll get an error. For instance, if you leave off any of the quotation marks in the previous DLookup() example, it won't work. If you omit the equals sign from the beginning of the expression, you may get this error as well. If you're unsure of the syntax, go into VB Help, find the function you're planning to use, read the description, study the examples, and copy the syntax precisely.

Use of Visual Basic Constants

You may be using a function that accepts a predefined VB constant as an argument. For instance, StrConv(string, vbConstant) expects a constant such as vbUpperCase or vbLowerCase as its second argument. It's right there in the Help file! However, you can't use a VB constant in an expression outside of VB code. Instead, you must use the literal value (which is also given in the Help file)—that is, instead of StrConv("myString", vbUpperCase), you must write StrConv("myString", 1).

Empty Query or Subform

In certain situations, a query or subform that returns no data can give rise to #Error?. For example, if you place a text box with a calculated control source (such as =0.15 * salary) on a report, it will produce an error if the query that the report is based on is empty. The fix is to use IsNumeric or IsDate to test values before you use them, like this: =IIf(IsNumeric(salary), 0.15 * salary, 0). This uses the Immediate If (IIf) function to choose one of two alternatives: if IsNumeric(salary) is true, then the query uses the salary expression; otherwise, it just returns zero. There is no equivalent test for text fields, but there is usually a numeric field available to test even if your expression doesn't use it.

A similar problem can arise on a subform with no records, and the fix is the same. In fact, if your subform is set to not allow records to be added (i.e., its Allow Additions property is set to "No"), you'll get #Error? if you refer to any of its controls from the main form.

Parameter Query Embedded in Expression

Suppose you have a query that expects the user to enter a value in an open form. Now you include that query in an expression, using DLookup(). If the referenced form is not open, there will be no parameter prompt—you'll just get #Error?. This applies to any parameter query, not just those based on forms.

Wrong Syntax for Subform Reference

If you're referring to a field on a subform, you must get the syntax right. See "Refer to Subform Properties" in Chapter 7.

Circular References

By default, Access gives a control the same name as the underlying control source. For example, if you have a startDate field in your jobs table, the wizard will give you a text box named "startDate" on your form. This is a potentially dangerous practice; most DBMS pros would change it to "txt-StartDate" to avoid any ambiguity (see Figure 1-20). The problem arises if you need an expression based on the underlying table. Suppose you want the start date on your form to be calculated as three days later than the startDate value in the jobs table. In the control source, you would write =DateAdd("d", 3, startDate)—and Access would give you #Error?. Why? Because it thinks you're referring to the value of the *control* on the form. That hasn't been calculated yet, so it's a circular reference. You can run into a similar problem with queries, if you use the names of table fields as aliases (e.g., LastName: StrConv([LastName], 3)).

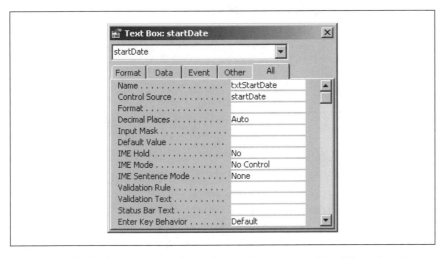

Figure 1-20. Good design practice is to change the control name to something different from the control source, usually with a prefix to indicate the type of control.

#Num!, #Div/0!, #Deleted, and #Locked

THE ANNOYANCE: I have a payroll report that calculates totals by month and by year. Some section totals just show #Num! instead of the amount. What does this mean? I tried searching for "#Num!" in the Answer Wizard, and it asked me to rephrase my question. I'll rephrase it all right!

THE FIX: These error tags that show up in fields are actually a good thing—they tell you more than if Access just left the fields blank. But Access's documentation is pretty poor, and because the Help search engine filters out special characters such as #, you're left guessing what the error codes mean. Here are some more helpful explanations (based on MSKB *209132*):

#Num!

> This is an overflow indicator. It means that the value you're trying to put in the field is too large, based either on the data type or the Field Size property—for instance, if you try to put a number like 1,250,000 into a Number field whose size is set to Integer, you'll get #Num!. (Yes, 1,250,000 is an integer, but Access's Integer data type maxes out at 32,767. For anything bigger, you need a Long Integer.) You can get info about field size limits by going into table Design View, placing your cursor in the Field Size property, and pressing F1. This error can also indicate that you are attempting to store text data in a numeric field.

#Div/0!

> This error indicates that you are attempting to divide by zero, which, of course, is strictly a no-no (see Figure 1-21). But what do you do when your expression *must* have zero as a divisor? Let's say you're calculating pay rates as CashSum/Hours, and Hours is occasionally zero. In this case, you must use the Immediate If (IIf) function, as follows, to test for this condition and avoid it: IIf(Hours = 0, 0, CashSum/Hours).

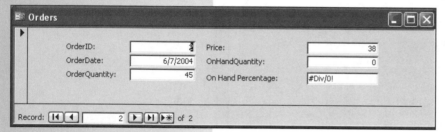

Figure 1-21. #Div/0! indicates that your expression is attempting division by zero.

#Deleted

> This error indicates that the record being referred to has been deleted (possibly by another user) since your view of the data was last updated. Hit Shift-F9 to requery the recordset, and this ghost record will be removed. Another cause may be a flaky ODBC driver. Make sure you have the latest driver installed. This error can also be a sign of data corruption.

#Locked

> This error indicates that the record you are trying to access is locked, either by you in another process (i.e., another form or query is using the data that you are trying to update) or by another user who is attempting to update the same record at the same time. The solution is to wait until the lock has been released. For settings that will minimize locking conflicts, see the discussion of record locking under "Global defaults" in the "Access's Bad Defaults" Annoyance earlier in this chapter.

Enter Parameter Value

THE ANNOYANCE: Access keeps prompting me to enter a parameter value, but I don't know what it's talking about. I'm pretty sure I didn't set up any parameters. I tried just clicking "OK," but then my query had no results. I am completely baffled!

THE FIX: Strictly speaking, the "Enter Parameter Value" dialog box is not an error message. Parameters are simply variables that let users customize a query at runtime. When you run the query, Access (properly) prompts you to type in a value for each parameter, which enables you to customize the query on the fly. For instance, parameters are often used to supply start and end dates, so that the dates don't have to be hardcoded into the query definition.

Unfortunately, Access handles parameters so loosely that whenever it sees certain kinds of expressions it doesn't recognize, it *assumes* you meant to create a parameter. Aargh! This is maddening, until you start thinking of it as Access's way of saying, "I can't find anything matching this name!" The "name" is whatever expression shows up in the dialog above the text box (see Figure 1-22).

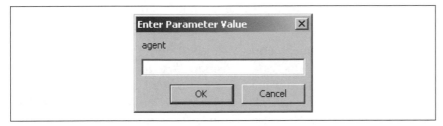

Figure 1-22. When Access prompts you to enter a value and you're not expecting to have to enter anything, it means there's some expression (in this case, agent) that it doesn't understand.

There are a zillion reasons why Access may not be able match the name. The most common one is that it's misspelled—for example, you may have typed "agent" in the query grid when the name of the field in your table is really "agents," or you may have created a query but then modified the field names in the table without updating the query. Another common problem is that you intended your query to pull a value from a form, using an expression such as Forms!frmBookAgents!agent. If your form is not *open* when you run your query, you'll get the dreaded parameter prompt. If it's a report that's causing the problem, are you sure that the field you're trying to use is available in the underlying query? Did you forget to use an equals sign in a calculated control?

> **TIP**
>
> To avoid typos in your queries, don't type field names. Instead, go to the appropriate table in the table pane and double-click the field names to insert them in the query automatically—or drag them directly into the query grid.

OK, so you've checked the obvious possibilities, and you're still getting the darn Enter Parameter Value prompt. You're absolutely sure that everything's spelled correctly, and you can't find a reference anywhere to this weird name. Here are some other things to check:

- Check your query to make sure that, in fact, no parameters have been created. In query Design View, go to Query→Parameters to see if any are listed.

- Is the missing name a query *alias*? In other words, does it show up in the query grid in front of a field name, like agent: bookAgentName or Expr1: employeeName? (Or in SQL using AS?) Access won't let you refer to an alias in query criteria, or anywhere else in the query.

- Check the query's properties sheet—especially the Filter and Order By fields—to see if they reference the errant name. If they do, delete it or change it to something that Access recognizes. (See "Find the Properties Sheet for a Query" in Chapter 4.)

- In a report, check View→Sorting and Grouping to see if the errant name is listed there. Again, if it is, delete it or change it to something that Access recognizes.

- Are you pulling a parameter from a subform and not using the correct syntax? See "Refer to Subform Properties" in Chapter 7.

- Did you create query criteria in code and forget to add quotes? (See ""Quotes", #Quotes#, and more #%&@!! """"Quotes"""""" in Chapter 7.) Or did you fail to supply a valid criteria string in your DoCmd.OpenForm statement? For example, this *looks* fine: DoCmd.OpenForm "frmCustomers", , ,"LastName = 'Price'"—but if there's no LastName field in the record source of the customers form, Access will prompt you for a value.

- If your report or form has any macros or code associated with it, check them for the errant name. You'll need to delete it or change it to something that Access recognizes.

- Still no luck? Check the bugs discussed in MSKB 8118600 and MSKB 298877.

No Access License

THE ANNOYANCE: I use Access XP for most of my work, but I recently installed Access 97 for compatibility with some older databases we use. Every time I try to run Access 97, though, I get the message "Microsoft Access can't start because there is no license for it on this machine." Both copies are fully licensed!

NOTE

Access has a built-in data documenter that will print out a description of any database object. If you can't find the parameter the error message refers to, click Tools→Analyze→Documenter and create a file for the relevant object(s). Then use a text editor to search the file for the errant name.

THE FIX: Oddly enough, this is probably caused by a font that trips up the Windows Registry (but see below, if you're running Windows NT 4.0 or Windows 2000). The fix is simple—hide the font and uninstall/reinstall Access 97 to force the Registry to be rewritten:

1. Search your system for a font called *hatten.ttf* (or possibly *Haettenschweiler.ttf*).

2. Rename it something like *hatten.bak*.

3. Use the Add or Remove Programs control panel to uninstall Access 97.

4. Reinstall Access 97.

5. Rename *hatten.bak* to *hatten.ttf*.

If you're running NT 4.0 or Windows 2000, it's a permissions problem. Your administrator will need to edit your Registry to give you read permissions for the license key. See MSKB 141373 for detailed instructions.

User-Defined Type Not Defined

THE ANNOYANCE: What the heck does the "User-defined type not defined" message mean? It sounds like some geek's version of the liar's paradox. I didn't define any types (at least, I don't think I did).

THE FIX: This error only relates to Visual Basic code, so if you haven't written any code yourself, it's a sure bet that there's a problem with the way Access's built-in code libraries are set up. For instance, if you encounter this error when using built-in functions such as Date() and Now(), Access is confused about where to find the VBA library and/or the Access Object Library (see the next annoyance, "Missing References").

On the other hand, if you *are* writing code, Access is telling you that you've used a data type it doesn't recognize. This could be as simple as a typo (e.g., you typed Strng instead of String), but more commonly, you're trying to use a DAO object when you're set up to use ADO, or vice versa. Remember that prior to Access 2000, the default was DAO; then Access switched to ADO. You can use both of them, but it's tricky, and you'll have to set your references explicitly. Do this in the VB Editor's Tools→References dialog—just check the box next to the library you need, and press OK. (For more information, see "DAO Versus ADO" in Chapter 0.)

All Cretans Are Liars

The liar's paradox is usually attributed to the Greek poet Epimenides, who famously declared "All Cretans are liars…one of their own poets has said so." (He hailed from Crete, so he could say that.) A few centuries later, Eubulides honed the paradox by simply stating, "This statement is false." Those guys obviously didn't have any real work to do!

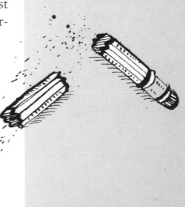

Missing References

THE ANNOYANCE: I moved my contacts database to a new PC, and now several references are marked as missing in the Available References dialog box. But I didn't change anything!

THE FIX: References are how you tell Access where to find external code modules or libraries. Some of these libraries are needed for Access to work at all, and others are used in custom applications. Here are some of the typical errors you'll get if Access can't find the libraries it needs:

- "Variable not defined."

- "Run-time error '5': Invalid procedure call or argument."

- "Microsoft Visual Basic: The library which contains this symbol is not referenced by the current project, so the symbol is undefined."

- "Compile Error: Can't find project or library."

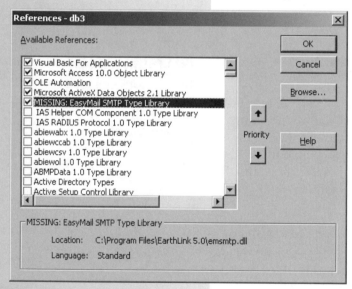

Figure 1-23. The Visual Basic references manager can show you which references are missing.

To see which references you're using, open the VB Editor (Ctrl-G) and click Tools→References to open the Available References dialog. You'll see checkmarks next to any libraries currently in use. If any of these are marked "MISSING," as in Figure 1-23, this means that Access can't find them. Occasionally this happens with a library that you're not actually using. Instead of fixing it, just uncheck the box to tell Access you don't need it. But how do you know if you *do* need a library? Choose Debug→ Compile. This compiles all your VB code; if it compiles fine, even with the libraries missing, you don't need them.

This error typically pops up when you change the version of Access or Windows that you're running. To fix it, first reset the reference. Write down its exact name, uncheck its box, and then close the Available References dialog. Reopen the dialog, find the same reference (it won't be in the same place in the list this time), and check its box again. This will often be enough to force Access to refresh its link to the library.

If this fails, uncheck *all* the references, both missing and non-missing (write them down first!), and reset them using the above procedure. Then choose Debug→Compile, and compile and save your project.

If there's a specific custom library that Access can't locate, and you know where it is, choose Tools→References and use the Browse button to show Access where to find it. Finally, if Access still can't resolve the reference, it's possible that the library really is missing. Perhaps it was inadvertently deleted, or was never properly installed. In that case, you'll need to reinstall the library, or possibly check the integrity of your whole installation. (See "Agonies of a Sick Installation," earlier in this chapter.)

Disk or Network Errors

THE ANNOYANCE: We have an Access 2000 backend running on a Windows NT file server. Users on client PCs get sporadic "disk or network" errors and must shut down in order to reconnect. I don't think there's a problem with the network.

THE FIX: Hmm. Maybe there is. These error messages indicate that Access cannot read the MDB file because of a disk or network problem. This is usually caused by flaky hardware, including cables, network interface cards (NICs), hubs, and so on. Since hardware problems are often intermittent, Access may work fine for a while and then disconnect abruptly. Access is much less tolerant of minor network instability than other apps (such as Word), which only need to write to a file now and then. In a split database model, Access is constantly writing across the network, and if a single write fails, it must give up the ghost or risk losing additional data. Diagnosing network hardware problems is beyond the scope of this book, but take a look at "Best Practices for Access on Networks" in Chapter 2.

Database corruption can also produce this message. Try compacting and repairing your MDB files (see "Flaky or Corrupted Database," earlier in this chapter). Also check to make sure your tmp environment variable points to a usable temp folder; see MSKB 251254 for more information.

Database Is Read-Only or File Is Already in Use

THE ANNOYANCE: We haven't even set a password on our database, but we're having permissions problems. This morning I tried to open our MDB and was not allowed to.

THE FIX: This is a common "gotcha" caused by the way Access keeps track of who's using a database at any given time. When a database is opened the first time, Access creates an LDB file (known as a "lock file") in the same directory, with the same name as the MDB file. A problem arises when some users don't have Windows filesystem permissions in the folder where the

MDB is stored. Even users who have only read-only access to the database itself must have read/write/create/delete permissions on the folder. *Create permission* is needed because the first user who opens the MDB creates the lock file. If no lock file is created, the database will be opened in exclusive mode, and all other users will be locked out. *Write permission* is needed because each subsequent user who opens the database must be able to update the lock file, or she'll be locked out. *Delete permission* is needed because whoever is last to close the MDB must delete the lock file.

Discuss this problem with your system administrator; she will be able to set up the requisite permissions.

Getting by Without a Lock File

There is one situation where Access may open an MDB *without* an LDB file: when it is opened in exclusive mode (by starting Access with no database, then selecting File→Open, clicking the arrow to the right of the Open button, and selecting "Open Exclusive"). In this case, only one user will be able to use the database at a time. (To complicate matters, recent versions of Access create the LDB even in exclusive mode. If anyone knows why, they're not talking.)

Performance, Versions, Security, and Deployment

2

As Access developers, we love creating elegant user interfaces and solving tough problems with ingenious code. But the evil Borgs who manage people like us know that most of the work goes into an Access application *after* it's written. The most effort and the biggest headaches arise during the unglamorous tasks of deployment and maintenance.

In this chapter we'll delve into the good, the bad, and the ugly of deploying a finished Access application. To start with, we'll look at how to diagnose and fix various performance issues. We'll show you how to avoid the embarrassment of having your beautifully crafted user interface become unusable because it can't handle a measly 10,000 records, and where to look for performance bottlenecks. Next, we'll step you through the delicacies of coping with multiple versions of Access. Then, since most projects require some form of security, we'll guide you through the stupefying maze of Access security—and give you the lowdown on just how (in)secure it really is. Finally, we'll show you how to move a multi-user application onto a network without the corruption that dogs so many projects, discuss best network practices and how to avoid the tedium of manual DSN setup on every user's machine, and maybe make replication a little less scary.

PERFORMANCE

Database Bloat from Images or OLE Objects

THE ANNOYANCE: We have a tiny employees database, and I thought it would be handy to store our ID photos with the rest of the employee data. These are small JPGs, no bigger than 100 KB each, and I only added five of them—but my database has gone from 400 KB to about 24 MB! What the heck happened?

THE FIX: Access provides an OLE data type that accepts objects such as pictures, sound files, spreadsheets, or Word documents, so you can do the kind of thing you tried to do. Don't do it. Even tiny objects will cause your database to bloat like a dead hog on a Texas highway. That's because Access is storing not only the object, but all the rendering (display) information, too. Rendering information can easily be larger than the object itself (see MSKB 123151 for more information).

Instead of storing pictures in your tables, link to them using the *image control*, which knows how to display them when the time comes. You'll find the image control in the standard toolbox. After you place it on your form or report, it'll prompt you for the location of the picture file to be displayed.

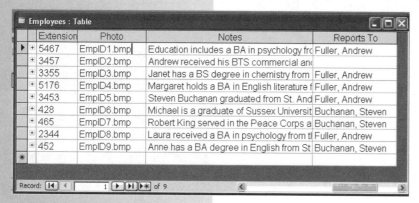

Figure 2-1. Only the name of the image file is being stored in the database. Code can be used to actually display the image on a form or report.

This solution is fine for simple applications, but it doesn't let you store and manage the picture locations as data within your database, which is often what you really want to do. If your image collection grows or moves, you don't want the file paths hardcoded in a control somewhere. Instead, set up the image control, then clear the Picture property, which is found on the Format tab of the image control's properties sheet. Next, add a dab of VB code to the Current event of your form that lets it read the picture location from a table (as in Figure 2-1), and set the image control to display it. The code might look like this:

```
Me![myImageControl].Picture = "fullPathToImageFile"
Me![myImageControl].Visible = True
Me.PaintPalette = Me![myImageControl].ObjectPalette
```

You may want to store your images with file paths relative to the location of your MDB file, which makes it easy to move the MDB and images without changing the code or data in your tables. The trick is constructing the full path for each image in your VB code, using the CurrentProject.Path property to look up where the MDB is currently stored.

For example, if your images were stored in an "images" folder in the same directory as your MDB, and you stored only the filenames in your database, you'd replace **"fullPathToImageFile"** in the previously shown code with this: **CurrentProject.Path & "\images\" & strNextFile**. In a real application, you'd probably want to add code to hide the image control if the picture doesn't exist, and so on. (Check out the code in the Current event of the Employees form in the sample Northwind database that comes with Access.) If you're doing a lot of work with images, you might consider using a commercial image control such as DBPix ($99; *http://www.ammara.com*). Also check out the web sites of Access MVPs Stephen Lebans (*http://www.lebans.com*) and Larry Linson (*http://members.tripod.com/accdevel/imaging.htm*) for more information and various approaches to working with images in Access.

To display non-image objects—such as Word docs, PDFs, Excel files, and so on—the best approach is actually to not display them within Access at all. Instead, use VB's Shell function to open the appropriate application for that file. For instance, here's a one-liner that you could put in the Click event of a button that will send a PDF file to Adobe Acrobat:

```
Shell "FullPathToAcrobatReader FullPathToPDFFile", vbNormalFocus
```

Why Is My Database So Slow?

THE ANNOYANCE: My database is running slower...and slower...and slower. There are only 10,000 records in the database. Is that more than Access can handle?

THE FIX: In the database world, 10,000 records is a drop in a teacup. We'll give you some tricks for improving Access performance, but first, let's check the basics. We'll assume that you're up-to-date on basic system maintenance (defragging your hard drive, installing sufficient RAM, and so on) and that you've been through the "Installation Checklist" section in the Appendix. Having your service packs up to date can make a big difference. Finally, we'll assume that you've manually set up the appropriate indexes for your tables (see "Speed Up Slow Queries" in Chapter 4).

> **NOTE**
>
> *If you're running a split database, also see the next Annoyance, "Why Is My Split Database So Slow?"*

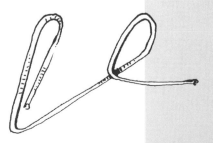

The Jet database engine upon which Access is built can easily handle tables with 10,000+ records, as long as the database is well designed. But of course, it's all a question of what you're trying to do with those records. If you want your application to perform well even as the amount of data grows, you must minimize data transfer by loading (or otherwise processing) only the records that are actually needed.

The following presents some useful tweaks to help you avoid the worst bottlenecks.

Name AutoCorrect and Subdatasheet Name

If you haven't already turned off Name AutoCorrect, do so (see "Access's Bad Defaults" in Chapter 1 for details). Similarly, by default all your tables have their Subdatasheet Name properties set to "Auto," which can cause performance problems. Set it to "None." If you want to adjust this setting on all your tables at once, try the code in MSKB 261000.

Queries

If SELECT queries are running slowly, make sure that you're indexing the criteria and sort fields. In other words, any fields in your query that have criteria in the Criteria line, or have their Sort lines set, can benefit from being indexed (see Figure 2-2).

> **NOTE**
>
> *Access Help also includes an extensive list of useful tips in an article entitled "Improve Performance of an Access Database." You can find it by doing an Answer Wizard search on "optimize performance."*

If UPDATE queries are bogging down, make sure you're not indexing any unnecessary fields. (Go to Tools→ Options, click the Tables/Queries tab, and clear the AutoIndex field.) See "Speed Up Slow Queries" in Chapter 4 for more information about indexes.

In a UNION query, use UNION ALL instead of UNION; UNION checks for and eliminates duplicate rows, which takes time.

Finally, it is much faster to sort on fields rather than expressions. For example, use **ORDER BY LastName, FirstName** instead of **ORDER BY LastName & ", " & FirstName**.

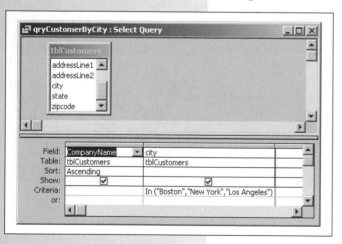

Figure 2-2. This query applies criteria to the city field and sorts on the CompanyName field. If it's running slowly, you could speed it up by applying indexes to those two fields.

Reports

As with queries, index the fields on which you sort or group, and avoid sorting and grouping on expressions. (To see if you are, open the report in Design View and go to View→Sorting and Grouping.) Avoid domain aggregate functions (such as DLookup)—instead, add the tables or queries you need directly to the report's underlying query.

Subreports (reports that are nested inside another report and linked on a specific field) can drastically slow down opening and printing a report. That's because a subreport gets opened anew every time it is called. You must either optimize your subreports or eliminate them. To optimize subreports, index the fields by which they're linked to the main report (see the link fields on the Data tab of the report's subcontrol). Also, base them on queries rather than tables, and don't include unnecessary fields in the queries; your table might have 25 fields, but if you need only 3 for the report, create a query that just has those 3 fields. If the subreport is still too slow, you may be able to eliminate it by pulling its data into your main report.

Finally, filter the main report to reduce the number of pages that must be printed or viewed at any one time. You'll speed up performance if you restrict your report to a narrower date range, a particular company, or some other relevant variable.

Forms

Forms, subforms, combo boxes, and list boxes—anything with a recordset or row source—will "scale" poorly—(that is, performance will degrade more and more as the amount of data grows) if bound directly to a table or query. For instance, if you set up a form to display all the Zip Codes in the U.S., by default Access loads the entire set of records at the outset. (And if your form has controls such as combo and list boxes, the data may actually load several times every time the form is opened.) To avoid this glut of record loading, follow these guidelines:

Limit recordsets.

> Your forms will hop through recordsets of arbitrary size if they only *load* one record at a time. For example, you can open the form with a single record displayed, and then allow users to select other records to display using a combo box (see "Find Records Faster" in Chapter 5). Simply set the form's Record Source property to an SQL statement such as this:

```
Select * From tblCustomers Where CustomerID = DLast("CustomerID",
"tblCustomers");
```

Alternatively, you can display a form that opens to a *new* (i.e., blank) record using an SQL statement such as the following, which returns no records:

```
Select * From tblCustomers Where False;
```

Place code in the Change event for the combo box to set the RecordSource property and show the selected record. Here's the standard way to do that, using the example of a customers form that has a combo box to select the customer:

```
Private Sub cboCustomer_Change()
    If Not IsNull(Me![cboCustomer]) Then
        Me.RecordSource = "SELECT * FROM tblCustomers WHERE " & _
                          "customerId = " & Me![cboCustomer]
    End If
End Sub
```

This fix prevents your form from loading more than one record at a time. If the combo box you use for selecting records is still too slow, see "Speed Up Slow Combo Boxes" in Chapter 5.

This fix assumes that you're comfortable constructing the appropriate SQL statement for your form's Record Source. If you're not, you can accomplish the same thing by referencing saved queries as your form's Record Source. For example, create a query based on the customers table, and save it as qryCustomersEmpty. Then add * to the Field line of the query, and add **customerId** as a second field, with its Criteria line set to "False." This query returns no records and can be used as your form's preset Record Source. (To link it to the form, put the name of the query into your form's Record Source property, on the Data tab of the form's properties sheet.) Save a second version of the query as qryCustomerLookup, and in customerId's Criteria line, put **Forms!frmCustomers!cboCustomer**. This query will use the combo box value to find a single record in the customers table. Then use the following code in the combo box's Change event to set the form's record source to the query:

```
Private Sub cboCustomer_Change()
        Me.RecordSource = "qryCustomerLookup"
End Sub
```

Load records on demand.

If a complex form has multiple subforms (or other controls) bound to large recordsets, chances are a user won't need all of these controls at the same time. If so, place the controls on distinct pages of a tab control, and leave the record source unset until the user clicks that page. For example, here's how you might set subform record sources for the second and third pages of a tab:

```
Private Sub tabMain_Change()
    If tabMain = 1 Then
    'Second page
        Me!sctlOrders.Form.RecordSource = "SELECT * " & _
                 "from tblOrders WHERE customerId = " & _
                                    Me!cboCustomer
    ElseIf tabMain = 2 Then
    'Third page
        Me!sctlSuppliers.Form.RecordSource = "SELECT * " _
                                "FROM tblSuppliers"
    End If
End Sub
```

Note that we skip the first page of the tab control, since it is visible immediately. Note that we don't use the Click event of each tab page, because those events don't fire when you click a tab; they fire when you click *inside* the page itself. Instead, we use the tab control's Change event. To determine which page was clicked, we test the value of the tab control, which gives the page number. Pages are numbered sequentially from 0, so the second page has a value of 1.

Hide, don't close.

Once a form is loaded, never close it. Instead, simply hide the form. First, disable the standard close buttons. In the form's properties sheet, click the Format tab and set Close Button and Control Box to "No." Now add your own "Close" button to the form, and in its Click event, make your form invisible, like this:

```
Forms!frmCustomers.Visible = False
Forms!frmMyMainMenu.Visible = True
```

Now instead of closing, the form just hides itself. When the user tries to reopen it, the form will automatically make itself visible again. You'll probably want to include the second line, as shown, which opens whatever switchboard or menu form you set.

A related trick is to open the most frequently used forms in hidden mode when the database itself is opened. Do this in two steps. First, open a single form at startup by going to Tools→Startup and selecting the form you want in the "Display Form/Page" box. Next, go to that form's Open event and open the other forms, like so:

```
DoCmd.OpenForm "frmCustomers", , , , , acHidden
```

Both of these tricks will speed up performance, since users won't have to wait for the forms to load when they "open" them. However, having lots of hidden forms open will rapidly use up RAM on your users' machines, so you may want to employ these techniques sparingly.

Functions

Domain aggregate functions such as DLookup, DSum, and so on are generally slower than the corresponding queries, which use the highly optimized Jet database engine. Domain functions simply perform calculations on sets of records (from tables or queries), and you can generally do the same calculations using a totals query. For example, if you're using DAvg in an expression in a query, instead you can create a separate totals query using the Avg function, add it to your first query (just like adding a table), and use the result. (For a complete list of these functions, see Table A-7 in the Appendix.)

Why Is My Split Database So Slow?

THE ANNOYANCE: We recently split our database and put the backend on a fast server. We have a moderate number of users and only 50,000 records, but it takes forever to do anything—open a form, find a record, and so on. This system is almost useless!

THE FIX: First, see the previous Annoyance for basic ways to optimize any Access database. In this fix, we'll look at a few tricks that are specific to speeding up split databases on networks. In general, remember that there are three places to look for performance bottlenecks: the client, the network, and the server. If any one of these is not running optimally, everything drags.

Maintain a Persistent Connection to the Backend

Locking problems on the LDB file can cause significant connection delays. To avoid these delays, your frontend should be set up to maintain a connection whenever it is open. An easy way to do this is to create a simple form (frmStayAlive) bound to any small table with a few records in the backend. You'll open this form at startup, hide it, and keep it open at all times. Put code such as the following in the On Open event of your startup form (or switchboard):

```
DoCmd.OpenForm "frmStayAlive", acNormal, , , , acHidden
```

This simple fix can make a big difference.

Make the Backend Easy to Get To

Use a short name for your backend, and place it on the root of a network share, rather than burying it deep in nested folders. Yes, this can make a difference.

Check Your Anti-Virus Software

Make sure that the anti-virus software running on client machines keeps an eye on local drives only, and doesn't attempt to scan the backend every time a connection is made.

XP Home Is Way Slow

THE ANNOYANCE: I recently deployed our database on some new Win XP Home Edition PCs, and the performance is much worse than on XP Pro systems. What's going on?

THE FIX: Home Edition allows only workgroup (i.e., peer-to-peer) networking, rather than NT domain networking, so it supports far fewer open connections to your server. It's not an Access problem, but Access does work better with more open connections. Of course, you should try all the performance optimizations discussed in this section, but in this case the most important fix is to update these PCs to XP Professional. The same applies to PCs running other flavors of Windows that only support workgroups, such as Windows 9x and Windows Me.

Access with SQL Server Is Still Slow

THE ANNOYANCE: We recently migrated an Access database with about 200,000 records to SQL Server, but we're still using Access as our frontend. We expected to see a dramatic performance improvement, but if anything, the darn thing is running slower! What are we doing wrong?

THE FIX: Part of the problem may be your expectations. Moving up to an enterprise DBMS enables much stronger data protection, more concurrent users, fewer corruption problems, and the ability to scale to very large data sets. But with this relatively modest amount of data, SQL Server isn't necessarily going to be faster than Access's Jet engine. If it's *slower*, the first thing to check is whether you're maintaining a persistent connection (see "Why Is My Split Database So Slow?," earlier in this chapter).

If your standard Access queries to the server are running slowly, try replacing them with *pass-through queries*. These queries are designed to be passed through to the server, rather than being processed in Access. When you use a standard query in a client/server setting, Access does try to pass the query to the server to be executed there. But in some situations (for instance, if you use native Access functions, or Access SQL that the SQL database can't translate), Access can't pass along the query. Instead, it must request the raw data from the server and process the query on the client PC. This works fine, but it's usually far more efficient to have the server process the query.

To create a pass-through query in Access, start with a blank query grid and choose Query→SQL Specific→Pass-Through. Access will open a big, blank window for the SQL code you want to pass to the server (see Figure 2-3). Just enter the SQL code, save the query, and give it a name.

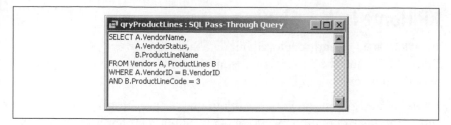

Figure 2-3. A pass-through query using Oracle syntax. Note the absence of the "AS" keyword for aliases and the absence of the semicolon at the end, which would be required if this were an Access query.

When constructing a pass-through query, remember to use SQL syntax appropriate for your server, rather than Access SQL. If you don't know SQL, you can use the Query Designer GUI to create the query. Once your query is working, convert it to a pass-through query by invoking the same Pass-Through menu sequence as above. By default, the Query Designer generates Access SQL, which may differ from the SQL used by your server. For better results, go to Tools→Options→Tables/Queries, and check the "This database" box under "SQL Server Compatible Syntax (ANSI 92)." This gives you a more portable flavor of the SQL language. Note: you can't convert a query that uses parameters; you'll have to handle parameters in code.

Once you've created the pass-through query, you must tell it how to connect to your server. Open its properties sheet (View→Properties), and set the ODBC connection string using the builder. The builder lets you choose a DSN, but a DSN-less connection string will also work. Set the Return Records property to "Yes" for select queries and to "No" for all others. (Some developers prefer to handle edits, updates, deletes, and inserts by calling stored procedures on the server; pass-through queries can do this, too.) You'll run the query like any other—double-click it or click on the Datasheet View.

Pass-through queries have two limitations:

- They are *never* updatable (see the sidebar "Updatable Queries" in Chapter 4), so you cannot use them as the record source for a form that is used to edit data. Instead, use a linked table or a standard query that minimizes the number of records returned (see "Why Is My Database So Slow?," earlier in this chapter).

- Access will not allow a pass-through query to be used as the record source for a subform (or subreport) that uses the Linked Child and Linked Master fields. Instead, either use a standard query, or don't use the linking fields.

VERSIONS, UPGRADES, AND CONVERSION

Access Works on One PC but Not Another

THE ANNOYANCE: The Access 2000 database I've been running for years on my Windows 98 PC craps out on my Windows XP Pro PC. It's a simple application—a couple of macros and a few buttons on forms. Sometimes the buttons work fine, but other times the program crashes.

THE FIX: First, make sure your version of Access is compatible with XP (see the next Annoyance, "Access/Windows Compatibility Issues"). XP and Access 2000 are indeed supposedly compatible, but in many cases problems arise anyhow. Why?

Assuming that bad karma is not the problem (you never know), the most likely cause is that something (software, hardware, installed patch files) is different on the two machines. But what? With Microsoft's elegant installation process, there are only a few thousand possibilities. That's why we created the "Installation Checklist" in the Appendix—run through it to ensure that the problematic machine is up to date in all respects. If you're running Access on a network, check your machine's Network Interface Card (NIC) and connection as well (see "Best Practices for Access on Networks," later in this chapter).

Access/Windows Compatibility Issues

THE ANNOYANCE: My boss wants me to install Access 2000 on our new Windows XP machines. Will this work? Why does Microsoft make it so hard to find out about compatibility?

THE FIX: What, you haven't upgraded to the latest version of everything? (Doing so would spare you this grief and fatten Microsoft's wallet—a win/win for everyone, no?) Well, you are right about one thing: Microsoft doesn't make it easy to find out about version compatibility. Table 2-1 shows what we were able to dig up. The general rule is that it's fine to run older versions of Access on newer versions of Windows, but don't do the opposite.

Table 2-1. Access and Windows compatibility

Access version	Compatible Windows versions
Access 2003	Microsoft Windows 2000 with Service Pack 3 (SP3), Microsoft Windows XP
Access 2002 (Access XP)	Microsoft Windows NT 4.0 with Service Pack 6.0a (SP6a), Microsoft Windows XP, Microsoft Windows Millennium Edition (Me), Microsoft Windows 98
Access 2000	Microsoft Windows NT Workstation version 4.0, Service Pack 3 or later, Microsoft Windows 95
Access 97	Microsoft Windows NT Version 3.51 with Service Pack 5 (SP5), Microsoft Windows 95

Converting Old Databases

THE ANNOYANCE: We're upgrading to Office 2003, but we have a lot of ancient databases running in equally ancient versions of Access. Do we have to convert all these old databases? It would be a nightmare!

THE FIX: Unfortunately, "legacy" databases put you between a rock and a hard place. Yes, conversion can be a pain. But if you don't convert, you enter the pity trail of supporting the multiple versions of Office necessary to run those older versions of Access, which can break even the most hardened system administrator.

While it's true that developers often run multiple versions of Access, this is not a good idea for end users. Best practice is to keep your users' desktops up to date and convert their frontends as needed.

To convert an old database, here's what to do. From your most recent version of Access, choose Tools→Database Utilities→Convert Database, and choose the file format you want to convert to (see Figure 2-4). If the version you want is not listed, that version is not compatible—it may just be too old. If the version you want is grayed out, you're running that version right now. Access will then prompt you for a new name for the database.

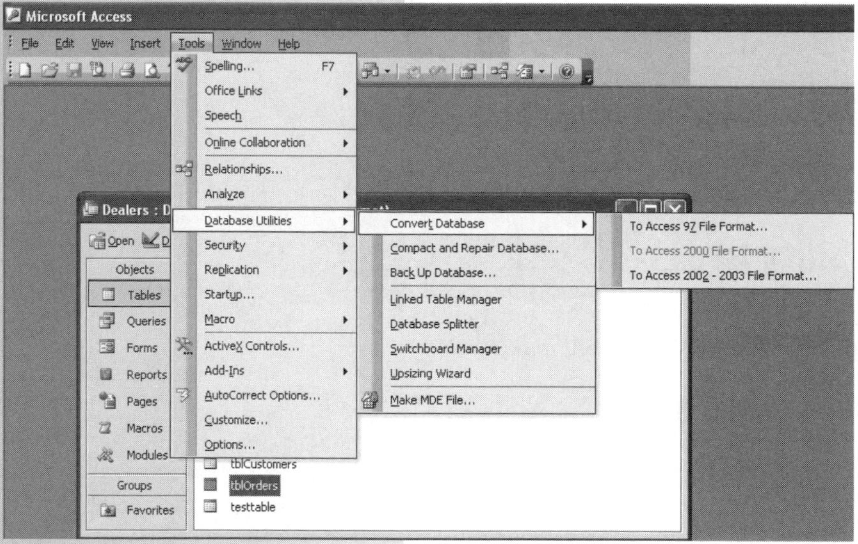

Figure 2-4. From the latest version of Access, you can convert your older database to a newer format.

Access's conversion tool will get you most of the way. The main gotcha arises because more recent versions of Access default to using the ADO code library, while older versions used DAO. If you have any custom VB code, this can cause some variable declarations to become ambiguous. (See "DAO Versus ADO" in Chapter 0 for more information.) Microsoft has white papers to help with the conversion process:

- For Access 97, see MSKB 151193.

- For Access 2000, see MSKB 237313.

- For Access 2002, see MSKB 319400.

In Access 2002 and later, there is a conversion errors table that you should check after each conversion; see MSKB 283849 for more information.

Running the Same Database in Multiple Versions of Access

THE ANNOYANCE: I have five users running five different versions of Access. I know this isn't ideal, but I don't want to upgrade all of them to the latest version.

THE FIX: They don't *have* to upgrade, but if they don't, they can't take advantage of Access's latest features, such as PivotCharts and PivotTables (both introduced in Access 2002).

If you need to support multiple versions of Access, split the database. (This recommendation is a no-brainer any time you're in a multi-user environment; sharing an unsplit MDB across a network is a sure recipe for corruption.) The key to making this work is that the backend—the part that contains your tables—*must be in the oldest format* that you want to support. That's because everybody uses the same backend, and you can't open an MDB file created in a format more recent than your version of Access. So, if even one user is running Access 2000, your backend must be in Access 2000 format (or older).

The frontends—the queries, forms, and reports that run on each PC—must be compatible with whatever version of Access is installed on the PC, but they don't all have to be the same version. Thus, the latest forms, reports, and such can be made available to those people running the latest version of Access, while those with older versions of Access can run the older frontends. The downside is that you'll have to create and manage multiple versions of the frontend, which is a chore.

Running Different Versions of Access on the Same PC

THE ANNOYANCE: I recently upgraded to Office 2002. I want to keep Access 97 on my system because I have to support users who still run Office 97, but the new Office installation seems to have clobbered the old one, and now Access 97 won't even start.

THE FIX: Given the compatibility issues between different Office versions, you'd think that Microsoft would acknowledge the need to keep older versions of Access around—and they do, sort of. The official stance is that running multiple versions of Access on the same machine is "not recommended," but they tell you how to do it anyway (see MSKB 241141). Many people run three or four different versions of Access on the same machine (under the latest version of Office, of course). It works fine; you just need to know how to do it.

If your installation of Office 2002 clobbered Access 97, it's probably because you accepted the default install directory. You must specify alternate

NOTE

Unlike Access, different versions of Outlook cannot coexist. The installer will remove the older versions no matter what you specify in the Removing Previous Versions dialog.

directories for different versions. Uninstall both versions of Office and Access and start over.

If you're starting from scratch, install the oldest version first and work forward to the newest. If you already have, say, Access 2002 on your system and you want to install Access 97, you can do so, but watch out for the Access 97 license bug (see "No Access License" in Chapter 1).

When installing additional versions of Access, pay attention during the install process. First, specify a different install directory. Second, you *must* tell the installer not to remove older versions. Depending on your Office version, you'll see some variant of a Removing Previous Versions dialog. Select the "Keep these programs" option.

Running the Right Version of Access

THE ANNOYANCE: I mostly work in Access 2002, but I keep Access 97 on my computer because occasionally I develop reports for users who still run this older version. But after I've worked with an Access 97 MDB, the next time I try to open an Access 2002 MDB (by double-clicking it) Access 97 starts up, can't recognize the newer format, and chokes.

THE FIX: By default, whatever version of Access ran last is the one that will be launched the next time you double-click an MDB or MDE file. This can be annoying, but fortunately there are easy workarounds. The simplest is to create a shortcut for each MDB file that specifies the full path to its appropriate executable. Create the shortcut, right-click it, select Properties, click the Shortcut tab, and in the Target field enter something like this:

```
"C:\Program Files\Microsoft Office\Office10\MSACCESS.EXE" "C:\Projects\
Contacts\contacts.mdb"
```

Your "Start in" field can be the same folder as the one in which your MDB file is located.

This technique works fine as long as you don't have tons of MDB files, or their names don't change frequently. If you do (or they do), you can turn to a helper utility that automatically checks the MDB version and opens the correct version of Access: check out Ezy Access Launcher (free; *http://www.aadconsulting.com/addins.html*) or AccVer ($15; *http://www.aylott.com.au/accver.htm*).

WARNING

Careful! If you adopt this file-naming convention, don't give two database files with different extensions the same name. Access creates an LDB file using your database name, and the two LDBs could collide.

If you don't want to install third-party software, use different file extensions for different versions of Access. (There's no law forcing MDB files to use an *.mdb* suffix.) For instance, you could name Access 97 MDB files with an *.a97* extension, Access 2000 files with an *.a2000* extension, and so on. Then go to Windows Explorer, select one of these files, select Tools→ Folder Options, click the File Types tab, click the New button, type in your new extension, and map it to the appropriate version of *MSACCESS.EXE*. Repeat for each type of file.

This Upgrade Is Killing Me!

THE ANNOYANCE: I recently upgraded to Access 2002, and now my database is broken. It worked fine in Access 97. What gives?

THE FIX: An upgrade should make your life easier, not harder. (Microsoft, are you listening?) So why does this one break your stable application? You may be running into a bug in the newer version of Access. As always, apply the usual safeguards (see the "Installation Checklist" section in the Appendix).

Also, make sure that references to VB code libraries haven't gone missing (see "Missing References" in Chapter 1). Open the VB Editor, then click Tools→References (see Figure 2-5). In Access 2000 and later versions, only the ActiveX Data Objects (ADO) library is included by default. If your code relies on DAO, you must add that reference by hand. Just check the box next to the latest version of the Microsoft DAO object library in the References dialog.

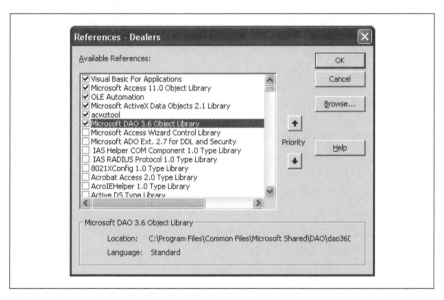

Figure 2-5. The Visual Basic References dialog lets you see which code libraries are included in your application.

Still having problems? You could be running into a compatibility problem between your old code and the new version of Access. The conversion from Access 97 to later versions causes the most problems, because of the switch from DAO to ADO. For example, every recordset must be declared as either a DAO.Recordset or ADODB.Recordset type—otherwise, your new version of Access won't know which one you want it to use. To avoid stumbling over errors at runtime (when the code is interpreted line by line), compile your code so you can track down and fix all the problems in one sitting. Open the VB Editor, and choose Debug→Compile *databasename*. Then work through the error messages one at a time. Typically, you'll need to add a reference to DAO and then change your Dim statements to make sure that your objects don't have the same names in both ADO and DAO.

Many Offices, Many Library Incompatibilities

THE ANNOYANCE: My Access database uses Office automation to interact with Excel, mainly to create charts. Our sales data is in Access, but the top office prefers the charts and analytical tools in Excel. Most of our users run Excel 2002, but some are still using Excel 97. If I set a reference to the object library in Access for Excel 2002, my Access application won't run on the systems using older versions of Excel. But if I use the older library, I can't tap into the new features in Excel 2002. Help me escape this Catch-22!

THE FIX: Office automation definitely becomes a bit more complicated when you do it across multiple versions of Office. You have two options. If you can live with the feature set that's available in Excel 97, just set a reference to the library that's compatible with that version and go home.

But if you want to use newer features available in, say, Excel 2002, and fall back on older features as necessary, you must take a different approach. The standard approach—binding your code to a given library by setting a reference—is known as *early binding* or *virtual table (VTBL) binding*. It is compile-time binding, and you should use it whenever possible. It results in better performance and allows you to catch many programming errors at compile time. However, when you need to support different library versions, you can't bind at compile time. In this case, you'll have to use *late binding* (a.k.a. *IDispatch*). It is slower, and you give up compile-time error checking.

In terms of the code you write (for the Click event of a button, say, that creates an Excel chart), the only difference between early and late binding is in the way that you declare your automation object. To bind at compile time, make the declaration fully explicit, like this:

```
Dim objExcel As Excel.Application
```

To bind at runtime, declare the object this way:

```
Dim objExcel as Object
```

The rest of your code is the same. You can call any methods on an object of type "Object," and you won't get compile errors. For more information, see MSKB 244167.

SECURITY

Access Security Is Weak

THE ANNOYANCE: I've heard that Access security sucks. Is it worth the trouble to master?

THE FIX: Access security is both weak (in a cryptographic sense) and poorly implemented. It's derided in the crypto community, and it's easy to crack with tools you can find on the Internet (see the "Database Lockout" Annoyance in this chapter). Still, it's useful in some situations. For example, it can protect your data from accidents—that is, the *unintended* actions of users. That's why it's important to grant users only those permissions they really need. Assuming you set it up correctly, Access security works just fine—for this purpose. The login will also keep out casual mischief-makers.

Beyond this, Access's security features are not enough to keep sensitive data safe. In addition to its security flaws, an even bigger vulnerability is that even read-only users must have write and delete permissions to the folder where the database is stored. A malicious user could easily delete the MDB file!

Upgrading Secured Databases

THE ANNOYANCE: We're about to convert several Access 97 databases to Access 2002 format. We have fairly complex user-level security applied to these applications. Do we have to recreate security after each conversion?

THE FIX: Nope. As long as you use the built in Conversion tool (Tools→ Database Utilities→Convert Database) Access will take care of migrating the security too. However, if you convert the application by importing all the objects into a database in the newer format, you will need to reapply security info; it does not import that way.

Database Lockout

THE ANNOYANCE: I've inherited a database that was created and maintained by an employee who has since left the company. I need to use this database, but the password I have doesn't work. I'm getting desperate!

THE FIX: Getting locked out of your own database is a common situation, and this may be the only time you are grateful that Access security is hard to apply correctly. First, identify what type of security has been applied to the database. If you're getting a password prompt with a single field (as in Figure 2-6), then you have simple security—one password for the entire database. If your prompt asks for both a name and a password (as in Figure 2-7), then you have user-level security, which is more complicated.

Figure 2-6. The login prompt under simple security requests a password but no username.

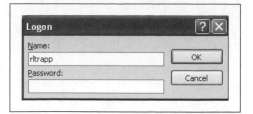

Figure 2-7. The login prompt under user-level security demands both a username and a password.

You may also run into database lockouts when you know the logins for your database but are being shut out because your workgroup file is either missing or corrupted. Fortunately, this too can usually be worked around.

Simple Security

If you're fairly sure that you have the correct password but still can't log in, your database is probably corrupted (see "Flaky or Corrupted Database" in Chapter 1). If you really have lost or forgotten the password, you'll need to recover it. Access guru Michael Kaplan provides free code for Access 97 or earlier versions that does this very neatly (see *http://www.trigeminal. com/lang/1033/codes.asp?ItemID=5#5*). If you're running a later version of Access, see below for information on commercial products/services that can break both simple and user-level security.

User-Level Security

To recover full control of a database protected with user-level security, you must log in as a user with administrator privileges. Assuming you don't know the login, here are some of the common security loopholes you may be able to exploit—*if* security was not properly applied:

Restore the original System.mdw.

> If the database was originally secured using the default workgroup file (*System.mdw*), restore this original (unsecured) file, and you'll be able to open the database without a login. Simply pluck *System.mdw* from your installation CD, rename the file you want to replace, and put the original unsecured copy in its place.

Use the Admin login.

> If the Admin user was not removed from the Admins group when the database was secured (see the next Annoyance, "Administering User-Level Security Correctly"), you can simply rejoin *System.mdw* (Tools→ Security→Workgroup Administrator), or *any* workgroup for which you know the Admin login, and the database will accept it.

Missing or Corrupted Workgroup File

If you know the logins for your database but can't use them because your workgroup file is missing or corrupted, you must repair or recreate the workgroup file. Since an MDW file is actually an Access database, you can repair it by running Tools→Database Utilities→Compact and Repair. First make a copy of the file, and store it in a different folder. Open Access without any database, and try repairing the copy. Then copy it back to the original folder and try to use it.

If this repair fails, or your MDW is missing, you'll need to recreate it. This is not hard to do, assuming you saved all the necessary information when you created it (namely, the exact username, password, and personal ID of at least one user with administrative privileges). You must also have the workgroup ID used when the file was created. Select Tools→Security→ Workgroup Administrator to create a new workgroup file using the exact same information and filename, and your MDB will accept it. If you didn't write down all that information...well, now you know why you should have. Your only hope is a password-recovery app.

Third-Party Products/Services

A Google search on "Microsoft Access password recovery" will find numerous companies offering both software and services for password recovery for both simple and user-level security. Just remember that if you are missing the workgroup file that secured your database, the job is substantially harder; get a guarantee (and a price) before handing over your cash.

Administering User-Level Security Correctly

THE ANNOYANCE: We have multiple users sharing a networked Access database, and I want to be able to assign different access levels to each one. I tried the Security Wizard on a test database, and I locked myself out! How can I properly secure the database without getting a Ph.D. in cryptography?

THE FIX: Administering user-level security in Access is a pain in the neck. It's complicated to set up, and if you miss one step, you can leave a gaping hole that will let users maliciously (or unintentionally) trample on your data. Follow the instructions below to the letter, and your security should be fine. If you're securing a split database, follow these steps for the frontend, then see "Frontend Secure, Backend Unprotected," later in this chapter for securing the backend.

> **NOTE**
> *The "Bible" of Access security is Microsoft's Security FAQ, which can be found at http://support.microsoft.com/ support/access/content/secfaq. asp. This doesn't cover Access 2002/2003, but it's still the best source around.*

Create a New Workgroup File

A *workgroup* is the set of users (and groups of users) for whom you will define permissions in your database. You can have multiple workgroups for different purposes. Each one is defined in a *workgroup file*, which stores the users, groups, and passwords in an encrypted format. To create a workgroup file, open Access without a database and follow these steps:

1. **Create the file.** Choose Tools→Security→Workgroup Administrator, then click the Create button.

2. **Fill in the name, organization, and workgroup ID.** You can use any name and organization that you want; these will be used along with the workgroup ID to uniquely identify the workgroup. (You'll definitely want to change the defaults, which can easily be guessed by anyone using your computer.) The workgroup ID can be any random string of characters; it will be used to create a unique identifier for the file. Be sure to write down these three fields in a safe place. If your workgroup file is ever lost or corrupted you will need them to recreate it.

> **NOTE**
>
> *Workgroup Administrator is not built into Access 2000 or earlier versions; it is included as a standalone utility, wrkgadm.exe, located by default in C:\Program Files\ Microsoft Office. Double-click the file in Windows Explorer to activate it.*

TIP

Use meaningful names for your workgroup files. Keeping them all in one directory makes it easy to switch between them.

Create a New Database Administrator

By default, every database you create is owned by Admin. You must change this. No database owned by Admin can be properly secured, and once your database *has* been secured, ownership can't easily be changed. Therefore, it's essential to change ownership *before you run the Security Wizard*. Start Access without any database, and follow these steps:

1. **Set up the login for Admin.** Choose Tools→Security→User and Group Accounts and click the Change Logon Password tab. (Note that you are currently logged on as Admin.) Leave the Old Password field blank and enter a new password for Admin. You're doing this because you can't remove the Admin user, so you need to create a login for it. Doing this also activates the login procedure for other users.

2. **Create a new database administrator.** Choose Tools→Security→User and Group Accounts, click the Users tab, and hit the New button. Enter any name and personal ID you like, and click OK to confirm. (As with the workgroup ID, the personal ID can be any random string.) Write down the name and personal ID. Now add this new user to the Admins group, giving him administrative privileges.

3. **Set the administrator login.** Once you have created the new administrator, restart Access, this time opening a database. You will be prompted to log in. Log in with the name of the new administrator, leaving the password blank. Choose Tools→Security→User and Group Accounts, click the Change Logon Password tab, and set up a password.

4. **Remove Admin from the Admins group.** Choose Tools→Security→ User and Group Accounts and click the Users tab. In the Name drop-down menu, make sure Admin is selected. In the Available Groups list box below, select the Admins group and click the Remove button (see Figure 2-8). This ensures that only accounts that you set up as administrators will have administrator privileges. (This step has to come last because the Admins group can never be empty.)

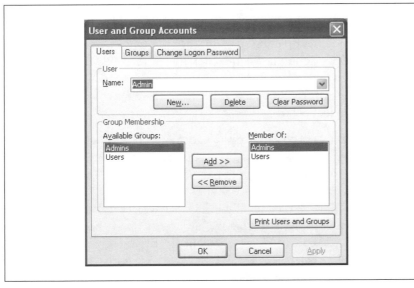

Figure 2-8. By default, the Admin user is a member of the Admins group. It's essential to remove this membership, so that Admin is only a member of Users. Since Access won't allow the Admins group to be empty, you'll need to create a new user with administrator privileges first.

Create a New, Secured Database

Access's Security Wizard can create a secured copy of your database, owned by the user that's currently logged in. The Wizard will remove all permissions from the Admin user and the Users group, and also encrypts the database. Here's how: open the database that you want to secure, logging in as the new administrator you just created. Choose Tools→Security→User-level Security Wizard and accept all of the Wizard's defaults (modify current workgroup information file, secure all objects, use no pre-defined groups, grant no permissions to Users, and add no users to workgroup). The Wizard automatically closes the unsecured database and reopens the secured one.

Admin Versus Admins Versus Users

There are three built-in entities in an Access workgroup: Admin, Users, and Admins. They cannot be removed.

Admin is the default user. It has no inherent privileges, except that by default it belongs to the Admins group.

Users is the default group. Every user belongs to it, even those who have not logged in. By default, it has all privileges except those of ownership.

Admins is a group that has irrevocable administrative privileges (consisting of defining users and groups and setting permissions). Only users that you wish to be administrators should be added to this group.

WARNING

The Security Wizards in Access 97 and 2000 have several bugs that will leave security holes. If you're using these older versions, see Microsoft's Security FAQ (http://support.microsoft. com/support/access/content/ secfaq.asp) for additional steps you must take.

Create Custom Groups

You already have an Admins group for database administrators. In a typical setup, you might also want a Writers group, for users with permission to add/modify data, and a Readers group, for users who only need to view data. (Putting a user in the Readers group doesn't mean you don't trust him; it just means there's no risk of him inadvertently changing data.) Here's the procedure: choose Tools→Security→User and Group Accounts, click the Groups tab, and click the New button. Once again, enter (and write down) name and personal ID information.

Assign Permissions to Groups

The Admins group already has its permissions set up correctly, but your new groups have no permissions. Here's how to set them up:

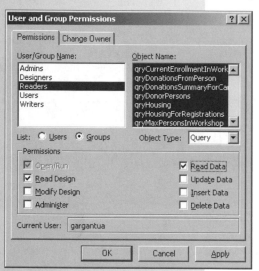

Figure 2-9. For each group and each object type (tables, forms, and so on), you can select some or all of the objects and apply permissions to the whole set at once.

1. **Open the Permissions tab.** Choose Tools→Security→User and Group Permissions, and click the Permissions tab. Change the view by selecting the Groups option button. You should now see a list that includes Admins and Users, plus the new groups you just created.

2. **Assign permissions.** Systematically work through all the objects in your database, assigning appropriate privileges to each group in turn (you can ignore Admins and Users). The interface is a bit clumsy, but here's one approach. Select your first group, then set Object Type to "Table." Under Object Name, select all the items (using Shift-click). Now check or uncheck permissions as needed (see Figure 2-9). Finally, hit the Apply button. Now, while that object type is still selected, go back and choose a different group, and set permissions for it the same way. Once you've done all your groups, go on to the next object type. Note that you cannot change permissions on the database object itself—just skip it.

Create Users

The last step is to create your user accounts—(that is, the login names that people will use):

1. **Create users.** Choose Tools→Security→User and Group Accounts and click the Users tab. Press the New button, and enter the name and personal ID for your first user. Then select the appropriate group(s), and click the Add button to add this user to those groups. If the user is in more than one group, she'll be granted the highest permissions that each group has. (In other words, you can restrict a user only by removing her from a group, not by adding her to a group. Note that you can't

remove anyone from the Users group.) Repeat this procedure for all of your users.

2. **Set logins for the new users.** Close Access and restart it without a database. Choose Tools→Security→User and Group Accounts. You'll be prompted for a login. Set the name to your first user, but leave the password blank. The User and Group Accounts tab will come up. Choose "Change Logon Password" and assign a new password, as in step 3 under "Create a new database administrator" earlier in this chapter. Close Access and repeat this process for each of your new users. We said this was going to be tedious!

Restore the Default Workgroup (Optional)

Once you've created your secured database, you may wish to restore the default workgroup. If you don't, the workgroup and logins you just created will be applied by default to all Access databases, and users will be forced to log into every one. If that is not what you want, go back to Tools→Security→Workgroup Administrator, and use the Join button to restore *System.mdw* as your default. (In older versions, the file extension will be *.mda*, not *.mdw*.)

If you try to open a properly secured database with *System.mdw*, Access will refuse. A secured database must be opened with its own workgroup file. To do this, create a shortcut that specifies the workgroup file, using the Target property of the shortcut. The syntax for the shortcut target is **"FullPathToMSAccess.exe" "FullPathToDatabase.mdb" /wrkgrp "FullPathToWorkgroup.mdw"**.

Undo Botched Security

THE ANNOYANCE: Aargh! I just ran the Security Wizard and botched it. How do I undo it so I can start over? This time I promise I'll follow your instructions....

THE FIX: Sure, that's what they all say. The easiest thing to do is to find the backup file created by the Security Wizard. This is an unsecured copy of your database; by default it is named something like *dbname_Backup.mdb*. Now, open Access, choose Tools→Security→Workgroup Administrator, and use the Join button to restore the *System.mdw* workgroup as your default, if it isn't already (see Figure 2-10). Discard the secured copy, rename the backup, and you're back to where you started.

If for some reason you can't use the unsecured backup (say, one of your underlings misplaced it), you can de-secure the secured version, but only if

Figure 2-10. Joining the default System.mdw workgroup information file.

you can log in as a member of the Admins group, or a user with Administrator privileges. (Otherwise, see "Database Lockout," earlier in this chapter.)

Once you're logged in, follow these three steps:

1. Add the Admin user to the Admins group. Choose Tools→Security→ User and Group Accounts, click the Users tab, and set the user to Admin. Then use the Add button to add Admins to the list of groups.

2. Grant the Users group full permissions to all objects in the database. Choose Tools→Security→User and Group Permissions and set the group to Users. (See "Assign Permissions to Groups" under "Administering User-Level Security Correctly," earlier in this chapter.)

3. Clear the Admin user's password. Choose Tools→Security→User and Group Accounts, set the username to Admin, and then press the Clear Password button.

Frontend Secure, Backend Unprotected

THE ANNOYANCE: I recently went through the hoopla of securing a split database. It required a lot of steps, but now I have groups of users with different levels of permission. This works fine as long as users go in through the frontend, but recently a temp in our office noticed that he could open the backend and do anything he wanted. This is security?

THE FIX: Yes, it *is* a bit disconcerting that when you apply security to the frontend of a split database, it has no effect on the backend. When you think you're applying security to tables in the frontend, for example, you're really just setting up permissions on *links* to the tables. In principle this makes sense, since it lets you set different permissions on multiple linked databases. Unfortunately, inexperienced administrators often set up security on the frontend and, thinking that they're done, leave the backend completely unprotected.

Here's how to secure the backend, assuming the frontend is already correctly secured. (Those steps are spelled out in "Administering User-Level Security Correctly," earlier in this chapter.) These are basically the same steps you use to secure the frontend, except that most of the work is already done because the owner and workgroup have already been set up.

1. Open Access without any database. Use the Workgroup Administrator (Tools→Security→Workgroup Administrator) to join the same workgroup defined in the file that you used for the frontend.

2. Log in as a member of the Admins group, and create a blank database. Import all the tables from the backend into the new database. (This ensures that a member of the Admins group, and not the pesky Admin user, owns the database.) This new database becomes your

Common Security Gaffes

The most common mistakes people make when setting up user-level security relate to the built-in Admin user and the built-in Users group, neither of which can be removed.

Is the Admin user a member of the Admins group? If so, the database will not be secure, because Admin is a member of *every* workgroup and should *never* have administrative privileges.

Have all permissions for all objects been removed from the Users group? If not, the database will not be secure, because even people who don't log in belong to the Users group. This is probably the single most common mistake people make (especially with Access 2000, because the Access 2000 Security Wizard fails to do this properly— Access 2002 and 2003 do it right).

new, secured backend; you can now delete or rename the old backend. Don't forget to relink the tables from your frontend (Tools→Database Utilities→Linked Table Manager).

3. Set permissions in the new backend for each of your groups.

4. An optional final step is to rejoin your default workgroup, which is usually stored in *C:\Documents and Settings\username\Application Data\Microsoft\Access\System.mdw*, and create a shortcut to your frontend. (See "Restore the Default Workgroup (Optional)" under "Administering User-Level Security Correctly," earlier in this chapter.)

First Login Fails After Securing Database

THE ANNOYANCE: I just used the Security Wizard to secure my database, and I can't log in! I used the right password, but it doesn't work!

THE FIX: Confused? We were too! One Access security "feature" is that each user's very first login does not require a password. There's no way to assign one in advance. You must log in with the correct username and *leave the password field blank*. (Some people try using the personal ID that's entered while running the Security Wizard, as in Figure 2-11. This is not a password.) Once you're logged in, go to Tools→Security→User and Group Accounts, click the Change Logon Password tab, and enter a password in the "New password" field. Leave the "Old password" field blank. The next time you open the database, you'll be prompted for a password.

Figure 2-11. The personal ID that you use to create new users looks like a password, but it's not. A user's password is blank by default the first time that user logs into a secure database.

Too Many Logins

THE ANNOYANCE: I use about 20 different databases. Recently I set up security on one of them, and now they're *all* prompting me for a login password. This is terrible. How do I turn it off?

THE FIX: When you set up security, you create a new workgroup file. This file stores the users, groups, and passwords that are used for setting permissions in your database. So far, so good. The maddening part is that when it creates this file, Access silently makes it your default workgroup. That means that when you open Access without specifying a workgroup file, that's the one it uses. You need to restore the old default. Here's how:

1. Reset your default workgroup. Choose Tools→Security→Workgroup Administrator and hit the Join button. Then browse to *System.mdw* (which is usually someplace like *C:\Documents and Settings\username\ Application Data\Microsoft\Access*), and accept it.

   Once you rejoin the old workgroup, it's a good idea to test the security on your secured database. Try opening it directly, by double-clicking the MDB or choosing File→Open. If you succeed in opening it, it hasn't been properly secured. The *only* way you should be able to open it is by going on to step two.

2. Create a shortcut to the secured database that specifies the new work-group file as part of its target. The syntax is **"FullPathToMSAccess.exe" "FullPathToDatabase.mdb" /wrkgrp "FullPathToWorkgroup.mdw"**. The only way to open this database should be via this shortcut.

See "Administering User-Level Security Correctly" for more information.

Splitting a Secured Database

THE ANNOYANCE: I assigned complex security permissions to my database. Then I split it, and when I opened it, I wasn't even prompted to sign in! The backend is no longer secure!

THE FIX: Yes, this is pretty silly. If you use the Database Splitter Wizard to split your lovingly secured database, it will produce a backend that's completely unsecured. Fortunately, doing it right is easy. Here are the steps:

1. Back up your MDB before you start.

2. Make a copy of your original, secured database, using Windows Explorer or the file manager of your choice. Name it something like *databasename_be.mdb*. In the copy, delete all objects *except the tables*. This will be your backend.

3. In your original copy, delete all the tables. This will be your frontend.

4. In the frontend, choose File→Get External Data→Link Tables, and choose your backend. Select all its tables.

Now you have both a frontend and a backend that are fully secured.

Security Fails on Network Deployment

THE ANNOYANCE: I created a secured database, and everything was fine until I moved it onto the network. Now either my users can't get in, or they can get into stuff they're not *supposed* to get into. What happened to my security?

THE FIX: Deploying a secured database in a multi-user environment is not that complicated—assuming your database has been secured correctly. But it's easy to run into just about every security gotcha there is.

If your users can't log in, this could indicate a problem with file permissions on the network share where the database is stored (see "Database Is Read-Only or File Is Already in Use" in Chapter 1). Or it might be due to a problem with deployment of the workgroup file where users, passwords, and so on get stored. Every user should be joined to the same copy of the MDW file that resides on the server. (You can check this by clicking Tools→Security→Workgroup Administrator on each workstation, as shown in Figure 2-12.) Finally, if users have permissions that they shouldn't have, you haven't secured the backend properly (see the previous Annoyance, "Splitting a Secured Database").

Figure 2-12. The Workgroup Administrator lets you find out what workgroup file you're joined to.

"Unsafe Expressions" Warning

THE ANNOYANCE: We upgraded to Access 2003, and now everyone is getting these idiotic warnings saying "Unsafe expressions are not blocked." It's exactly the same database we've been running for the past year, and there are no unsafe expressions in it. We tried to change the security level, but the Tools→Macro→Security command seems to be missing from our version of Access.

THE FIX: Microsoft takes a lot of flak over the poor security implementation of Windows and Internet Explorer, so someone in marketing must have decided that it was time to lock down the Visual Basic functions that could be security threats. This is driving users crazy. As usual, you have a couple of options for fixing this problem.

To disable these warnings entirely, choose Tools→Macro→Security and set Security Level to "Low" (see Figure 2-13). Of course, do this *only* if the macros and code you're running come from a trusted source. (If you seem to be missing the Security option from your Tools→Macro menu, reset the menu: choose Tools→Customize, click the Toolbars tab, select "Menu Bar," and press the Reset button.)

> **NOTE**
>
> *The macro security setting applied to Access will be applied to all your Office applications.*

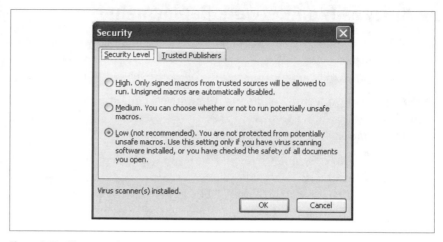

Figure 2-13. Macro security settings.

A safer alternative, especially if you sometimes run MDBs that you don't know to be from a trusted source, is to install Jet 4.0 Service Pack 8 and run Access with medium or high security in "sandbox" mode. (In sandbox mode, Access evaluates only those expressions in field properties and controls that are safe.) Running in sandbox mode disables potentially harmful functions and expressions, so Access will stop bugging you. (See Microsoft's FAQ at *http://office.microsoft.com/assistance/preview.aspx?AssetID=HA011 225981033&CTT=98.*)

Finally, if you are distributing an application and don't want your users to see this warning, digitally "sign" your application using a trusted certificate. (See "Creating Digital Signatures" below for more information.)

Creating Digital Signatures

THE ANNOYANCE: The new security warnings in Access 2003 practically force us to sign every app with a digital certificate. I'm supposed to shell out $400 for a certificate, tweak every frontend I've created, and go through the signing process again? Let me off this bus!

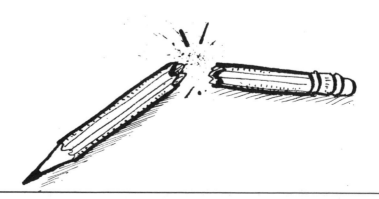

THE FIX: As you probably know, the *idea* behind the digital signature is a good one: it allows you to create an essentially "unforgeable" seal identifying yourself and proving that the code has not been tampered with after you signed it. Some day, the tools for generating certificates and signing applications will be integrated into Access, and using digital signatures will be as routine as using a key to open your front door.

Unfortunately, that day has not arrived. Right now, for example, if you make any modifications to your application, you must remember to re-sign it, or it won't work. As usual, Microsoft has left us with a bit of a headache. One option is to disable security warnings entirely (see the previous Annoyance). But if you need to digitally sign your app, you don't have a lot of choices. You can, however, save money by using a self-signed certificate.

To sign your own certificate, use the *Selfcert.exe* application that comes with Office 2000 and later versions. You may have to install it from the CD. Open the Add or Remove Programs control panel, find the Microsoft Office entry, and click the Change button. Then, in the Setup Wizard, locate "Digital Signature for VBA Projects" under Office Shared Features or Office Tools, and add this feature.

Your users will still see a warning message about trusting your certificate, but once they accept it they won't be warned again. Of course, avoiding that warning is what you pay the certificate vendors for. Once you have your certificate, you can use it to sign your MDB by going to the VB Editor (Ctrl-G) and choosing Tools→Digital Signatures (see Figure 2-14). Either choose a new certificate or accept the one that's previously been used.

Figure 2-14. Inserting a digital certificate.

ENTERPRISE DEPLOYMENT AND NETWORKED DATABASES

Keeping Access Running Smoothly

THE ANNOYANCE: I'm responsible for ensuring that our sales database is up, running, and as happy as possible. The problem is, I'm no database administrator. I know Access can get cranky; what can I do to take a proactive, preventive approach?

THE FIX: Your options will vary a bit depending on whether or not you've split your database. (For more information, see "Multi-User Databases and Split Design" in Chapter 0.)

In the unlikely case that you're administering an unsplit single-user database, with all the tables, queries, and so on in one MDB, there's not much to do. Some rules to live by:

- Back up your data as often as possible. How often? Ask yourself, what's the most data you can afford to lose forever?

- Compact the database regularly (Tools→Database Utilities→Compact and Repair Database). How often? Compact once per week if your data changes daily. (See the sidebar "What Is Compacting?" in Chapter 1.)

- To avoid headaches in the long run, it helps if you design your database properly in the first place. See "Table Design 101" in Chapter 3 for guidelines.

If you're running a split, multi-user database over a network, there's quite a bit more to be concerned about. One common error is putting the frontend (i.e., queries, reports, forms, and so on) on the server and having users open it across the network. This is never a good idea; it puts unneeded demands on the server, makes for poor performance, and increases the risk of database corruption. Instead, install a copy of the frontend on each user's desktop machine. Only the backend (i.e., the tables) belongs on the server.

In multi-user environments, some form of record locking is essential to avoid having users overwrite each other's data. Click Tools→Options, click the Advanced tab, and set "Default record locking" to "Edited record." Be sure to leave the "Open databases using record-level locking" box checked. (For more information on these choices, see the discussion of record locking in the "Global Defaults" section of "Access's Bad Defaults" in Chapter 1.)

If your database is being actively developed while users are entering data, separate the copy that's in use from the copy where design changes are being made. And don't write code or try out design changes on live data! Your developers should each have a copy of the backend on their own desktops, or on a development server. Only when design changes are finalized should you distribute the new frontend to users and (if needed) port backend changes to the production copy on the server. Remember to compact the MDB after making changes; if you make changes in the backend, remember to refresh the links on each frontend (Tools→Database Utilities→ Linked Table Manager) and compact them, too.

In general, a complete database administration strategy will bring together various recommendations made elsewhere in this book:

Backup and compacting
    See the next Annoyance, "Automating Maintenance Chores."

Preventing corruption
    See "That Darn Corruption" in Chapter 1.

Installation maintenance
    See the "Installation Checklist" section in the Appendix.

Performance tuning
    See the "Performance" section in this chapter.

Automating Maintenance Chores

THE ANNOYANCE: Every week I try to make backups of our patient visits database and compact both the frontend and backend. But sometimes the office gets really busy, and I forget. There must be some way to automate these chores, right?

THE FIX: What? You don't have a 24/7 IT department dedicated to handling your maintenance chores? Automating backups is the easy part. If nothing else, you can use Windows's built-in backup software to protect your MDB and MDW files—simply click Start→Programs→Accessories→ System Tools→Backup. (On some flavors of Windows, the backup utility is not installed by default; MSKB 302894 and 152561 tell how to find and install it.)

Daily (or nightly) data backup should be standard operating procedure. Since your backups protect not only against database corruption but also against hard disk failure, back up to a network drive, a second internal hard drive, or removable media. You can use Windows's built-in scheduler (Start→Programs→Accessories→System Tools→Scheduled Tasks) to automate the backup at a convenient time. Think about having some off-site storage for your data as well. When that meteorite hits your office building....

You can use the same approach to automate a compact and repair operation, with two small complications:

- An MDB file can't be compacted when it's in use. If you can set Scheduler to perform the compact at a time when you're *certain* no one will be using the database, you're all set. Otherwise, you'll need some way to notify your users to log off until the maintenance is done.

> **WARNING**
>
> *The Windows Scheduler will silently fail—i.e., scheduled tasks will not run—if you are not logged in when you schedule them. In other words, unless you have defined a login password on your PC (Start→Settings→ Control Panel→User Accounts), you can't use Scheduler.*

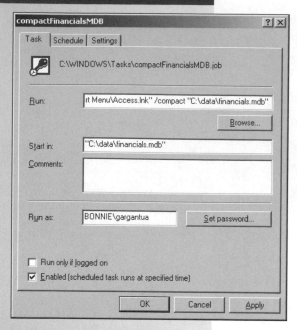

Figure 2-15. Use the Windows Scheduler to schedule compact and repair operations for your databases.

• You'll need to use a command-line switch when loading the Windows Scheduler. To do so, create the basic task using the Scheduled Tasks Wizard, then right-click the task's icon and open its properties sheet. On the Task tab in the Run field, add **/compact *fullpathtodatabase*** after the path to the LNK file that Scheduler generates (see Figure 2-15).

If these Windows utilities don't meet your needs—perhaps you need to do backups while your database is running, or back up multiple databases at the same time—there are other options. For instance, if you're an experienced VB programmer, you can compact from Visual Basic using DAO's CompactDatabase method. Be aware, however, that because of the way Access 2000 and later versions store system information, DAO's CompactDatabase does not reclaim all unused space (although the built-in Access menu command still does).

If you're interested in rolling your own solution, check out Access guru Michael Kaplan's Compactor and SOON utilities (go to *http://www.trigeminal.com* and click the "TSI Utilities, Components, and Tools" link). There are also commercial maintenance utilities, such as Total Visual Agent ($299; *http://www.fmsinc.com/products/Agent*) and Access Autopilot ($129; *http://www.access-autopilot.com*). Both utilities offer flexible scheduling and easy handling of logged-on users, but since Autopilot relies on DAO's CompactDatabase, it suffers from the same limitations noted above.

Finally, there's one more chore that you may wish to automate: managing and distributing frontends. In a multi-user scenario with the backend on a server, it can be a hassle to distribute frontend updates and have users install them without your help. Access MVP Tony Toews has created a free utility, Auto FE Updater (*http://www.granite.ab.ca/access/autofe.htm*), that runs on your server and automatically updates client frontends. It works, it's free, and Tony would love to get feedback and new feature requests.

Best Practices for Access on Networks

THE ANNOYANCE: Ever since we moved our Access 2002 database to the network, we've been plagued with sudden disconnects, corruption, and other errors. I thought Access was designed for a multi-user environment!

THE FIX: Access was originally a standalone desktop database system, and an MDB database is still just a single file that must be shared by all users; it'll never take the hundred-requests-per-second pounding that true multi-user databases can handle without a hiccup. However, if properly designed and deployed, an Access database can scale well to fairly large amounts of data and serve a reasonable number of concurrent users. The following sections present several best practices tips that will help keep your networked database running smoothly.

Minimize Network Connections

Whenever your frontend reads data from or writes data to the backend (say, when a form loads and records are edited), it needs a network connection. Constantly opening and closing connections leaves you more vulnerable to data corruption than just leaving the connection continually open. To minimize stress on the network (and your database), minimize the number of distinct connections used by your frontend. If you're writing VB code, you can either use a global variable to store a persistent connection or simply reuse a connection that's already open. This will also speed up your application, because Jet enforces a five-second delay for successive read/write operations on the same data when a given frontend has multiple connections open.

Optimize Your Design

A well-maintained and well-designed database will survive the hazards of network life far better than one that is overweight and out of shape. Remember, the frontend must reside on client PCs, not on the server. For proper design and deployment techniques, see "Keeping Access Running Smoothly" and "Why Is My Split Database So Slow?," earlier in this chapter.

Hardware Considerations

It's an inescapable fact that network instability causes database corruption—so keep your network hardware (NICs, cables, hubs, and so on) healthy, and don't even consider using Access across a WAN or a modem connection. One phone-line dropout during a write operation, and your database can be corrupted. An overstressed server can also be a source of instability, especially since IT departments often stick databases on the oldest, tiredest server. Convince IT to install a database server that's up to the job (if you can afford it).

Oplocks

To complicate matters, Windows networks may use a file-sharing protocol known as *opportunistic locking* (or *oplocks*) to improve performance. This protocol, which allows multiple users to share locks on a single file, is a prime source of network database corruption. The fix depends on what flavor of Windows you're running; a Windows Service Pack update may do the trick, or you may need to disable oplocks entirely. See MSKB 300216 for more information.

> **NOTE**
>
> *If you're using ADO libraries, connect via the OLEDB driver rather than using Open DataBase Connectivity (ODBC). ODBC is not thread-safe—it isn't stable in a multi-user environment and can cause data corruption. (For the specific, gnarly OLEDB syntax that lets you define a connection in code, look for "OLE DB Provider for Microsoft Jet" at Carl Prothmann's site, http://www.carlprothman.net/Default.aspx?tabid=81.)*

What Is Jet?

Microsoft Access is really two applications rolled into one. First, it's a tool for building database frontends (forms, reports, and so on). This tool can be used to build a frontend for *any* database (including Access, Oracle, MySQL, or SQL Server) that can be connected to via ODBC. Typically, these enterprise-strength database systems don't come with frontend builders as powerful or as easy to use as Access.

But there's more—you don't need to use an external database system, because Access has its own: the Jet database engine. When you define tables within Access, you're using Jet. Jet is a sophisticated tool in its own right, and it can be used separately from Access via automation (if, say, you were writing a VB application and needed an embedded database).

Getting Around Jet's 2-GB Limit

THE ANNOYANCE: Our inventory and sales records are stored in an Access database that has slowly grown to nearly two gigabytes. I know that Access's Jet database engine tops out at 2 GB for any one MDB file. What can we do? This data is vital to us, and we have years of application development effort invested in our frontend.

THE FIX: Two gigabytes is a lot, but having that much data isn't unheard of. To get around Jet's 2-GB file size limit, there are a couple of options you can consider. The easiest is to break the backend into two smaller files. (We'll assume that with a database of this size, you've already split it into front- and backends.)

To do this, create a blank database and import some of the tables from your original backend; this will be your second backend. Then delete those tables from the original. Use the Linked Table Manager (Tools→Database Utilities→Linked Table Manager) to redefine the links to the tables that you moved: simply select all of the tables, and press OK. You'll be prompted for the new location, and the manager will do the rest. *Voilà*—more space!

There are a couple of limitations to this method, however. You can't split a single table into two or more files, so if most of your data growth is in a single, huge table, this method won't work. Also, you can only enforce referential integrity—that is, maintaining the ties between related records in different tables—within a single MDB file (see "Relationship Angst" in Chapter 3). Consequently, this method works best on table designs that can be split into two parts that don't need to be related (e.g., if you had both your parts tables and your contacts tables in the same database).

A second approach is to archive any data beyond a certain age that is rarely used, thereby freeing up space in your database. (Of course, you can still access the archived data.)

To move data into "cold storage," you must create a separate MDB file with tables identical to those whose data you want to archive. Then you connect these archival tables into your active MDB as linked tables. Once done, you can create an append query to copy data from the active tables to the archival tables, and follow it with a delete query that deletes the archived data from the active database. (Never heard of an append query or a delete query? See the sidebar "Types of Queries" in Chapter 4.) Obviously, this is an advanced exercise, not only because of the deletes, but because of the need to observe the referential-integrity rules.

In short, you can get around Jet's 2-GB limit, but only to a limited extent. If you've accumulated a lot of data in a small number of related tables, and you need all of it in production, once you hit that 2-GB limit, you must migrate your data to an enterprise DBMS. Access has a built-in wizard for migrating to SQL Server (a process known as "upsizing"), via Tools→Database Utilities→Upsizing Wizard. As long as you're only migrating data, the process is relatively painless. A good third-party export tool will even take care of indexes and relationships for you. Best of all, you can continue to use Access as your frontend to any DBMS via ODBC; it's just like running a split database, except your backend is not an MDB file, but some other database system.

Avoiding Manual DSN Setup for ODBC

THE ANNOYANCE: We use Access as a frontend to an Oracle database via ODBC. We have hundreds of client machines, and each one needs its own Data Source Name (DSN) set up for the ODBC connection to work. This will take forever to do by hand (see Figure 2-16). Is there any way to automate the process?

THE FIX: One way is to create the DSN for each PC automatically, by using a bit of Visual Basic code. We won't go into details here (see MSKB 184608 if you're interested), because a far better solution is to automate a *DSN-less* connection. This solution is preferable because it's more flexible and portable. You don't have to create a DSN on everyone's computer; instead, users just connect directly to the database.

There's nothing magic about using a DSN-less connection. It's what we used to do before there *was* DSN. Remember that DSN basically just hides the connection details from the developer and the application. That's a boon, because you don't have to worry about the details of the connection string; it "just works." By contrast, to make a DSN-less connection, you must make the connection explicitly in your VB code. The upside? Instead of being stored on every machine, the connection information can be distributed in the frontend sitting on every PC. No more machine-by-machine DSN setup!

We'll assume a typical scenario, where you want to deploy a frontend on each PC. This frontend would normally use linked tables, which link via a DSN to a backend stored on a server. And that's how you'll set it up when you're developing it. But when it's time to deploy your application, you'll switch it to use DSN-less connections. All you need to do is run a little VB code that steps through your linked tables and rewrites their connection strings. (See the sidebar "A Guide to Connection Strings" for details on what they are and how to find the ones you need.) The following code sample uses an SQL Server-trusted connection rather than a username and password. It steps through all your table definitions, but it acts only on

- **NOTE** -

If you're upsizing to SQL Server, you might want to look at the Upsizing PRO utility, which reports on potential compatibility and performance problems (http://www.ssw.com.au/ssw/UpsizingPRO/).

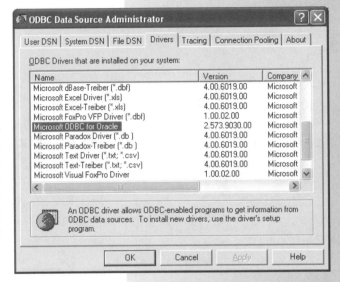

Figure 2-16. Setting ODBC drivers for every machine by hand, as shown here, can be a real headache.

tables that already have connection strings—that is, your linked tables. Local tables on your PC won't be affected by this code.

```
Sub createDSNLess(strServerName As String, strDatabaseName As String)
    Dim dbCurrent As DAO.Database
    Dim tdfTable As DAO.TableDef
    Dim strConnect As String

    Set dbCurrent = DBEngine.Workspaces(0).Databases(0)
    strConnect = "ODBC;DRIVER={sql server};" & _
                 "SERVER=" & strServerName & ";" & _
                 "DATABASE=" & strDatabaseName & ";" & _
                 "Trusted_Connection=Yes;"

    For Each tdfTable In dbCurrent.TableDefs
        If Len(tdfTable.Connect) > 0 Then
            tdfTable.Connect = strConnect
            tdfTable.RefreshLink
        End If
    Next
End Sub
```

To run this code, copy the code into any public module and call it from the Immediate window, like this: **createDSNLess** *"myServerName"*, *"myDatabaseName"*.

If you'd like to delve further into the nuances of DSN-less connections, check Paul Litwin's free DSNStripper add-in (*http://www.mvps.org/access/modules/mdl0064.htm*) and Doug Steele's free DSN-less code (*http://www.accessmvp.com/djsteele/DSNLessLinks.html*).

A Guide to Connection Strings

A *connection string* tells Access how to connect to a remote database. For a DSN connection, the connection string is the DSN name, and possibly a username and password. For a DSN-less connection, it's whatever information is required for the connection, such as the server name, database name, ODBC driver, and possibly port, username, password, and more. For example, here's a string for connecting to MySQL:

```
DRIVER={MySQL ODBC 3.51 Driver};SERVER=myServerName;DATABASE=
myDatabaseName;USER=myUsername;PASSWORD=myPassword;
```

You can see why DSNs are so popular; they spare you from these gory details. But don't panic; it's really not so bad. You can get the connection string from the vendor of the system you're connecting to, or from Carl Prothman's incredibly useful site: *http://www.carlprothman.net/Default.aspx?tabid=81*.

VB Code Fails After Split

THE ANNOYANCE: I recently split an Access database that has some custom Visual Basic code, and now when I open a form, I get a "Current provider does not support the necessary interface for Index functionality" runtime error. Why didn't anyone warn me that splitting would break my application?

THE FIX: There's one major gotcha when splitting a database that has VB code: code that uses the Seek method to locate records won't work. That's because Seek can only work with recordsets opened directly on tables (so-called *table-type recordsets*)—but you can't open table-type recordsets on linked tables, and linked tables are what you get when you split your database. Any code that tries to index a linked table using the Seek method will generate a runtime error. Here are two possible fixes:

1. Use FindFirst (in DAO) or Find (in ADO) instead of Seek—these work fine on non-table-type recordsets. The only drawback is that these functions are less efficient on large numbers of records.

2. Use Seek, but first open the backend database directly. In ADO, create a Connection object like this:

```
Dim conn As ADODB.Connection
conn.Open "Provider=Microsoft.Jet.OLEDB.4.0;" & _
          "Data Source=c:\fullpath\myBackendDatabase.mdb;"
```

Now, instead of opening your recordset using CurrentProject.Connection, use the Connection object you just created, like this:

```
rst.open "tblOrders", conn, adOpenStatic, adLockOptimistic
```

In DAO, call OpenDatabase instead of using CurrentDb:

```
Dim db As DAO.Database
Set db = DBEngine.Workspaces(0).OpenDatabase("c:\fullpath\
myBackendDatabase.mdb")
```

Then call OpenRecordset on this database, instead of the local one.

Directly opening the backend database enables you to use table-type recordsets as usual.

Merging Two Frontends

THE ANNOYANCE: Every six months, our company's Access developers issue an updated frontend to our customer database, and I'm stuck with having to import all my custom queries and reports into the new version. There's gotta be a better way.

THE FIX: The easiest option is to create your own frontend, and link it to the same backend everyone else uses. You can then use yours or theirs, according to what you're doing. Of course, this assumes you don't need to use your custom objects with the company's standard frontend.

A better solution would be to automate the process of exporting your custom objects into the official frontend. Exporting a single object is a one-liner (put this code into the Click event of a button on any convenient form):

```
DoCmd.TransferDatabase acExport, "Microsoft Access", _
        "C:\My Documents\FrontEndLatestRelease.mdb", _
        acReport, "MyCustomReport", "MyCustomReport"
```

Note that minor variations are needed for other types of objects. Instead of acReport, use acForm, acQuery, and so on.

If you're serious about this, you'll probably want to set up a table (see Figure 2-17) to track your custom objects. Record each object's name and type, and write some code to loop through the table and export each one. It will look something like this:

```
Sub MyExport()
    Dim db As DAO.Database, rst As DAO.Recordset
    Dim strObjName As String, strObjType As String
    Dim intObjTypeConst As Integer
    Dim varData As Variant, intI As Integer
    'Open the table
    Set db = CurrentDb()
    Set rst = db.OpenRecordset("tblMyCustomObjects")
    'Loop through table
    Do Until rst.EOF
        strObjName = rst![objectName]
        strObjType = rst![objectType]
        If Ucase(strObjType) = "REPORT" Then
          intObjTypeConst = acReport
        ElseIf Ucase(strObjType) = "FORM" Then
          intObjTypeConst = acForm
        ElseIf Ucase(strObjType) = "QUERY" Then
          intObjTypeConst = acQuery
        ElseIf Ucase(strObjType) = "MODULE" Then
          intObjTypeConst = acModule
        End If
        DoCmd.TransferDatabase acExport, "Microsoft Access", _
              "C:\My Documents\FrontEndLatestRelease.mdb", _
                  intObjTypeConst, strObjName, strObjName
        rst.MoveNext
    Loop
End Sub
```

Figure 2-17. Set up a table to keep track of your custom objects. Then you can automate the process of importing them into new releases of the company frontend.

This code just opens a recordset for the table of custom objects and loops through every row, exporting the objects one at a time. The only complication is that the TransferDatabase method requires Visual Basic constants such as acQuery, acReport, and so on, which are integers—so we translate the more user-friendly object type information in the table ("Query," "Report," and so on) into these constants.

Can't Get Replication to Work

THE ANNOYANCE: We have several employees who need to take copies of our database with them when they travel. We implemented replication to synchronize all the data changes in those remote copies with the database on the server in the office, but when we actually try to *do* the synchronization (either over the Internet, or here at the office on the LAN) we keep getting "failed to synch" errors.

THE FIX: We feel your pain. Replication is arguably the single most difficult thing to implement in Access. (For more on replication, see the sidebar "What Is Replication?") In fact, many pros regard the entire replication process as unworkable and won't touch it. So first, ask yourself if you really need it. Full-blown replication requires sophisticated conflict resolution that can handle multiple users trying to update the same data. But in many cases, remote users aren't updating the same data; they're just adding different data, or perhaps updating their own data. In this case, all you need is code that merges each user's records in any valid copies of the database. You can write code that does this, or turn to third-party software. (For example, FTI Data Replication Tools, available at *http://www.ftisystems.com/MainFrame/ftidr_intro.html*, implements a very simplified version of data sync for $40. These tools merge remote data into the master copy and sync the remotes against the master; they also perform conflict resolution.)

Another alternative is to create a web-based interface for your database (see "Putting Data on the Web" in Chapter 3), so both local and remote users can access it. After all, the optimal multi-user scenario is where every user talks directly to the same copy of the database. However, if only true replication suits your needs, and you can't get Access replication to work, there are third-party solutions available (such as those from Progress Software, at *http://www.progress.com/realtime/products/dataxtend_re/index.ssp*).

Finally, if you decide replication is too big a pain, you can undo it. For more information, see MSKB 208394. Also check out Michael Kaplan's free Un-Replicator utility (*http://www.trigeminal.com/lang/1033/utility.asp?ItemID=7#7*), which will convert your replicated database back to something anyone (not just a mother) could love, removing all the gunk (globally unique identifiers and so on) that the replication process adds.

Replication Fails on Frontend Objects

THE ANNOYANCE: I have a master database with two simple macros in it. I replicated the database, and I now get errors in my replicas saying they can't find the macros. But they're right there!

THE FIX: Although the Replication Manager lets you replicate *all* the objects in a database, you should *never* replicate forms, reports, or macros. You're just asking for corruption problems. To have a prayer of getting replication to

Want to Replicate an Access 2003 Database? Not So Fast!

When you can't directly connect two replicas over a LAN or the Net, you need to perform *indirect replication*, and that means you need the Replication Manager. The only problem? Access 2003 no longer ships with the Replication Manager. This has quite a few developers scratching their heads. The good news is that since replication depends only on Jet 4.0, you can use the Replication Manager that comes with Access 2000 or 2002 Developer Edition. The bad news is that unless you already have a copy of one of these versions, you may be out of luck—Microsoft doesn't sell the older versions of Access any more. (Can you spell e-B-a-y?)

work right, you must split your MDB into front- and backends, and replicate the backend *only*. Replication is for data. Period. No exceptions.

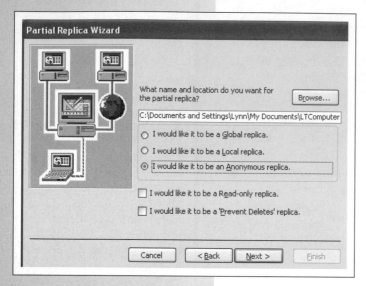

Figure 2-18. Although the Replication Wizard lets you set up local or anonymous replicas, don't do it!

Corrupted Replicas

THE ANNOYANCE: Our replicas get the error "The Search Key cannot be found." We have installed all the Office 2003 patches and the latest Microsoft Data Access Components, and we compacted twice before the replication, yet the replicas still get corrupted.

THE FIX: You could be suffering from a bug that was fixed in Jet 4.0 Service Pack 5. It's more likely, though, that you're using local or anonymous replicas (see the sidebar "What Is Replication?," and also Figure 2-18) that have been cut off from the replica set. Since local/anonymous replicas can synchronize only with the replica that created them (the parent), if anything happens to that parent, they are locked out—and since there's no way to change the parent once they've been created, they are locked out forever. Alas, there is no good fix. For this reason, it is strongly recommended that you do not use local or anonymous replicas.

What Is Replication?

Replication enables users to share a database even when they're off the local network. For example, each member of a company sales force can have his or her own copy of the sales database to take on the road. Periodically, they can synchronize their copies with the other copies (over either the Internet or the company LAN) to ensure that everyone has the latest data from other team members. Of course, until you sync up, your data can be somewhat out-of-date.

When you fire up replication (Tools→Replication→Create Replica), you take the unreplicated master copy of the database and convert it to what's known as a *design master*. All design changes to the database must be made in the design master. The same command can be used to create additional copies of the database that can be synchronized with each other and with the master. All together, these copies of the database form the *replica set*.

Note that some types of replicas (*local* and *anonymous*) can synchronize only with the particular replica that created them; this is a dangerous situation and should be avoided (see "Corrupted Replicas," later in this chapter). By default, replicas are *global*, which means they can synchronize with any other global replicas.

Synchronization (Tools→Replication→Synchronize Now) is the exchange of data between two replicas. It can be one-way or two-way. When Access synchronizes two replicas, it must perform *conflict resolution*—that is, it must resolve the cases where both replicas have changed the same data. This can be done automatically, by assigning priority levels to different replicas, or it can be done manually. For a good starting reference on Access replication, see "Database Replication in Microsoft Jet 4.0," at *http://msdn.microsoft.com/library/default.asp?url=/library/en-us/dnacc2k/html/dbrepjet.asp.*

Data, Tables, and Database Design

3

GIGO—Garbage In, Garbage Out—means that all the fancy forms and reports in the world don't mean a thing if the data in your base ain't got that swing. In this chapter, we tackle the annoyances that prevent you from getting and keeping good data.

Chief among these annoyances is the fundamental issue of good database design. The average Access user quakes at the thought—mostly because so-called "normalization" rules are usually explained in terms so arcane that transmuting lead into gold seems simple by comparison. If you cut through the techno-speak, though, database design is simple—and we'll show you how to do it right. Then we'll help you ensure that the data that goes into your lovely design is valid. Finally, we'll address the myriad migraines that Access causes when you try to move data around using import, export, and linking.

DATABASE DESIGN AND DATA INTEGRITY

Table Design 101

THE ANNOYANCE: I've heard that I'm supposed to "normalize" my tables, but the books that discuss this are really confusing. "Primary keys," "foreign keys"...what are they talking about? And "Boyce-Codd normal form" sounds like a disease. Why do I need an advanced degree to create a simple contacts database?

THE FIX: *Normalizing* basically means organizing data to reduce redundancy. As the esteemed Webopedia (*http://www.pcwebopedia.com*) pithily puts it, it involves "dividing a database into two or more tables and defining relationships between the tables. The objective is to isolate data so that additions, deletions, and modifications of a field can be made in just one table and then propagated through the rest of the database via the defined relationships."

Such well-designed tables are essential to maintaining data integrity and the long-term health of your database. They also make a big difference in performance as your database grows. Fortunately, you can leave the theoretical stuff to the experts; following a few simple rules will suffice for most needs. The essence of data normalization is just this: pull out repeating and reusable items and put them in their own, separate tables.

Some table-design rules to follow:

1. **Split up your data by topic.** Think of tables as file folders in a filing cabinet. Identify the main topic headings for your data, and create tables for each distinct topic. For example, if you were running a business, you wouldn't file your customer data in the same folder with suppliers' addresses and price lists, nor would you mix accounts payable with receivables. Apply the same organizational logic to the information you plan to store in your Access database.

OK, that sounds sensible enough, but when it comes time to do it it's hard to know where to start. For instance, you have a customers table (see Figure 3-1), but what data should be stored there? Orders, billing addresses, shipping addresses, phone numbers, everything? That's where the other data normalization rules come in.

CUSTOMERS

businessName	address	phone	order1	order2
Bob's Diner	14 Rialto St. Boston, MA 02119	617-447-0106 617-499-0976	4 doz. handbraided Guatemalan placemats	8 basic curtains (floral) and curtain rods
Turpelo Cleaners	205 South St. Roxbury, MA 02334	617-547-0098	1 basic curtains (floral) and curtain rods	
...	...	...	...	...

Figure 3-1. A customers table in an early stage of design. It has no extraneous topics (such as vendor data) but is not yet normalized. Note the multiple phone numbers in a single field; this should never be done.

2. **Give every item of data its own field.** For example, many customers will have both a cell phone and a land line. You might be tempted to create a single "phoneNumber" field and put both numbers into it, separated by a comma. This is *never* a good idea. Instead, create a "cellPhone" field and an "officePhone" field, and let each field hold a single item of data (see Figure 3-2). Similarly, in good database design mailing addresses are typically broken up into "addressLine1," "addressLine2," "city," "state," and "zipCode" fields.

businessName	officePhone	cellPhone	addressLine1	...
Bob's Diner	617-447-0106	617-499-0976	14 Rialto St.	
Turpelo Cleaners	617-547-0098		205 South St.	
...	...	...	...	...

Figure 3-2. A normalized customers table. Note that the address and phone numbers have been split into separate fields holding one item of information apiece.

3. **Put repeated items into separate tables.** If your customer has two or more phone numbers, you should create distinct phone number fields in the customers table. But what if you need to record something that repeats indefinitely, such as customer orders (including customer order numbers)? If you stored them in the customers table, you'd have to create fields such as Cust_Order1, Cust_Order2, Cust_Order3, and so on, ad infinitum. The obvious problem here is that you don't know how many orders you'll need to provide fields for. This clearly indicates that you need to create a separate table just for orders. In a properly designed database, *new data adds rows, not fields*. (When you're designing tables, you have to think about how they're going to be used. If, in the course of normal use, you envision your users adding new fields, something's very wrong.)

4. **Put reusable information into separate tables.** Any information that you'll be entering multiple times is "reusable" information. Your goal in database design is to avoid entering the same data twice. Instead, find a way to reuse the data that's already been entered. Not only does this save work, but it avoids data entry errors or discrepancies that will make it difficult to maintain a database.

An example is a product description. You might be tempted to put that right into the orders table (Figure 3-3), but the product descriptions don't change, and you'll find yourself entering the same descriptions again and again for each new order. This is a sure sign that this information belongs in a separate table (Figure 3-4).

ORDERS

orderDate	productDescription	unitCost	quantity
2004-01-07	handbraided Guatemalan placemats	$12.00	48
2004-01-22	basic curtains (floral) and curtain rods	$17.80	1
2004-02-01	basic curtains (floral) and curtain rods	$17.80	8
...	...	...	...

Figure 3-3. This orders table is not yet fully normalized. Note that product information is repeated verbatim in records 2 and 3. This reusable information should be stored in its own table.

ORDERS

orderDate	productCode	Quantity
2004-01-07	GUA0571	48
2004-01-22	CUR0008	1
2004-02-01	CUR0008	8
...	...	...

PRODUCTS

productCode	productDescription	unitCost
GUA0571	Handbraided Guatemalan placemats	$12.00
CUR0008	Basic curtains (floral) and curtain rods	$17.80
...	...	...

Figure 3-4. Normalized orders and products tables. The product descriptions have been replaced with product codes that refer back to the products table.

These rules don't cover every situation, but you can go pretty far with them. However, there's one important concept that we haven't yet addressed. Normalizing is all about splitting up your tables the right way—but once they're split, you need a way to connect them. For instance, if you create a separate table for orders, you need a way to track which orders go with which customers. This is done by forming "relationships" among your tables (the subject of the next Annoyance).

MSKB 234208 is a good, non-technical article on normalization. For a slightly more technical tutorial, check out *http://dev.mysql.com/tech-resources/articles/intro-to-normalization.html*. It's not written about Access, but normalization is the same in any relational database.

Relationship Angst

THE ANNOYANCE: I just designed my first database, but when I tried to put data into it, Access gave me a "primary key violation" error message. What's wrong? More to the point, what is a key, and what is a *primary* key, and why should I care?

THE FIX: Setting up correct table relationships is the second half of good database design. (The first half is defining your tables correctly; as discussed in "Table Design 101.") In this fix, we'll look at relationships from the ground up.

When you designed your database, you sorted your data into separate tables—you "normalized" it. Defining relationships between tables is how you pull that related data back together again. The links you create ensure you don't forget how the data is related, and they remind you to enter (and prevent you from accidentally deleting) data that's needed to complete the picture.

Field Names and Data Types

Once you have designed your tables, creating them in Access is pretty straightforward. In table Design View, give each field a name (see "Bad Field Names," later in this chapter). Field names must be unique *within* a table but can be reused in other tables.

The trickier part is assigning a data type to each field. Unlike with a table In a Word document, for example, with an Access table you must specify what *kind* of data you intend to put in each field. Databases are very strict about this—and for good reason, because exercising maximum control over the classification of data is at the heart of a database's power. Because a database knows what kinds of values are in a specific type of field, it can sift, collate, sort, and view different slices of data in myriad ways and can prevent some kinds of data from interacting in certain undesirable ways. For instance, you can multiply the values from two fields, but only if they're numeric fields; it wouldn't make sense to multiply two text strings.

Here are some simple rules to follow when choosing data types:

- For names, addresses, and other text, if your data won't exceed 255 characters in length, make it a Text field; otherwise, it must be a Memo field. Text is for words, Memo is for paragraphs—but remember that Memo fields can't be indexed, so searching for Memo data (and sorting it) may be slower.

- For money, use the Currency data type.

- For numbers that are neither money nor foreign keys (see the final bullet in this list), you'll need to take a bit more care. Most of them will be the Number data type, but you may need to adjust the Field Size property setting to ensure that the field matches the

kind of numbers you're using. Here are some very basic guidelines. If your numbers are integers (i.e., don't contain decimal points), use the Number data type with the Field Size set to Long Integer. If your numbers have decimal points, setting Field Size to Double will be fine—unless you're concerned about rounding that might occur in scientific applications that use floating-point data. In that case, you may want to use the Currency data type (see "Flaws in the Decimal Data Type," later in this chapter).

- For text that looks like numbers but isn't actually numeric, use the Text data type. For example, data such as phone numbers, Zip Codes, and Social Security numbers looks numeric but isn't. A simple test: if it doesn't make sense to add, subtract, and multiply it, then it's not a number, it's (numeric) text. So make it a Text field.

- For dates and times, there's only one choice: the Date/Time data type. Use this for simple dates (1/14/2005), simple times (5:45 PM), and true date/times (1/14/2005 5:45 PM). See "Dates! Dates! Dates!" in Chapter 7.

- For fields that can have only two values (Yes/No, True/False, On/Off), use the Yes/No data type. However, if you might need to add one or more additional values later (such as Don't Know), use Text instead.

- For foreign keys, you must use the data type of the primary key that the foreign key refers to. For example, if the primary key is an AutoNumber, use the Number data type with the Field Size set to Long Integer for the foreign key. (See "Relationship Angst" for more information on primary and foreign keys.)

Primary Keys and Duplicate Records

Some database experts recommend using a meaningful field rather than an AutoNumber ID as a primary key. That's because when you use an AutoNumber as your primary key, nothing prevents you from adding the same record multiple times—the only difference between the records will be their ID numbers. And duplicate records cause all sorts of headaches.

If you *do* use something meaningful—such as the customer name or employee ID—as a primary key, you'll be prevented from adding the same record twice by the unique index that's enforced on the primary key. But you can run into different problems with using meaningful fields. For instance, two customers might have the same name, or you might need to add someone to the employees table who doesn't yet have an employee ID. And even with a meaningful key, you can still enter duplicate records if, for example, you use a slightly different spelling of the name.

For these reasons, we recommend using an AutoNumber ID field in most cases. It's simple, it's easy, and it works.

The element that forges the relationship between two tables is the "key." It's like a Social Security number—a unique identifier for each record in that table. Good table design requires that every table have at least one field that acts as a unique key. We call this the *primary key* field. In Access, you designate it by right-clicking the field in Design View and selecting "Primary Key."

Be vewy, vewy careful when you pick the primary key field—its value must be unique for each record. You might think that the businessName field in a customers table would make a good primary key, but it probably won't. (After all, you could have two customers with the same business name in different states.) The simplest approach is to add an "ID" field to every table (for the customers table, we'll call it "customerId") and use the AutoNumber data type for that field. Every time you add a new record to the customers table, Access will enter a new, unique number into that record's customerId field. The numbers are meaningless—they simply serve as unique identifiers. (See the sidebar "Primary Keys and Duplicate Records" for deeper thoughts on ID fields.)

To see how keys are used to create relationships, consider two tables: one listing customers and the other listing orders. As we saw in the previous Annoyance, the orders table should not have any customer information in it (such as shipping address, business name, and so on), because that's all reusable information that you don't want to retype into each order. So how do you create a report that tracks which order goes with which customer, and presents all that information on one screen? You simply add a field to the orders table that refers to the primary key of the customers table. You may as well call it by the same name, customerId (see Figure 3-5). Now you can see why it's essential that the primary key be unique. Every order in the orders table has a customerId, and that is the *only* way you'll know which customer the order belongs to. Incidentally, the customerId field in the orders table is known as a *foreign key*; it refers to the value of a primary key field in another table.

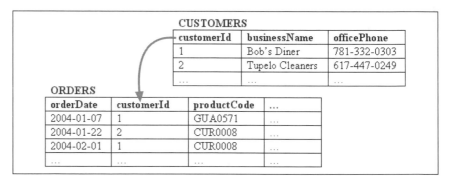

Figure 3-5. Customers and orders tables, related by customerId. customerId is the primary key in customers and the foreign key in orders.

Once you've defined primary and foreign keys, you will probably want to set Access to enforce these relationships. For instance, you can tell Access to prevent you from adding customerId values to the orders table that don't already exist in the customers table. This is a very good idea, because if you don't, a typo could leave you with no way to determine which customer an order belongs to.

To define a relationship, choose Tools→Relationships. Right-click anywhere in the Relationships window and select Show Table. Add the tables you want to relate to the Relationships window by highlighting them and clicking the Add button in the Show Table window. Then drag the primary key field from one table and drop it onto the matching foreign key field in the other table. The Edit Relationships dialog will open. Make sure the field names look right, and then check the "Enforce Referential Integrity" box. This will prevent you from deleting a record that's related to a record in another table. (You can safely ignore the other options, but you may want to check out the discussion of the Cascade Delete option in "Can't Delete Records," later in this chapter.) Click the Create button, and Access will draw a line connecting the two tables. If you ever need to edit or delete the relationship, you can do so by right-clicking the line.

The customers/orders relationship used here as an example is a very common type of relationship—a *one-to-many* relationship, where every order belongs to exactly one customer, and one customer can have many orders. But there's another important kind of relationship—the *many-to-many* relationship. Consider the relationship between suppliers and products. Several suppliers might supply the same product, and one supplier might supply several different products. If you followed the customers/orders example and added a supplierId field to the products table, each product could have only a single supplier. Likewise, if you added a productCode field to the suppliers table, each supplier could supply only a single product.

The problem is that when two tables are directly related, only one of the tables can be on the "many" side. But you need a way to enable both sides of the relationship to be "many." To do that, you'll have to introduce a *linking table* that will serve as an intermediary. Both products and suppliers will have one-to-many relationships to this linking table, enabling each product to have many suppliers and each supplier to supply many products (see Figure 3-6).

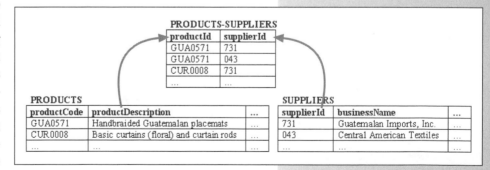

Figure 3-6. Products, suppliers, and products-suppliers tables. Products and suppliers are in a many-to-many relationship.

A linking table typically just contains the foreign keys from each of the tables that it links. For example, to link suppliers and products, you'd add a products-suppliers table with just two fields: productCode and supplierId. Each supplier will appear in this table once for each product supplied, and each product will appear in this table once for each supplier who supplies it. The primary key for this linking table will be a composite key using both fields. (In table Design View, hold down the Ctrl key and click both fields to select them, then right-click and choose "Primary Key.") To define this relationship in the Relationships window, simply treat this many-to-many relationship as two one-to-many relationships.

I Don't Want to Design a Database from Scratch

THE ANNOYANCE: I run a small business, and I just need a simple database to handle sales contacts. I don't need anything fancy or customized. Surely this application has been designed a thousand times by people who know Access better than I ever will. Isn't there some way to avoid building it from scratch?

THE FIX: There sure is. You have a variety of options, depending on your needs and how much you can afford to pay. For a very generic contact database, take a look at the prefab database templates that come with Access. Choose File→New, and in the New Document task pane select one of the template options (such as "On my computer" in Access 2003, or "New from template" in Access 2002). Figure 3-7 shows the Databases tab, with choices such as Contact Management, Expenses, and so on. Selecting one of these will start the Database Wizard, which lets you customize the template a bit. They're not fancy, but they're a decent starting point. If you don't see the kind of database you're looking for here, there are more choices at *http://office. microsoft.com/templates/default.aspx*. You'll also find a few full databases you can download at web sites such as *http://www.rogersaccesslibrary.com and http://www.mvps.org/access/resources/ downloads.htm*.

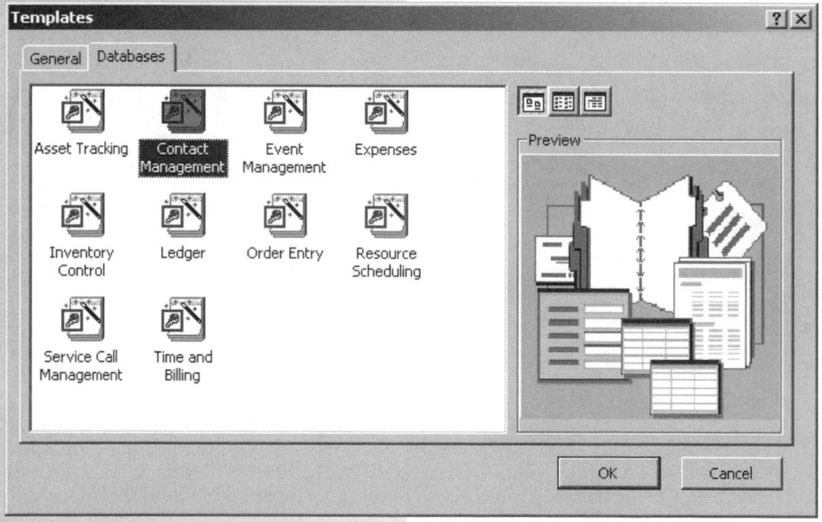

You might also poke around in newsgroups or at Utter Access (*http://www. utteraccess.com*) to see if anyone has a database they'd be willing to share.

Figure 3-7. Access comes with templates for common database applications that you can customize with the Database Wizard.

If your needs are more complex, or you don't want to take your chances with a homegrown job, consider paying for a commercial solution. Many off-the-shelf Access packages are available for common business needs, and in many cases the seller will customize upon request. A Google search for "off-the-shelf Access contact database" should find quite a few, but it can be hard to sift through the chaff. Alternatively, try posting a query in Google groups; many vendors read these groups. For most businesses, many of your database needs (such as A/R, order entry, inventory control, and so on) fall under the rubric of accounting packages. Access MVP Tony Toews maintains a list of such off-the-shelf packages at *http://www.granite.ab.ca/accsacct.htm*.

Finally, if you can't find the right off-the-shelf solution, there are many professional Access developers who will be happy to put together a custom solution for you at a reasonable price. ("Reasonable" varies, of course, depending on the complexity of the project—but you'll probably end up paying between $25 and $100/hr, and it might take anywhere from a week to a couple of months.)

Bad Field Names

THE ANNOYANCE: I've just been brought in to rescue a half-finished database design. Among other things, the field names are a mess, with spaces and many reserved words. Why does Access allow this sort of thing?

THE FIX: Microsoft tried to make Access user-friendly by allowing you to name your database objects, fields, and controls just about anything that fits into 64 characters. For instance, names can include spaces and apostrophes, like this: "Employee's and temporary staff's benefits table." What Access doesn't tell you is that using spaces or apostrophes in names can cause major headaches with Visual Basic. For example, when you're creating SQL queries you'll have to surround everything with brackets (and your SQL will be nonstandard), since SQL does not allow spaces.

Another common mistake is choosing field names such as "date" and "name," which are reserved words in Visual Basic; using them can cause unexpected problems, some of which can be very hard to track down. Most of the time VB will think that you're referring to a built-in method or object when, in fact, you're simply trying to refer to one of the fields you've created. Worse yet, problems may not show up until later, and they can be quite difficult to debug. If your database already has poorly chosen field names, see "Find/Replace for Database Objects" in Chapter 1 for a way to fix the problem.

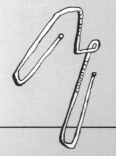

NOTE

Camel case is what you get when you run words together and use capitals where the second word begins, to form theHump.

If you need to *suggest* a space, either use an underscore (as in "total_payments") or use "camel" case (as in "totalPayments"). Whatever you do, avoid using VB reserved words—you can find a list of these in MSKB 286335. While you're at it, replace generic field names such as "error" or "sum" with more specific names such as "accountingError" or "paymentSum."

There is one downside to using names such as "leasePaymentsSum" for fields in tables: although they aren't meant to be seen by end users, these names become the default display labels in Datasheet View, or when you create a form based on the table. Of course, you can go into form Design View and change the label to anything you want, but that's an extra step. To make life a bit easier, use the field's Caption property. For example, when working in table Design View, you can set the caption of the leasePaymentsSum field to "Sum of Lease Payments." Then controls based on that field will automatically have understandable labels.

Adopt a Naming Convention

To save time and anguish later on, adopt a consistent naming convention for your database objects—it's what all serious developers do. The Reddick VBA naming convention (*http://www.xoc.net/standards/*) is widely used by Access developers.

Reddick uses prefixes to distinguish different types of database objects and controls, such as "tblEmployees" (for a table) and "qryEmployees" (for a query). Access doesn't *insist* that you do this, but the practice can save you headaches later on—for instance, when you're looking at a list of tables and queries and trying to remember which is which. Using prefixes for control names (such as "txtLastName" for a text box) is especially important; if you don't intervene, Access will default to giving a bound control the same name as the underlying field, which can easily cause a circular reference problem (see "#Name? and #Error?" in Chapter 1).

Other examples of prefixes include "frmEmployees" (for a form), "rptEmployees" (for a report), "cboEmployeeName" (for a combo box), and "lstTowns" (for a list box).

Here are some of the most commonly used prefixes:

- Checkbox: chk
- Combo box: cbo
- Command button: cmd
- Form: frm
- Label: lbl
- List box: lst
- Macro: mcr
- Module: bas
- Query: qry
- Report: rpt
- Subform: sfr
- Subreport: srp
- Tab control: tab
- Table: tbl
- Text box: txt

Flaws in the Decimal Data Type

THE ANNOYANCE: We use Access 2003 for our weather database, and we store temperature data using the Decimal data type. But when we try to sort those temperatures from high to low, Access treats negative temperatures as if they're higher than positive ones! (See Figure 3-8.)

qryTemperaturesSorted : S...	
Date of reading	Degrees Celsius
9/5/2004	-2.3
9/6/2004	-5
9/7/2004	12.5
9/3/2004	11.9
9/4/2004	5.7

Record: 1

Figure 3-8. Problem: Access sorts negative decimals as if they're higher than any positive number.

THE FIX: There are a number of problems with the Decimal data type, and this sorting bug is one of the worst. (See MSKB 837148.) As a workaround, you can add an index to the field, which will enable Access to sort the values in the field correctly. But if you use the data in expressions, aggregate queries, and so forth and try to sort on the calculated values, you'll run into the same problem—and the index won't help. Another workaround is to convert everything to the Double data type before you sort; just wrap the expression to be sorted in CDbl(), like this: CDbl(temperature).

A better solution is to avoid using the Decimal data type at all (or at least where possible). Decimal is a scaled integer data type, which means that although it displays numbers with a decimal point, it stores them internally as an integer and a scaling factor. (The scaling factor is a value that represents the number of decimal places to the right of zero. So, 15, 1.5, and 0.15 all get stored as a pair of values; the integer is always 15, but the scaling factor is 0, 1, or 2, respectively.) This enables Access to avoid the rounding errors that occur with the Single and Double floating-point types. If absolute accuracy is important to you, and you only need four places to the right of the decimal point, enter the data as the Currency data type, which is also a scaled integer. Despite its name, its wide range (−922,337,203,685,477.5808 to 922,337,203,685,477.5807) and fixed-point accuracy make it a good choice for many numeric applications. Simply set the format of your currency field to General Number to get rid of the dollar signs and display the numbers as entered.

Decimal Data—Not

The Decimal data type has other problems as well. For example, if you view Decimal data in a PivotTable or PivotChart, everything to the right of the decimal point is ignored (MSKB 310264). Furthermore, if you're writing VB code, it's awkward to work with Decimal data because there's no corresponding type in Visual Basic; you must store Decimal data in variables of Variant type.

There's another problem, too. If you're not familiar with the Decimal type, you may be surprised to see it swallow up the fractional parts of your numbers. For instance, type in 100.7, and Access stores it as 100. That's because by default, the number of decimal places a Decimal type supports is *none*. Oh, happy day! To change this, go to table Design View and set your field's Scale property equal to the number of decimal places you want to the right of the decimal point. The Precision property sets the total number of digits that will be stored on both sides of the decimal point. Its maximum is 28.

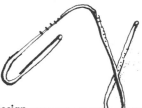

AutoNumber Nightmares

Custom Counters

In some cases, you may want more control over your autoincrementing value—for instance, if you need an alphanumeric such as ADZ-10001, or you want to reuse discarded values. The most typical case is where you need to mirror a numbering convention that's used elsewhere in the company. In a single-user situation, one very simple solution is to define your primary key field as a Number data type, with the Field Size set to Long Integer. In your data entry form, set the field's Default Value to something like `DMax("IDNumber", "myTable") + 1`. Of course, this only works if all data entry is through your form (as it should be—you don't want users entering data directly into your table's datasheet), and it can cause problems with subforms. In some cases, a better solution will be to use a plain old AutoNumber field as the primary key field, and to provide an incrementing ID field based on DMax (as above) as an extra field. That gives you the counter you need, and your primary key takes care of itself.

If you're an experienced programmer, the most complete solution is writing a custom counter that stores the primary key values in its own table and increments them as needed. One problem you may run into, however, is contention for the "next" number among multiple users sharing the database. For the full monty on implementing this solution, see "Create and Use Flexible AutoNumber Fields" in *Access Cookbook*, Second Edition, by Ken Getz, Paul Litwin, and Andy Baron (O'Reilly).

THE ANNOYANCE: We use an ID field set as an AutoNumber data type as the primary key field in our orders table. The problem? To match our hard copy records, we need the ID field to start numbering at 11001, and not skip values between records. But Access always starts AutoNumbers at 1, and if we delete a record, it creates a gap in the sequence.

THE FIX: Access doesn't let you set the starting value of an AutoNumber field; nor does it guarantee there won't eventually be gaps. If the AutoNumber field's New Values property is set to "Increment" (the default), Access will generate sequential numbers, but it won't *reuse* numbers that get discarded when you delete a record or undo the creation of a new record. What AutoNumber does guarantee is that you'll get a unique number that can be used as a primary key—and for most purposes, that's all you need. (In Access 2002 and earlier versions, compacting the database resets the AutoNumber ID to the last one used, recovering any deleted numbers. However, a bug in the current Jet service pack removed this feature in Access 2003.)

Given how AutoNumbers are normally used, you shouldn't be concerned about their actual values, or about gaps in the sequence. Still, if these issues are a problem for you, there are steps you can take. Setting the start value of an AutoNumber field is easy to do with an SQL statement, but ensuring that there are no gaps—despite deletions or undos—is considerably more complex, especially in a multi-user scenario.

Check to see if your database is set to use the ANSI SQL-92 extensions. To find out, select Tools→Options, click the Tables/Queries tab, and look in the SQL Server Compatible Syntax area to see if the "This database" box is checked. If it isn't, check it now. (This feature is not available in Access 2000.) Once you're using the ANSI SQL-92 extensions, you can specify both the start value and increment of an AutoNumber field using an SQL Create Table statement, like this one:

```
CREATE TABLE tblMyTable (myAutoNumber AUTOINCREMENT (11001, 1));
```

Create a blank query and paste this code into SQL View; then run it. It creates an AutoNumber field that starts at 11001 and increments by 1. You can add your other fields in Design View. (Or, if you're good at SQL, you can specify all your fields in this statement.)

If you're not using SQL-92, you can set the start value of an AutoNumber field by using this SQL statement:

```
INSERT INTO tblMyTable (myAutoNumber) VALUES (11000);
```

Simply paste it into the SQL View of a blank query, edit it to suit your specifics, then run it. After running this query, go into the table and delete the record. The next record will start at 11001.

Can't Create a Relationship

THE ANNOYANCE: No, I'm not trying to get on Oprah. I'm trying to define a relationship between patients and visits tables so I can enforce referential integrity—that is, prevent users from accidentally deleting records in one table that are related to still-existing records in the other table. The problem is that there's a ton of existing data in these two tables, and apparently someone has *already* done exactly the thing I'm trying to prevent from happening in the future...and Access won't let me enable referential integrity unless the tables are already ship-shape. How can I repair the messed-up data so I can turn on the Enforce Referential Integrity option?

THE FIX: Sometimes when you try to add a relationship between tables, Access won't let you because the existing data has invalid foreign keys. In this example, you probably have some patient IDs in the visits table that aren't found in the patients table. Finding and extracting the records that are causing the problem can be a real headache—the trick is to let Access do it for you, by running a query that finds unmatched records.

Run the Unmatched Query Wizard (Figure 3-9) from the database window by choosing Insert→Query→Find Unmatched Query Wizard and clicking OK. In the wizard's first screen, add the table that has the foreign key (in this case, the visits table), and in the second screen add the table that has the primary key (in this case, patients). Tell the wizard to match on the foreign key field. When the wizard finishes, Access will run the query; it will find all the records in the first table where the foreign key doesn't match a primary key in the second table. You can then select the problematic records, and delete them or fix them by hand.

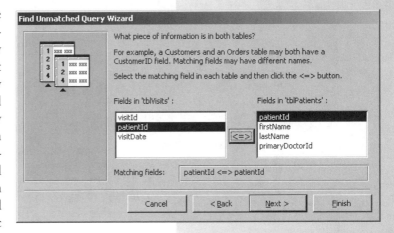

Figure 3-9. Match the foreign key field to the primary key field, and then click the <=> button.

Can't Delete Records

THE ANNOYANCE: I need to delete erroneous records from my clients table, but because it has an enforced relationship with the active projects table, I get the following error: "The record cannot be deleted or changed because table <tblProjects> includes related records." Why can't Access just delete these related records, too? I know they're related, and Access does too, so shouldn't there be some way for Access to just blow them all away?

THE FIX: By default, Access doesn't automatically delete records that are related to the record you're trying to delete. This is a reasonable default—otherwise, it would be too easy to create orphaned records (i.e., records containing foreign keys that point to nonexistent other records). But, if you really know what you're wishing for, you can have it that way. Choose Tools→ Relationships and right-click the relationship line that connects the two tables. Choose Edit Relationships, and check the "Cascade Delete Related Records" box (Figure 3-10). This tells Access that when you delete a record whose primary key is linked to a foreign key in a related record, the related record(s) should be deleted, too.

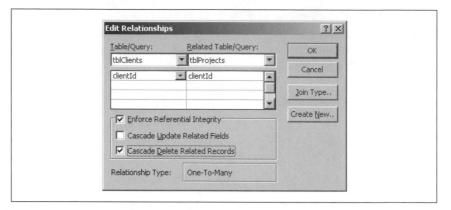

Figure 3-10. When you select the Cascade Delete option, if you delete a record whose primary key appears in another table as a foreign key, the related record will be deleted automatically.

Default Values Don't Apply to Existing Records

THE ANNOYANCE: I set the default value of our leaseDate field to 2002-02-10, which is the date that most of our leases started. However, the records don't show this date at all—not in the form, and not in the table, either.

THE FIX: Remember that default values are applied only when a record is *created*. This means that defaults will *not* be applied to records that already existed when you set them up.

If you want to add a default value to preexisting records, you must use an update query. How? Create a regular (select) query that finds all the records with null values in the field. In the database window, click Queries→Create Query in Design View, and put "Is Null" in the Criteria line. Then convert the select query to an update query by choosing Query→Update Query, and enter the default value in the Update To line. Running this query replaces nulls with your default. Alternately, if you're entering data in a form (new or preexisting) and you come to a field that has a default value set up for it, use Ctl-Alt-Space to fill in the default value.

Setting up defaults that are fixed values (such as "Unknown" or "25") or are based on simple expressions (such as =Date()) is easy. Just open the table in Design View, click in the field's Default Value property, and type in the default value. For example, to mark every record in a table with its creation date, add a createDate field to the table and set its Default Value to **=Date()** (Figure 3-11). Just be sure that your field size is large enough to accept the default you specify. You can apply defaults to fields in a table, or controls in a form, but be aware that some functions (such as DLookup, DSum, CurrentUser, and so on) cannot be used at the table level; you'll know immediately, because Access will give you an error when you try to save the table. If you need to use one of these functions, apply the default at the form level.

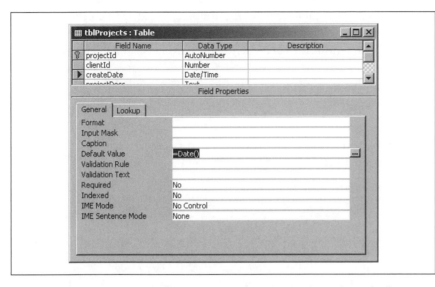

Figure 3-11. Setting the createDate field default to "=Date()" ensures that each record will automatically be marked with its creation date.

Defaults that are derived from other data in the same record can't be set using the Default Value property. For example, suppose you have a transactions form, and you want the default commission to be equal to the transactionAmount times the commissionRate—values that are stored in the same record. The problem is that you can't reference other fields in the same table in a field's Default Value, and you can't reference other controls in the same form in a control's Default Value. That's because the default gets applied when the record is created; it can't derive itself from other values in the same record because they don't exist yet. The fix is to add some code to the After Update event of the controls on your form that your calculation depends on. Once the other controls are filled in, the code computes the result and inserts the default value into the calculated control. Here's some sample code:

```
Private Sub txtTransactionAmount_AfterUpdate()
  If Not IsNull(Me!txtTransactionAmount) And _
          Not IsNull(Me!txtCommissionRate) Then
      Me!txtCommission = Me!txtTransactionAmount _
                  * Me!txtCommissionRate
  End If
End Sub
```

> **NOTE**
>
> *If the calculated value will never be changed by hand, it's not a default value; it's just a calculated value—and generally it shouldn't be stored in the database at all, since it can always be calculated.*

Simple Validation Rules

THE ANNOYANCE: I'm trying to define a validation rule for Zip Codes that will catch the occasional data entry error on my form. But Access's #@$#! Help system doesn't tell me a darn thing. Help!

THE FIX: Simple validation rules can be applied via the properties sheets of fields (in table design) or controls (in form design). As a general rule, it's better to do it at the table level, to ensure that the same rule gets applied no matter what route the data takes to the table. Either way, Access's help on data entry validation rules definitely comes up short. What they say is true: you can use just about any expression for a validation rule. But—Hello? Come in?—that doesn't help much if you don't know which expressions to use in the first place.

In practice, just a few kinds of expressions solve most common validation needs. Table 3-1 gives some examples, and the following sections discuss the various operators.

Table 3-1. Validation rule examples and usage

Rule	Usage
>=25	Greater than or equal to 25.
<>0	Not equal to zero.
<#2004-01-01#	Less than (i.e., prior to) January 1, 2004.
Like "#####" OR Like "#####-####"	Accepts both 5-digit Zip and Zip+4 Codes. You combine the two patterns with the OR operator.
Like "541-###-####"	Matches specific characters with a pattern of numbers. This example accepts only phone numbers starting with area code 541.
Like "54[1369]-###-####"	Accepts a *set* of characters, that you specify using brackets. This example accepts phone numbers with area codes 541, 543, 546, and 549.
Like "21[0-9]-###-####	Accepts phone numbers whose area codes start with 21. Character sets also allow the use of a hyphen (-) to indicate a range of characters. Ranges don't have to be numeric: [A-D] is the same as [ABCD]. Character ranges always go from low to high, and character sets are not case-sensitive.
Like "BL????"	Accepts any six characters, as long as the first two are B and L.
Like "BL*5"	Accepts any string of characters, of any length, beginning with BL and ending with 5.
Like "SKU[0-2]###[ABD]	Accepts four-digit numbers prefaced by SKU and followed by the letter A, B, or D. The first digit must be 0, 1, or 2.
Between #2002-03-15# And Date()	Accepts any date between March 15, 2002 and today.
In (1, 10, 100, 1000)	Accepts any number in this list. Note that numbers don't require quotation marks.

The Like Operator

When you want the input to match a certain pattern, turn to the Like operator. For example, for a string of five digits (such as a Zip Code), use **Like "#####"**. (The quotation marks are required.) For a string of five characters (digits, letters, or punctuation), use **Like "?????"**. Like recognizes three wildcard characters:

? Represents any single character

Represents any single digit

* Represents zero or more characters

For example, **"###"** means three digits, but **"###*"** means three digits followed by anything else.

The Between Operator

To restrict input to a continuous range of values, use the Between operator. For instance, **Between #2004-02-01# And #2005-02-01#** will restrict input to dates within the year between February 1, 2004 and February 1, 2005. (Note the special syntax required for bracketing dates.) To restrict numerical input to values between 100 and 500, enter **Between 100 and 500**. Between can be applied to dates, numbers, and even text (to restrict entries to, say, words starting with letters between B and L—this is used primarily in queries). It is inclusive, which means that the endpoints are always included.

The In Operator

To restrict input to a set of discrete values, use the In operator. For example, **In ("MA", "CT", "RI", "VT", "NH", "ME")** restricts input to these state abbreviations. (The quotation marks are required.) A better solution might be to provide a combo box with a value list on your data entry form; that way, users are guaranteed to follow the rules. (See "Activating the Wizards" in Chapter 5.)

Record-Level Rules

Sometimes you want a validation rule to enforce a relationship between different fields in a record. For instance, you might want to ensure that proposedFee is greater than the sum of fixedCosts and variableCosts. The rule is simple: **> fixedCosts + variableCosts**. (As you might expect, > means "greater than.") Note, however, that you can't assign this validation rule to the proposedFee field in your table, because field-level rules can't reference other fields. Instead, open the table in Design View, click View→Properties to display the properties sheet, click on the Validation Rule field, and enter this rule: **[proposedFee] > [fixedCosts] + [variableCosts]** (see Figure 3-12). The brackets tell Access you're referring to fields.

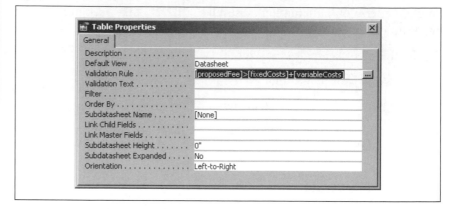

Figure 3-12. In the table's properties sheet, you can enter a validation rule that references different fields from the table.

Complex Validation Rules

THE ANNOYANCE: I've ended up with some duplicate entries in my contacts database, and it's my fault; when I enter a "new" person, I often forget to check to see if she's already in the database. I tried to create a validation rule to check if the person I'm entering is already there, but I just couldn't figure out how to do it. Help!

THE FIX: Validation rules do a good job of catching data entry errors in fixed patterns, such as Social Security and phone numbers. But for more complex rules, you're better off writing a bit of VB code and placing it in the control's Before Update event. By doing the validation there, you enable Access to catch bad data, display a custom error message for the user (see Figure 3-13), and cancel the update.

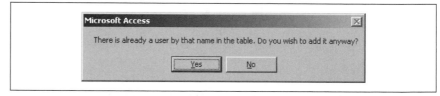

Figure 3-13. Use a message box in your code to communicate with your users and enable them to respond to data validation issues that arise.

You can also allow the user to override the rule. The following example checks for duplicate names in a contacts table, issues a warning, and allows an override in case two different people have the same name. (You'll need to have at least a little VB knowledge to adapt it—it's not just a question of replacing placeholders.)

```
Private Sub Form_BeforeUpdate(Cancel As Integer)
   If DCount("*", "tblContacts", "lastName = """ & Me!txtLastName _
      & """ And firstName = """ & _
      Me!txtFirstName & """") > 0 Then
         If MsgBox("There is already a user by that name in the" _
            & "table. Do you wish to add it anyway?", _
            vbYesNo) = vbNo Then
      Cancel = True
   End If
   End If
End Sub
```

Subtypes and Supertypes

THE ANNOYANCE: I'm designing a database for a retreat center that hosts many different kinds of events—workshops, weddings, and so on. I'm pretty sure that each kind of event needs its own table, because the kind of information we collect for each event type varies. Do I create a single table with everything in it, or multiple tables that I somehow relate to each other?

THE FIX: Workshops, weddings, and the like are all subtypes of one supertype: events. Since subtypes and supertypes are common in the world, they're pretty common in databases as well. For example, employees can be subdivided into union, temporary, and exempt. All events have some common attributes (name, location, and so on), but different kinds of events have their own unique attributes as well (weddings have caterers, workshops have instructors, and so on). When faced with organizing this kind of information, a database designer must choose between using a single table, using multiple unrelated tables, or creating a supertype table (which includes the common attributes) that's related to multiple subtype tables (which include the unique attributes).

The simplest option is a single table that accommodates all the types. This works if the data you collect is mostly the same for all event types. For example, if every type of event has a start date, an end date, a sponsor, and so on, then just go ahead and create a single events table with a field that specifies the event type. As discussed above, you'll probably need a few extra fields for attributes that are specific to certain event types. That's fine; just leave those fields blank when they're not needed.

However, if event types vary significantly, using one table doesn't make sense. Weddings and workshops, for example, may require a completely different set of fields, so you could just go ahead and create separate tables for them. This is not a bad solution, but it can lead to complications later. For example, you'll need to collect payments for both types of events, so your payments table will need to have a foreign key field for the ID of the event—but how do you know whether that ID refers to the weddings table or the workshops table?

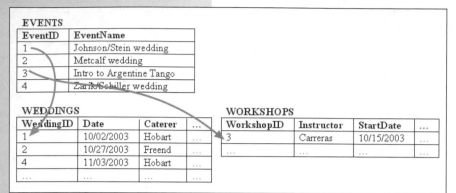

Figure 3-14. The events table is the supertype. Weddings and workshops are subtypes, linked on their primary key fields.

A better solution is to use supertypes and subtypes in your design, as shown in Figure 3-14. This gives you the best of both the single table and multiple table solutions.

First create an events table, and create the fields common to all event types. Then create subtype tables, such as weddings, workshops, and so on. Give each subtype a primary key that's compatible with the primary key of your supertype. For example, if your events table uses an AutoNumber ID field, give each subtype table an ID field that's a Number data type, with the Field Size set to Long Integer. (The foreign key field must be able to hold any data that would be valid in the primary key field, and generally speaking, you make the foreign key the same data type as the primary key. It's not obvious, but AutoNumbers are Long Integers.) Next, create a relationship between the supertype and each subtype by linking the primary keys of the two tables (one supertype, one subtype) in the Relationships window. When Access sees you linking two primary keys, it knows that this is a one-to-one relationship—i.e., that each record in the supertype table will correspond to exactly one record in one of the subtype tables.

For most purposes, you can treat tables that are in a one-to-one relationship as if they are a single table. Add them both to a query, and the join on the primary key field makes them behave just like a single table. Similarly, there's no need to use a subform when including both tables on a form. Just base the form on a query where they're joined—that's what the Form Wizard does.

The benefit of this design reveals itself in situations where you need to base a foreign key on the supertype's primary key. For example, every row in the payments table needs the ID of the event that the payment is for. As we saw above, without a supertype table you'd have to mix keys from different tables in the same foreign key field. With a supertype table, the design becomes a simple one-to-many relationship between the events (supertype) table and the payments table.

Duplicate Records

THE ANNOYANCE: In our equipment database, we enter most equipment by serial number—but we can't use serial numbers as our primary key, because some items don't have them. Unfortunately, we don't always remember to check first to see if a serial number is already in the database, so we're getting duplicate records. How can we prevent this?

THE FIX: As you suspected, the best way to avoid duplicate records is to use a "natural" primary key, such as serial number or employee badge number, that is uniquely associated with the data you're recording. Since Access won't let you add duplicate primary keys, you can't add the same item twice. In practice, though, it's rarely this easy, because usable natural keys are hard to find. And as you've discovered, you may need to record data where the natural key is missing, or there may be duplicates of natural keys that you thought were unique (such as two people with the same Social Security number—it happens!). That's why we usually recommend that you use an AutoNumber ID field as a primary key (see "Relationship Angst" and the sidebar "Primary Keys and Duplicate Records," earlier in this chapter).

If you're sure that the serial numbers will be unique, you can avoid duplicates by adding a unique index to the serial number field. In table Design View, simply set the field's Indexed property to "Yes (No Duplicates)." Unlike a primary key field, a unique field can have null values, but Access will still prevent you from adding duplicate values. (If you sometimes need to allow duplicate values but want the system to warn you before accepting them, see "Complex Validation Rules," earlier in this chapter.)

Relationships Window Ghosts

THE ANNOYANCE: I'm trying to delete a table from my database, and Access is telling me that I can't because the table is involved in relationships with other tables. But when I look in the Relationships window, no such relationships are listed.

THE FIX: The Access Relationships window is at best a crude tool, and it can be misleading. Remember that it doesn't automatically show *all* relationships—it just shows relationships for tables that you've added to the window. That means that in order to see a relationship, you first have to add the relevant tables to the Relationships window. If you don't mind discarding your current Relationships layout, choose Edit→Clear Layout, then choose Relationships→Show All. If a relationship exists, it will show up.

Before you discard your current layout, look for tables that may have scrolled off the screen. Select any visible table in the Relationships window, and then tab through all your tables. Each time you tab, watch carefully to see if the highlight vanishes; if it does, that means that the current selection is offscreen. Hit Delete to remove that table, and its relationships, from the Relationships window (since it's offscreen and there's no way to get it back on!). Do this for any offscreen tables, then add back any tables you need, putting them somewhere you can see them. Once you've found the ghost relationships, you can alter them so Access will allow you to dump that table.

Relationships Window Layout Distress

THE ANNOYANCE: Our inventory database has 103 tables and 95 relationships. I've spent hours laying them out in the Relationships window just the way I want. Recently, I needed to import everything into a new database. The relationships imported fine, but the layout is gone. I want to smash something....

THE FIX: You're not the first person to go ballistic over this one, and fortunately, Michael Kaplan was mad enough to fix the problem. His free SysRel Copy Utility (Figure 3-15) lets you transfer Relationships window layouts between databases (which also means you can share layouts between two users of the same database). You can download this utility from *http://www.trigeminal.com/lang/1033/utility.asp?ItemID=12#12*. You might also want to have a look at Stephen Lebans's free code to save and restore multiple relationship layouts (*http://www.lebans.com/saverelationshipview.htm*). If you need a professional tool for viewing, documenting, and analyzing your design, check out Total Access Analyzer (*http://www.fmsinc.com/products/analyzer/*), which costs $299 and up.

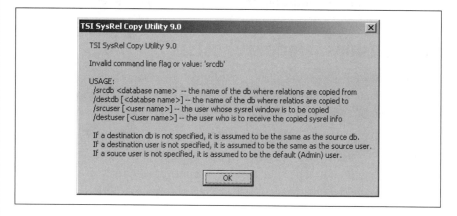

Figure 3-15. To get usage instructions, run the SysRel Copy Utility without any options. It ain't pretty, but this is what you'll see.

Attack of the Nonexistent Tables

THE ANNOYANCE: Much to my horror, Access has populated my Relationships window with tables that don't exist. I do have an Orders table, but where did Orders_1 and Orders_2 come from!?

THE FIX: Whenever a table has more than one relationship to another table, Access adds extra copies of that other table to the Relationships window. Maybe Access thinks this makes it easier to lay out the relationship lines. In any case, the extra copies are distinguished by adding an incremented suffix—if Orders is the first copy, Orders_1 is the second and Orders_2 is the third (see Figure 3-16). The underlying tables are not affected; these names show up only in the Relationships window. The issue typically comes up when you use the Lookup Wizard "data type" in table design, because the wizard adds a relationship (not to mention an index) as part of the lookup process. (This is one more reason many people avoid the use of lookup fields. See "Hide Foreign Keys" in Chapter 5 to see how to avoid them.) The bottom line is, don't worry about the extra tables; they're just visual clutter in the Relationships window.

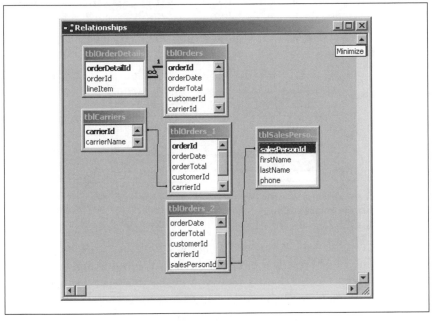

Figure 3-16. Access appends _1, _2, and so on to a table name in the Relationships window when multiple copies of that table are added.

Errors with Imported Data

THE ANNOYANCE: I'm trying to import a parts inventory into Access from an Excel worksheet. The Import Wizard (File→Get External Data→Import) runs fine, but then it gives me a "Not all of your data was successfully imported" message. The ImportErrors table shows a lot of "type conversion" errors, and some of the data is just plain wrong. But the wizard never asked me to specify data types!

THE FIX: The single biggest problem with importing data is getting the data types right. If you have type conversion errors, or if garbage data appears in the imported table, either the imported file has bad data or the receiving table has incorrect data types.

Let's look at bad data first. Suppose you're trying to import a column of numbers into a field that's set up to be a Number type—but a few of the numbers have feet or inches symbols attached, like 3" or 5.5'. The extra characters disqualify these values from being stored as the Number data type and cause conversion errors. Fortunately, the ImportErrors table (see Figure 3-17) points to the errant field (i.e., column) and row, making it easy to track down the bad data in the source file. You can then clean up the data and import it again.

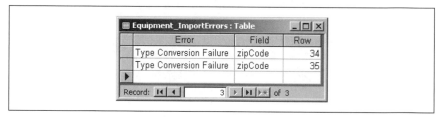

Figure 3-17. The ImportErrors table gives you the reason for the error, the field in which it occurred, and the row of data in which it occurred.

The other common problem is specifying the wrong data type at the receiving end, which is especially a problem when you're importing worksheets. For some reason, Access doesn't allow you to specify data types during the import. Instead, it tries to *guess* the correct types for each field based on the first rows of data. (Depending on your version of Access, it will examine as many as 25 rows before making a decision.) If the Import Wizard sees any text, it sets the data type to Text (unless the text is more than 255 characters long, in which case it'll choose Memo). If it sees both numbers and dates, it chooses Number, and if it sees only dates, it chooses Date/Time.

These rules make sense—except when the first rows of data are not representative of the rest of the data in the column. For example, a list of part numbers could, by chance, start out with all numbers (10012, 11201, 23113...) and then, further down, become alphanumeric (AQ12013, E4320...). You'd need a Text data type for that field, but what you'll get is a Numeric field—and all those alphanumerics will generate conversion errors.

A simple fix is to set up your Access table with the correct data types *before* you do the import. But not so fast! If you *import* the worksheet into your Access table, Access will ignore the data types you so lovingly crafted and will spit out errors. (For some reason known only to the kids in Redmond, Access does allow you to set data types when importing, but only if you're importing a text file.) Instead, once you've set up your Access table with the correct data types, simply *copy and paste* columns from your Excel worksheet into your Access table. Select a column in Excel, then open your Access table in Datasheet View and choose Edit→Paste Append. This way, your data types will be preserved. Note: if you have fields in your Access table that aren't in your Excel worksheet, first open your table in Datasheet View and arrange your columns to match your Excel worksheet. Then select those columns before you paste.

Another simple solution is to insert a single dummy row at the top of your spreadsheet with the desired data types. For instance, a text value in that row will coerce Access into assigning the Text data type to the whole column. Once you've imported the data, just delete the dummy row. Yet another trick is to precede the first value in an Excel column with an apostrophe. Excel will ignore the apostrophe but will be forced to store the number as text, which will then import as the Text data type in Access. (You can also use Excel's TEXT() function to tell Excel to store numeric values as Text.)

Finally, a clean, flexible solution is to save your worksheet as a text file (say, CSV) and then import it, setting the data types in Access's Import Specification dialog. If you have a lot of spreadsheets to import, consider a commercial tool such as 4TOPS Excel Import Assistant (*http://www.4tops. com*), a $99 Access add-in that gives you full control over the process.

Linked Spreadsheet Woes

THE ANNOYANCE: I have an Access table that's linked (through Access's Get External Data dialog) to an Excel worksheet containing student data from our registrar. The data in the worksheet is fine, but when I view it in Access, some fields are truncated, some have garbage, and some appear only as #NUM!. All I wanted it to do was *link*.

THE FIX: Linking to an Excel worksheet presents many of the same problems as importing data from an Excel worksheet (see the previous Annoyance), because Access must likewise assign specific data types to the worksheet's

NOTE

If you only need to display (not edit) the worksheet data in Access, you can simply link to or embed an Excel object in your Access form or report; there's no need to import the data or create a linked table. In form or report Design View, click Insert→Object, choose "Create from File," and then browse to your worksheet file and click OK, then OK again. The Excel worksheet will show up as a read-only (i.e., static) image—but if you check the "Link" box when you insert it, it will be kept in sync with the original worksheet, and the data will always be current.

data. If you're seeing nonsense data or #NUM! values, either you've got bad data, or Access has chosen the wrong data type.

Bad data results when you have items of one data type mixed in with items of another data type (e.g., a single numeric value mixed into a column of dates). Databases, Access included, do *not* like items of different data types in the same column. As an example of Access guessing the data type wrong, let's say you have a column of Zip Codes, and the rows that Access analyzes when trying to determine the data type happen to hold only 5-digit codes. Access will assign the Numeric data type to the field—and then shriek #NUM! when it encounters Zip+4 Codes later in the worksheet. (Since Zip+4 numbers include hyphens, they must be stored as Text.)

Access assigns each column in a linked spreadsheet a "data type" in order to treat it as a "table." And once Access assigns that data type, there's no way to change it. Instead, you must change the way the data is represented in Excel. Usually this means representing numbers as text. You *can't* do this by simply formatting the cells, which doesn't change the underlying data. You must do it by adding a preceding apostrophe (which will be ignored by Access but will cause it to display the numbers as text), or by using Excel's TEXT() function. Note that it's not enough to adjust only the first row of data in Excel; you must alter at least 25 rows so that Access thinks the majority of them are Text.

As for truncated data, if fixing your data types doesn't solve the problem, we'll guess the data is coming from worksheet cells that hold more than 255 characters. Access maps such cells to the Memo data type. Memo fields can contain up to 65,535 characters, but by default Access formats the field to show only up to 255 characters. The data is still there, but Access ignores it, and you can't change the design of a linked table. If you want a ton of text data in Access, you'll have to import it, rather than linking to it—which is often a better solution in the long run, anyway. If you must have your data available in spreadsheet form, import the data into Access and then link to it from Excel.

Data Incorrectly Imported as Dates

THE ANNOYANCE: All our spreadsheets use our company's internal (and nonstandard) date format of "yyyymmdd." These are not dates, they are numbers stored as text—don't ask me why. When I try to import them into Access, they are assigned the Text data type, but I need them to be dates in Access. And the Import Wizard doesn't let me specify the data type!

THE FIX: The easiest solution is to save each worksheet as a text file (e.g., in CSV format) and then run the Import Wizard (File→Get External Data→Import). Why save the worksheet as text? The wizard won't let you specify data types if you try to import a worksheet, but it will if you import a text file. Here are the steps:

1. As soon as you attempt to import the text file, the Import Text Wizard will open. Click the Advanced button to create the specification (see Figure 3-18) and set up the dates to match your format.

2. For "yyyymmdd," set the Date Order to "YMD," clear the Date Delimiter box, and make sure that both the "Four Digit Years" and "Leading Zeros in Dates" boxes are checked. (If you think you'll need to do this import again, click the Save As button and give this import spec a name. Next time, just click the Specs button to recall it.)

3. Once the import spec is completed, step through the wizard, assigning appropriate data types to each column of your data. The wizard will apply your date specification to any columns that you specify as dates.

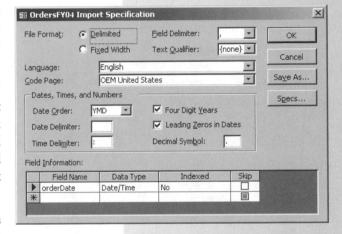

Figure 3-18. The Import Specification dialog lets you specify data types for your import fields, and gives a fair amount of flexibility in interpreting date fields.

An alternative solution—useful if your dates are in a format that the wizard can't parse—is to import the spreadsheet into a dummy Access table, leaving the dates as Text. Then create an append query (open a new query in Design View, then click Query→Append Query) that pulls the data out of the dummy table, formats the dates correctly, and appends them to the true table. To do this, first create an append query as if you were going to simply copy the data between the two tables, then replace the date field (i.e., the date that you've added to the Field line) with an expression similar to this one:

```
CDate(Mid([myDateField],5,2) & "/" & Right([myDateField],2) & "/" &
Left([myDateField],4))
```

This expression parses out month, day, and year from the text string and then coerces the result into a Date/Time data type (for instance, it will convert 20051203 to 12/03/2005).

Obscure Excel Import Errors

THE ANNOYANCE: I often need to import Excel worksheets created by our financial people into Access. Most of the time it works fine, but occasionally I get obscure errors such as "Unparsable Record" or "Subscript out of range." I have no idea what these errors mean.

THE FIX: The ImportErrors table's error messages are usually fairly meaningful (see Figure 3-19).

Figure 3-19. The ImportErrors table devotes a row to each error, noting which field caused it and which row it occurred in.

However, your error messages require further explanation. According to Microsoft, a record is "unparsable" when the text delimiter character (e.g., a quotation mark) is included in the data itself. (Such delimiters should be doubled, as in "This is a ""sample"" with internal quotes.".) But this is only a problem with text file imports. Your problem is due to a more common obstacle: too many characters in the record. Records in an Access table are limited to 2,000 characters each (except for Memo or OLE fields, which are stored separately). A row in a large worksheet can easily exceed this amount. If it does, Access populates as many fields as it can, leaves the rest empty, and slaps an unparsable error in the ImportErrors table.

When a "Subscript out of range" error shows up in the Import Wizard, it typically indicates that you're importing a worksheet with too many columns. An Access table can have a maximum of 255 fields; a worksheet, up to 256 columns. (Note that if you get this error after seeing another message, such as "ActiveX component can't create object," it's not a problem with your worksheet; some other index is out of range, and your Access installation has gone awry. Follow the procedures in "Agonies of a Sick Installation," in Chapter 1, to fix it.)

For more information on these errors, check out the "Troubleshoot importing and linking" section in Access Help. It's listed under Working with Data→External Data→Importing, Exporting or Linking to Data in the Table of Contents—but not in Access 2000 (sigh). It can also be found online at *http://office.microsoft.com/en-us/assistance/HP051885461033.aspx*.

Unhelpful Error Messages During Import

THE ANNOYANCE: I have some old data stored in a worksheet that I'm trying to import into an existing table in Access. The Import Wizard seems to go along fine, but then, when it's all done, I get the brilliant, informative message: "An error occurred trying to import file <filename>. The file was not imported." Grrr!

THE FIX: This error message is really dumb. If this is the *only* error message you're getting, check that your column headings in Excel match your field names in Access *exactly*; if there is so much as an extra space, the import will fail. Access doesn't care about the order of the columns, and you don't have to put data in every field in the table. But Access must be able to find a matching field in your table for every column heading in Excel. If the column headings and field names do match up precisely, there may be extraneous data in your worksheet, outside the columns you're trying to import.

Sometimes a stray keystroke far offscreen is the culprit. Deleting the cell's contents isn't enough—you must delete the empty columns, too. And wait—it gets better. Often this error is preceded by a long error message (see Figure 3-20) that begins: "Microsoft Access was unable to append all the data to the table." Then it goes on to explain the reasons why *zero* records might have been deleted or lost!

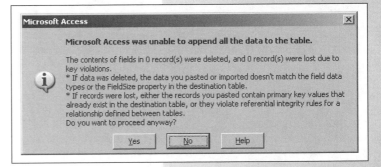

This would be hilarious if you hadn't needed to finish your conversion 20 minutes ago.

What's it mean? Most likely, your worksheet has data that violates an existing validation rule, or is missing data in a required field. You'll need to fix your data.

Figure 3-20. This marvelous error message, reporting zero errors, does indicate some problem with your data. Usually data is violating a validation rule, or data is missing from a required field.

Can't Import Word Tables

THE ANNOYANCE: I'm embarrassed to admit that I have years' worth of business data stored in Microsoft Word tables. I've tried to import this data into Access, but the Import Wizard doesn't recognize Word files. Don't tell me I'm going to have to type all this data into Access!

THE FIX: Access can't directly import Word documents (or their tables). One possible fix is to copy the tables from Word and paste them directly into an Access table. Another is to copy the tables into a format that *can* be imported, such as an Excel worksheet.

For the former process, copy your table in Word, open the Access table in Datasheet View, and choose Edit→Paste Append. Access will add rows as needed. Of course, the data coming from Word must be compatible with the data types of the fields in Access—otherwise, you'll get a PasteErrors table, and Access will skip those rows. Note that you can paste into any contiguous region of your table, so if you have fields in Access that aren't in Word, simply open your table in Datasheet View and arrange your columns to match your Word table. Then select those columns before you paste.

Since data in Word tables is seldom arranged to match an Access table, it's often useful to move it to Excel first, using Copy and Paste Special (Text). Put each table on a separate worksheet and massage the data as needed (see the sidebar "Massaging Word Tables") before importing the Excel sheet into Access. As you can see from the preceding Annoyances, importing from Excel is not without its tribulations, but it's doable.

Copy/Paste to Excel Is Broken

THE ANNOYANCE: When I used Access 97, I didn't have any problems copying and pasting from a datasheet to an Excel worksheet. (I like to use Excel's statistical functions for computations.) But since I "upgraded" to Access XP, my numbers show up in Excel as text, and I have to fiddle with them before I can use them. This is an improvement?

THE FIX: It isn't! In fact, it's a bug in Office XP (see MSKB 328933). Fortunately, it was fixed in Office XP Service Pack 3 (for details, see MSKB 307841). In the meantime, the workaround is to Paste Special into Excel, choosing Excel's BIFF5 (Binary Interchange File Format) format.

Massaging Word Tables

Before importing your data into Access, it can be useful to do a little massaging in Excel. First of all, if you're storing, say, all of your dates or all of your product codes in the same row, you'll need to use Excel's transpose function to turn those rows into columns, since Access expects like items to be stored in columns. Simply select your data, then copy and paste it into a new worksheet, again using Paste Special but this time checking the Transpose box (Figure 3-21). Once your data is in columns, check each column to be sure that all the items match the data type you're intending to import them to. Then open Access and run the Import Wizard by clicking File→Get External Data→Import.

If you don't have Excel, open Word, select Table→Convert→Table to Text, click "Separate text with commas," click OK, and import the resulting text file. This may be a good solution if there are line breaks in your data within table cells. Managing these isn't trivial, but if you need to do it, consult MSKB 290169 for detailed instructions.

Figure 3-21. It's common for Word tables to be organized in columns, but Access needs rows. Excel's Paste Special with Transpose is just what the doctor ordered.

Exporting Reports Produces Weird Numbers

THE ANNOYANCE: I'm trying to export an Access 2003 report to Excel. The Access report includes a text field of internal accounting codes (such as 002-00001-003) that show up as weird numbers (e.g., 37653 and 38018) in Excel. Why is this happening, and how can I stop it?

THE FIX: Oh, the woes of exporting Access reports! For some reason, when Access exports text fields in a *report*, it perversely tries to interpret these fields as something numeric or date-like—despite the fact that they're clearly defined as text. Access considers anything with one or two hyphens (or slashes) as a date, and strings such as 6a or 20P will be interpreted as times. (Why the weird numbers? That's how Excel represents dates and times! If you apply a date/time format to those cells, you'll see what's going on.) To make matters worse, Access interprets text strings such as 20E070 or 5D4 as if they were numbers in scientific notation, and they'll show up in Excel as 2E+71 and 50000. Ridiculous!

If it makes you feel better, this is a known Access bug (see MSKB 823222) and is just one more reason to avoid exporting reports. As a general rule, you'll have much better luck exporting tables and queries to Excel. But if you absolutely must export a report, the workaround is to append an apostrophe to your text field. Open the report in Design View, and open the properties sheet of the text box that contains your field. If, for example, the name of the text field is acctCode, set the Control Source to `=[acctCode] & "'"` (see Figure 3-22). The ampersand character concatenates two strings, so this expression appends an apostrophe to whatever's in your text field. Make sure that you name the text box itself something different from the control source (e.g., txtAcctCode), or you'll get #Error!.

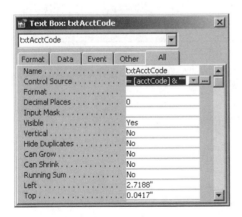

Figure 3-22. Append an apostrophe (in quotes) to the control source to force Access's exporter to interpret the data as text.

Now your data will export to Excel as text. The only problem is that it will show up in Excel with apostrophes. To get rid of them, you can use Find/Replace and replace the apostrophes with nothing, or run the snippet of code that Microsoft provides in the above-mentioned Knowledge Base article, which will remove them automatically. We admit it: this fix is ugly. Try to avoid it.

Hidden Apostrophes in Exported Data

THE ANNOYANCE: I exported my table to Excel (using Excel 97-2002 format), and all the text strings have appeared with an apostrophe in front, like this: '*my text*. Whose idea was that?!

THE FIX: It's not well advertised, but Access and Excel both use this cute apostrophe trick to ensure that text data isn't mistakenly interpreted as numbers or dates. What you're seeing are "hidden apostrophes," and you can't get rid of them with Find/Replace. But you don't need to—they display only in the formula bar, and they don't print out. You can prevent these rogue characters from appearing by checking the "Save formatted" box in Access's File→ Export dialog box (see Figure 3-23). Note that this box is grayed out when you're exporting a report, but it's available for tables and queries.

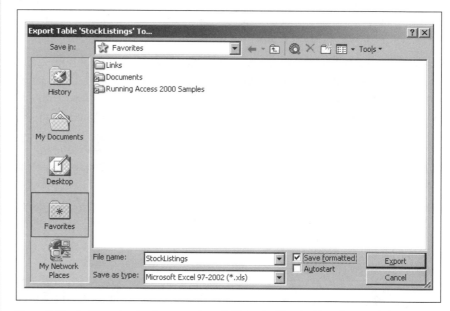

Figure 3-23. Avoid apostrophes in exported text fields by checking the "Save formatted" box in the Export dialog.

If you're running an older version of Access or Excel, and "Save Formatted" isn't available, you can remove the apostrophes using this simple code:

```
Sub RemoveApostrophe()
    Dim CurrentCell As Range
    For Each CurrentCell In Selection
            If CurrentCell.HasFormula = False Then
                    CurrentCell.Formula = CurrentCell.Value
            End If
    Next
End Sub
```

In Excel, save this code as a macro by choosing Tools→Macro→Visual Basic Editor and pasting the code into a module. If there's no module available, choose Insert→Module to create one. It will be saved as part of your worksheet. Before you run the code, select the range of cells in the worksheet that you want to clean. Then choose Tools→Macro→Macros and run the RemoveApostrophe macro.

Exported Numeric Data Is Truncated

THE ANNOYANCE: We've got three years' worth of geophysical data stored in an Access database using the Double data type—a floating-point type that can handle very big numbers (such as 1.0034×10^{23}) with any number of decimal places (e.g., 1.930024). We need to export the data as text files, but Access truncates all our numbers to two decimal places!

THE FIX: According to Microsoft, this is a feature, not a bug (see MSKB 153364). Fortunately, there's a simple workaround: set up a query for your table, and use the Format function to preserve your decimal places. For example, suppose your table has a field called sensor13, which represents the reading of the global subterranean frammelstat sensor, and you want to preserve four decimal places to the right of zero. Add that field to your query, and apply formatting such as the following to it:

```
exportSensor13: Format([sensor13],"##0.0000")
```

Then export the query as text. Choose File→Export, and in the "Save as type" drop-down, select "Text Files." Then click Save, Save All, or Export. This summons the Export Text Wizard. By default, the wizard will surround your data with quotes—which you probably don't want. Click the Advanced button and set the wizard's Text Qualifier field to "{none}" (see Figure 3-24). You can save this setting as an export specification from this dialog, using the Save As button.

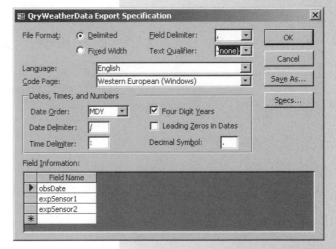

Figure 3-24. When exporting to text, by default the wizard will surround your data with quotes—which you probably don't want. To get rid of them, set Text Qualifier to "{none}."

Exported Text Data Is Truncated

THE ANNOYANCE: I set up a macro in Access to export a table to Excel. The table has several memo fields, and they all appear chopped off in Excel. What's the problem?

THE FIX: There are two possible causes:

- If you're exporting to an older Excel format (that is, anything before Excel 97), cells are limited to 255 characters.

- If Access interprets your data as a text field rather than a memo field, it will truncate the data before it reaches Excel.

When you're designing this kind of macro, the OutputTo action seems like a good choice—it even lets you select Excel 97-2002 format. Unfortunately, because it's an old function (and has now been superceded), OutputTo is actually limited to the older Excel 95 format—so it treats memo fields like text fields. Instead, you must use TransferSpreadsheet, with its export option (see Figure 3-25). Set the Spreadsheet Type to "Microsoft Excel 8-10" (i.e., 97-2002). For export, the Has Field Names field is ignored. The same goes if you're using these functions in VB code.

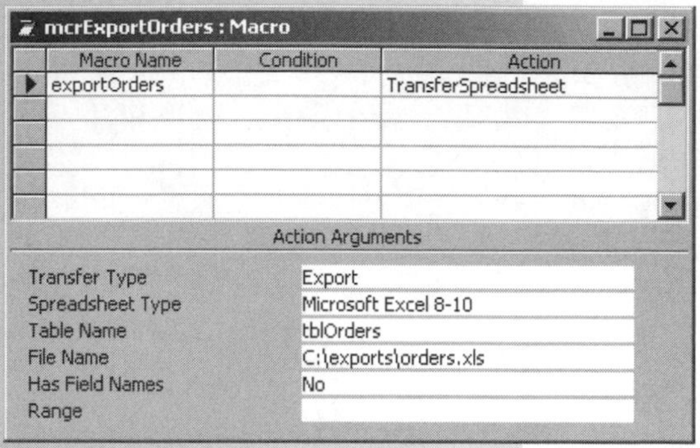

When exporting reports (and only reports), Access *always* uses the older (Excel 95) format, regardless of your choices in File→ Export. This virtually guarantees that memo fields will be truncated. The best approach is to avoid exporting reports to Excel; export the underlying query instead.

You may find other data, such as calculated expressions that exceed 255 characters, truncated as well. Likewise, if you concatenate text fields—for instance, if you export mailing addresses as a single expression—Access will treat the expression as a text field and truncate it. The workaround is to convert your query to an append query that stores its results in a table with a memo field. Then export the memo field data; it won't be truncated.

Figure 3-25. To avoid truncation, use the TransferSpreadsheet action, instead of OutputTo.

Miscellaneous Export Annoyances

THE ANNOYANCE: We have a dozen Access 2003 databases containing clinical research data. I just noticed that when I export a table or query with null fields to Excel, and those Access fields turn into Excel cells, data from the adjacent cell slides over to fill the empty cell produced by the null Access field. The ultimate result is that several subjects' blood pressure numbers become their ages, and their ages become their heights. Do I need to call our malpractice attorney?

THE FIX: Put down that phone. This is one of Access's many maddening export annoyances. This is a known bug (see MSKB 294410) that shows up only if certain conditions are met. To swat it, simply install the latest Jet service pack. Here are a few more export annoyances of note, and how to get around them:

Junk in hyperlink fields

When you export hyperlinked fields, such as URLs or email addresses, you may see junk such as this: *phil@yahoo.com#http://phil@yahoo. com*. That's because Access stores hyperlink data in multiple parts, including a display part, a full address, a subaddress (if needed), and so forth. At least, that's the idea—the meaning of *http://phil@yahoo.com* is beyond us. If you want to strip out the junk, create a query using an expression like this:

```
expEmailAddress: HyperlinkPart([EmailAddress], 0)
```

Put this expression in the Field line of the query grid to include it in your query results. You can get more information about the HyperlinkPart function in VB Help. See "Create Email Links" in Chapter 7 for an alternative to using the Hyperlink data type.

"Too many rows" error when exporting to Excel

Excel 97 and later versions are limited to 65,536 rows. You can't export more than that number of rows to a single worksheet. But if you're getting this error with fewer rows, it's because Access thinks you're exporting to an *older* version of Excel (the limit used to be 16,384 rows). This happens if you use the OutputTo function or action (calling the function with a macro); instead, use the TransferSpreadsheet action. It also happens if you're exporting a report; export the underlying query instead.

Wrong data type

When exporting Access data to Excel, or another brand of database, the data types that appear in the result are sometimes incorrect. For instance, your query may output a perfectly proper Access date string that Excel insists on interpreting as text. The fix is to use a VB function in your query to coerce the data type so it will wind up in the appropriate format in Excel (or wherever). These coercion functions all begin with "C," such as CDate, CStr, CInt, and so on. For instance, to coerce a text string to be treated as a date, add CDate(myDateText) on the Field line of the query grid, instead of the raw date field. Of course, Access will throw an error if the text string isn't something that can be interpreted as a date.

Can't export to a specific worksheet in an Excel workbook

When you export to Excel using File→Export, or a macro, the only thing you can specify is the name of the workbook. If you need to place data on a specific worksheet, or even in a specific location on a specific worksheet, and you don't mind digging into some VB code, use TransferSpreadsheet. Despite what Access's Help file says, you *can* export to a *named* range using the "range" argument. This enables you to specify exactly where in your Excel workbook the data goes. Depending on your versions of Access and Excel, you may also be able to use sheet names and unnamed ranges. See "Automating Import/Export," later in this chapter, for details.

Putting Data on the Web

THE ANNOYANCE: We want to make the data in our bibliographic database available on the Web. We tried exporting static HTML, but our data changes too frequently and no one wants to maintain the static pages. We would use ASP pages, but our IT department doesn't run an IIS server. Aargh! Access has so many different ways to do this, but none of them seem to fit. Why couldn't they just give us one *good* way to get our data on the Web?

THE FIX: The ability to publish data that's always up to date and is readable by anyone with a browser and an Internet connection is transforming our information culture. It's no accident that Microsoft tried to make Access web-friendly; it's just too bad they didn't do a better job. In this fix, we'll go over your options for putting Access data on the Web, and make some recommendations.

Two primary factors determine how you generate web pages from Access data: whether your data is static or dynamic, and whether you want it to be read-only or editable.

Static and Read-Only

If your data doesn't change (e.g., if it's a collection of historical data) or changes only infrequently, and your goal is to publish it on the Web so people can view (but not edit) it, then static HTML pages are a reasonable solution. Using File→Export, you can export tables, queries, and reports; just set the "Save as" type to "HTML Documents (*.html; *.htm)." For tables and queries, Access creates an HTML page that looks like Datasheet View. In older versions of Access, exported reports also look like datasheets, but starting with Access 2002, they look like reports. Forms still export as datasheets based on the underlying record source.

Left to its own devices, Access creates very basic HTML pages. There are a couple of options that let you enhance them. For tables and queries, checking the "Save formatted" box on the Export dialog usually produces a nicer result: more polished visually, with shading, borders, and other professional touches. (Reports always have this option checked.) You'll get an HTML Output Options dialog that lets you choose both a character encoding and a template. If you need to handle international characters (with diacritics, etc.), you'll want one of the Unicode options. The template is any web page that you want Access to embed the data into; without a template, Access will just create a standalone page.

To tell Access how to embed the data in your template, simply include the special tags in your web page: use <!–AccessTemplate_Title–> for the title and <!–AccessTemplate_Body–> for the data; if the export spans multiple pages, you can also use the FirstPage, PreviousPage, NextPage, LastPage, and PageNumber tags. Access replaces the tags with their corresponding items. Only reports will be broken into multiple pages by Access.

Dynamic and Read-Only

If your data changes frequently, static HTML pages are a poor solution. A better option is to build the web pages on the fly. With this approach, every time a browser requests data, the database is queried and the results are built into a nice, neat page. This is how most database-backed web sites work, and it's something almost any web developer can set up for you.

> **NOTE**
>
> *While all of these solutions produce some kind of web page, that alone doesn't actually get your data on the Web. For that, you'll also need a web server—that is, a computer that's connected to the Internet and is running server software such as Apache or IIS. The server responds to browser requests by delivering your web pages.*

In Access, you can create dynamic web pages by exporting tables and queries in Active Server Pages (ASP) format. Use File→Export and set the file type to "Microsoft Active Server Pages (*.asp)." You'll get the same display options as with static HTML. The difference is that ASP pages don't include a snapshot of your data; instead, they use code that knows how to retrieve the data from the database. During the export, you'll need to specify a Data Source Name (DSN)—that is, the name of the ODBC data source on your web server that connects to your database.

ASP has one significant limitation: it only works with Microsoft's web servers (IIS Version 3.0 or later, and Personal Web Server). If you don't want to be locked into that choice, see our recommendation in the next section.

Dynamic and Editable

A fully interactive web application allows users to view *and* edit data on a web page. Microsoft's solution is Data Access Pages (DAP)—but the technology comes up short.

The goal of DAP is to deploy Access-like functionality in Internet Explorer. When your browser loads a DAP page, a suite of ActiveX controls known as the *Office Web Components* is loaded. These provide database connectivity and an enhanced user interface. In the Access 2000 version of DAP, users had to have an Office 2000 license to view and edit the data. With Access 2002 or 2003, unlicensed users can view, but not edit, data. As you can see, DAP is not a general-purpose web technology, but rather a web-based extension of Microsoft Office. It tends to be used mainly on intranets, as an alternative to giving everyone a copy of Access. DAP pages are complex to design and tricky to debug, and we don't recommend using them.

Besides, web developers solved this problem years ago, with an open source scripting language called PHP. (PHP was designed precisely to make it easy to put data on the Web.) For example, the following is the complete HTML and PHP code for a web page that queries a database and then displays the results in a table. Even if you don't understand the details, you can see that the amount of code required is very small and is mostly self-explanatory. The code connects to the database, submits the query, then loops through the results row by row and outputs the data in apple-pie order. Although this example only displays data, it is equally easy to accept input using an HTML form and then write it to the database.

This code builds an HTML table with all the authors and titles found in the tblBooks table:

```
<html>
<body>

<?php
$conn=odbc_connect("MyDateStoreName", "user", "pwd");
if (!$conn)
{
```

```
    exit("Connection Failed: " . $conn);
}
$sql="SELECT * FROM tblBooks";
$result=odbc_exec($conn,$sql);
if (!$result)
{
    exit("Error in SQL");
}
echo "<table><tr>";
echo "<th>Author Name</th>";
echo "<th>Book Title</th></tr>";
while (odbc_fetch_row($result))
{
    $author=odbc_result($result,"AuthorName");
    $title=odbc_result($result,"Title");
    echo "<tr><td>$author</td>";
    echo "<td>$title</td></tr>";
}
odbc_close($conn);
echo "</table>";
?>

</body>
</html>
```

We don't expect you to write your own PHP code based on this example, but it's reasonably easy to do—and worth a small investment of time to learn how. (A good place to start is David Sklar's *Learning PHP 5*, also published by O'Reilly.) With a little HTML and PHP wrangling, you can make your Access data web-accessible. You'll also be able to use any platform (Windows, Linux, and so on), any web server (Apache, IIS, and so on), and any browser. That's a big win.

Automating Import/Export

THE ANNOYANCE: Every week we get the same worksheets from human resources and have to import them into an Access database. Isn't there some way to automate this dreary process?

THE FIX: If you just want to click a button that imports or exports a specific file, it's pretty easy. In this example we'll discuss importing, but you can export using the same methods. Depending on the target of your import, you'll use either TransferSpreadsheet (for importing data from an Excel or Lotus worksheet), TransferText (for importing from a text file), or TransferDatabase (for importing from another database). To put these methods (which belong to the DoCmd object) into the Click event of a button, see "How to Create an Event Procedure" in Chapter 0. To add a custom error handler, see "Better Error Handling" in Chapter 7.

For instance, to import the A1:G12 range from Sheet1 of the *hr_weekly.xls* worksheet, you'd use something like this:

```
DoCmd.TransferSpreadsheet acImport, acSpreadsheetTypeExcel8, _
"tblEmployees","C:\data\hr_weekly.xls", True, "Sheet1!A1:G12"
```

"True" here means that the first line of the worksheet has column headings. To import the whole worksheet, just omit the last argument. As always, consult VB Help for more information on the various arguments. If you need to let the user choose the file to import, see "File Choosers" in Chapter 7. Note that while Help insists that you can't use the "range" argument with an export, this is a lie. All Access versions covered in this book can export to a *named* range, and later versions of Access and Excel (2002 and later) can export to specific sheets and unnamed ranges as well.

If you want to automatically import or export the same *set* of files each week, it takes a little more work. Start by creating a table, say "tblMyImportFiles," that lists the names of the files you want to import and the receiving tables (see Figure 3-26). Then iterate through the table in code, importing each file into its table. If you need to support multiple file types, just add a column to the table to store that information.

The following code iterates through the tblMyImportFiles table and imports each spreadsheet listed in the fileName column into the matching table listed in the import-Table column:

Figure 3-26. Importing the same worksheets into Access? Define a table to hold the names and import destinations of your files.

```
Public Sub cmdImport_Click()
    Dim db As DAO.Database
    Dim rst As DAO.Recordset
    Dim strFileName As String
    Dim strImportTable As String
    Set db = CurrentDb()
    Set rst = db.OpenRecordset("tblMyImportFiles")
    With rst
        If .RecordCount > 0 Then
            Do Until .EOF
                strFileName = ![fileName]
                strImportTable = ![importTable]
                DoCmd.TransferSpreadsheet acImport, _
                    acSpreadsheetTypeExcel9, strImportTable, _
                    strFileName, True
                .MoveNext
            Loop
        End If
        .Close
    End With
End Sub
```

Put this code in the Click event of a button, as shown here. Note that TransferSpreadsheet will *append* to your table. In some cases, you may want to delete the old records first before doing the import.

One last thing: if you receive an error such as "Field 'F3' doesn't exist in the destination table," this means that Access thinks there's an extra column in the worksheet, and it doesn't match any field in the table. There probably was data in a column that has since been cleared. Remember that *clearing* a cell's contents isn't enough—you must *delete* the column, or Access will attempt to import it. Just select the whole column and select Edit→Delete.

Exporting Data on the Fly

THE ANNOYANCE: I'm trying to write a VB application that lets users export specific data, on the fly, from our HR database to a spreadsheet. I thought TransferSpreadsheet would do the job, but it only works with static tables and queries, and I'm building my recordset on the fly. There must be some way to do this.

THE FIX: There is—but note that this fix is only for those who are comfortable writing VB code. The trick is to automate Excel (not Access) and use its CopyFromRecordset method to assemble the data for your export on the fly. As you can see from the following code, once you've defined your worksheet range, a single call to CopyFromRecordset sucks your recordset into Excel:

```
Sub exportRecordset()
    Dim rst As ADODB.Recordset

... 'Create recordset

    Dim objApp As Excel.Application
    Dim objWorkbook As Excel.Workbook
    Dim objWorksheet As Excel.Worksheet
    Dim objRange As Excel.Range

    Set objApp = New Excel.Application
    Set objWorkbook = objApp.Workbooks.Open("c:\fullPath\myExport.xls")
    Set objWorksheet = objWorkbook.Worksheets("ExportSheet")
    objWorksheet.Range("namedRangeForExport").Clear
    objWorksheet.Range("namedRangeForExport").CopyFromRecordset rst
    objWorkbook.Close True
    objApp.Quit
    Set objApp = Nothing
    rst.Close
End Sub
```

Note that although we used an ADO recordset, CopyFromRecordset accepts DAO recordsets as well. We exported the data to a named range in the worksheet, but you could have used a literal range. (The range only needs to be cleared if it has old data in it.) By default, CopyFromRecordset copies the entire recordset. If you supply it with optional row and column arguments, it will take that number of rows and columns.

Queries

4

I don't know how to fix my own car, which is why I pay somebody to do it for me. This arrangement suits me just fine. But if I didn't know how to *drive* my own car, that would be a different story entirely. It would be almost as bad as, well, having a database and not being able to write my own queries.

That said, I'm sorry to tell you that query Design View can be one of Access's most baffling interfaces—but if you want to go anywhere, you've gotta use it. In this chapter, we'll do our best to get you over the speed bumps, and we'll offer fixes and workarounds for query Design View's idiosyncrasies and deficiencies. We'll also offer guidance for creating queries that may seem impossible, but can generate some very useful results. When you're done with this chapter, you'll know some of the tricks that hard-core Access stunt drivers use—tricks you *should* try at home.

QUERY BASICS

Query a Single Table

THE ANNOYANCE: I need to generate a list of names and phone numbers for just those employees who live in Massachusetts—but our employees table includes workers in eight states. I can't make any sense out of query Design View. Where do I start?

THE FIX: Access's query Design View really drives people crazy. It's not intuitive, but once you get used to it it's really pretty useful. Since querying data is what it's all about, you must learn how to make query Design View dance to your tune. (Incidentally, Access does have a Simple Query Wizard, which you can find by clicking Insert→Query, but it's so simple that it's almost useless.)

To make sense out of the query Design View interface, remember that *Access thinks in terms of tables*. Tables, and nothing but tables. Even when your query produces a single number, Access thinks of this as a table with one field and one row. So designing a query is really about translating your question into terms that define a new (virtual) table—a.k.a. a *recordset*. That's what query Design View helps you do. Here's how to use it, step by step:

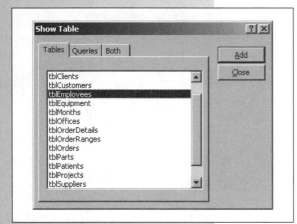

Figure 4-1. In the Show Table dialog, double-click the table name to add a table to your query.

1. **Tell Access where to find the data.** First, specify the existing table that holds the info you're seeking. In this case, that's the employees table. To open query Design View, go to Insert→Query, select "Design View," and click OK. When the Show Table dialog box opens, simply double-click the table you want (see Figure 4-1). The table you choose will appear in the upper pane of the Query Design window, with a list of all its fields.

2. **Define the fields you want.** Next, specify which fields in the table hold the data you want to suck out. In the field list in the upper left of the Query Design window, double-click the field names you want to use in the query; they will appear in the query design grid in the lower half of the Query Design window (see Figure 4-2). You can also drag a field from the list and drop it on the query design grid. In this example, you'd choose firstName, lastName, and phoneNumber.

At this point, you've defined a "virtual" table consisting of three fields. Choose View→Datasheet View to preview your results; you'll get a window filled with the data you requested from those three fields in the employees table.

But how do you restrict the results to Massachusetts?

3. **Add criteria.** To constrain or filter your data, go back to query Design View (if you're not already there) and locate the Criteria row. You can add just about any expression you like to this row (for example, `< Date()`, which means prior to today's date). Whatever the expression, Access will populate your virtual table with just the data that matches it, and nothing else. (For more information on the expressions you can use, see "Simple Validation Rules" in Chapter 3 and the "Expressions" section in Chapter 7.)

   In this example, since you want to base your criteria on the table's State field, you must add that field to the grid, just as you did the other fields. Then, in the Criteria row, add the line `="MA"` under the State column. (When you save the query, Access will remove the equals sign.) Since you don't need to show the state in your results, uncheck the "Show" box in the State column.

> **NOTE**
>
> *If your criteria expression references fields in your table, you must use brackets around the field names—otherwise, Access will treat the field name as literal text. For instance, use [productName], not productName, to refer to the product name field.*

Types of Queries

Select
  Select queries find and display data from your tables. This is Access's default type of query.

Totals
  Totals queries allow you to summarize data by calculating averages, sums, minimum and maximum values, and so on. For example, you can find sales totals based on all orders for the past month. See "Create a Totals Query," later in this chapter.

Crosstab
  Crosstab queries let you summarize data using multiple variables. For example, you can break out sales totals by salesperson *and* by month. See the sidebar "Crosstab Traffic," later in this chapter.

Parameter
  Parameter queries limit the records chosen based on variables that users supply every time the query is run. See the sidebar "Queries That Accept Parameters," later in this chapter.

Action
  Action queries change or delete data; they actually modify the database itself. They're useful because you can use complex query criteria to identify a precisely defined set of records, and then apply an action to it—for example, you can use a delete query to find and delete duplicate records. There are four kinds of action queries:

Update
  Edit existing data

Append
  Take the results of a query and store them in an existing table

Delete
  Delete existing data

Make-Table
  Take the results of a query and create a new table to store them in

---

Figure 4-2 shows the finished query in Design View. Switch to Datasheet View, and you can see the query populated with results. Once you understand that all Access ever does is repackage and display data drawn from your underlying tables into new, *virtual* tables, based on your instructions, you'll be on your way to Indy 500 query writing—and query Design View will actually start to make sense.

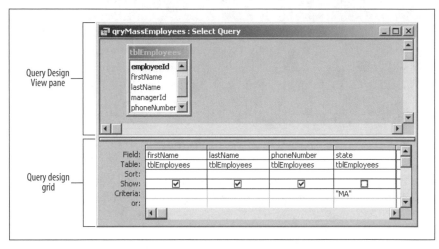

Figure 4-2. This simple query lists the names and phone numbers of employees who live in Massachusetts.

Query Multiple Tables

THE ANNOYANCE: We need to generate a list of teachers and the names of the classes each one teaches. We have a teachers table and a classes table, but how do we get them together?

THE FIX: You need to create a multi-table query, and that involves using *joins*. Joins take a little getting used to, but they are the backbone of complex queries. If you drag multiple tables into the Select query pane without using joins, Access will create one big table with all possible combinations of records. In this example (see Figure 4-3), Access has paired every teacher in tblTeachers with every class in tblClasses, whether a given teacher teaches that class or not. This is known as a "Cartesian" product.

Figure 4-3. All together now! If you drop tables in the query Design View pane and don't join them, Access will combine them into one big table—not the result you want. Using joins, you can accurately query related data in multiple tables.

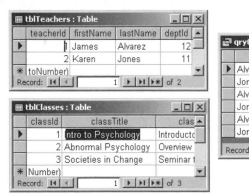

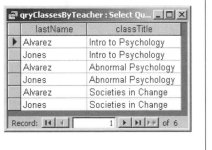

Although Cartesian products can sometimes be useful, in this example you really only want rows from tblTeachers (names) to be paired with rows from tblClasses (classes) *if the teacher teaches those classes.* In other words, you want to match teachers with the classes they teach. That's where a join comes in—in this case, a join that links the teacherID field in each table.

To create a join in query Design View, go to the upper pane of the Query Design window, then drag the field to join from one table and drop it on the matching field in the other table. The field names do not have to match; the data types must be compatible, but they don't have to be identical (e.g., you can't join text to numbers, but you can join Long Integers to Short Integers). Access will create a thin line connecting the two tables (see Figure 4-4). Compare Figure 4-5 with the Cartesian product created earlier, and you can see how the results have been pared down—each teacher only appears with the classes that he or she teaches. You can join on more than one field, but one field often suffices.

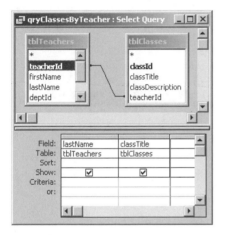

Figure 4-4. Tables with joins. Drag-and-drop the join field (here, teacherId) from one table to the other to create a join. This tells Access to include only those rows where the data in the join fields is the same. (The names of the fields do not have to be the same, although in this case they are.)

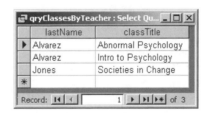

Figure 4-5. The result of joining tblTeachers and tblClasses on teacherId. Now each teacher appears only with the classes that he or she teaches.

> **NOTE**
> *You can also add queries to the upper pane of the Query Design window (via the Queries tab or the Both tab of the Show Table dialog) and treat them just like tables: you can drag fields from them to the query design grid below. See "Divide and Conquer," later in this chapter, for more information.*

The key to complex queries is understanding that no matter how many tables you add to the upper pane of the Query Design window, Access merges them into a single virtual table. You use joins to tell Access what data you want to cull. Once you've specified the joins, you complete your query by adding fields and criteria, exactly as you would in a single-table query. For more on the nuances of joins, see "Data Is Missing from a Multi-Table Query," later in this chapter.

In a well-designed database, Access may actually create the joins for you automatically. It does this with any fields that are connected by *relationships*; usually, the related fields are the ones that you'd typically want to use for joins. (If, on the other hand, Access automatically creates lots of joins that *don't* represent relationships, turn off the AutoJoin function; see "Spurious Joins," later in this chapter.)

If your data is properly normalized (see "Table Design 101" in Chapter 3), it's not uncommon for a query to require you to join three or more tables. This can seem daunting at first, but Access can really help. Add one table at a time, create the join you want, and then switch to Datasheet View to make sure you're getting the data you want. In this way, you can build a complex query in small steps.

Meaningless Column Names

THE ANNOYANCE: I created a simple query to extract names and phone numbers from our employees table. I used an expression to concatenate first names and last names, and Access named the column "Expr1." Can't the field have a more meaningful name?

Updatable Queries

Access's designers figured that since the result of a query is really just a virtual table, why not let people update the data in the underlying tables by editing the data in the query results? Good figurin'. Not only can you create a query that shows, for example, product descriptions for all your products that cost more than $100, but you can type changes to those descriptions right into the query datasheet, and Access will propagate them back down to the tables that underlie the query!

This may seem like a good idea, but we don't recommend the practice—nor do we recommend directly editing data in a table. As a general rule, to protect your data it should be edited via forms. But the fact that you *can* edit data in query results means that you can assemble just the data that you want via a query, then generate a form based on that query and update the data in the much easier-to-use form. This technique is often used to simplify potentially complex data entry processes, by letting you enter data into multiple related tables from a single form.

But there are limitations: the results of some queries are not updatable, and some are only partly updatable. Here's why:

- The results of totals queries are never updatable, because these queries process and summarize groups of records—and Access has no way of knowing which individual records to update. For example, what would it mean to update the average of all student test scores? In fact, if you include a totals query as part of a larger query, the whole query becomes uneditable.

- The results of queries that use expressions are not editable. If a select query includes an expression such as `Full Name: lastName & ", " & firstName`, the results can't be updated because Access doesn't know what field should get the data you enter.

In addition, the results of crosstab queries, pass-through queries, and queries where the Unique Values property is set to "Yes" are not editable. For a full list of reasons, search for "updatable queries" in the Answer Wizard in Access Help.

THE FIX: When you enter an expression in the Field row of the query design grid, Access generates a generic column name such as "Expr1" or "Expr2" (see Figure 4-6). In queries that run totals, you'll see names like "CountOfOrderId" and "SumOfTotalAmount." None of these column headings are very user-friendly. Fortunately, you can change them to any unique name you like. For example, instead of writing your expression as **Expr1: [firstName] & " " & [lastName]**, you could use **Full Name: [firstName] & " " & [lastName]**. You can also add column names for any fields in the query grid, not just for expressions or aggregate columns—just insert the name, followed by a colon, in the Field line of the query grid. But avoid names that are the same as field names in your tables; this creates ambiguous references that can cause problems. For example, you might be tempted to do something like this: **Amount: Nz([Amount]).** This is no good. Instead, do something like **Amount of Payments: Nz([Amount]).**

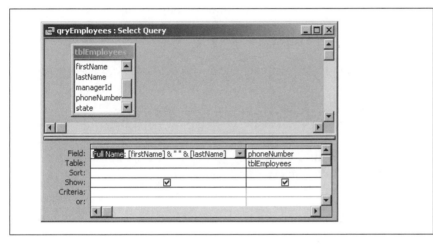

Figure 4-6. You can replace the generic column name that Access assigns with any unique name you choose.

Create a Calculated Field

THE ANNOYANCE: When I created our products table my Access guru told me to leave out the retail price field, since that can be calculated based on other information in the table. Now I need that field in my query, and my guru is on vacation. How can I get it?

THE FIX: Your guru was right. You shouldn't store data that can be derived from other data by a calculation. The reason comes down to our ever-burning desire to *store data in only one place*. Experience shows that otherwise your data will eventually get out of sync. In short, you're doing the right thing—but, of course, you still need that calculated field. Here's how to create it.

In the Field line of the query design grid, click in a blank column and enter an expression such as **RetailPrice: [WholesaleCost] * [MarkupPercent]**. (Of course, you'll use the names of the real fields.) Note that the term before the colon (in this case, "RetailPrice") can be any unique name you choose. What comes after the colon is the calculation, based on existing fields, functions, constants, and so on. The brackets indicate fields in the table; if you forget to type in the brackets in the Field line, Access will add them for you. When you run the query, Access builds a virtual table with a field named **RetailPrice**, populated with values based on the expression you wrote. It's just as if you had a table with that field in it, except that the data in this calculated field will always be up to date.

Create a Totals Query

THE ANNOYANCE: I need a query that computes our average monthly sales figures. I know I have to use a totals query, but I can't find the command to create it. This is embarrassing.

THE FIX: It *is* dumb that the Query menu doesn't have a totals command... but that's Access for you. The command exists all right, but some brilliant programmer put it on the View menu. In query Design View, click View→ Totals, or, if your Query Design toolbar is showing (reveal it by clicking View→Toolbars→Query Design), click the Σ button. Either way, you'll see a Total line added to the query design grid (with "Group By" in the first cell). Now you've got a totals query.

Understanding the Group By Clause

If you were curious enough to click the down arrow to the right of "Group By" in your new Totals row, you'll have seen a drop-down list of mathematical operators (Sum, Avg, Min, and so on). These operators get applied to *groups* of records, but that begs the question, how do you define which groups they get applied to? When you set Group By on a field, Access divides all the records selected by the query into groups, based on the value of that field. For example, if you group on gender, you'll have one group of males and one of females. If there are null values, they'll be lumped into their own group. Your query results will devote a row to each group.

You can group on more than one field; for instance, you could use both gender and occupation. Access then takes the groups defined by the first field and subdivides them using the second field. You might wonder whether the order of Group By columns matters. It doesn't. Whichever way you do it, you'll wind up with groups of male lawyers, female lawyers, male teachers, female teachers, and so on.

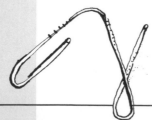

Find the Properties Sheet for a Query

THE ANNOYANCE: I'm trying to find the properties sheet for a query so I can set the Unique Values property to "Yes" and prevent duplicates from coming up. I pressed F4, but nothing happened. I right-clicked the query, but that didn't display any meaningful properties, either. Where the heck is it?

THE FIX: F4 is such a convenient way of displaying properties sheets that it would have been *too* sensible for Microsoft to use this technique for opening *all* properties sheets. As you've discovered, it doesn't work for queries, nor does it work for tables. To display table properties, open the table in Design View (View→Design View) and then click View→Properties. For a query, open it in Design View, right-click in the blank background of the upper pane of the Query Design window, and choose Properties. Note: if you open the properties sheet in SQL View and you click View→Properties, you'll see *some* of the properties, but not all of them (see Figure 4-7). Dumb, isn't it?

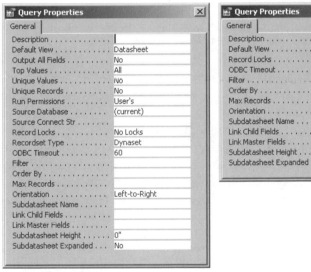
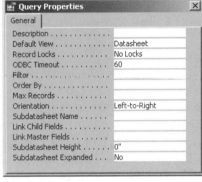

Figure 4-7.   The properties sheet for the same query, shown in Design View on the left and in SQL View on the right.

Divide and Conquer

THE ANNOYANCE: I need a query that summarizes customer information—specifically, total orders, year-to-date orders, and best month of orders (i.e., the month with the most dollars' worth of orders). I'm going batty trying to figure out how to combine these into one totals query.

THE FIX: Whenever a query stumps you, the way to start is by looking for one piece of the problem that you know how to solve. In this case, for example, you might already know how to find total orders in a query by itself. That's going to come in handy, because in query Design View you can use saved queries as building blocks for other queries (see Figure 4-8). This lets you build a complicated solution out of smaller, simpler pieces.

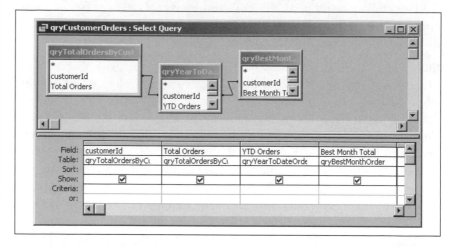

Figure 4-8. This summary query for customer orders is composed of three other queries, joined on customerId. Using simple building blocks can make a complex query easy to create.

While your query may seem dauntingly complex if you think of it as one operation, it becomes simple if you approach it as three separate totals queries (one for total orders, one for year-to-date orders, and one for best month of orders). Once you have these three components, create a blank query and add each of them to it, using the Queries tab of the Show Table dialog. Access treats them just as if they're tables: you can add any of their fields to the query, and you can join them as appropriate. In a typical case, you'll want each component query to have a primary key field (such as customerId) that you can join on.

Spurious Joins

THE ANNOYANCE: I added tables in the upper pane of the Query Design window, and Access created a bunch of spurious join lines. What's gone wrong, and how can I fix it?

THE FIX: You have AutoJoin enabled, which allows Access to automatically "suggest" joins based on matching field names. Access creates AutoJoins when the data types are compatible, and when one of the fields is a primary key.

To disable AutoJoin, choose Tools→Options, click the Tables/Queries tab, and uncheck the "Enable AutoJoin" box. If relationships are set up properly on your tables, you'll automatically get joins for those anyway. To remove a spurious join line, simply select it, right-click, and select "Delete."

Limit the Number of Records Returned

THE ANNOYANCE: I wrote a parameter query (see the earlier sidebar "Types of Queries") so users can pull specific information from our company's products database on the fly. The only problem? If you make a poor choice of parameters, you can wind up retrieving 250,000 rows—a huge waste of time and network bandwidth. How can I limit the number of records a user gets?

THE FIX: There are two ways, and the one you'll choose depends on whether you're querying an Access database directly, or retrieving records from an enterprise database via ODBC or OLEDB. Both settings can be found in the query's properties sheet. To view the properties sheet, choose View→Design View, right-click in a blank area of the upper pane of the Query Design window, and choose Properties.

If you're directly querying an Access database, use the Top Values property. Click in the field and choose the value you want from the drop-down list, or type in a custom value (see Figure 4-9). If you use this on a sorted field, you'll get the first N or N% of the values in sort order; if the field is unsorted, you'll simply get the first N or N% of the records. For an Access project (a special kind of Access frontend that's designed for talking to SQL Server) or an ODBC query, use the Max Records property instead. It's similar to Top Values, but you can specify only absolute numbers, not percentage values.

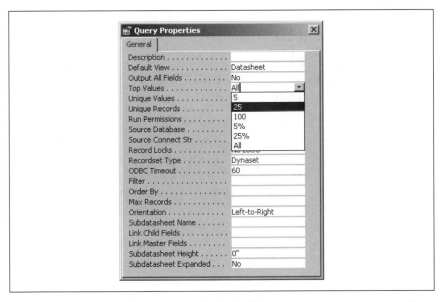

Figure 4-9. You can select from preset values for the Top Values property, or type in your own value.

Avoid Duplicates in a Query

THE ANNOYANCE: I created a query that finds all customers who have bought something in the past month, but some customers appear multiple times in the list. Setting Unique Values in the query's properties sheet doesn't seem to help. Why not?

THE FIX: When you set the Unique Values field to "Yes," this tells Access to remove duplicate rows from your results. If Access still gives you duplicate values, it's usually because you've included at least one field in your query that's different in every record. For instance, if you included a transaction ID in your query, customers with more than one transaction will show up more than once. A row is a true duplicate only if *every* column is the same as some other row.

Once you find the field that's different, you have two choices. If you don't need the field in your query results, uncheck the Show box under that field in the query design grid. If you do need it, make your query a totals query (press the Σ sign on the Query Design toolbar) and group your results by the fields that aren't changing. For instance, if you want each customer to appear only once in the results, set the Total line to "Group By" for customerId and customer name. But since *every* field in a totals query must have something on its Total line, you'll have to choose some aggregate function other than Group By (perhaps First or Last) for the fields that do change.

Find Duplicate Records

THE ANNOYANCE: I just inherited a mailing list database with over 30,000 records, and it has lots of duplicate entries. I'm trying to create a query to find the duplicates, but nothing works.

THE FIX: Queries that find duplicates are tricky to write. Even the pros are glad that Access has a built-in wizard just for this purpose. Choose Insert→ Query→Find Duplicates Query Wizard and click OK. It's easy to use. Let's say you're looking for duplicate last name and first address line entries in your customers table. Start the wizard, choose the customers table, and click the Next button. To add both fields to the query, select each field in turn from the "Available fields" list, and click the > button, then the Next button. In the next dialog box, you can add additional fields to the results; you'll want to add your primary key field so that you can easily find the original records. Click the Next button when you're done, give the query a name, click the "View the results" radio button, and then click the Finish button. The duplicate fields will appear in a nice, neat tabular form, and since the query is updatable, you can even delete the records you don't want.

Count Yes/No Answers

THE ANNOYANCE: Our table of survey results has many Yes/No fields. I tried creating a totals query to count the Yes answers, but it just counts the number of records.

THE FIX: The Yes/No data type is stored in Access as numeric values: 1 (Yes) and 0 (No). It has three variants—Yes/No, True/False, and On/Off—which you can use interchangeably. A simple way to show the Yes/No counts in a totals query is to add the field that contains your Yes/No data to the query design grid twice. In the first column, set the Total line to "Group By"; in the second column, use "Count." If you don't want both groups (e.g., if you only want Yes values), change Total in the first column to "Where," and add **=Yes** to the Criteria line. An equivalent expression, which is sometimes useful in calculated fields on reports, is =Sum(IIf(myYesNoField=Yes,1,0)). This tells Access to add 1 to the sum if the value of myYesNoField is "Yes," and otherwise to add 0. In other words, it counts Yes answers. You can tweak it easily to count No answers.

For example, look at a query that counts the number of workdays between Christmas and Valentine's Day (see Figure 4-10). This query uses a calendar table (see "Working with Calendar Dates," later in this chapter) that has a Yes/No field that indicates whether a date is a workday or not. The query groups on the workday field, and also counts the workday field. The Where column limits the date range.

By default, the query results display checkboxes (as in Figure 4-10), but you can change the display format in the properties sheet of the particular field in the query. To display text (Yes/No, True/False, and so on), click the Field line in the query design grid and open its properties sheet (View→Properties). On the Lookup tab, set Display Control to "Text Box"; on the General tab, choose the format you want.

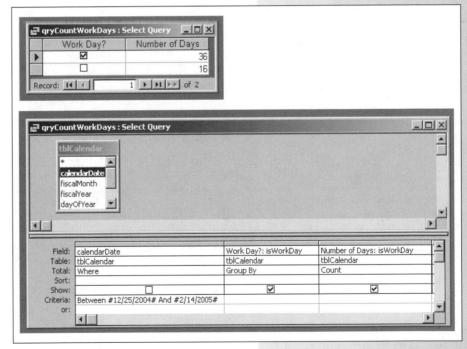

Figure 4-10. A query to count the number of workdays between Christmas and Valentine's Day. The results are shown above.

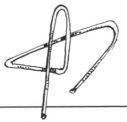

Jump to SQL View

THE ANNOYANCE: I want to write SQL code so I can run ad hoc queries on our sales and customers databases—using SQL is faster than fiddling with query Design View, and it's more powerful. But it's a pain in the neck to get to an SQL window—it takes too many steps.

THE FIX: Access doesn't make it easy for those who want to use SQL—but it *can* be done. For ad hoc queries, probably the easiest thing to do is to keep an old query lying around that you can quickly load and change. Call it qryAdHoc and save it in SQL View. The next time you need to whip up some SQL, select the query and press Ctrl-Enter (or right-click it and select "Design View"). The query will open in SQL View. Now just remove the old code, type in the new code, and run it. Unfortunately, you can't save a blank or incomplete query, so you'll have to overwrite your old code each time you want to make a new query.

A better solution is to set up a VB function that creates an SQL View. Assign this function to an AutoKeys macro (see "Create Keyboard Shortcuts" in Chapter 1), and you'll have an SQL window available at a keystroke. Here's the function that'll do it—just save it in a module and call it from your macro:

```
Public Function NewSQL()
    On Error Resume Next
    CurrentDb.CreateQueryDef "Enter SQL"
    DoCmd.OpenQuery "Enter SQL", acViewDesign

    DoCmd.RunCommand acCmdSQLView
    DoCmd.RunCommand acCmdDelete
End Function
```

Of course, compared to modern code editors, using Access's SQL window is like scratching marks on a clay tablet. Also, it occasionally gets confused and won't let you select code or copy and paste. For any significant amount of SQL editing, use a tool with more smarts (syntax highlighting, auto-indent, and so on), such as Emacs (free; *http://www.gnu.org/software/ emacs*), UltraEdit-32 ($39.95; *http://www.ultraedit.com*), or TextPad ($30; *http://www.textpad.com*).

Speed Up Slow Queries

THE ANNOYANCE: I have a simple query I use for our database of market indicators. It used to run fine, but the database has grown to about 100,000 records, and now it takes 10 minutes to run. I'm losing patience....

THE FIX: The most common way to speed up a query is to add *indexes* to pertinent fields in the underlying table(s). When you index a field in a table, Access creates a sorted copy of the data in that field, along with pointers to the original records. Since searching sorted data is much faster than searching unsorted data, indexing the fields used in query criteria can greatly speed up the query.

Before adding any indexes, though, be aware that Access automatically indexes primary key fields and join fields used in relationships. (If you haven't turned off AutoIndex, it may be indexing other fields, too. Select Tools→Options, click the Tables/Queries tab, and clear the list of field names in the "AutoIndex on Import/Create" box.) There's no point in indexing fields that are already indexed; note, too, that you can't index memo, hyperlink, or OLE object data types.

Also, avoid unneeded indexes—they bloat the database and can slow down updates or edits, because the indexes must be updated, too. Just index those fields that will be part of your search criteria, or those that you sort on or group by. If your query includes joins that are not based on defined relationships, you should index the join fields. This is especially important if one of your join tables is an ODBC-linked table.

Adding an index to a field in a table is simple. Open up the table in Design View, select the field, and set its Indexed property (on the General tab at the bottom) to "Yes." If you want Access to also enforce uniqueness on the values in the field, choose "Yes (No Duplicates)"; otherwise, choose "Yes (Duplicates OK)." To see all the indexes on your table, choose View→ Indexes. You can add, edit, and delete indexes in this view.

In situations where you place query criteria on multiple fields (for instance, on both lastName and firstName fields), a single *compound index* on those fields may run faster than separate indexes on each field. To create a compound index (see Figure 4-11), choose View→Indexes, create a new index by clicking in a blank Index Name cell (give it any name you want), and add your first field by clicking in the Field Name cell to the right and selecting the field from the drop-down menu. Add successive fields by clicking in Field Name cells in the rows below. These fields will be added to the new compound index you just created in the Index Name cell (as long as you don't add an additional Index Name to match the additional fields; as soon as you add another Index Name, you start adding a completely new index).

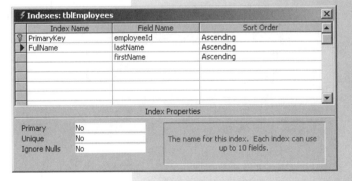

Figure 4-11. This employees table has two indexes: a primary key index on the employee ID (which prevents duplicates), and a compound or multi-field index on the first and last name fields.

Note that the order of fields in a compound index is significant; if you use the wrong order, the index won't work at all. Use the order that fields will naturally be sorted or searched in. (MSKB 209564 discusses some significant limitations of compound indexes.)

Should you use a compound index, or separate indexes on each field? There's no hard and fast rule. Experiment to see what gives you the best performance. You *may* be able to speed up your query using a compound index, but it's not guaranteed. Try it and find out—it's not hard to do, and you can always delete it if you don't like the results.

In addition to indexes, there are other ways to speed up queries. Two simple things you can do are:

1. Compact your database, if you haven't done so recently.

2. Avoid using domain aggregate functions (such as DLookup, DSum, DAvg, and so on) in query expressions; the Jet engine can't optimize them. Instead, add the underlying table or query to your query.

For more tips, go to MSDN (*http://msdn.microsoft.com*) and search for "Ways to optimize query performance." The article is also included in some versions of Access Help.

QUERY MISFIRES

Data Is Missing from a Multi-Table Query

THE ANNOYANCE: I created a query that generates a list of teachers and the classes they teach (see "Query Multiple Tables," earlier in this chapter). The query is based on a join of a teachers table and a classes table. But for some reason, Access leaves out some of the teachers. What's wrong?

THE FIX: This isn't an Access error, but a faulty design choice. The art of successfully joining tables involves anticipating which data doesn't match between the two tables. For instance, in Figure 4-12, you'll see that while Sue Levin is in the teachers table, her teacherId doesn't appear in the classes table. When you join these two tables, you have to make a choice. Do you want teachers who have no current classes to show up in your results? Maybe not. But in some cases, you may want the unassigned teachers to show up, perhaps with "UNASSIGNED" next to their names. You can do this easily by modifying the type of join that you use. Figure 4-13 shows the two different results.

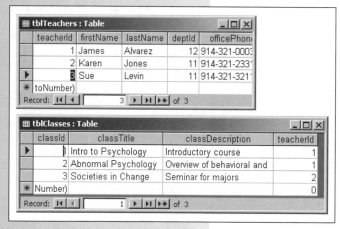

Figure 4-12. The teachers table includes one teacher, Sue Levin, whose ID doesn't appear in the classes table.

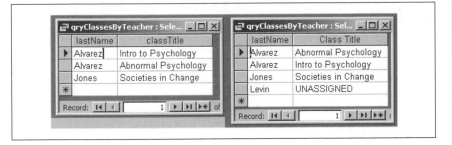

Figure 4-13. The query results on the left are based on an inner join between teachers and classes. It omits teacher Levin, because there's no record with her teacherId in the classes table. The query on the right uses an outer join, which includes all teachers regardless of whether there are records for them in the classes table.

Here's how to generate each result. In query Design View, right-click the join line that connects the two tables and select "Join Properties." Default option 1 is "Only include rows where the joined fields from both tables are equal." This means that rows (such as Sue Levin's) where there's no matching value will be omitted. (A join that omits nonmatching rows is known as an *inner join*.) To show all teachers regardless of any matches in the classes table (what's known as an *outer join*—also termed a left or right join), you'd pick option 2 (see Figure 4-14).

If you need nonmatching rows from both tables, see "Full Outer Joins," later in this chapter.

When you use an outer join, you'll often want to set up an expression to handle the null values that can arise in your results. For example, in place of className in the query design grid, use an expression like:

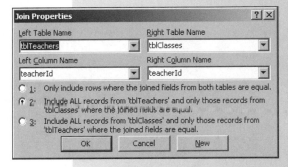

Figure 4-14. To change an inner join into an outer join, right-click on the join line and open its properties dialog. The second option makes it a left join, the third option makes it a right join.

```
Class Title: IIf(IsNull(className), "UNASSIGNED", className)
```

This tests the className field and, if it is null, replaces it in your query results with the text string "UNASSIGNED."

Query Has No Data or Has Wrong Data

THE ANNOYANCE: My company leases construction equipment, and I'm trying to generate a list of contracts where the closing date is after the lease date (in other words, where the rental started before the deal was signed). Simple, right? The Criteria line for my closing date field in the query is > "leaseDate", but I get no results—and I know they're there!

THE FIX: It's baffling when you pull together all the pieces of a query and it comes up empty. A query can really seem like a black box—you just push the button and hope it works. Fortunately, queries *aren't* black boxes: you can open them up, look inside, and figure out what's going on. There are two things to look at: the table joins and the criteria. Save a backup copy of your query so that you can edit it without losing your original work, then start digging.

Open the query in Design View and check the items listed on the left side of the query design grid. Make sure there isn't any "Append To," "Update To," or "Delete" line; those kinds of queries do not return data. If one of these lines appears, click Query→Select Query to make it a select query. Also make sure that at least one box is checked in the Show line.

If your query has joins, it's possible that null values in your join fields are causing data to be omitted. Remove *all* criteria from the Criteria line in the query design grid, then switch to Datasheet View. If your data is still missing, either it's simply not in your tables, or there's a problem with your joins. (See "Query Multiple Tables," earlier in this chapter, for help with joins.)

Now add back your criteria expressions one at a time. After each one, switch to Datasheet View to make sure you're getting the data you expect. Remember that Access is strict about the way it interprets your expressions. If you tell it =`"California"` but your data is stored as "CA," you won't get a match. In your case, the problem is with the quotation marks around `leaseDate`, which make Access interpret the string as *text*. Instead, use

> **[leaseDate]**; the brackets tell Access to interpret the string as a field name (see "[Brackets] Versus "Quotes"" in Chapter 7).

While you're at it, look to see if the fields in the tables you're searching have formats applied to them. (In table Design View, click the field name in the upper pane of the screen and look at the Format property listed on the General tab at the bottom.) Why does this matter? Formats only affect the way data is displayed, so they won't affect search results. But since the data you search for may be based on the way the values are displayed, you may be confused by the results you see. For example, if you see many entries of $100 in the table, you'd expect the search criteria =`100` to find those records. If none show up, it's possible that the numbers in the table are actually $99.95, $100.03, and so on, but the format is set to round them to the nearest dollar.

If you're using one or more "or" lines underneath the Criteria row (see Figure 4-15), there's another gotcha. The criteria for additional fields must be repeated on *every* "or" line, or they will apply only to the data in the line on which they appear. You can avoid this problem by combining the separate lines into a single expression, using the `OR` operator to connect them. For instance, instead of putting `"CA"` and `"NV"` on separate lines, simply use `"CA" OR "NV"` on the first line.

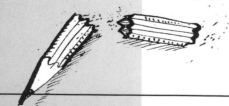

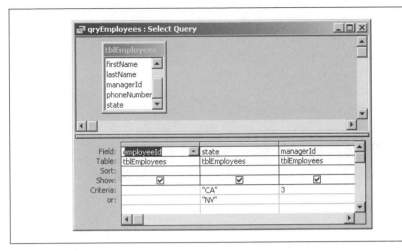

Figure 4-15. Think this query finds employees who live in California or Nevada, and whose manager's ID is 3? Nope. It finds all the employees who live in California and whose manager's ID is 3, plus all employees who live in Nevada, regardless of their manager's ID. The "3" must be repeated in every "or" line.

Getting expressions right is tricky, and Microsoft makes it doubly hard because Access Help barely covers the subject. You can find some examples by going to Help's Contents tab, opening Queries→Using Criteria and Expressions to Retrieve Data, and reading the "Examples of Expressions" article. (In some versions of Access, look in Working with Expressions→ Examples of Expressions.) Also see "Simple Validation Rules" in Chapter 3, and the "Expressions" section in Chapter 7.

"Aggregate Function" Error

THE ANNOYANCE: I'm trying to create a totals query that shows the total payments from each of our facilities. I'm grouping on the facilityID field, and I want to include the name and address for each facility as well. But Access keeps giving me this error: "You tried to execute a query that does not include the specified expression <expr_name> as part of an aggregate function."

THE FIX: What you're doing makes sense, but it isn't quite right. It makes sense because *you* know that for every record where the facilityID is the same, the name and address will also be the same. The problem is that Access doesn't know this—and that's what the error means. Those fields that don't have an aggregate function applied to them (in other words, that don't have anything in the Total line of the query design grid) are causing the problem. The fix in your case is easy: just set those fields to use "Group By" in the Total line. Grouping on redundant fields will cause no harm. For instance, grouping on name and address fields in this example won't change the groups created by simply grouping on facilityID.

Sometimes, however, this fix is not appropriate. If the additional fields are *not* all the same within each group, and you need to use them for query criteria *before* any aggregate functions are applied, use the "Where" choice in the Total line, and enter the criteria below as usual—for example, total payments from facilities located only in New York, Rhode Island, and Pennsylvania. Otherwise, these fields don't belong in a totals query, or you must apply some appropriate aggregate function to them (see Figure 4-16).

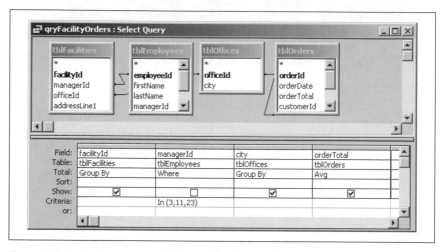

Figure 4-16. In a totals query, every field on the Total line must have a setting. This query uses a WHERE clause to restrict the search to a small set of manager IDs; then it groups on facility ID and city, and calculates the average of the order total field.

If you're writing SQL code and getting aggregate function errors, you're probably trying to use an aggregate function in a WHERE or GROUP BY clause. They don't belong there; aggregate functions can be used only in clauses that apply to groups of rows (or to the entire table, if there's no grouping). These clauses include the SELECT list, and the HAVING and ORDER BY clauses when used with GROUP BY.

Totals Query Gives Incorrect Result

THE ANNOYANCE: I have a totals query that computes an average score for every soccer team I track. But when I checked some of the averages by hand, I found Access wasn't calculating them right!

THE FIX: If the calculations are coming out wrong, some of your records might have null values. Access will ignore those records, and that will change the average (or count, and so on) it computes. To include those records, in the Field line of the query design grid replace the field name (such as team-Score) with an expression such as **Nz(teamScore)**. This converts null values to zeros and ensures that every record will be included in the calculation.

Sort Order Is Out of Order

THE ANNOYANCE: I have a crosstab query with monthly column headings formatted as Jan-05, Feb-05, and so on. Instead of sorting the columns in date order, Access sorts them alphabetically! This is absurd.

THE FIX: Access lets you apply nice formats to dates, but then it stops treating them as dates. This is darned annoying—and the quirk isn't limited to Date/Time fields, either. The fix involves convincing Access to interpret your sort field using the data type that *you* have in mind, rather than the one that it thinks it sees.

When you're working with dates, the Format function is the usual culprit. It allows you to apply custom formats, but it returns a string value—which Access treats alphabetically. The best workaround is to omit the formatting from your query and apply it later—for instance, by using the Format property of a text box in a report. But sometimes you really need the field sorted within the query itself—say, if you're using the query as the control source for a combo box. Often, the easiest thing to do is add another copy of your date field, uncheck the Show box, leave it unformatted, and sort on that field. But this won't work with your crosstab column headings. If your crosstab columns must be sorted within the query, pick a date format that you can live with *and* that sorts correctly alphabetically (for instance, yyyy/mm/dd or yyyy-mm)...and live to fight another day.

> **NOTE**
>
> *If you run into this problem with other numeric data, use a function such as CInt or CDbl to coerce the text into a numeric data type before sorting. This approach isn't as useful with dates, however, because CDate limits you to using the default date format (e.g., "3/2/2005").*

Left Join Doesn't Work

THE ANNOYANCE: All I want is a list of my clients and any active projects they have. I joined my clients and projects tables, using a left join so I get all my clients. That works fine, except that my results include tons of inactive projects, and I only want the active ones. But when I add criteria (on the Criteria line) to filter out inactive projects on the projects side, I don't get the full client list.

THE FIX: It's easy to confuse how left and right joins work. When you set up your left join, you selected the option that said "Include ALL records from tblClients and only those records from tblProjects where the joined fields are equal." You probably thought that no matter what else you defined in your query, you ought to get all of your clients. Wellll, it doesn't quite work that way. That's because the join gets done first, and your query criteria get applied after. Let's look at your example.

If you look at the results of your clients/projects join before adding any criteria, you should see all of your clients. But you also may see that some clients have all nulls in the projects fields. That's to be expected, because the whole point of the left join was to pull in *all* the clients, even if they don't match anything in the projects table.

But now what happens when you set criteria such as **"ACTIVE"** on the project status field? Your clients that don't have any projects at all certainly don't have any active projects, and this test will filter them out. You can pull them back in by changing the criteria to **"ACTIVE" OR Is Null**. This limits your results to clients that have active projects, or no projects at all—but it doesn't pick up clients who have only inactive projects.

To get exactly the results you want, define a separate query on your projects table, and set the criteria to **"ACTIVE"**, as above. This pulls all active projects out of the projects table. Now, instead of adding the projects table to your main query, add this active projects query, and create your left join between clients and active projects. Your results will show *all* of your clients, and any active projects that they have.

"Join Expression Not Supported" and "Ambiguous Outer Joins" Errors

THE ANNOYANCE: I created a simple query to get class registration records for our students—just three tables and two joins—and I did it all in query Design View. But when I run the query, Access says, "The SQL statement could not be executed because it contains ambiguous outer joins." In SQL View, I get "Join expression not supported"—but Access generated the darn SQL statement, not me!

THE FIX: These errors can arise for two completely different reasons: one when Access generates the SQL, and the other when you do. If Access generated it, it means there's an ambiguity in your use of inner and outer joins that Access can't resolve. If you wrote it, there's probably a problem with the ON clause of your join. We'll look at the latter case first, because it's simpler.

The problem with the ON clause (which occurs only if you're writing your own SQL) can be as simple as forgetting to put parentheses around a compound condition, such as (tblTrials.trialCode = tblExp.trialCode AND tblTrials.facet = tblExp.facet). You'll also get this message if the ON clause is incomplete or contains "too many" tables—but, of course, Microsoft doesn't say how many is too many.

The other cause of these join errors may be ambiguous combinations of inner and outer joins in either SQL View or query Design View (see Figure 4-17). If your SQL code uses parentheses correctly, your joins are *not* ambiguous; the problem is that Access ignores parentheses when interpreting the order of joins! To make matters worse, Access's error handling is ridiculous. If you're working in the SQL window, you'll get a "Join not supported" error when you try to save or switch back to the query design grid. But if you're in the grid and you try to run the query, you'll get the "ambiguous outer joins" error.

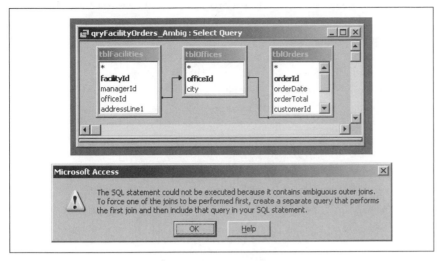

Figure 4-17. This query won't run, because Access considers the join order to be ambiguous. The fix is to break the query into two parts, and have the first one call the second.

Consider these two joins: (A LEFT JOIN B) INNER JOIN C and A LEFT JOIN (B INNER JOIN C). In SQL, the parentheses indicate which join should be performed first—and the order matters. In the first join, the left join preserves all the rows of A, but then the inner join may discard some of them. In the second, you may lose some rows from B and C, but you're guaranteed to get all the rows of A. The problem is that Access ignores the parentheses, and tries to interpret the SQL like this: A LEFT JOIN B INNER JOIN C. But as we've seen, this statement is ambiguous, because it has two different outcomes depending on which join gets executed first. It's a real pain in the Access.

The workaround is to create a separate query that forces Access to interpret the joins in the order that you want. For example, if you want the inner join to be performed first, create a query such as B INNER JOIN C and save it as qryBC. Then recast the original query as A LEFT JOIN qryBC. This works in query Design View as well as in SQL View, since you can treat a saved query like a table in either place (see Figure 4-18).

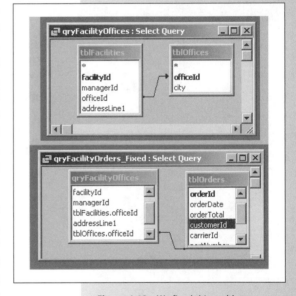

Figure 4-18. We fixed this problem query by creating a separate query, qryFacilityOffices, which does the left join. Then we added that "subquery" to our main query and created the remaining inner join. Now Access knows to do the left join first.

Input Mask Nixes Queries

THE ANNOYANCE: I added input masks to the phone, Zip Code, and Social Security Number fields in my table to make data entry easier and more accurate. The input mask seems to work properly for data entry, but queries that include these fields aren't finding all the records.

THE FIX: Input masks are a handy way to force users to enter data in a fixed format. For example, to prevent users from entering phone numbers in a mix of styles, such as (413) 222-1111, 413-222-1111, and 413.222.1111, you can give them a data entry form like the one shown in Figure 4-19. But if you store mask characters such as parentheses or hyphens in your data (or conversely, only use them for display) and your query doesn't reflect this, you'll get just the problem you describe.

Figure 4-19. An input mask for the phone field automatically presents the user with parentheses and a hyphen, and allows only numbers to be entered.

When you create an input mask, the value following the first semicolon specifies whether to store the mask characters in the table or not: 0 means store mask characters, and 1 means don't store them. For example, with an Input Mask property setting of \(000") "000\-0000;0;_, the value stored in the table will be (413) 222-1111. With an Input Mask setting of \(000") "000\-0000;1;_ or \(000") "000\-0000;;_, the value stored will be 4132221111. The problem, of course, is that it's easy to forget which you've chosen, since the formatting appears in forms and datasheets with no indication of what's stored in the field.

Because queries search the underlying data, not the formatted values, your query criteria must precisely match the way the values are stored (with or without mask characters, in this case). The problem gets worse if you add an input mask to a table that already contains data: Access doesn't update the existing records, so older values might be stored with formatting, while newer ones are not. For this reason, we recommend that input masks be applied at the form level rather than at the table level. That way, you can see exactly what's in your table.

If you've already applied a mask at the table level, here's what to do:

1. Make sure all the values are stored in the same way. Open the table in Design View, click in the Input Mask field, and delete the field's contents. Access will prompt you to save the table. Do so.

2. Switch to Datasheet View, select the column where mask characters appear, and do one of the following:

- If you want to store values *without* formatting, select Edit→Replace, enter the mask character (such as "-") in the Find What field, and leave the Replace With field empty. In the Match drop-down box, select "Any Part of Field," and click the Replace All button.

- If you want to store values *with* formatting, you must add mask characters wherever they are missing. If there are too many records to do this manually, reapply the mask, select the column in the datasheet, click Edit→Copy, remove the mask, then select the column in the datasheet again and click Edit→Paste.

3. Return to Design View. Set the Input Mask property again, restoring the original settings you deleted in step 1. If you want to store the mask characters in the table, make sure the value following the first semicolon is 0; if not, set it to 1.

PARAMETER AND CROSSTAB QUERIES

Parameter Queries with Wildcards

THE ANNOYANCE: I have a simple parameter query that lets users input a phone number and receive any matching records. But I can't figure out how to make the query use wildcards.

THE FIX: The trick is using the Like operator. (It's hard to find, but the Like operator *is* documented in Help: see Microsoft Jet SQL Reference→ Overview→SQL Expressions. (In Access 2000, on the Index tab, search for "Like.") If you want users to enter the wildcard characters, put **Like [Enter phone number]** in the Criteria line of the phone number field. If a user enters **212***, she'll get all the phone numbers that begin with 212. Enter **#** to match any single digit, and **?** to match any single alphanumeric character. For instance, entering **21#-323-4100** returns 210-323-4100, 211-323-4100, and so on.

If you don't want users to enter wildcards, enter criteria such as **Like "*" & [Enter phone number] & "*"**. Adding the wildcard to both ends of the input string ensures that your query will automatically return all matches. For instance, if a user enters **212-432**, he'll get back any phone numbers that contain those digits, such as 212-432-3323 and 441-212-4324.

Parameter Queries and Blank Responses

THE ANNOYANCE: I have a simple parameter query that accepts a state abbreviation and returns matching records. If users leave the parameter blank, I'd like it to return *all* records, but I can't make this work.

Queries That Accept Parameters

You've just a designed a wonderful query that shows sales data for the past year. There's only one problem: your users don't always want a year's worth of data. Sometimes they want the data from a three-month period, say, or for six months starting in the second quarter of the previous year. Making a separate query for each scenario is way too much work, though, and creates maintenance problems.

That's why Access lets you use *parameters* in your queries. A parameter is simply a variable. When you run the query, it prompts you to provide a value for the variable, and then the query runs based on that value. For instance, instead of hard-coding dates into your sales query, you could provide start date and end date parameters and let users specify the date range when the query runs.

Access makes it easy to specify parameters. Anything that looks like a field name (namely, anything in brackets) that Access can't locate in your tables is treated as a parameter. For example, if you put [CustName] on the Criteria line in the query design grid, when the query runs Access will prompt you for a value, and then use it as query criteria for that field. (When you want a parameter, this is great; if you don't, and you see the parameter dialog box, it's really an error message. See "Enter Parameter Value" in Chapter 1.) A common trick is to name parameters something like [Last name of customer?], which makes the "Enter Parameter Value" prompt a bit more user-friendly (see Figure 4-20).

In certain cases—crosstab or action queries, queries that underlie charts, criteria for Yes/No fields, and fields in external databases—you must declare the data type of the parameter. In query Design View, choose Query→Parameters and fill in the name (e.g., [Last name of customer?]) and data type, such as Text or Integer. Even when

it's not required, it's good practice to specify parameter data types for anything other than text. That way, users who enter invalid data will get a reasonably sensible error message; if you don't, they'll get pure gobbledygook (see Figure 4-21).

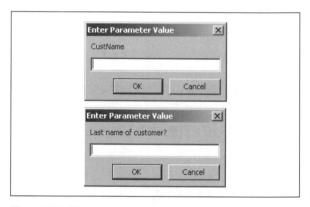

Figure 4-20. When you use a query parameter, Access presents the parameter name as part of the input prompt. For user-friendliness, use a name like "Last name of customer?" rather than "CustName."

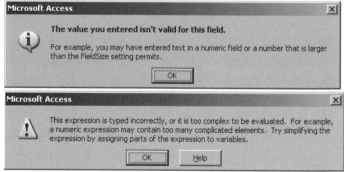

Figure 4-21. Two different error messages when a user enters invalid data for a parameter. If you specified the data type, users will get the pleasant message above. If you didn't, they'll get the forbidding one below.

THE FIX: When the parameter prompt is left blank, its value is null. Since null values require their own tests (see "Tangled Up in Null" in Chapter 7), you'll need to add query criteria so Access can handle this situation. For example, to return all records, put something like **[Enter state abbreviation] Or [Enter state abbreviation] Is Null** on the Criteria line in the query design grid (see Figure 4-22). Because an Or statement is true if either condition is true, if the parameter comes back null, every record will satisfy this criterion. This technique also works with Like statements and Between ... And criteria.

---- **N O T E** ----

If you save and reopen this query, it will split the **[Enter state abbreviation] Or [Enter state abbreviation] Is Null** *statement, placing the* **Is Null** *test in a separate column.*

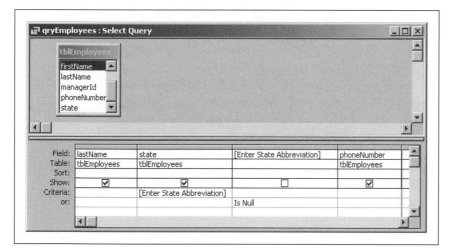

Figure 4-22. To include all records when the parameter is left blank, add the Is Null test as an alternative Criteria row.

User-Friendly Parameter Queries

THE ANNOYANCE: Our sales database has a massive amount of information in it, and I need to give users the ability to select data by specifying multiple parameters, such as date range *and* region of interest, and so on. But Access's built-in query parameters are far too simple to handle this task.

THE FIX: No kidding. Access's built-in parameters are useful if you need, say, data from a single date, but not for much more. If there's more than one parameter, the prompts come one after another, rather than all on one page, and there's no way to add error handling, drop-down lists, or other conveniences to make parameter entry more user-friendly and reliable. Fortunately, you can do all this (and more) with forms—and it's easy to use form data as parameters for queries.

First, create an unbound form (see "Create Dialog Box Input Forms" in Chapter 5) and add the controls that you'll need for user input (see Figure 4-23). Use text boxes for free-form data entry, combo and list boxes to constrain users to predefined values, and any other controls you need. All the usual "good design" practices apply, so use format and validation rules where appropriate to help your users submit valid parameters. Don't forget to add a "Run query" button.

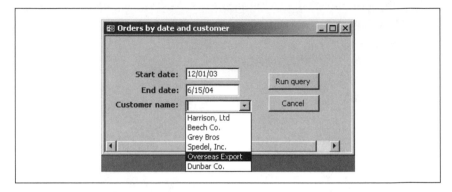

Figure 4-23. A simple unbound form lets you gather user input on which you can base the query criteria. It's far friendlier than "Enter Parameter Value" boxes.

Once the form is complete, you can reference its data in your query by placing fully qualified control names such as **Forms!frmMyParamForm!txtMyParamField** on the Criteria line of your query. ("Fully qualified" simply means using the whole path, not just the short name; in this example, txtMyParamField is the short name.) Here, frmMyParamForm is the name of your unbound form, and txtMyParamField is the name of a field on that form. For example, to use a date range as a query criterion, you'd enter something like **Between Forms!frmMyParamForm!txtStartDate And Forms!frmMyParamForm !txtEndDate** on the Criteria line of your query. When the user hits the "Run query" button, the query will pull those values (namely, the start and end dates she's entered in the form) from the data entry form. If your data entry form uses a combo box rather than a text box, you can use its value, like this: **Forms!frmMyParamForm!cboMyComboBox**. The usual rules about declaring parameter data types apply here. (See the sidebar "Queries That Accept Parameters," earlier in this chapter.)

In order for this to work, the form must be open, with the date range already entered, when the query is run. (If it isn't, Access won't be able to resolve the control names and will resort to the "Enter Parameter Value" prompt. You don't want that.) The simplest way to ensure this is to put the "Run query" button on the form itself. You can use the Command Button Wizard to do this (see "Activating the Wizards" in Chapter 5). Once the wizard starts, choose the Run Query action in the Miscellaneous category on its first page.

Parameter Queries That Accept Lists

THE ANNOYANCE: I want to create a parameter query that computes sales statistics for a set of cities. I built an input form (as described in the previous Annoyance) with a nice list of cities for users to choose from, but there seems to be no way to get the list into my query!

THE FIX: Letting users choose from a parameter list makes sense, but alas, Access doesn't support this very well. There are a couple of workarounds, but neither one is completely satisfactory. The first solution is relatively easy, but it sticks the user with a crude user interface (manually entering a comma-separated list of parameters). The better solution uses a multi-select list box, but this requires writing some VB code. Figure 4-24 shows both alternatives.

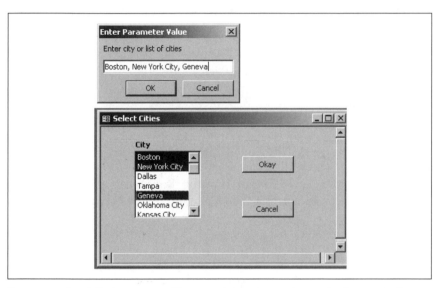

Figure 4-24. Two different ways to enable users to input parameter lists. In the above approach, which is much more error-prone, the user must enter a comma-separated list. The multi-select list box below is far more user-friendly.

If you don't mind asking your users to type in a comma-separated list (as opposed to choosing from a list), you can use the first approach. On the Field line of your query grid, put **[Enter city or list of cities]**, and on its Criteria line, put **Like "*" & [cityField] & "*"** (where cityField is the field that contains the city names). This is the opposite of how you usually use the Like operator—instead of saying **cityField LIKE "Boston"**, we're saying **"Boston, New York, Springfield" Like *cityField***. Adding wildcards to the field value ensures that each city will match when compared to the whole list.

This works fine with some data being queried, but in other situations the wildcards may yield false hits. For instance, a user who searches for Dayton will retrieve both Dayton and Daytona Beach. To prevent this, add a delimiter such as a comma to your expression. For example, type **","** & **[Enter city or list of cities]** & **","** on the Field line, and **Like "*,"** & **[cityField]** & **",*"** on the Criteria line. This forces the query to match the entire field. However, the match will fail if the user enters a space after the comma by accident—a common mistake. Change the criteria to **Like "*[,]"** & **[cityField]** & **"[,]*"**, and it should work. (Remember that brackets inside quotes are not defining a field name, they're defining a character set—in other words, telling Access to match both comma and/or space.)

For most users, a multi-select list box on an unbound input form is a far better choice; there's no fussing with commas and no risk of misspelling a name. Though you're probably more familiar with combo boxes, list box controls are very similar and have a similar wizard. (If you're unsure of how to use an unbound input form, see the previous Annoyance, "User-Friendly Parameter Queries.") To make this fix work, though, you'll need to write a bit of VB code.

By default, list boxes have their Multi Select property—which allows a user to make multiple selections—set to "None." From the Other tab in the list box's properties sheet, change this to "Simple" or "Extended," depending on which style of multiple selection you prefer.

The problem now is that there's no easy way to get the user's selections back into your query from your form; you need a bit of VB code to loop through the selections and construct a criteria string. Run Access's VB Editor, pop in this code, save it, and tie it to the OK button's Click event:

```
Dim varItem As Variant
Dim strInClause As String
If Me!lstCities.ItemsSelected.Count = 0 Then
    MsgBox("Please select at least one city.")
Else
    strInClause = "[city] IN("
    For Each varItem In Me!lstCities.ItemsSelected
        strInClause = strInClause & """" & _
            Me!lstCities.Column(0,varItem) & """" & ", "
    Next varItem
    'Remove the trailing comma and space from the last item
    strInClause=left(strInClause,len(strInClause)-2) & ")"
End If

[PAGE 197]
Private Sub Form_Current()
    If IsLoaded("frmInvoices") Then
        Forms!frmInvoices.Filter = _
                "ClientID = Forms!frmClients!ClientID"
        Forms!frmInvoices.FilterOn = True
    End If
End Sub
```

This code starts with the string fragment "[city] IN(", and then builds up the list of cities for the IN clause by looping through the ItemsSelected collection, which provides a list of the selected rows. In this example we use the Column property to extract column 0 (the first column) for each row, but you can extract any column. Also, note that the Column property's arguments are the reverse of what we usually expect: (col, row) instead of (row, col).

Once you've created this string—which in this case looks something like [city] IN("Boston", "New York City", "Geneva")—you can use it as a filter criterion applied to a form or report. For example, to open a report with this criterion, use DoCmd.OpenReport "rptSalesSummary", acViewPreview, , strInClause. If you need to open a query, as in this Annoyance, construct the entire SQL string and use CreateQueryDef, like this:

```
Dim qdf As QueryDef
Set qdf = CurrentDb.CreateQueryDef("qrySales", _
            "Select * From tblSales Where " & strInClause & ";")
DoCmd.OpenQuery "qrySales"
```

Parameters in Crosstab Queries

THE ANNOYANCE: I have a crosstab query that displays suppliers by product category, and I want to let users filter the output by region. But when I try to add a region parameter to the query, Jet says it can't recognize the field name. I can add parameters to other queries without any problem.

THE FIX: If Access doesn't recognize something in the query design grid, it usually assumes it's a parameter. But with crosstabs, the rules are changed: if you want to use parameters, you must declare them explicitly. Choose Query→Parameters, fill in the same parameter name that you used in your query (e.g., **[Enter region]**), and specify its data type (see Figure 4-25). Note that if your crosstab query is based on any other queries, parameters in *those* queries must also be declared.

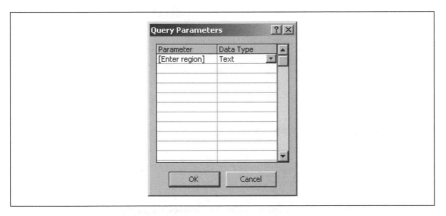

Figure 4-25. The Query Parameters dialog lets you explicitly specify the parameter data type. You must do this for certain types of queries (such as crosstabs and action queries) and certain data types (such as Yes/No fields), but it's good practice to do it for all your parameters.

Sorting Crosstab Rows Based on Totals

THE ANNOYANCE: I have a crosstab query that shows accident data. The rows represent different facilities, and the column headings are teams at each facility. I want to sort the facilities by the total number of accidents (showing the most accidents at the top), but Access gives me an error when I try to do this.

THE FIX: If you've survived the rigors of the Crosstab Query Wizard and have actually produced a working crosstab query... congratulations! Presumably, you then opened it up in Design View and tried to set the Sort line on one of your totals fields to sort the output (ascending or descending). This sounds simple, but when you try it Access spits out an error—and for good reason.

Crosstab Traffic

When working with data, you often want to see how two different variables are related. For instance, you might want to see sales data broken out by customer *and* by quarter, or student enrollment by region *and* by family income. This kind of analysis is called *cross-tabulation*, or *crosstab* for short. One variable spans the columns while the other variable goes down the rows, producing a rich cull of information.

Access has a Crosstab Query Wizard (Insert→Query) that makes it easy to create crosstabs. If all the data you'll need is in a single table, you can apply the wizard to that table; otherwise, you'll need to combine the data from multiple tables into a single query first (see "Query Multiple Tables," earlier in this chapter) and base the crosstab on that. When the wizard asks you to specify row headings, it's asking which field in your table will provide the headings for each row. In Figure 4-26, that's company name. Next, the wizard asks for the field that will supply "column headings" along the top of the query; in this example, that's the order date. Since this column heading is a date field, Access asks if you want to group dates into units such as years, quarters, or months. (As you can see in Figure 4-26, we said yes to quarters.)

Next, the wizard asks what number should appear at each row/column intersection. That's because, in a typical crosstab query, you'll have more than one data item at each intersection. For instance, in our sales crosstab, each customer might have multiple orders in a given quarter. You might want to display the average, maximum, sum, and so forth. We chose sum. On the same page, you can add a summary column (the Total Orders column) that totals the figures for each row (as in Figure 4-26).

Company Name	Total Orders	Qtr 1	Qtr 2	Qtr 3	Qtr 4
Beech Co.	$7,315.00	$2,335.00	$4,400.00	$580.00	
Grey Bros	$568.00	$568.00			
Harrison, Llc.	$4,564.00	$330.00	$3,671.00		$563.00
Johnson	$3,005.00			$3,005.00	
Spedel, Inc.	$1,828.00		$1,003.00	$324.00	$501.00

Record: I◄ ◄ 1 ► ►I ►* of 5

Figure 4-26. A crosstab query allows you to view your data using multiple factors at the same time. In this example, order totals are broken out by company name and by fiscal quarter.

Access doesn't support this feature! (Of course, you can reference an aggregate column alias, such as a Count of Accidents in SQL using the ORDER BY clause, but Access SQL won't do it.) The workaround is to base a new query on your crosstab query, and do the sort there. Here are the steps:

1. Create a new query and add your crosstab query to the query Design View window.

2. Double-click the asterisk (*) to add all its fields, and then double-click the totals field that you want to sort on.

3. Uncheck the Show box, choose the sort order you want, and run the query.

Crosstab Queries with Multiple Values

THE ANNOYANCE: I'm designing a crosstab query to summarize sales data for different offices over the past 12 months. I want to display more than one aggregate statistic at the intersection of each row and column, but I can't figure out how.

THE FIX: PivotTables were invented to solve this very problem. A PivotTable is a dynamic, interactive table—really, a kind of report—that lets you explore different views of complex data. A powerful alternative to static reports, PivotTables allow you to quickly see "what if" without modifying the underlying data. PivotTables aren't updatable, which means you can play with them without worrying about messing up your data. They can't be used for data entry, but they're a very valuable tool for interactive data analysis. PivotTables have been available for years in Excel and were first introduced in Access 2002. If you're using an older version of Access, we discuss some alternatives at the end of this fix.

PivotTables (and PivotCharts) are complex beasts; we won't tackle them here. But to get a feel for their capabilities, try this: open the table (or query) that your crosstab is based on in Datasheet View, and then select View→ PivotTable View. You should see a PivotTable field list. (If not, select View→ Field List.) Now drag the row and column fields and drop them into the places reserved for them (you'll see labels such as "Drop Row Fields Here"), as if you were manually creating your crosstab. (If you're looking at a blank screen, see MSKB 307905 for the bug fix.)

This creates your framework. Populate the framework by dragging other fields into the areas marked for them (see Figure 4-27). To apply an aggregate function, right-click the field name in the column heading and choose "AutoCalc." To show only the aggregate values, right-click the column and choose "Hide Details." You control everything via the PivotTable menu and by right-clicking. The trickiest part of the interface is that there's no way to throw away your work and start over—not even by quitting (because you're defining a view, and Access remembers it)—and sometimes it's not obvious how to return to an earlier view. However, you can always right-click your row and column headers, and select "Remove." This empties your PivotTable so you can start over.

tblOrders : Table				
Drop Filter Fields Here				
	Years ▾ Quarters			
	⊞ 2002	⊞ 2003	⊞ 2004	Grand Total
	+│−	+│−	+│−	+│−
customerId ▾	Total Amount ▾	Total Amount ▾	Total Amount ▾	Total Amount ▾
1	$221.00	$330.00	$350.00	$350.00
	$30.00	$8,330.00	$120.00	$221.00
				$30.00
				$330.00
				$8,330.00
				$120.00
	$251.00	$8,660.00	$470.00	$9,381.00
2	$430.00	$2,000.00	$150.00	$150.00
		$4,400.00		$2,000.00
				$4,400.00
				$430.00
	$430.00	$6,400.00	$150.00	$6,980.00

Figure 4-27. This PivotTable view of the orders table was generated with just a few clicks—dragging customer ID to the "Drop Row Fields Here" area and order date to the "Drop Column Fields Here" area. The grand totals were created by clicking the plus sign under Grand Total and then right-clicking and choosing AutoCalcSum.

If you're using Access 2000 or an earlier version, or you don't want to use a PivotTable, there are a few tricks that let you display multiple values in a crosstab. By design, a crosstab can have only one Value column in the query grid, but you can combine multiple aggregate values in a single column. For example, an expression such as Sales Avg and Sum: Avg(sales) & "/" & Sum(sales) would give you both average and total values, concatenated into a single string: $5,770/$48,908. (The first term is the average; the second term is the sum.) Of course, if you need to use these values in a report, you'll have to write some code to parse them back out. Another workaround is to create a separate crosstab query for each value that you want, and then join those crosstabs into a third query, arranging the fields as you wish. (See MSKB 209143 for details.)

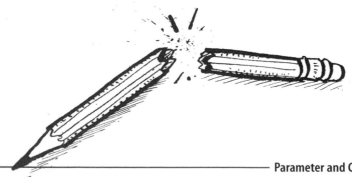

TECHNIQUES FOR DIFFICULT QUERIES

In this section, we'll look at a handful of fairly difficult query problems. These solutions—from self-joins and non-equi-joins to auxiliary tables and subqueries—illustrate techniques used by professional developers. Although advanced, you may find these procedures useful when untying knotty query conundrums.

Comparing Different Rows

THE ANNOYANCE: I need to generate a list of all my projects whose dates overlap with other projects going on in the same city. All this info is in my projects table, but when I try to create a query that compares different rows, it doesn't work. Are Access queries truly limited to looking at one row at a time?

THE FIX: Like every relational database, Access is row-oriented. When you set criteria in a query, those criteria get applied one row at a time—not across different rows. But to compare the date ranges of different projects, you must examine pairs of rows at the same time. It seems impossible in Access, until you know the trick.

Since you can't change Access's one-row-at-a-time mentality, create a virtual table that has the information you need in each row. You'll do this using a join (see "Query Multiple Tables," earlier in this chapter). Since you must look at each project paired with every other project, add the projects table to the query Design View window *twice*. Adding the same table to a query more than once is known as a *self-join*.

Notice that Access adds "_1" to the name of the second copy. This lets Access distinguish which field you're referring to when you add fields to the query design grid, since otherwise, the fields in both tables would have identical names. For example, if you add the project title field from each table, Access will represent them as tblProjects.projectTitle and tblProjects_1.projectTitle. You'd be well advised to give them more meaningful names, such as Project 1: tblProjects.projectTitle and Project 2: tblProjects_1.projectTitle.

With no join lines between the two copies of the table, Access generates a list combining every row with every other row (see Figure 4-28). To include only rows where projects are in the same city, join on the city field. (It's a good idea to join on the state field, too, to avoid mix-ups with identically named cities in different states.)

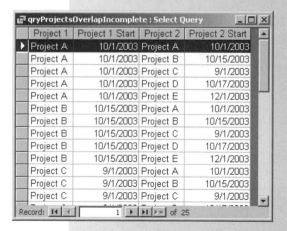

Figure 4-28. When you add two copies of the same table to a query, you start out with all possible pairs of rows in the two tables, including each row paired with itself. Use join lines and criteria to restrict which rows remain in the query.

Now add the fields that you want in the results (project title, city, state, and so on), and you get Figure 4-29.

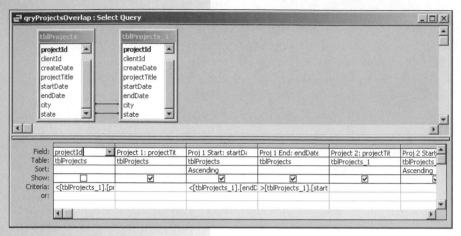

Figure 4-29. The final query, which detects date range overlaps, is not complicated—but getting the details right is tricky.

The hardest part of this query is picking the criteria that will detect a date range overlap. (See "Dates! Dates! Dates!" in Chapter 7 for full details.) You can start by adding tblProjects.startDate to the grid, and in its Criteria line adding **< tblProjects_1.endDate**. Then add tblProjects.endDate, and in its Criteria line put **> tblProjects_1.startDate**. In other words, Project A overlaps with Project B if A's start date comes before B's end date *and* A's end date comes after B's start date.

This works great, except that every pair of overlapping projects appears in the results twice. That's because the criteria are symmetrical: if Project A overlaps Project B, then Project B overlaps Project A, so the results include both row orderings. And since every project overlaps itself, these show up as well. To exclude these redundant rows, add tblProjects.projectId to the query design grid, and set its Criteria line to **< [tblProjects_1].[projectId]**. This may seem like an odd addition, since whether a project's ID is less than any other project's ID is totally arbitrary. However, this trick excludes self-matches, and it (arbitrarily) eliminates one of the redundant entries in each pair.

Working with Hierarchies

THE ANNOYANCE: We have a managerId field in our employees table that points to the manager for each employee. But data on managers is also stored in the employees table. How can I generate a list of employees with the appropriate manager's name next to each employee?

THE FIX: When a foreign key (see "Relationship Angst" in Chapter 3) refers back to its own table, it creates a type of relationship that is useful for representing trees and hierarchies. The classic example is managers and employees, where managers are employees whose IDs show up in other employees' managerId fields. This type of recursive relationship can nest within itself an arbitrary number of times (managers who have managers who have managers, and so on).

In the days before the advent of relational databases, hierarchical database systems ruled the roost, and they made it easy to work with these kinds of data. But relational databases are not optimized to work with trees or hierarchies, and there's a limit to what you can do without creating some kind of procedural code (whether stored procedures or application code) that reconstructs the hierarchy from the raw data. In this fix, we'll stick to the basics.

To show a list of employees and their supervisors, use a self-join (see the previous Annoyance, "Comparing Different Rows"). Add two copies of the employees table to the query Design View window, and drag the managerId field from the first copy onto the employeeId field from the second (see Figure 4-30). The first copy of the table will contribute employee names, while the second will add their managers. If you want to include employees who don't have managers, turn this join into an outer join by right-clicking the join line, choosing "Join Properties," and then choosing option 2 ("Include ALL records from 'tblEmployees' etc.").

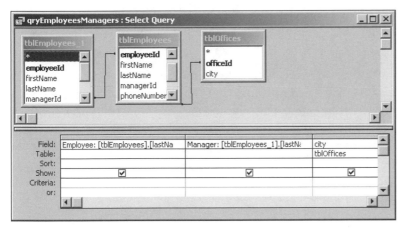

Figure 4-30. This query uses a self-join on the employees table on employeeId, as well as a simple join on the offices table on officeId. The employee names come from tblEmployees, and the manager names come from tblEmployees_1.

Self-joins are not limited to only two copies. If you need to show the managers of the managers, you can do it by repeating this process and adding a third copy of the table to the query Design View, and so on for more levels. Note, however, that if you don't know in advance how deep your org chart is, there's no good way to finish the problem—that is, to show the complete hierarchy—using this approach. For a general solution, you must add procedural code.

Still, there are a few other questions that are readily solved with this design. To find the big boss(es), look for employees with nulls in the managerId field. To find the employees who don't manage anyone, use a subquery (see "Divide and Conquer with Subqueries," later in this chapter):

```
SELECT *
FROM tblEmployees As e1
WHERE NOT EXISTS
    (SELECT *
    FROM tblEmployees As e2
    WHERE e1.employeeId = e2.managerId)
```

Working with Ranges

THE ANNOYANCE: I need a report that summarizes our purchase orders, broken into groups based on the size of the order. What I can't figure out is how to create groups based on ranges such as $0 to $100, $101 to $500, and so on.

THE FIX: When you want to create groups, you need a *grouping field*—in other words, a field whose value will be the same for every row in the group. There are two different ways to do this: using an expression or an auxiliary table. An expression offers more flexibility, but the auxiliary table performs faster.

To use an expression, you need a function that maps each range into a constant value. You'll add this function to the Field line of the query design grid, and then group on it. The built-in Partition function, which slices a range into fixed categories, is intended for just this purpose, but unfortunately it's not flexible enough to be very useful. For simple cases, the Switch function is usually a better choice. For example:

```
AmountRange: Switch([orderTotal] Between 0 And 100, "$0 to $100",
[orderTotal] Between 101 And 500, "$101 to $500", [orderTotal] Between
501 And 5000, "$501 to $5000")
```

The Switch function evaluates every range expression (Between...And) and returns the label associated with the one that is found to be true. For example, all order totals less than $101 will be mapped to the AmountRange "$0 to $100" (the Between...And operator includes both ends of the range). Now you can group on the AmountRange expression. Pay attention to the points where your ranges meet. They shouldn't overlap, but you don't want values falling between the cracks, either. Sometimes it's easier to specify conditions explicitly, like this: [orderTotal] >= 100 AND [orderTotal] < 500.

For more complex conditions (say, orders that are less than $101 *and* come from the West Coast), the Switch function is unwieldy. Instead, define your own Visual Basic function, save it in a module, and call it from your query with whatever input you need, like this: AmountRange: createOrderPartition([orderTotal], [postalCode]). This function should accept any order total and postal code and return a range label that allows the query to put it into a group.

A different approach to creating ranges is to add an auxiliary table to your query. A typical range table has three fields: minValue, maxValue, and rangeLabel (see Figure 4-31).

tblOrderRanges : Table

minValue	maxValue	rangeLabel
0	100	$0 to $100
101	500	$101 to $500
501	5000	$501 to $5000
0	0	

Record: 1 of 3

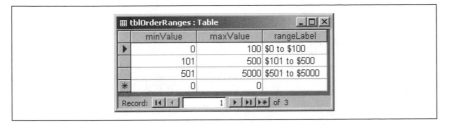

Figure 4-31. A simple range table defines ranges and provides a text label for each range.

Add this table to the query Design View window, but don't create a join. Add the rangeLabel field to the query, and in its Criteria line put something like **`[orderTotal]>=[minValue] And [orderTotal]<[maxValue]`**. Group on the rangeLabel field. Figure 4-32 shows the result *before* you group on rangeLabel, and Figure 4-33 shows the result *after* grouping.

qryOrdersByRange : Select Query

Range	Order ID	Total Amount
$0 to $100	1	$5.00
$0 to $100	2	$13.00
$0 to $100	3	$4.00
$0 to $100	16	$30.00
$101 to $500	5	$150.00
$101 to $500	6	$350.00
$101 to $500	14	$430.00
$101 to $500	15	$221.00
$101 to $500	17	$330.00
$101 to $500	19	$120.00
$501 to $5000	9	$2,000.00
$501 to $5000	10	$4,400.00

Record: 1 of 13

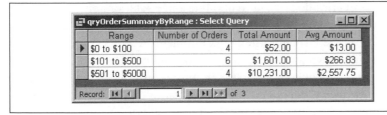

Figure 4-32. Regardless of whether you use an expression or a range table, the effect is to add a range field to your query that is the same for every row that falls in the range. This gives you a field that you can group on to create a summary query.

qryOrderSummaryByRange : Select Query

Range	Number of Orders	Total Amount	Avg Amount
$0 to $100	4	$52.00	$13.00
$101 to $500	6	$1,601.00	$266.83
$501 to $5000	4	$10,231.00	$2,557.75

Record: 1 of 3

Figure 4-33. Once you have established a grouping field, you can create a totals query that provides summary statistics based on that grouping.

If you are writing SQL code, note that the standard way to express this query is using a join expression, like this:

```
tblOrders As t INNER JOIN tblOrderRanges As tor
ON t.orderTotal >= tor.minValue AND t.orderTotal < tor.maxValue
```

Full Outer Joins

THE ANNOYANCE: I'm joining two tables: publishers and articles. Some publishers have no associated articles, and some articles have no publishers, but I need them all to appear in my results. Why doesn't Access support a full outer join?

THE FIX: Access doesn't fully support the SQL-92 standard—not in SQL View, and not even when you've enabled SQL-92 syntax. It would be handy if it did, since full outer joins preserve both sides (left and right) of the join, whether there's a matching row on the other side or not. The most straightforward workaround is to create a UNION query, combining left and right joins. This can be done only in SQL View, and the result isn't updatable. The code (which you'd run from your query's SQL View) would look something like this:

```
SELECT * FROM tblPublishers LEFT JOIN tblArticles
ON tblPublishers.publisherId = tblArticles.publisherId
UNION
SELECT * FROM tblPublishers RIGHT JOIN tblArticles
ON tblPublishers.publisherId = tblArticles.publisherId
```

You might think this would produce a lot of duplicate rows, but UNION automatically removes them. To retain every row, use UNION ALL.

Divide and Conquer with Subqueries

THE ANNOYANCE: I'm trying to find the names of all staffers who live in the same town as any one of our vendors. We have a staff table and a vendors table, but I can't figure out how to join them to get this result.

THE FIX: Many queries don't yield to an all-at-once solution, but if you break the problem into parts you can then piece together for the desired result. For example, if you were solving the above problem by hand, you'd probably start by writing down a list of all the vendors' towns. Do the equivalent in Access by creating a query that finds the unique cities in the vendors table. Now add that query, along with the staff table, to a new query, and create a simple join on the cities field. Set the query's Unique Values property to "Yes," and you're done.

This divide-and-conquer approach is best implemented using a *subquery*—a query embedded in another query. In Access, subqueries can only be created using SQL. For the example above, we could simply have said:

```
SELECT DISTINCT fullName, city
FROM tblStaff
WHERE city IN
    (SELECT DISTINCT city
     FROM tblVendors);
```

The `(SELECT DISTINCT city FROM tblVendors)` part is the subquery. The subquery says, "Give me a list of the cities that are in the vendors table," and the main query says, "Give me just the staffers whose cities are on that list." Subqueries are often used with the `IN`, `EXISTS`, `ANY`, and `ALL` operators, in addition to the simple comparison operators. Here are a few examples:

IN/EXISTS/NOT EXISTS

To list any customers who have not placed an order within the past three months, first create an SQL query that finds all orders placed within the past three months:

```
SELECT orderId
FROM tblOrders
WHERE orderDate > DateAdd("m", -3, Date()));
```

The `DateAdd` function is used here to subtract three months from today's date.

Now embed your SQL query in the main query, like this:

```
SELECT customer
FROM tblCustomers
WHERE NOT EXISTS
        (SELECT orderId
         FROM tblOrders
         WHERE tblCustomers.customerId = tblOrders.customerId
         AND orderDate > DateAdd("m", -3, Datc()));
```

Notice that we added a match on customerId to the `WHERE` clause of the subquery. By referencing a field within the subquery, we force the subquery to be reexecuted for each row of the main query. Why do that? This query could have been written using only an `IN` clause. However, if the orders table is large, executing the `IN` over and over will take forever. This correlated subquery should be faster, especially since customerId—as a primary key—is an indexed field.

ANY/ALL

To list customers whose single orders exceed $1000, use a query such as this:

```
SELECT customer
FROM tblCustomers
WHERE 1000 < ALL
        (SELECT orderTotal
         FROM tblOrders
         WHERE tblCustomers.customerId = tblOrders.customerId);
```

Adding ALL to the comparison means that it must be true for every row in the subquery. ANY means that it must be true for at least one row in the subquery. Substitute ANY for ALL in the example, and you'll list the customers with at least one order above $1,000.

Simple comparisons

To find vendors whose average shipping cost is greater than five percent of their deposit, use a query such as this:

```
SELECT vendor
FROM tblVendors
WHERE (.05 * deposit) <
        SELECT AVG(shipCost)
        FROM tblOrders
        WHERE tblVendors.vendorId = tblOrders.vendorId);
```

Here we use the subquery to calculate average shipping costs for each vendor, and then embed those results in a select query that compares those averages with the calculated value (5% of deposit).

Finding Rows That Don't Exist

THE ANNOYANCE: Our satellite offices submit monthly transaction reports that get recorded in a transaction reports table (tblTransactionReports). I'm trying to generate a list of offices with missing reports, but it doesn't seem possible.

THE FIX: In a relational database, it's easy to test for *fields* with missing data, but it's impossible to directly test for missing *rows*. Since they're not there, there's nothing to select on. If you manually added a row to the reports table every month for every office, and simply left the date submitted field blank if the report was never submitted, it would be easy; you could just test for null values in that field. But that's a lot of extra work, and there's a better way: let Access generate your list of expected reports. This is both easier and less error-prone, and once you have that list, it's a simple matter to write a query that combines it with your actual table to see what's missing. Here are the steps.

1. **Generate expected rows.** To find rows that aren't there, you need to generate a list of the rows that you expect to find. In this case, you must create a query that has a row for every office and every month. It's easy to produce a row for every office, since you undoubtedly already have an offices table. It's less obvious how to produce a row for every month, but the solution is simple: use a table of months.

   This can be just a simple table with a month field and a year field, and a row for every month in every year you want. Create a query (qryOffices-ByMonth), and drag your offices table and the new months table to the query Design View window. Don't join them. The result is a Cartesian product—a row for every office and every month, which is what you need (see Figure 4-34).

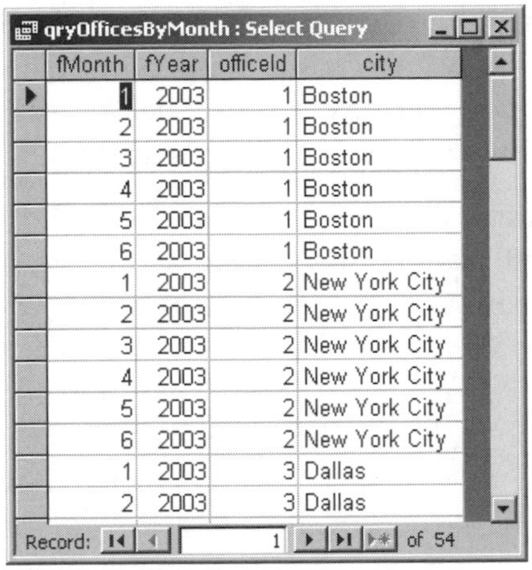

qryOfficesByMonth : Select Query

fMonth	fYear	officeId	city
1	2003	1	Boston
2	2003	1	Boston
3	2003	1	Boston
4	2003	1	Boston
5	2003	1	Boston
6	2003	1	Boston
1	2003	2	New York City
2	2003	2	New York City
3	2003	2	New York City
4	2003	2	New York City
5	2003	2	New York City
6	2003	2	New York City
1	2003	3	Dallas
2	2003	3	Dallas

Record: 1 of 54

Figure 4-34. This simple office/months query contains a row for every office and every month in the range we're interested in, making it easy to detect the missing rows that will result if an office fails to file a report.

2. **Match to missing rows.** For every row in the office/months query, see if there's a matching row in the transaction reports table (tblTransactionReports), using a subquery, like so:

```
SELECT office, month, year
FROM qryOfficesByMonth As t1
WHERE NOT EXISTS
        (SELECT *
        FROM tblTransactionReports As t2
        WHERE t1.office = t2.office
        AND t1.month = Month(t2.submitDate)
        AND t1.year = Year(t2.submitDate))
```

This subquery says, "Give me rows from the transactions table that match a row in the office/months query." Then the main query says, "Give me the offices, months, and years where that subquery is empty." It may seem strange to refer to the table (actually, here, a query, qryOfficesByMonth) in the main query from within the subquery, but it's not uncommon—this is known as a *correlated subquery*, and it allows you to essentially loop through the office/month rows and find the ones without a match. Is there a Design View solution that non-SQLers can use? Yes. The key is to create a view of the transaction reports table that can be directly joined to the office/months query. (You'll still need to create qryOfficesByMonth, as above, first.)

3. **Create a transaction reports query.** You need to join the transaction reports on all the fields of qryOfficesByMonth. You may run into one snag here: your reports table probably has a single submitDate field, but your qryOfficesByMonth query has separate month and year fields—you can't join them directly. Fortunately, this is easy to solve. Create a new query (qryTransactionReports) based on the transaction reports table, and give it three fields: officeId; submitMonth: Month(submitDate); and submitYear: Year(submitDate).

4. **Create outer joins.** Create a new query and add both qryOfficesByMonth and qryTransactionReports to it. Join on all three fields, and make each join an outer join, preserving all the rows from the qryOfficesByMonth side. Add the fields that you want from qryOfficesByMonth, and sort them appropriately. Then, add all the fields from qryTransactionReports, but uncheck the Show boxes and type **Is Null** in the Criteria line for each field. This says that you want only the *missing* rows from qryTransactionReports.

Working with Calendar Dates

THE ANNOYANCE: I need to generate monthly patient counts, based on the fiscal calendar that the hospital uses. In addition, I'm supposed to create a separate report to count how many patients show up on holidays. All I have to work with are the raw dates from the patient visits table, and I'm at a complete loss.

THE FIX: Calendars are beasts; only idiot savants really understand them. Don't tackle problems like this with complicated date expressions—let the database do the work for you. The trick is to create an auxiliary table that has the calendar information you need (see Figure 4-35). Set up this calendar table once, and you'll never have to worry about it again. (If for some reason—say, you're extremely short on storage space—you do need to use an approach based on date expressions, see MSKB 132101.)

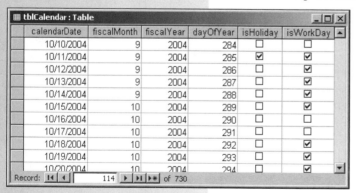

calendarDate	fiscalMonth	fiscalYear	dayOfYear	isHoliday	isWorkDay
10/10/2004	9	2004	284	☐	☐
10/11/2004	9	2004	285	☑	☑
10/12/2004	9	2004	286	☐	☑
10/13/2004	9	2004	287	☐	☑
10/14/2004	9	2004	288	☐	☑
10/15/2004	10	2004	289	☐	☑
10/16/2004	10	2004	290	☐	☐
10/17/2004	10	2004	291	☐	☐
10/18/2004	10	2004	292	☐	☑
10/19/2004	10	2004	293	☐	☑
10/20/2004	10	2004	294	☐	☑

Record: 114 of 730

Figure 4-35. A typical calendar table. By simply storing the calendar information in a readily usable format, you avoid the agony of computing date relationships using expressions within queries.

If you need only a small date range, you can set up the calendar table by hand, but if you want years' worth of rows, create it via VB code.

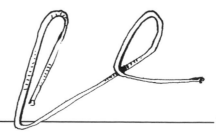

You'll need to create the calendar table (tblCalendar) first, with all its necessary fields. Then copy this code into any module, and customize it for your needs. The following code (createCalendar) supplies the fiscal month and year, as well as a Yes/No field indicating workdays:

```
Public Sub createCalendar(dateStart As Date, dateEnd As Date, _
    intFirstFYMonth As Integer, intFirstFYDayOfMonth As Integer )
    Dim rst As ADODB.Recordset
    Set rst = New ADODB.Recordset
    rst.Open "tblCalendar", CurrentProject.Connection, adOpenKeyset, _
    adLockOptimistic, adCmdTableDirect

    Dim lngNumDays As Long
    lngNumDays = DateDiff("d", dateStart, dateEnd)

    Dim dateNext As Date
    Dim lngCnt As Long
    Dim intMonthNext As Integer
    Dim intDayOfMonthNext As Integer
    Dim intYearNext As Integer
    Dim intFiscalYear As Integer
    Dim intFiscalMonth As Integer
    Dim DateCurrentFYStart As Date
    Dim boolWorkDay


    For lngCnt = 0 To lngNumDays
            dateNext = DateAdd("d", lngCnt, dateStart)
            intMonthNext = Month(dateNext)
            intDayOfMonthNext = Day(dateNext)
            intYearNext = Year(dateNext)
            DateCurrentFYStart = DateSerial(intYearNext, _
                    intFirstFYMonth, intFirstFYDayOfMonth)

            'COMPUTE FISCAL YEAR
            If dateNext < DateCurrentFYStart Then
                    intFiscalYear = intYearNext - 1
            Else
                    intFiscalYear = intYearNext
            End If

            'COMPUTE FISCAL MONTH
            If intDayOfMonthNext < intFirstFYDayOfMonth Then
                    intFiscalMonth = intMonthNext - 1
                    If intFiscalMonth = 0 Then
                            intFiscalMonth = 12
                    End If
            Else
                    intFiscalMonth = intMonthNext
            End If

            'COMPUTE WORKDAY
            If DatePart("w", dateNext, vbMonday) > 5 Then
                    boolWorkDay = False
            Else
                    boolWorkDay = True
            End If
```

```
'WRITE TABLE
With rst
        .AddNew
        .Fields("calendarDate") = dateNext
        .Fields("dayOfYear") = DatePart("y", dateNext)
        .Fields("fiscalMonth") = intFiscalMonth
        .Fields("fiscalYear") = intFiscalYear
        .Fields("isWorkDay") = boolWorkDay
        .Update
    End With
    Next lngCnt
End Sub
```

To populate your calendar table with data, run the createCalendar code from the Immediate window of the VB Editor. For instance, to populate your table from June 2004 to June 2010, with a fiscal year that starts on September 15, call it like this:

```
createCalendar #2004-06-01#, #2010-06-01#, 9, 15
```

Note that this routine doesn't populate the isHoliday field. Since holidays are so irregular, you'll have to add that information by hand. Also note that it does populate a day of year field (for example, October 10 is the 284th day of the year), even though this is easily computed on the fly using DatePart—summoning this information from a table is faster than recomputing it every time you need it.

To use a calendar table, you'll typically join to it on its date field. For instance, you'd add it to your query of patient counts by joining the calendarDate field in tblCalendar to the visitDate field in the tblVisits table (see Figure 4-36). Now add tblCalendar's fiscal month field to the query design grid, and set its Total line to "Group By." Instead of grouping by calendar month, you're now grouping by fiscal month—it's as easy as that. To exclude holidays, add the isHoliday field and set its Criteria line to "False."

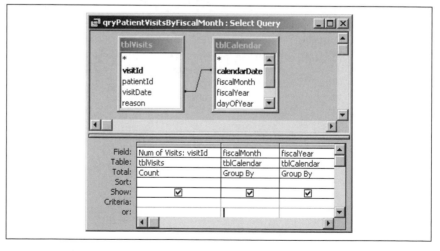

Figure 4-36. You can easily create a query that groups on fiscal month and year by joining the visits table's visitDate field to the calendar table's calendarDate field.

Missing SQL

THE ANNOYANCE: My old MySQL database let me use a CASE expression to create meaningful output in queries. For instance, in a query of student test scores, I could set it up so that scores greater than 90 showed up as As, and so on. But Access doesn't support CASE.

THE FIX: Like most database systems, Access supports only a subset of ANSI SQL-92—and CASE is one of the glaring omissions. Let's take a look at how you can (sometimes) jury-rig Access to more or less deliver the same functionality as CASE and some other missing SQL expressions:

CASE *expressions*

In situations where you need to return a simple value (an "A," a "B," and so on), you can easily replace CASE expressions using VBA's IIf or Switch functions. For example, Switch(score > 90, "A", score > 80 And score <= 90, "B", score <= 80, "Pass") tests the value of score and returns "A" if it's above 90, "B" if it's between 80 and 90, and so forth. CASE can do a bit more than this, but for most needs, this workaround suffices.

Full outer joins

Jet SQL does not support full outer joins. See "Full Outer Joins," earlier in this chapter, for a workaround

Row-valued constructs

SQL-92 supports row-valued expressions such as WHERE (office, location) = (SELECT office, location FROM tblOffices. Such expressions let you make comparisons between sets of fields, rather than comparing one field at a time. This functionality is not available in Access, but you can always translate it into a field-by-field comparison.

Check constraints

Adding check constraints to a table definition is a powerful data-validation technique. Check constraints operate like validation rules, but they are more flexible. For instance, they let you refer to data outside the current table. Access supports check constraints, but only if they are created in code (see MSKB 201888); in other words, you can't create a check constraint in the SQL window. And unlike with validation rules, there's no way to specify validation text—a user who violates the constraint will receive an ugly error message. If you do use check constraints, remember that the constraint must be dropped (i.e., removed in code) before the table can be deleted. Because of these hassles with check constraints, validation rules (or validation in code) generally provide a better solution.

Forms

5

In many offices, forms for data entry and data viewing are where users spend most of their time. Well-designed forms make work easier and help ensure the quality and integrity of data.

Access makes it easy to crank out *basic* forms, but adding the tweaks and touches that make your forms truly user-friendly can be maddening. In this chapter, we'll start off with some usability tricks for you, the designer (in form Design View), and show you how to take full advantage of various form designs, including multi-table forms, subforms, and pop-up forms. The largest section in the chapter is devoted to usability tweaks your users will love, such as forms that enter data automatically and combo boxes that work the way they should.

WORKING IN DESIGN VIEW

Activating the Wizards

THE ANNOYANCE: Call me stupid, but I've been using Access for weeks and I haven't seen a Combo Box Wizard yet.

THE FIX: The wizards for combo boxes and other controls, such as list boxes and option groups, are easy to miss if you don't know where to look. At the top right in the Toolbox in Design View (see Figure 5-1), there's a Control Wizards button that activates the wizards. It looks like a magic wand with stars. (If you don't see the Toolbox, select Tools→Customize, click the Toolbars tab, and check the Toolbox box.) Click the button, and when you add a control to a form the appropriate wizard fires up. To deactivate the wizards, just press the button again.

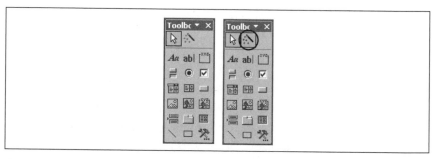

Figure 5-1. The Toolbox and the Control Wizards button. In the box on the left, the button is not selected; on the right, it is.

Edit Many Controls at Once

THE ANNOYANCE: My form has 50 controls—25 text boxes and 25 labels. I'm trying to standardize our look and feel, and all of these need a slight size adjustment. Doing this one item at a time is tedious—there's got to be a faster way!

THE FIX: Fortunately, Access lets you edit controls en masse. With the form displayed in Design View, select all the controls by using Edit→Select All. (To select specific controls, Shift-click, or click and hold and wrap a selection box around the controls you want to grab.) To adjust the size of the items, use Shift-Arrow keys. To change the position of the selected controls, use the arrow keys; use Ctrl-Arrow keys for finer movement. (In Access 2000, the arrow keys alone don't work, but Ctrl- and Shift-Arrow do.) If you want to align controls, or make them all the same size, select the controls, then use Format→Align or Format→Size and choose a predefined adjustment from the menu.

Editing multiple controls at once isn't limited to size and position adjustments, though. Open the form's properties sheet while multiple controls are selected, and you'll see that many properties can be applied en masse (see Figure 5-2). For instance, you can change the Font Size or Locked properties of all the selected controls at once—it's an easy and an indispensable option.

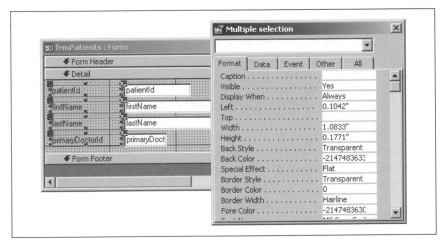

Figure 5-2 All the labels on this patients form have been selected at once. The Multiple selection properties sheet lets you change properties for all of them at once.

Leaving the Properties Sheet Open

THE ANNOYANCE: When I'm in form Design View, I find myself constantly going back and forth between controls and their properties. If I have to open and close one more properties sheet, I'm going to go cra-a-azy!

THE FIX: The properties sheet looks like a dialog box, so you naturally think that it must be opened and closed for each form or control. But it ain't necessarily so. Properties sheets are more like detachable toolbars that float above everything (see Figure 5-3). It'd be nice if they had a roll-up feature, a là Photoshop, because they take up a lot of screen real estate—but in any case, you can leave them open. In fact, if you open a properties sheet for any control and then click a different control, the contents of the sheet magically change. This is very handy if you're fiddling with different controls in a session. (You can also change the selected control on the properties sheet by clicking the Control Source drop-down menu at the top of the Data tab. Click in the background *outside* the form area to return to the form itself.) You can even leave the properties sheet open when you close your form, and it'll be there the next time you open it in Design View.

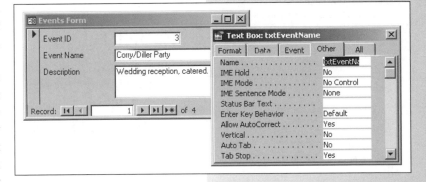

Figure 5-3. You can leave the properties sheet open when you switch between Design View and Form View. Sometimes this is a convenient way to modify properties and see the results immediately, though you must be in Design View to modify most properties.

There are two gotchas that we should mention. First, if you leave properties sheets open on different forms, they *stay* open, even when you switch to Form View—and you probably don't want that. You can change this behavior by setting the form's Allow Design Changes property (on the Other tab) to "Design View Only." Second, properties sheets can misbehave and intercept Alt-Tabs; if you leave them open, when you try to return to Access from the VB Editor, or from another application, all you may get is a properties sheet. You'll have to close the sheet to return to Access.

Where Are the Form's Properties?

THE ANNOYANCE: In Access 2002, I can easily get to any control's properties sheet by clicking the control and then pressing F4. Even better, if a properties sheet is already open, all I have to do is click a control to see its settings. Why can't I summon a form's properties sheet just as easily? When I click the form's background, it doesn't select the form; it selects a section.

THE FIX: It's just bad design that you can't select the form by clicking its background. But it's easy enough to select the form once you know how. In Design View, open the properties sheet of any control in the form, open the drop-down menu at the top of the properties sheet, and select "Form." Quicker still, click in the gray background *outside* the form and hit F4. If the ruler is visible (View→Ruler), you can also right-click the form selector button in the upper-left corner and select "Properties" (see Figure 5-4). All totally non-obvious, unintuitive solutions to a very common task.

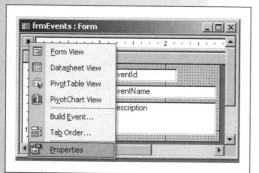

Figure 5-4. The form selector button is in the upper-left corner of the ruler. Right-click and select "Properties" to open up the form's properties sheet.

Attached Labels

THE ANNOYANCE: My order entry form looks pretty nice, but I want to create more space between the text boxes and their labels. When I move the text boxes over, the labels tag along!

THE FIX: Those attached labels have baffled many a user. But the fix is easy, and it applies to any controls, including combo and list boxes, that have attached labels.

To adjust the distance between an attached label and its text box, click each item and locate the larger black box that appears in the upper-left corner of the surrounding frame (see Figure 5-5). When you mouse over one of these boxes, the cursor turns into a finger pointer. Grab the appropriate box to move the label or the text box wherever you want. Go wild.

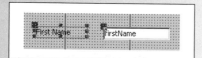

Figure 5-5. "Move handles" in the upper-left corner of a text box and its attached label let you move these controls independently.

To *detach* a label, click the label and press Ctrl-X, which cuts the label; then press Ctrl-V to paste it back in. When you do this, the label is detached from its text box. Now you can move the text box anywhere you like. (You can do this en masse by selecting multiple labels first.) To *reattach* a label to a text box, cut the label, select the text box, and then paste. The downsides, of course, are that this works on only one label at a time, and when you reattach it the label goes back to its default position vis-à-vis the text box.

Incidentally, you can specify various label defaults in the default properties sheet for text boxes. (Click the Text Box tool in the Toolbox, and then click View→Properties→Format tab.) For instance, if you don't want attached labels at all, set Auto Label to "No." Eliminate the colons in labels by setting Add Colon to "No." To specify the label position, use the Label X and Label Y properties; Label X is the distance the label starts from the left edge of the box, and Label Y is the distance between the label's lower edge and the lower edge of the text box. For example, to have your labels just above and left-aligned with your text boxes, set Label X to **0"** and Label Y to **-0.2"**.

Fix Combo and List Box Names

THE ANNOYANCE: Our orders form has a combo box that allows you to look up orders by customer. I changed the control name, and now the combo box doesn't work.

THE FIX: By default, Access gives controls meaningless names, like "Combo17" or "List3." It's good design practice (see "Bad Field Names" in Chapter 3) to change them to something meaningful, like "cboFindCustomer." This is easy to do—just use the Name property, which is on the Other tab of the control's properties sheet. The problem arises when there's code that uses the old control name—often, code written by a wizard. It's just dumb that the wizard doesn't let you name the control before it writes the code (see Figure 5-6).

For example, if you use the wizard to create a combo box that finds records on your form, the wizard will add code to the combo box's After Update event. That code will refer to the original name of the combo box and won't work properly with the new name. The fix? Open the combo box's properties sheet, and click the Event tab.

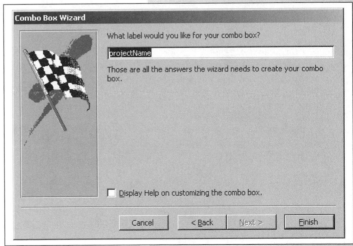

Figure 5-6. The Combo Box Wizard lets you specify the label for the combo box (i.e., the text that will appear next to the control), but it doesn't let you specify the name of the combo box (the internal name of the object, used when you need to refer to it in code)—and that's a major pain.

You'll see that the After Update event has a procedure in it. Click in the After Update field, then click the Build (...) button to the right to jump to the code window. (If you get a Choose Builder box, select the Code Builder option.) In the Visual Basic Editor, you'll now see two After Update procedures, one for the original combo box name, and one for the new name. Copy and paste the code from the old procedure into the new one, then delete the old one. You'll see that the old name appears in one line of this code; change it to the new name.

Subform Is Blank in Design View

THE ANNOYANCE: My registration form has a payments subform. Normally, I can see and edit the subform's controls in Design View—but sometimes all I see is a big white box. What's going on?

THE FIX: Let's just say Access has a bit of a problem handling subforms in Design View—but it's nothing too serious. To get to the root of this problem, open your subform in Design View, and then open your main form in Design View. You'll see the white box (Figure 5-7), because Access won't let you have the subform open in two different Design Views. Fair enough. But why does this happen when the subform is *not* open in its own window? We don't know, but our best guess is that Access is confused; it's been known to complain that a subform is open even when it isn't. To get rid of the white box, try toggling into Form View and back again. If that fails, close your form and reopen it directly into Design View.

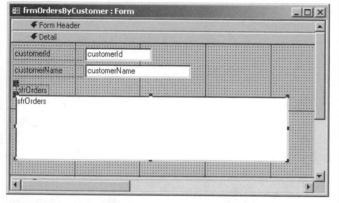

Figure 5-7. The subform goes blank in Design View when Access thinks it's already open in a separate window. Refresh the view by toggling in and out of Form View, or close and reopen your form.

Form Opens Slowly in Design View

THE ANNOYANCE: I built a fairly complex form to handle student registration payments. The form works fine, but it takes a lonnnng time to open in Design View. Is it loading records even in Design View?

THE FIX: Forms don't load records in Design View, so that's not the problem. First, make sure that Name AutoCorrect is turned off—it's the usual culprit. Select Tools→Options, click the General tab, and uncheck the "Track name AutoCorrect info" box. (See "Access's Bad Defaults" in Chapter 1 for more info.) Also, if you're running Access 2000, there's a known bug that slows down forms. Seek out MSKB 269698.

If your form is *still* opening slowly, the problem becomes a bit murkier. Do you have enough RAM? Has your hard disk been defragged? Are other memory-intensive applications running? If everything's up to snuff, consider the VB factor. If the form has VB code, make sure that it's compiled (Debug→Compile in the VB Editor). While you're at it, run Tools→Database Utilities→Compact and Repair Database.

If this is the only form that's opening slowly, has it become so big and complex that you're approaching the limit of 754 controls that can be added to a form? If so, you should break the form into multiple forms that are activated via button presses. On the other hand, if *all* your forms and reports are opening slowly, there could be a problem with your Access or Office installation (see "Agonies of a Sick Installation" in Chapter 1).

FORM DESIGN

Building the Right Form

THE ANNOYANCE: We have a persons table and a households table in our mailing list database. Mailing addresses are stored in the households table, because several persons can share the same mailing address. The problem is that all the rest of our data entry is person-centric. I'm trying to build a persons form that has households as a subform, but I get "related record" errors.

THE FIX: The key is understanding how table relationships dictate form design. If you design your forms properly, Access will manage foreign keys for you. You'll never have to worry about having a persons record with an incorrect or missing household ID. This is a big plus. (For more information about relationships, see "Relationship Angst" in Chapter 3.)

In your case, you want a persons form with a households subform, because that's how your users conceptualize the data—a mailing address belongs to a person, rather than vice versa. But when you put a subform on the "one" side (households) of a one-to-many relationship, Access doesn't know how to handle the foreign key. When you try to create a new person record, it expects that a corresponding household record already exists. (See below for more on this design.) In what follows, we take a look at common form designs, based on the table relationships that underlie them. To solve your particular problem, see the many-to-one discussion below.

Unrelated Table

If your table has no foreign keys in it, creating its form is simple. Use the Form Wizard (Insert→Form) if you're not sure how to start.

One-to-Many

Access makes it easy to base a form on the one side of a relationship and put the many side into a subform (typically with the subform in Datasheet View, as in Figure 5-8—see the sidebar "Creating Subforms" for details). To make this work, ensure that the Link Child Fields and Link Master Fields properties of the subform control are set to the foreign key and the primary key, respectively. You can link on multiple fields; just put a semicolon between the fields in the property setting. If your main table has other one-to-many relationships, these can go in separate subforms on the same form.

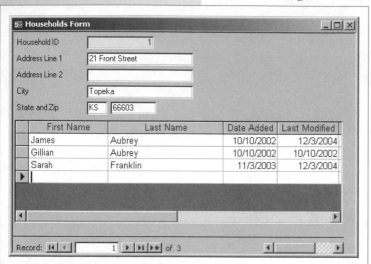

Figure 5-8. A typical one-to-many form, with the many side in a subform in Datasheet View.

One-to-Many-to-Many

Another common design adds a third table to a subform on the many side of a one-to-many relationship. You can nest this third table as a subform inside your subform, but it's better interface practice to place both subforms side by side on the main form and synchronize them. When the first subform changes, its child subform will update automatically. (See the next Annoyance, "Synchronizing Subforms," for details on how to do this.)

Many-to-One

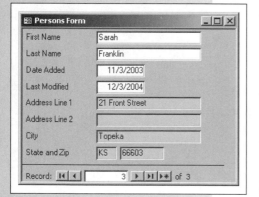

Figure 5-9. This is a many-to-one form based on a query that joins the persons and households tables. This type of form doesn't let the user distinguish between editing the household address and moving the person into a different household. Consequently, we've locked the one side (households) to prevent confusion.

In your situation, you'd like your form to be based on a table that's on the many side (persons) of a one-to-many relationship, and you'd like the one side (households) to show up in a subform (see Figure 5-9). Access is not set up to handle this design. The best workaround is to have a button that opens the one-side table in a separate form. (For example, you might have a persons form with buttons that let you create households, add persons to households, and remove persons from households.) If you want both tables on a single form, base the form on a query that joins the two tables—which is what the Form Wizard does by default (in Access 2002 and later). This works fine if you set the one side to be read-only (see the sidebar "Enabled Versus Locked") or to support partial edits. But you won't be able to manage the full creation and editing of related records between the two tables, because Access doesn't know what to do when you need to clear the foreign key field. You could write code to manage changes and updates to the one side, but we don't recommend it.

Many-to-Many

When your tables are in a many-to-many relationship (related via a link table), you'll need a separate form for each table. For example, suppose patients and doctors are in a many-to-many relationship. (A patient may have many doctors; doctors certainly have many patients!) You'll need one form to create new patient records, and a separate form to create new doctor records—it wouldn't make sense to do both on the same form. If you need to display all of a patient's doctors, or all of a doctor's patients, put the link table into a subform, based on the one-to-many relationship.

Creating Subforms

It often makes sense to include related data on the same form. For instance, a households form might include a list of persons in that household, or a suppliers form could have a products list. One good way to accommodate all this information is to nest a second form within a main form.

Subforms are just regular forms that are used in a nested form design. It's useful to have a naming convention to distinguish main forms from subforms: we use the "frm" prefix for main forms and the "sfr" prefix for subforms. Here are the steps to create a subform (again, we'll use the example of households and persons):

1. Design the main form, leaving space where you want to put the subform. In this example, this is a households form (frmHouseholds) with fields for address information.

2. Design a separate subform for the related data. In our example, this is a persons form (sfrPersons) that we set to use Datasheet View (View→Properties, click the Format tab, and, in Default View, select "Datasheet").

3. With the main form open and the subform closed, drag the subform from the Database window and drop it onto the main form, where you want it. Access adds a subform control that contains the subform (see the sidebar "Subforms Versus Subform Controls," later in this chapter).

4. Set up link fields. Subforms are often used to display related data, and in order to do this Access must know what fields to relate. Often, this will be primary and foreign key fields. For instance, in this example, the persons table has a foreign key field (householdId) that matches the primary key field of the households table. Linking on this field ensures that the persons subform will display only the persons that match the household currently being displayed on the main form. If you've already created a relationship between underlying tables, Access will fill in the link fields for you automatically. If you need to set link fields manually, they're on the Data tab of the subform control's properties sheet. The Master field is on the main form (which typically provides the primary key), and the Child field is on the subform (which typically has the foreign key). If you click in one of them (say, Link Master Fields), you'll see the Build button, which brings up the Subform Field Linker. As shown in Figure 5-10, you can set the link fields there.

Figure 5-10. The Subform Field Linker makes it clear how the link fields will work.

Synchronizing Subforms

THE ANNOYANCE: We have two subforms side by side on our customers form: orders and line items. The idea is that you can see all the orders for each customer, and if you click an order, you can see the line items. But when I click on an order, the line items subform doesn't update.

THE FIX: You can readily handle this kind of one-to-many-to-many design with subforms, but you've got to get them linked up correctly (see Figure 5-11). If your subforms aren't linked, one won't know what the other's doing. The key is in the Link Child Fields and Link Master Fields properties (found on the Data tab of the subform's properties sheet). Access can sometimes set these fields automatically for a subform that's linked to a main form, but to link side-by-side subforms, you'll have to set them up by hand. Don't worry, it's not hard to do.

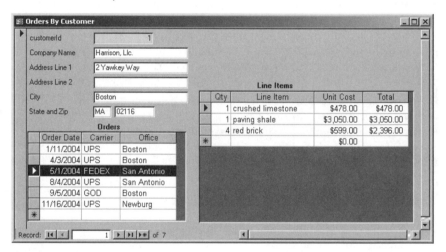

Figure 5-11. When a specific order is selected in the orders subform, that order's line items appear in the line items subform. The two subforms are synchronized with a hidden link field on the main form, which reads the order ID from the orders subform.

NOTE

You could drag your line items subform onto the orders subform, nesting it down one level. But in general, subforms that are nested within subforms are less flexible (for example, you're pretty much stuck with Datasheet View) and make for a more cluttered user interface. We recommend sticking with the side-by-side, synchronized design discussed here.

When you link using child and master fields, you're telling Access to synchronize the subform based on the master key(s). For example, when your customers form is showing customer ID = 1, you want to display all the orders that have that customer ID. This is easy to do in a main form/subform design—you just put the name of the customer ID field in each of the link fields. The child customer ID refers to the foreign key in each orders record, and the master customer ID refers to the primary key in each customer record. Access does the rest.

However, it's not so simple when you're synchronizing two subforms. If you try putting an order ID in the link fields, you'll get an "Enter Parameter Value" prompt. That's because the line items subform can't find the master field—the order ID field—that's in the orders subform. It can't "see" the other subform; it can only look on the main form for the master key, and there's no order ID there. The solution is to add an order ID field to the main form.

First, add an unbound text box to your main form, naming it something like "txtLinkOrderId." Open its properties sheet and set its Control Source property to the field you want to use as your master link field; in this case, it's the primary key of the orders subform. Note that you must provide the full pathname of that field, prefixing it with the name of the subform control (e.g., =[sctlOrders]![orderId]). Now open the properties sheet of the other subform (line items), and set its Master Link Fields property to "txt-LinkOrderId" and its Child Link Fields property to "orderId." That should do it. Once everything is working, set the Visible property of txtLinkOrderId to "No."

Synchronizing Two Forms

THE ANNOYANCE: I want to synchronize my invoices form with my clients form, so that the invoice details always relate to the client that's currently being displayed. The only way Access seems to support this is by using a subform, but this invoice form is too complex to nest into another form. I want separate forms.

THE FIX: Unlike subforms, which Access can synchronize automatically, keeping two separate forms in sync requires a macro or code. If you want to filter records like a subform does (i.e., have one form show only records related to the other form), use code in the "main" form's Current event to set the Filter and FilterOn properties of the "detail" form. For example, this code keeps an invoices form synchronized to the same client ID as a clients form:

```
Private Sub Form_Current()
    If IsLoaded("frmInvoices") Then
        Forms!frmInvoices.Filter = _
                "ClientID = Forms!frmClients!ClientID"
        Forms!frmInvoices.FilterOn = True
    End If
End Sub
```

If your detail form is used to add new records, you might also want to automatically set the foreign key value from the main form when adding records. Place this code in the Before Insert event of the detail form:

```
Private Sub Form_BeforeInsert(Cancel As Integer)
    If IsLoaded("frmClients") Then
        Me!ClientID = Forms!frmClients!ClientID
    End If
End Sub
```

If you always want the two forms to appear together, you can open the detail form in the main form's Open event, and close it later in the main form's Close event:

```
Private Sub Form_Open(Cancel As Integer)
    DoCmd.OpenForm "frmInvoices"
End Sub

Private Sub Form_Close()
    DoCmd.Close acForm, "frmInvoices"
End Sub
```

If you simply want to move to the matching record in one form every time the current record changes in another form, turn to the Bookmark property of the second form's recordset, which identifies the current record. If the forms are based on the same underlying records, or have a one-to-one relationship, you might even use this strategy in *both* forms, so that changing records in either form moves the other form as well. For example, if you look up a new invoice, the clients form could load the appropriate client automatically. Here's how you'd do that:

Put code in the form's Current event that sets the Bookmark property for the other form's recordset. In this example, we take the ClientID from the clients form and set the bookmark of the invoices form to match it:

```
Private Sub Form_Current()
    Dim rst As DAO.Recordset

    If IsLoaded("frmInvoices") And Not IsNull(Me!ClientID) Then
        Set rst = Forms!frmInvoices.RecordsetClone
        rst.FindFirst "ClientID = " & Me!ClientID
        If Not rst.EOF Then
            Forms!frmInvoices.Bookmark = rst.Bookmark
        End If
    End If
End Sub
```

The IsLoaded Function

All of these samples employ a user-defined function called IsLoaded, which determines whether a second form is currently open—a must when you're synchronizing forms. The standard syntax for this function is:

```
Function IsLoaded(ByVal strFormName As String) As Boolean
    If CurrentProject.AllForms(strFormName).IsLoaded Then
        If Forms(strFormName).CurrentView > 0 Then
            IsLoaded = True
        End If
    End If
End Function
```

This function uses the built-in IsLoaded method to test whether a form is loaded, and also tests what view it's loaded in. If it's loaded in Design View (CurrentView = 0), then it may as well not be loaded, because it won't have loaded any data or calculated any values. The IsLoaded function can be found in the Northwind sample database that comes with Access, in the "Utility Functions" module.

Create Dialog Box Input Forms

THE ANNOYANCE: I want to create an input form that will let users specify what report they want to view and which parameters should be used to filter that report's results. But the wizards only create forms that are bound to data in the database. I want something that behaves like a dialog box. What do I do?

THE FIX: A dialog box form—or any menu or unbound form that allows users to input unbound data—is different from a data form in several ways. And no, Access wizards don't help here. To create an unbound form, you start with a blank form and make some important changes (see Figure 5-12).

Here are the basic steps:

1. In the Database window, create a new form by clicking Forms→ New and double-clicking "Design View."

2. Click View→Properties and set the properties listed in Table 5-1 in the Format and Other tabs.

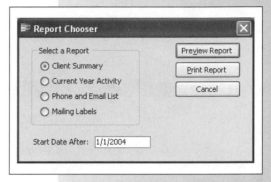

Figure 5-12. An unbound form designed to open and filter reports.

Table 5-1. Properties and settings for creating an unbound form

Property	Setting
Caption	`<Text you want in the form's title bar>`
Scroll Bars	`Neither`
Record Selectors	`No`
Navigation Buttons	`No`
Auto Center	`Yes`
Border Style	`Dialog`
Popup	`Yes`, if you want the form to always appear in front of other windows
Modal	`Yes`, if you will always close the form before displaying another form or report
Allow Design Changes	`Design View Only`

> **NOTE**
>
> *If you plan to create more than one unbound form, save a copy of the empty form as a template so you won't have to set these properties again.*

3. Build your form, adding the usual elements (text boxes, option groups, and so on) to collect information from the user. As always, good design principles (meaningful labels, useful defaults, and so on) apply.

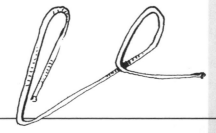

4. Add command buttons that perform the actions you want. For example, you might include buttons that open other forms or reports, or run action queries. (The Command Button Wizard can be helpful here; see "Activating the Wizards," earlier in this chapter.)

On most unbound forms, you'll at least want a Cancel command button. The wizard will put `DoCmd.Close` in the button's Click event procedure, but you may also want to set the button's Cancel property (on the Other tab of its properties sheet) to "Yes." This makes it behave like a standard Cancel button, which can also be activated by pressing the Escape key.

Using the Information You Collect

Once users enter information into an unbound form, what's the best way to use that information in other forms and reports? For example, in "Create Dialog Box Input Forms" we showed you how to create a form where users select from a list of reports and enter dates for filtering records. But how do you actually make use of this user input when opening the report?

Here are three common strategies:

Pass filters with the OpenForm or OpenReport methods.
The `OpenForm` and `OpenReport` methods are designed to accept a `Where` condition and use it to filter the form or report that gets opened. You can place a button on your unbound form and use the `OpenReport` or `OpenForm` action in its Click event to pass the date along in the `Where` condition argument:

```
DoCmd.OpenReport "Orders", acViewPreview, ,
"StartDate = #" & Me!txtStartDate & "#"
```

This code assumes that StartDate is a field in the underlying table or query and txtStartDate is the control on the unbound form. The `OpenReport` action will filter the report's set of records based on the `Where` condition (i.e., "StartDate = #" & Me!txtStartDate & "#").

Hide the unbound form and refer to its controls from other places.
Rather than closing the form when a user is finished, set its Visible property to "False." The data will persist as long as the unbound form is not closed, and in other forms, reports, or queries, you'll be able to refer to the values entered. For example, to filter a report based on a date entered in an unbound form, you would add criteria such as `>=Forms![frmFilterDialog]!StartDate` to the report's underlying query.

Set global variables.
If you don't want to leave your unbound form open and hidden, you can store values to be used throughout your application. To do this, first declare the variables you need (such as gdateStartDate) in any standard module, so they are available anywhere in your application:

```
Public gdateStartDate As Date
```

Then, in the Click event of a button on your unbound form, set the value:

```
gdateStartDate = Me!txtStartDate
```

Now you can use the variable via code anywhere in your application. To use it in queries and expressions, you'll need to create a user-defined function that returns the value. Again, put this definition into any standard module:

```
Public Function StartDate() As Variant
    StartDate = gdateStartDate
End Function
```

Then you can use `StartDate()` in expressions and query criteria; it will return the value of the global variable that was set in your unbound form.

Display Subform Values on the Main Form

THE ANNOYANCE: Part of our customers form is a subform that lists the selected customer's orders. I'm trying to provide order totals on the main form, but I get #Name? errors when I refer to values on the subform.

THE FIX: Subforms are typically used to display the many side of a one-to-many relationship, and one common need on the many side is to compute totals and other aggregates and display them on the main form. This is readily done in Access, but it requires some nonobvious steps. Basically, you need to compute the totals in text boxes you add to the subform, then reference those totals in text boxes you add to the main form (see Figure 5-13).

Here's how it works:

1. **Compute summary values.** Open your subform in Design View. (If your main form is already open in Design View, right-click the subform and select "New Window.") If the form footer is not visible, choose View→Form Header/Footer. With the mouse, grab the bottom of the subform and drag downward to open a small area of the footer. Put one or more unbound text boxes from the toolbox into the footer, and in their properties sheets set the control sources, using aggregate expressions such as **=Max([orderTotal])** to calculate the totals that you want. Check your results by viewing your main form in Form View; you should see these aggregate values in the footer of your subform.

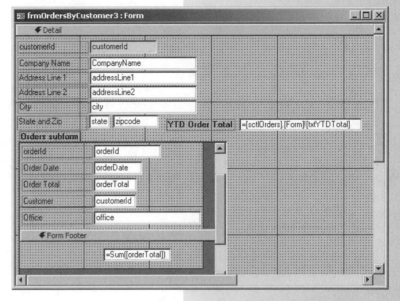

Figure 5-13. Use the form footer of the subform to calculate totals (or other aggregate values). Display them on the main form by using the fully qualified name of the subform control.

2. **Reproduce the footer values on the main form.** Now that the subform's text boxes are calculating the totals correctly, put them on the main form. Simply add new unbound text boxes to your main form, and set their control sources to the text boxes you just created in the subform's footer. Remember that you must qualify the names of each of the subform's text boxes with the name of the subform control, like this: =[sctlOrdersSubform].[Form]![txtSumTotalOrders]. (See "Refer to Subform Properties" in Chapter 7 for detail on this syntax; see "#Name? and #Error?" in Chapter 1 for info on avoiding errors when the subform control is blank or the subform has no records.)

3. **Hide the footer values.** Once your form is working properly, hide the subform footer by opening the footer's properties sheet and, on the Format tab, setting its Visible property to "No." *Don't* accidentally set this on the entire subform; just click the footer bar when you open the properties sheet.

Hide an Empty Subform

THE ANNOYANCE: My orders form has a subform that displays an alternate shipping address. I want to hide it when there is no alternate shipping address, but the HasData property gives me a "method not found" error.

THE FIX: It's not your fault—it's Microsoft's. According to most versions of VB Help, you can use the HasData property to determine if a form or report is bound to an empty record set. But that's a lie—only reports can use the HasData property.

Hiding a subform is easy—just change its Visible property to "False." However, to do this based on a condition, you'll have to use VB code, which you typically add to the main form's Current event. That much is straightforward. What isn't straightforward is determining whether your subform is empty. To do that, your VB code will have to explicitly check the size of its recordset. You'll know it's empty if it has no records. For instance, you could enter something like this in the form's Current event:

```
If Me!sctlAltShipAddr.Form.RecordsetClone.RecordCount = 0 Then
    Me!sctlAltShipAddr.Visible = False
End If
```

Reusing Subforms

THE ANNOYANCE: Our events database has many different forms (rentals, workshops, weddings, and so on) that all use the same basic subform design to record payments. I've created subforms for each of these forms (a rentals payments subform, a workshop payments subform, and so on), but now every time we want to tweak the design I have to make the changes on all of them. This is a total waste of my time.

THE FIX: It's never a good idea to duplicate the same work in multiple places, and subforms are a case in point. If you want to use the same subform for multiple main forms, you don't have to duplicate the subform—instead, just reuse the same subform, adding it to the various main forms. The key is that the link properties are stored in the subform *control*, not the subform itself—so they can be set separately for each main form.

The complications that can arise with this technique have to do with the ways that your foreign keys may be set up, and therefore with what you may need to do in order to link your subforms correctly. For example, you might need to link on multiple fields, which you can do using semicolons to separate the field names in the link properties. You may also need to add a hidden control to your main form to provide a necessary link field. To best take advantage of this approach, you may want to adopt a subtype/supertype design for your database (see "Subtypes and Supertypes" in Chapter 3).

Subforms Versus Subform Controls

OK, what's the difference between a subform and a subform control? Well...as the names imply, a subform is a *form*, and a subform control is a *control*. You can't directly add a subform to a form; you can only add a control, which is essentially a container for the subform. That's why when you refer to a subform in your main form, you should ignore the subform name and use the name of the subform control instead. (For more information, see "Refer to Subform Properties" in Chapter 7.)

CREATE FORMS YOUR USERS WILL LOVE

Simplify Data Entry

THE ANNOYANCE: I'm designing a patient intake form for a doctor's office. Since I actually have to use this form myself, I'd like to have it automate as much of the data entry as possible, but I have no idea where to start.

THE FIX: A well-designed form makes data entry easy and efficient. There are various tricks, but consider the essentials first. In general, forms should be neat, uncluttered, and well organized. Use combo and list boxes, or option groups, whenever you can so that users can choose from a list rather than typing in data; it's faster, easier, and far less error-prone. Setting the Auto Expand property will allow your users to type one or more letters in a combo box and jump straight to the appropriate spot in the list, without having to scroll through all the choices. For example, a clients list might have 1,000 names—but when you type "Sm..." you jump right to Smith. (For more on using Auto Expand and type-ahead in combo boxes, see "Limit Rows with Type-Ahead" in "Speed Up Slow Combo Boxes," later in this chapter.) The Combo Box, List Box, and Option Group Wizards make it easy to set up these controls and load them with data taken from a table or a list of values entered by hand.

The following outlines some other tweaks that can help you streamline data entry and put together a clean, coherent form (as illustrated in Figure 5-14).

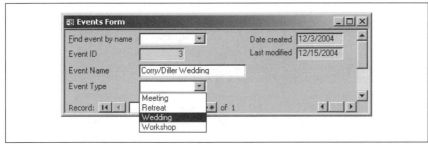

Figure 5-14. This simple form illustrates several important usability tweaks. The Event Type dropdown lets the user choose from a list, rather than typing. The "Find event by name" box has a keyboard shortcut (Alt-F) defined for it. The "Date created" and "Last modified" fields are autofilled, and all noneditable fields are distinguished by being grayed out.

Autofill Dates

Records often have fields that capture their creation dates and last modified dates. These fields should almost never be filled in by hand. To autofill the creation date field, open the form in Design View, right-click the field, and select "Properties." On the Data tab, set its Default Value property to

=Date(). This assigns today's date to the creation date field. To autofill the last-modified field, insert code such as **Me!lastModified = Date()** in the form's Before Update property. (Me is a handy VB name that, in this context, refers to whatever form is currently active.) This code will run every time a record is edited and saved—including the initial data entry. If you want the date to include the time (in *hour:minute:second* format) as well, use Now() instead of Date().

Autofill Related Fields

Often, once a user inputs some data, a form can "guess" the values of related fields and automatically fill them in. For example, you might want to automatically fill in a spouse's last name with the name entered earlier on the form for the patient's last name. To do so, place code such as **Me!txtSpouseLastName = txtLastName** in the After Update event of the patient's name field. This copies the value from the last name text box to the spouse's last name text box. The user can edit or clear this value as needed.

Sometimes Access needs to look up or compute related information before it can autofill a field. If you enter a lot of addresses, you'll appreciate having a Zip Code table that lets you autofill city and state fields based on Zip Codes. To implement an autofill such as this, enter the following code in the After Update event of the Zip Code field:

```
Private Sub txtZipcode_AfterUpdate()
    Dim rst As ADODB.Recordset
    Dim strSQL As String

    Set rst = New ADODB.Recordset
    strSQL = "SELECT city, state FROM tblZipcodes " & _
        "WHERE zipcode = """ & Me!txtZipcode & """"
    rst.Open strSQL, CurrentProject.Connection
    If Not rst.BOF And Not rst.EOF Then
        Me!txtCity = rst!city
        Me!txtState = rst!state
    End If
End Sub
```

This code reads the Zip Code entered on your form, looks up the associated city and state in the Zip Code table, and writes that information back to the form. You can subscribe to Zip Code data directly from the U.S. Postal Service, or you can purchase it from vendors such as *http://www.fmsinc. com* and *http://www.zipcodeworld.com*, who sell it prepackaged for quick deployment in Access.

Define the Tab Order

You probably know that you can adjust the tab order (that is, the order in which the insertion point moves from field to field in a form when the user presses the Tab key) by going to form Design View, selecting View→Tab Order, and changing the order of the list that appears in the dialog box. The process is a little clunky: you have to select and then release the little box on the left before you can drag the controls to new positions in the list. Clicking the Auto Order button will create a "natural" left-to-right, top-to-bottom tab order—but there are cases when the natural order isn't best. If you autofill one field based on another field, you'll probably want the source field to come first in the tab order. For instance, if you autofill city and state based on Zip Code, Zip Code should probably come first, even though that's not the "natural" order. You should also remove noneditable controls (or fields) from the tab order, by setting their Tab Stop properties to "No" (on the Other tab of the controls' properties sheets).

Distinguish Noneditable Fields

Most forms have fields that aren't editable because they are calculated, are part of a non-updatable query, and so on. It's good practice to make these fields visually distinct from fields that can accept input. In form Design View, click the field you want to change, then click View→Properties. On the Format tab, set the Back Color property to an appropriate background color. (For maximum readability, you may want to define a custom color, such as R=225, G=225, B=225. Click the Back Color property, then click the Build button on the right. Click the Define Custom Colors button, and enter the RGB values in the Custom Color dialog.) If you use the same color consistently throughout your application, your users will understand how your forms work without having to learn each one.

If you want to make a control (such as the last-modified date) *behave* as if it's not editable, even though the underlying data is, set its Locked property (on the Data tab) to "Yes." See the sidebar "Enabled Versus Locked" for more info on the Enabled and Locked properties.

Keyboard Shortcuts for Find Boxes

Many forms have combo boxes that are used to jump to specific records. These combos should normally be left out of the tab order, since they're not part of the data entry or edit workflow. Instead, create a shortcut (triggered by pressing the Alt key and a letter) that lets users go directly to the combo box. To do this, open the properties sheet of the combo box's *attached label*, and in its Caption property (on the Format tab) type **&** before the shortcut letter, like this: **&Find customers**. (For more about these labels, see "Attached Labels," earlier in this chapter.) The label will display the shortcut letter underlined (in this case, F). Press Alt-F, and you jump to the combo box.

Enabled Versus Locked

You may have noticed two properties on the Data tab of a control's properties sheet: Enabled and Locked. What's the difference? The Enabled property determines whether the control can receive focus—i.e., whether you can even put your cursor into it. If it can't receive focus, the user can't do *anything* with it, and Access grays it out. But this makes the data hard to read, which defeats the purpose of having it on the form at all. For this reason, we avoid Enabled entirely.

The Locked property allows the control to receive focus and allows the data in the control to be copied, but prevents the data from being *changed*. By default, Access does not gray out locked controls. In fact, if you set Locked to "Yes" and Enabled to "No," Access will display data in the control as normal (not grayed out) even though the control can't even receive focus—not that we can think of a case where this makes for good user interface design. We do, however, recommend changing the background color of locked controls, to distinguish them visually to your users. (See "Distinguish Noneditable Fields" in this Annoyance for details.)

Open a Form to a New Record

THE ANNOYANCE: When I open our customers form, it always shows the first record—which I almost never need to see. How can I make it open to a new, blank record, but let me go back to existing records if I need to?

THE FIX: Simple. Just add one line of VB code to the form's On Load event:

```
RunCommand acCmdRecordsGoToNew
```

To open to the last record in the recordset, use this:

```
RunCommand acCmdRecordsGoToLast
```

If you want to start with a blank record and prevent users from viewing or editing existing records, you can do it without any VB code. In Design View, open the form's properties sheet, choose the Data tab, and set both the form's Data Entry property and the Allow Additions property to "Yes."

Refresh Data Automatically

THE ANNOYANCE: Our registrations form has a subform that lets us record multiple payments. When a new payment is added, the totals on the main form should update—but they don't. We have to close the form and then open it again.

THE FIX: It's useful (even elegant) to have totals on the main form update automatically as subform data is changed (see Figure 5-15). Normally, Access does this without any extra effort on your part—controls on the main form that refer to subform values will refresh automatically *when the subform is saved*. There's the catch. A subform record is not saved until you move to another record or explicitly save it (using Records→Save Record). People sometimes expect the totals to update as soon as they enter values, but that's not how Access works. However, with a bit of code, you can *make* it work that way.

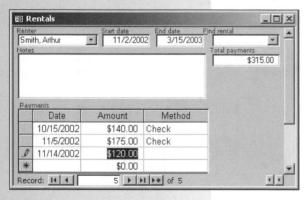

Figure 5-15. The Total payments field on this form refreshes automatically when a new payment is added. The refresh will occur as soon as the new subform record is saved.

Usually, a control on a main form gets subform values via a function or query, which is why Access will not refresh these values automatically. You can recalculate totals by pressing F9, or, with a little bit of Visual Basic code, you can have Access do this automatically.

Open the payments subform in Design View, and add one line of code to its After Update event: **Forms!*myMainForm*.Recalc**. (Of course, you'll need to substitute the name of your main form for ***myMainForm***.) That's it.

You have several choices when it comes to refreshing data, and you can apply them to individual controls rather than to the entire form. The three options are:

Recalc (F9)

Recalculates calculated controls based on most current data.

Refresh (Shift-F9)

Updates current recordset based on most current data. Does not show new or deleted records (i.e., records added or deleted by other users).

Requery

Requeries recordset, reflecting changes to existing records as well as additions and deletions. Note that Requery moves the bookmark (i.e., the current record pointer) to the first record in the recordset; don't use requery when your user is in the middle of looking at some other record (or, if you must, save the bookmark first so that you can return your user to his original place).

Hide Foreign Keys

THE ANNOYANCE: Our patient visits table has two foreign keys: patient ID and doctor ID. But our visits form will be incomprehensible if we display those ID numbers instead of patient and doctor names. What can I do?

THE FIX: This problem arises in any properly designed database, because foreign keys are almost always meaningless numbers. So how can you display them in a meaningful way? Access has two built-in solutions that apply not only to foreign keys, but to any place where the data you want to display is different from the data you want to store.

One solution is to use the Lookup Wizard. You can find it by going to table Design View, clicking the down arrow in any Data Type field, and selecting "Lookup Wizard." This effectively hides the foreign key value, so that the only values the user sees are the ones that you specify. In addition, lookup fields will automatically show up in forms as combo boxes (with display values) rather than text boxes—which saves you the trouble of creating them yourself.

This approach has some notable downsides, though, and consequently we don't recommend it. First, hiding the actual data in your tables is a bad idea. Months later you're going to look at a field and not be sure whether what you're seeing is the stored value or just its representation. And for every lookup field, Access adds an extra relationship and index, complicating the design and bloating the database. (For more on the complications of lookup fields, consult "The Evils of Lookup Fields in Tables" at *http://www.mvps.org/access/lookupfields.htm.*)

Using the Combo Box Wizard is a much better solution. Instead of masking the data in your tables, you can simply create a combo box that presents a nice display to users. On your visits form, delete the patient ID text box (if you have one), choose the Combo Box tool from the Toolbox (View→ Toolbox), and then click on your form; this starts the Combo Box Wizard. Then follow these steps:

1. Choose "I want the combo box to look up the values in a table or query," and click the Next button.

2. Select the table that the foreign key points back to (e.g., the patient ID points back to the patients table). Click Next.

3. Select the primary key field from that table from the Available Fields list on the left. This is the value that gets stored in the foreign key field, along with the display fields that you want. In this example, we'll add patientId, and then lastName and firstName. Click Next.

4. Adjust the height and width of the display to suit your data, by grabbing and dragging the column separators at the top and the row separators on the far left. Click Next.

5. Select "Store that value in this field," and select your foreign key field (e.g., patientId). Then click the Finish button.

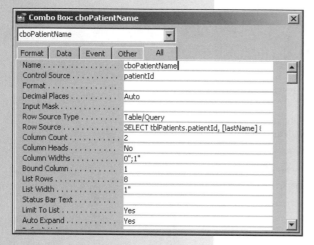

Figure 5-16. This combo box is set up to display patient names, even though it's bound to the patient ID field as a foreign key.

The wizard creates a combo box that is *populated* with all the names and IDs from the patients table and *bound* to the patientId field in the visits table (see Figure 5-16). Users of the form see the patient names, but the patient IDs are what get stored in the visits table.

Although the wizard does most of the work for you, it helps to understand how the properties work. In Control Source, you indicate the field the combo box is bound to. Row Source is where it gets its data (in this case, a select query from the patients table). The Column Count property specifies the number of columns (two, in this case), Bound Column indicates which column is bound to patient ID (the first), and Column Widths indicates just that. We've made the bound column 0" wide, effectively hiding it. The second column (1" wide) displays the patient names.

It's a simple and very user-friendly solution—but there are a few things you'll need to fix before you're done. First, in the Name field on the All tab of the properties sheet, give the combo box a meaningful name, such as cboPatientName. This combo box doesn't have any associated code, so you don't have to worry about updating its name in the VB Editor. Second, you'll want to sort and possibly rearrange the data that's displayed in the combo box. To see how, check out step 2 of the fix in the next Annoyance.

Find Records Faster

THE ANNOYANCE: Users of our employees form need to be able to jump to different records based on employee name or ID. They're using the Find function, but it takes way too many steps. There's gotta be a quicker way!

THE FIX: The Edit→Find command is useful for one-off searches, but for regular use, you should provide a custom lookup box that lets users jump directly to the records they need. This is usually implemented as a combo box with an autocompletion drop-down display that users can type into. And as it turns out, Access has a wizard that makes it easy to set up. Here are the steps:

1. **Run the Combo Box Wizard.** Choose the Combo Box tool from the Toolbox, and then click on your form; this starts the wizard. Choose "Find a record on my form based on the value I selected in my combo box," and click the Next button. Select the field(s) on which your users will search. For instance, if they're going to search on employee name, add both the first name and last name fields. You should also add the primary key. Click Next, and then click through the rest of the wizard's screens, accepting the defaults; we'll adjust them later.

   Access is smart enough to *display* the search field(s) but *search* on the primary key field, which ensures that things will work right even if several employees have the same name. Note, however, that if users need to search on different fields (e.g., name *or* employee ID), you must set up a separate combo box for each type of search.

2. **Fix the combo box display.** At this point your combo box should work, but it clearly needs some tweaking. Figure 5-17 shows the combo box that the wizard creates for you (left), and our improved version (right). As you can see, the Combo Box Wizard does not sort the records, and if you add multiple fields (first name and last name) it presents them in separate columns. Although your users will probably expect to search by last name, when they type in the combo box only the first column—in this case, first name—will respond. You'll want to make some changes to the combo box to improve its performance and make it more user-friendly. You should also give it a more obvious name than "Combo12" (see "Fix Combo and List Box Names," earlier in this chapter).

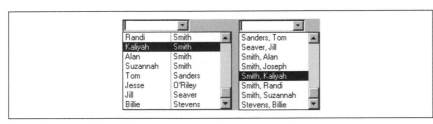

Figure 5-17. A tale of two combo boxes. On the left, you see what the Combo Box Wizard gives you if you add both first and last name fields. On the right, the names have been merged into a single field, type-ahead works the way it should, and we've sorted the query so the names appear in alphabetical order.

Here's how to fix the sorting and typing problems. In form Design View, open the combo box's properties sheet, click the Data tab, click in the Row Source field, and then click the Build (...) button. You'll see that Access is using a query to populate the combo box, pulling its fields from the row source of your form. You can tweak this query to make it work just the way you want.

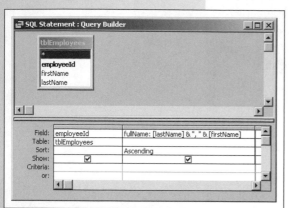

Figure 5-18. The query that supplies rows to the combo box. We've replaced the separate firstName and lastName columns with a single column that combines these two fields into the full name.

In our example, cboFindEmployeeByName displays first and last names in separate columns. Unfortunately, when users type in the combo box, only the first column (holding the first name) responds. In the combo's query, replace those two fields with a single expression such as this: **fullName: lastName & ", " & firstName** (see Figure 5-18). In the Sort line of the query design grid, put **Ascending**. When you're done, close the Query Builder. Access asks, "Do you want to save the changes made to the SQL statement and update the property?" Click Yes, and then save your form.

Try the combo box, and you'll see that the names have been merged into a single field, type-ahead works, and the names appear in alphabetical order. But now there's an empty column to the right. In form Design View, open the combo box's properties sheet. In the Format tab, adjust the Column Count property to match the number of fields in your query, and adjust the column widths. In this example, we reduced the column count from three to two and combined the last two 1" columns into a single 2" column. (We can do this, even though we still have two columns defined, because we've given the first column a width of 0".)

3. **Synchronize and refresh (optional).** A few more lines of code can be used to keep the combo box synchronized and up-to-date. If you want the combo box to show the same name as the current record, put this line in the form's Current event:

```
Me!cboFindCust = Me!CustomerID
```

If you want the contents of the combo box to be updated to reflect new records, put these lines in the form's After Update event:

```
Me!cboFindCust.Requery
Me!cboFindCust = Me!CustomerID
```

Create Forms Your Users Will Love

Handle Items Not in a Combo Box

THE ANNOYANCE: Our orders form has a combo box that lets us select a customer by typing in the customer's name. But if I type a name that isn't in our database, I get an error, "The text you entered isn't an item in the list." Is there some way I can get Access to just open a blank customers form?

THE FIX: As long as the combo box's Limit To List property (found on the Data tab) is set to "Yes," whenever users type in an unrecognized entry they'll get the "not in list" error. If Limit To List is set to "No," and the combo box is bound to a table or query, then users can type in anything they want, and their input will be stored in the underlying field. Normally, turning off Limit To List is a little risky, since it lets users add data a bit too freely. Instead, you'll want to use the combo box's Not In List event. This event fires up when a user types an unrecognized value into a combo box and presses Enter, or tries to leave the combo box. Plug a little code into the Not In List event, and you can handle this situation elegantly. Here's some skeleton code:

```
Private Sub cboCustomers_NotInList(NewData As String, Response As
Integer)
    If MsgBox("That customer is not in the list." & _
            "Would you like to add a new customer?", vbYesNo) = vbYes
Then
        'User said yes, so add the new customer here...
        Response = acDataErrAdded
    Else
        Response = acDataErrContinue
    End If
End Sub
```

You can see from the above code that Access provides two parameters: NewData and Response. NewData gives you the value that was typed into the combo box. The Response parameter lets you tell Access what to do once this code finishes running. You can set Response to any one of these values:

acDataErrAdded

Tells Access that you've added a new value and that Access should requery the combo box. This ensures that the combo box will display the value you just added.

acDataErrContinue

Indicates that you've notified the user of the error and that Access should return focus to (i.e., put the cursor back into) the combo box.

acDataErrDisplay

Tells Access to display the usual "not in list" error.

The skeleton code above doesn't do very much yet—it just displays a message, asking if the user wants to add a new customer (Figure 5-19).

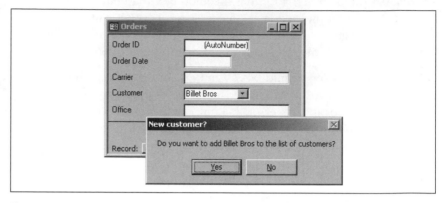

Figure 5-19. When a user types a value not in the combo box list, it's either a typo, or the user needs to add a new value. If the latter, then you'll either add the value directly, or open a form and let the user create a new record.

Click No, and the focus goes back to the combo box. Click Yes, and two different things can happen, depending on whether you're adding a single value to the list or more information. If the combo box is a simple lookup list of, say, cities, you can just add the new value within the Not In List event procedure. Here's one way to do it:

```
Private Sub cboCity_NotInList(NewData As String, Response As Integer)
    If MsgBox("Do you want to add " & NewData & _
            " to the list of cities?", vbYesNo, _
            "New city?") = vbYes Then
        DoCmd.RunSQL "INSERT INTO tblCities(City) VALUES ('" & _
                NewData & "')"
        Response = acDataErrAdded
    Else
        Response = acDataErrContinue
    End If
End Sub
```

If the user needs to enter data in several fields in a separate form—say, if you have a combo box that lists customers—Access could respond to the Not In List event by opening a customers form:

```
Private Sub cboCustomer_NotInList(NewData As String, Response As
Integer)
    If MsgBox("That customer is not in the list." & _
            "Would you like to add a new customer?", vbYesNo) = vbYes
Then
        ' Open the form to add the new customer.
        DoCmd.OpenForm "frmCustomers", , , , acFormAdd, acDialog,
NewData
```

```
        If IsNull(DLookup("CustomerID", "tblCustomers", _
                "CompanyName = """ & NewData & """")) Then
            Response = acDataErrContinue
        Else
            Response = acDataErrAdded
        End If
    Else
        Response = acDataErrContinue
    End If
End Sub
```

This code opens the customers form and, once the user has entered all the necessary information, uses DLookup to check whether the item was actually added. This is essential. If the user changes her mind and closes the form without doing anything, she'll get the "not in list" error unless you "trap" this condition.

Note the parameters of OpenForm:

acFormAdd

> Opens the form in data entry mode—existing records cannot be viewed or edited. To allow users full access to the form, leave this parameter blank.

acDialog

> Opens the form in dialog mode, which means that everything else stops until the user closes the open form. This is essential, since otherwise your code will keep running—and exit before the user has a chance to do anything.

By including the NewData value, we pass the data to the form we're about to open. It's up to the form being opened to do something with that data. For instance, you can add code like this to the Load event of the new form to autoload the data that the user has already typed. It retrieves that data in the OpenArgs parameter:

```
Private Sub Form_Load()
    If Not IsNull(Me.OpenArgs) Then
        Me!CompanyName = Me.OpenArgs
    End If
End Sub
```

One Form, Many Screen Resolutions

THE ANNOYANCE: Some of my users have 21" monitors set at high resolution, and others are low-end desk jockeys with 14" screens. If I size my forms to fit the small screens, they look minuscule on the high-res systems. But if I match them to the big monitors, the desk jockeys have to constantly scroll to do anything. Either way, my forms look terrible on *somebody's* machine.

THE FIX: It's really a shame that Access doesn't adapt to different screen resolutions (see Figures 5-20 and 5-21). You can zoom in Word and Excel; why not in Access?

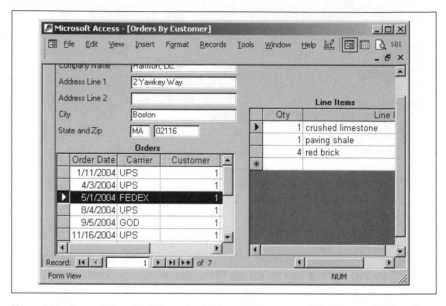

Figure 5-20. Forms designed to look good on high-resolution screens will look cramped and require scrolling on low-resolution screens...

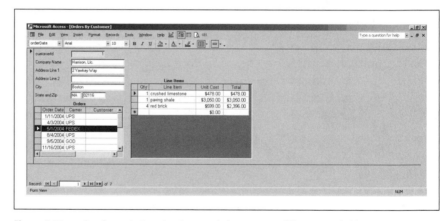

Figure 5-21. ...but forms designed on low-resolution screens will be surrounded by empty space when viewed on high-resolution screens.

Until Access gets a DoCmd.FitToScreen function, there are a couple of home-grown solutions. One is to have two versions of each form: a wide-screen edition and a regular one. You can let users choose which version to open, or open them conditionally after detecting the current screen resolution.

To do the latter, place the following line of code into any standard module (Insert→Module will zap you over to the VB Editor; you can name the module anything you like):

```
Public Declare Function GetSystemMetrics Lib "user32" _
      (ByVal nIndex As Long) As Long
```

This code is a declaration for the Windows API call GetSystemMetrics(). Since this function is not in any Access library, you must tell Visual Basic where to find it. GetSystemMetrics() is a function that looks up the current screen resolution. You'd use it like this (place this code in the Click event of the button that opens your form):

```
Private Sub cmdCustomerForm_Click
    Dim intScreenWidth As Integer

    intScreenWidth = CInt(GetSystemMetrics(0))
    If intScreenWidth < 1024 Then
        DoCmd.OpenForm "frmCustomers"
    Else
        DoCmd.OpenForm "frmCustomersWide"
    End If

End Sub
```

This code looks up the screen resolution, and then—depending on the screen width—opens either the regular or the wide-screen form.

But this solution is unwieldy if you have to maintain a lot of forms in multiple-resolution versions. If you want to maintain only one version, you'll need code that automatically resizes your forms based on the current screen resolution. This code is a bit beyond the scope of this book, but you'll find it in *The Access Developer's Handbook*, by Litwin, Getz, and Gunderloy (Sybex)—look at the section "Automatically Resizing Forms" in the "Topics in Form Design" chapter).

Finally, if you'd rather buy (or download) code than write it, you have a few options. Form Resizer is a free code module that automatically resizes forms based on your screen resolution. It's available at *http://www.jamiessoftware.tk*, but it requires a working knowledge of Visual Basic. The shareware ShrinkerStretcher program also resizes forms automatically, and it lets Access 97 through 2003 users zoom forms in and out. It's available from *http://www.peterssoftware.com/ss.htm* for $35.95.

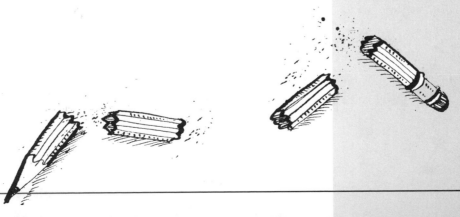

Option Groups Don't Allow Text Values

THE ANNOYANCE: We want our patients form to look like our printed intake form, which, among other things, has two checkboxes for gender: male and female. An option group seems like the logical way to go, but it can only store numeric values. Why!?

THE FIX: There's no good reason why option groups are limited to numeric values, but that's how they work in Access. The easy fix is to use a combo box instead, setting its Row Source Type to **Value List** and its Row Source to the list of values you want to offer, separated by semicolons—for example, **"Male";"Female";"Just confused"**.

However, if your user interface design requires an option group, a little bit of VB code can take numeric values and translate them into text. For example, the option group in Figure 5-22 is bound to text values, via the "txtHiddenGender" box (which would normally be hidden). The "Option value" box is included to demonstrate that the option group still uses numeric values—it's our code that translates them into text values.

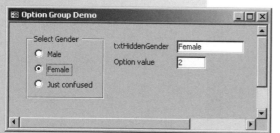

Figure 5-22. If necessary, you can bind an option group to text values.

Let's look at how this works. First, you'll create an unbound option group. You'll use its After Update event to map numbers into text, and you'll use the form's Current event to translate back from text into the option group display. A hidden, bound text box provides an easy way to write the text values into the table. Here are the steps:

1. **Create an unbound option group.** Use the Option Group Wizard (activated by clicking the magic wand icon in the Toolbox in form Design View) to create your option group. Without the wizard you'll just get an empty frame, and you'll have to construct your option group by hand, out of labels and option buttons. The wizard is pretty self-explanatory—just be sure to leave the option group unbound by choosing "Save the value for later use" on the fourth page.

2. **Create a bound text box.** This text box is bound to the field where you want to store the data. An easy way to create it is by choosing View→ Field List, and then dragging the field name from the pop-up list onto the form. Give it a meaningful name, such as txtHiddenGender. You'll eventually hide this text box, but it's a good idea to leave it visible until all the code is working.

3. **Add After Update code.** Click on the option group's frame in Design View, and open its properties sheet. On the All tab, give the group a meaningful name, such as grpGender. Then go to the Event tab and create an After Update event with code similar to this:

```
Private Sub grpGender_AfterUpdate()
    Me!txtHiddenGender = Choose(Me!grpGender, _
                    "Male", "Female")
End Sub
```

The Choose function maps a numeric index (1, 2, 3, and so on, supplied by grpGender) into a list of values. Here we only have two values (Male and Female), but you can have as many as you need. The resulting text value is assigned to the text box. Open the form in Form View, and click through all the option buttons. You should see the value in the text box change to match the option button you click; you may need to change the order in which you list the values in the Choose function.

4. **Add On Current code.** Open the form's properties sheet, and in the On Current event, enter code such as this:

```
Private Sub Form_Current()
    Select Case Me!txtHiddenGender
    Case "Male"
        Me!grpGender = 1
    Case "Female"
        Me!grpGender = 2
    Case Else
        Me!grpGender = Null
    End Select
End Sub
```

The Select Case statement compares the value in the table (via the bound text box) with the list of cases ("Male" and "Female") and executes the statement under the case that matches. If there's no match—say, because the field is empty—it executes the Case Else line, which clears the option group.

Now open the form in Form View and page through your records, checking to see whether the option group tracks the same values as those shown in txtHiddenGender. If not, adjust the numeric values in your case statement until they do. The option group values are set in the Option Value property of each option button, on the Data tab. If you used the wizard's defaults, they go from 1 to N, where N is the total number of options.

5. **Hide the text box.** Once your code is working, open the text box's properties sheet, and on the Format tab, set its Visible property to "No."

Can't Change Column Headings for Datasheet View

THE ANNOYANCE: I always use my payments subform in Datasheet View. This works great, except it displays the field names as column headings. There's got to be a way to change the column headings, but I can't find it.

THE FIX: It's a bit obscure, but here's how it works. If the controls on your form have *attached* labels, those labels will be used as column headings in Datasheet View. Otherwise (that is, if your labels are unattached), the *control* names—not the underlying field names—will be used. It only looks as though the field names are being used because, by default, controls get the same names as the fields to which they're bound. Since best practice suggests using standard control names, such as txtDepositDate (see "Bad Field Names" in Chapter 3), you should use attached labels and give them useful names, so you likewise end up with useful column headings. (If you need to reattach your labels, see "Attached Labels," earlier in this chapter.)

Set Focus Doesn't Work

THE ANNOYANCE: I have an employees form with a text box where users enter an employee ID. In the text box's After Update event, I entered some code that checks whether it's a valid ID; if not, it's supposed to display a message and return focus to the text box. But no matter what I do, the focus goes to the next control on the form.

THE FIX: Setting focus in Access can be maddening, because there are subtle—and mostly undocumented—timing issues and idiosyncrasies involved. For example, while you can use a control's After Update event to set focus somewhere else, you can't set focus back to a control in its own After Update event. This is probably because the control hasn't yet lost focus, and Access is unable to "remember" that a control that's *about* to lose focus should get it back. However, using the After Update event for data validation is not a good solution, anyway. Normally, data validation should be done in the Before Update event. If the data is invalid, just set the Cancel parameter in the event procedure to True. This cancels the subsequent events (i.e., After Update→Exit→Lost Focus) and returns focus to the control.

On the other hand, you can't change the focus in a control's Before Update event. Access will not allow this, because the data has not yet been saved. This is generally not a problem, because if the data is invalid, you usually want to leave focus where it is and have the user fix it. If you need to prompt the user to fix related data in a *different* control, use the Before Update event of the form itself. From this event, you can cancel the update and set focus to any control.

Need to move focus from a main form to a control within a subform? Use code like this, which first sets focus on the subform control itself:

```
Forms!frmMainForm!sctlSubForm.SetFocus
Forms!frmMainForm!sctlSubForm!txtSomeControl.SetFocus
```

Note that if a control is not enabled, or is invisible, it can't accept focus. By the same token, a subform that has its AllowAdditions property set to False and has no records cannot accept focus. SetFocus will issue an error if you attempt to set focus on a control that can't accept it (see Figure 5-23).

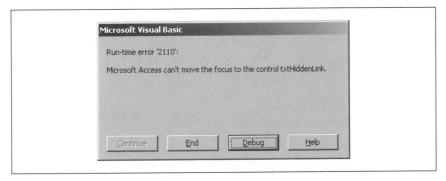

Figure 5-23. A runtime error will result if you attempt to move focus to a control that can't accept it (because it is not visible, not enabled, and so on).

Enable Null Values in a Combo Box

THE ANNOYANCE: A combo box on our patients form lets us specify marital status, which is left null if unknown. The problem is that if you select a value by mistake, there's no way to change it back to null.

THE FIX: Most people don't realize it, but there *is* a way for users to input a null—just select the value you accidentally entered in the combo box, and clear it. Still, a good user interface should make this choice obvious by including an "N/A" or "Unknown" value that the user can select (see Figure 5-24).

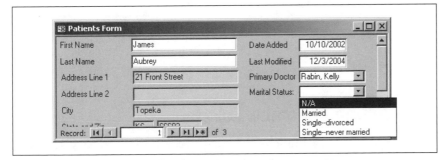

Figure 5-24. It's good design practice to add an N/A value to combo boxes that represent optional fields. This way it's obvious how to clear the value if it's incorrect.

So, the fix is to add "N/A" to the combo box choices, and then, since you don't want to store that value in the table, trap it in the Before Update event and replace it with null. Here are the steps:

1. **Add "N/A" to the combo box.** If your combo box gets its entries from a value list, simply add "N/A" to the Row Source list on the Data tab of the properties sheet. If your combo box gets its entries from a query, you'll need to replace that query with a union query. For example, suppose your combo box row source is a query such as SELECT tblCities. cityName FROM tblCities. To include "N/A" in the query results, open the combo box's properties sheet, choose the Data tab, click the Row Source field, and click the Build (...) button. In the Query Builder, choose View→SQL View, and then change the query to something like this:

   ```
   SELECT tblCities.cityName FROM tblCities
   UNION
   SELECT "N/A" FROM tblCities;
   ```

   If your combo box has a hidden key field in the first column, the code should look something like this:

   ```
   SELECT tblCities.cityId, tblCities.cityName FROM tblCities
   UNION
   SELECT Null, "N/A" FROM tblCities;
   ```

   Either way, both SELECT statements must have the same number of columns. Match the null column to whichever column in the first SELECT statement is bound to the underlying table.

2. **Trap "N/A" values.** If the display column of the combo box is also the bound column, you'll need to trap the "N/A" values to prevent them from being written to the database. Place this code in the combo box's Before Update event to translate "N/A" into a null value in the database:

   ```
   Private Sub cboCity_BeforeUpdate(Cancel As Integer)
       If cboCity = "N/A" Then
           cboCity = Null
       End If
   End Sub
   ```

   If the display column is not the bound column, this translation happens automatically.

Fix Scrolling in Combo Boxes

THE ANNOYANCE: My registrations form has a combo box filled with a few thousand student names. But for some reason, when I drag the scroll box it doesn't go all the way to the bottom of the list; it just shows the first few records.

THE FIX: Access only scrolls records that it has pre-loaded. This speeds up the initial loading of the combo box, but it makes for weird scrolling behavior if you have a large number of records (see Figure 5-25).

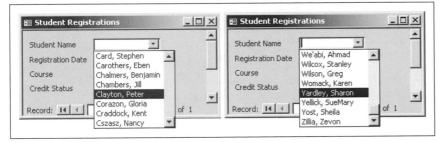

Figure 5-25. Combo boxes with a lot of records don't scroll properly. In the box on the left, the scroll box was pulled all the way to the bottom—but it bounces part way up, and the displayed names are still in the Cs. The box on the right has been fixed: when you pull the scroll box down to the bottom, it goes to the bottom of the list and stays there.

The solution is to force the combo box to load everything up front, which you can do by asking it to count how many items it has. Put this code in the form's On Load event, replacing *cboMyComboBox* with the name of your combo box control:

```
Dim lngCount As Long
lngCount = cboMyComboBox.ListCount
```

Of course, loading everything up front will take time. If the slowdown is unacceptable, see "Speed Up Slow Combo Boxes," later in this chapter.

Use Arrow Keys in Combo Boxes

THE ANNOYANCE: When I tab into a drop-down menu on the Web, I can use the arrow keys to cycle through the choices. But with a combo box, I have to open the box by clicking it with the mouse before the arrow keys work. My data entry would be a lot easier if I could keep my hands on the keyboard.

THE FIX: Little details like this can make a big difference in ease of data entry. You could, of course, open the combo box by pressing F4 or Alt-Down Arrow, but a more convenient fix is to add this code to the On Got Focus event of your combo box: **Me!cboMyCombo.Dropdown**. This pops open the combo box as soon as it receives focus (i.e., as soon as you tab to that field), and then the arrow keys work.

An alternate and more elegant solution is to use the combo box's Key Down event to trap the pressing of the arrow keys and manipulate the combo box appropriately. Since you'll probably want to do this in many of your combo boxes, we'll present it as a function that you can save in a public module. Here's the function:

```
Public Function handleKeyDown(KeyCode As Integer, cboControl _
    As ComboBox)
    Dim curIndex As Long
    curIndex = cboControl.ListIndex
    Select Case KeyCode
    Case vbKeyUp
        If curIndex > 0 Then
            cboControl = cboControl.ItemData(curIndex - 1)
        End If
        KeyCode = 0
    Case vbKeyDown
        If curIndex < cboControl.ListCount - 1 Then
            cboControl = cboControl.ItemData(curIndex + 1)
        End If
        KeyCode = 0
    Case Else
    End Select
End Function
```

Note that this sets KeyCode to zero, which means "no keypress"—ensuring that Visual Basic won't pass these arrow keypresses along to some other module to process. To use this function, type this line of code into your combo box's On Key Down event (substituting the name of your combo box for *cboMyCombo*): `Call handleKeyDown(KeyCode, Me!cboMyCombo)`.

Speed Up Slow Combo Boxes

THE ANNOYANCE: I have a combo box that lists over a hundred thousand part numbers—and it takes forever to load. How can I speed it up?

THE FIX: Combo boxes don't perform well with that many records, and users can't interact with that many records, either. We'll look at two different ways to restrict the number of records that your combo box loads—and we'll assume that you've already indexed those fields, as we suggested in "Speed Up Slow Queries" in Chapter 4.

The first approach uses a separate control to narrow the search field. This is especially useful when it's important for the user to be able to open the combo box and view the choices. The second approach uses the first few letters the user types to limit the rows retrieved. This is more useful when a user typically types a choice into the combo box. Both approaches leave the row source of the combo box unset until the user enters additional information that Access can use to filter the list. If you're starting from scratch, you may want to use the Combo Box Wizard to create your combo box, and then clear its row source (on the Data tab of the properties sheet). If your SQL skills are a little wobbly, copy the Row Source property before you clear it, and use that SQL statement as a starting point.

Restrict with a Separate Control

A typical tack for a parts database is to narrow the choices by supplier. Add a second combo box to your form that lets users specify the supplier first, and populate the parts combo box with only parts from that particular supplier. In the code below, we use the After Update event of the supplier combo to grab the supplier ID specified by the user. The SELECT statement filters the parts list by supplier ID, and assigns it to the combo's row source. If it's null, the code just clears the parts combo's row source.

```
Private Sub cboSelectSupplier_AfterUpdate()
    If IsNull(cboSelectSupplier) Then
        cboSelectPart.RowSource = ""
    Else
        Dim strSelect As String
        strSelect = "SELECT partNumber, partDescription " & _
            "FROM tblParts WHERE supplierId = " & cboSelectSupplier & _
            " ORDER BY partDescription;"
        cboSelectPart.RowSource = strSelect
    End If
End Sub
```

Limit Rows with Type-Ahead

With this approach, nothing loads into the combo box until the user starts entering data. To see how this works, suppose part numbers can begin with any digit (0–9), and the user enters a "7." Since we now only need to load part numbers that begin with "7," we've radically reduced the number of records we need to display, to roughly only 10 percent of the total. If we have 250,000 parts and we wait for the user to enter the first three digits, on average we'll only need to load about 250 records—which makes for a speedy combo box. We'll use the combo box's Change event to detect when the user starts typing. Here's some sample code:

```
Private Sub cboPartNumber_Change()
    Dim strTyped As String
    Dim strSelect As String
    strTyped = Nz(cboPartNumber.Text,"")
    If Len(strTyped) = 3 Then
        strSelect = "SELECT partNumber FROM tblParts " & _
            "WHERE partNumber LIKE """ & strTyped & "*"" " & _
            "ORDER BY partNumber;"
        cboPartNumber.RowSource = strSelect
    End If
End Sub
```

Note that we use the Text property of the combo box to grab what the user types. That's because until the user leaves the combo box, its Value property isn't set. There are a couple of other subtleties in this code. First, we don't assign any row source until the user types three characters. There's nothing magic about this number—depending on your total number of records, which characters are being typed, and the number of records you'd like displayed in your combo box, you can use fewer or more. You might wonder why we don't continue to narrow the rows as the user types additional characters, which we could easily do using "greater than" instead of "equals" as the length condition. That's because we want to leave the combo box's Auto Expand property on. Once Auto Expand finds a match, it fills in the combo box's Text property with the first match, so we'd wind up filtering on an entire part number—our row source would be reduced to a single record, and not necessarily the one the user is seeking.

A final note: you must match the number of columns in your SELECT statement to the number of columns in your combo box, and you must make sure that the order of the columns corresponds to the display order you specified. The first code example in this fix uses two columns in the SELECT statement; the second code sample uses only one. This technique works fine with or without hidden columns in your combo box.

The Limits of Conditional Formatting

THE ANNOYANCE: I want to highlight records in our articles form whenever an article title contains any of the search terms entered in a text box. Is this possible?

THE FIX: You bet. Conditional formatting is pretty easy to use, and in many situations it works well—but it can only be applied to text and combo boxes. In form Design View, select your control, choose Format→ Conditional Formatting, and use the drop-down menu (Condition 1) and parameter fields. If the condition is based on the field getting focus, or on the value of the field being compared to some other value, the dialog is pretty self-explanatory. What trips people up is that to refer to the value of *another* field or control, you must enclose the name in brackets—otherwise, Access will treat it as a text string.

If the condition you want is more complex, select "Expression Is" from the drop-down Condition 1 menu. Whatever expression you place here will be evaluated, and if it's true, the conditional formatting will be applied. For instance, to solve your problem (say, looking for all articles that relate to the Red Sox winning the World Series), you'd enter something like this: **[articleTitle] Like "*red*" OR [articleTitle] Like "*sox*" OR [articleTitle] Like "*world series*"**. Figure 5-26 shows the result.

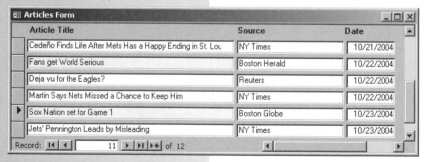

Figure 5-26. Conditional formatting helps users make sense of a mass of information.

So what's the biggest limitation of conditional formatting? You can put as many conditions as you want into a single expression, but you're limited to four distinct display formats. People sometimes want to apply five or more different colors, depending on what range a value falls into, and that just isn't supported. If you really need more than four display formats, and your form is in Single Form View, you can use VB code to set as many control formats—based on as many conditions—as you like. However, this won't work for forms in Continuous View, since Access stores only one copy of its control properties for all the rows of a continuous form. There are various (complex) hacks to get around this limitation; if you're dead set on doing it, search Google groups for the code.

NOTE

Access 2003 has a conditional formatting bug that can bite you. When formatting is applied to a calculated control, Access can go into an infinite recalculation loop and never finish displaying the form. See MSKB 555033 for workarounds. Applying the latest service pack is sometimes all you need to do.

Form Is Blank in Form View

THE ANNOYANCE: I have a form that takes its data from three different tables: patients, doctors, and office visits. It looks fine in Design View, but when I switch to Form View, it's completely blank.

THE FIX: There are a few reasons why Form View comes up blank. Typically this occurs when there are no records to display *and* new records are not allowed. When both conditions are true, Access hides the controls in the detail section (see Figure 5-27). It's like your car's steering wheel disappearing when you run out of gas!

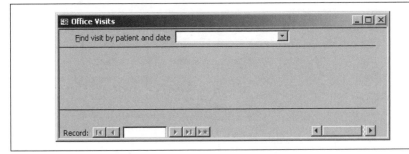

Figure 5-27. The entire detail section of this form is hidden, because it's based on a query that is not updatable and there are no records yet. Only the form header is visible.

Since these two conditions can each have multiple causes, let's break them down:

No records to display

You'll have no records if the table is empty, the query results are empty, or the filter results are empty. You often encounter this problem when you're just starting a design and don't have any data yet. But remember, the form won't be blank unless the second condition is also met.

Can't add new records

You can't add new records if the table or query on which your form is based is not updatable. For instance, totals queries are not updatable, multi-table queries without joins are not updatable, and complex joins are often not updatable. In your case, patients have a one-to-many relationship with both doctors and office visits, and Access won't update a many-one-many relationship. (For more info, see the sidebar "Updatable Queries" in Chapter 4.) There may be other reasons why you can't add new records, too. Make sure that permissions are set correctly and that the database isn't set to read-only. Also make sure that the form's Allow Additions property is set to "Yes."

There are a few other, less common reasons that a form may come up blank. Make sure that the form's Visible property is set to "Yes." Also, if you're using a form header and/or footer, make sure that they're not too large. Headers and footers will cover the detail section if there isn't enough room for both, and the form will appear blank. (For more possible causes, see MSKB 209734.)

Edit User-Entered Data

THE ANNOYANCE: On our customers form, some people enter company names using all caps, and others use upper- and lowercase. I want to apply StrConv() to standardize each new entry to upper- and lowercase, but Access won't let me edit the data.

THE FIX: You're trying to use the Before Update event to grab the data and apply a string conversion to it *before* it goes into the database. This is totally logical, but it won't work. Access has already started an update process, and it won't let you tinker with the data. Instead, it'll hit you with runtime error 2115. The solution is easy: let Access complete the update, and then make your changes in the After Update event.

Can't Save Changes to Data

THE ANNOYANCE: When I try to edit data in a form, save a form, or even exit a field, either I can't or I get an error message. What am I doing wrong?

THE FIX: There are many reasons why you can't edit or save data. In some cases, Access is protecting you or your data in appropriate ways; in other cases, an editing snafu indicates bigger problems with your database. Depending on the cause, you may or may not see an error message; and if you *do* see such a message, it may not be very helpful. Welcome to the Wonderful World of Access!

If you can't edit a field in a form or datasheet, here are some possible causes:

Locked or disabled control

If a control's Locked property is set to "True," you can't edit it. If its Enabled property is set to "False," you can't cursor into the control at all. (See the sidebar "Enabled Versus Locked," earlier in this chapter.)

Can't edit form

If the form's AllowEdits property is set to "False," you can't edit any controls on the form.

AutoNumber or calculated field

AutoNumber fields and calculated fields are not editable. When you try to edit them, a "Control can't be edited" message appears. To change the value in a calculated control, you must edit the underlying fields instead.

Query isn't updatable

If the query aggregates data, contains certain types of joins, or gets its data from an external database, the data may be read-only. If the query's Recordset Type property is set to "Snapshot," the data is read-only. If you want to update this data in your form, change its Record Source to an updatable query. (See the sidebar "Updatable Queries" in Chapter 4.)

Record is locked by another user

If another user is editing the same record or table that you are, you might not be able to make changes. Try again later, or ask other users to save their changes and close the table or form.

Entire database is read-only

If the database (*.mdb*) file is read-only or was opened in read-only mode, or you don't have write permission for it, all the data will be read-only. Check your network permission settings as well as the properties of the database file.

When data can't be saved, Access insists that you fix the problem before you leave the field or close the form. To undo your changes, press Esc—once for changes to the current field, and a second time to undo all changes to the record. Then, if you suspect that the data type or validation settings are inappropriate for the field, open the form or underlying table in Design View to change them.

If you can't leave a field you've changed, here are some possible causes:

Data type

If the data you've entered is inappropriate for the field's data type—for example, you're trying to enter text into a numeric field—Access will reject the change.

Combo box list

A combo box whose Limit To List property is set to "Yes" requires you to select a value from the list, not enter your own.

Field validation

The field's Validation Rule property setting in the table or form might specify a condition that you failed to meet.

BeforeUpdate or Exit event procedures

If one of these procedures contains code that sets `Cancel = True`, you won't be able to leave the field.

If you can't save a record or close a form, here are some possible causes:

Primary key or unique index

You can't save a record if it contains a value that already exists in the table's primary key field, or any field with its Indexed property set to "Yes (No Duplicates)."

Record validation

If you have failed to meet a condition specified in the table's Validation Rule property, you won't be able to save the record.

Required field left blank

If the Required property is set for one or more fields, you can't save a new record without entering values in those fields.

Referential integrity

When relationships between tables enforce referential integrity rules, Access won't let you break them. For example, you can't create a record on the "many" side of a relationship unless a related record exists on the "one" side. (For more information, see "Relationship Angst" in Chapter 3.)

BeforeUpdate or Unload event procedures

If one of these procedures contains code that sets `Cancel = True`, you won't be able to save or close the form.

Write conflict with another user

In a multi-user environment, another user might change a record while you are editing it. In that case, Access displays a "Write Conflict" message asking whether you want to overwrite the other user's changes (see Figure 5-28). To avoid this situation in the future, change locking options so that Access won't let you edit data at the same time as another user. (For more information, see "Access's Bad Defaults" in Chapter 1.)

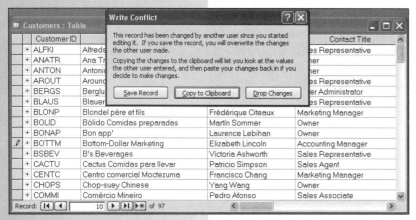

Figure 5-28. You'll see this Write Conflict message when two users are editing the same record.

Some Forms Shouldn't Be Editable by Default

THE ANNOYANCE: While viewing data in a form I created, I discovered that some users had accidentally changed the data! How can I stop this?

THE FIX: While some database systems require users to take special action before editing data, Access makes it easy—maybe too easy—to edit data. If you want to prevent users from editing data inadvertently, you can set properties to lock controls in your form. Then you can add a command button that resets these properties to allow editing (see Figure 5-29).

If you *never* want users to edit data in the underlying tables, simply set the form's Recordset Type property to "Snapshot." Be aware, however, that if you do this with VB code, Access will requery the entire recordset and move focus back to the first record.

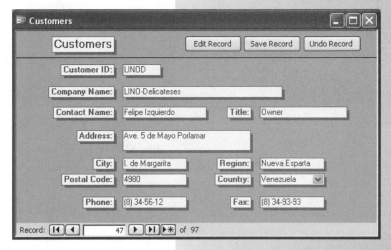

Figure 5-29. Read-only form with a button to allow editing.

On the other hand, if you sometimes need to let users edit data, you'll need code to toggle the controls between the locked and unlocked states. You can do this for the entire form at once, by setting its Allow Edits property to "False." However, if your form includes any unbound controls (such as a combo box that helps users find records), you won't want to lock them. Instead of locking the whole form, lock specific controls by setting their Locked properties to "True."

To allow editing, create a command button on the form that sets the form's Allow Edits property to "True." Then, in the form's Current event procedure, reset the property to lock the controls again:

```
Private Sub cmdEditRecord_Click()
    Me.AllowEdits = True
End Sub

Private Sub Form_Current()
    Me.AllowEdits = False
End Sub
```

To allow editing of individual controls, set the control's Locked property to "False." To toggle a control between locked and unlocked, you'd use something like the following code, where *myControl* is the name of your control:

```
Private Sub cmdEditRecord_Click()
    Me!myControl.Locked = False
End Sub

Private Sub Form_Current()
    Me!myControl.Locked = True
End Sub
```

NOTE

If your code sets Allow Edits to "False" when the record has been changed but not saved, edits will still be allowed until the record is saved. To avoid the problem, save the record programmatically (see "Save a Record" in Chapter 7) before setting Allow Edits to "False."

If you want to prevent users from editing subforms whenever you've locked the main form, use code like this in the Enter and Exit events for the subform control:

```
Private Sub sfOrderDetail_Enter()
    Me!sctlOrders.Form.AllowEdits = Me.AllowEdits
End Sub

Private Sub sfOrderDetail_Exit(Cancel As Integer)
    Me!sctlOrders.Form.AllowEdits = False
End Sub
```

Too Many Controls on One Page

THE ANNOYANCE: My form has too many controls to fit on a single page—users have to scroll down to view fields. Isn't there a better way to organize the fields?

THE FIX: Unless the fields at the bottom of your form are seldom used, you don't want users to have to scroll down to find them. Fortunately, there are other options:

Use tabs.

Programs from Excel to Firefox use tabs to organize related features. You can likewise use Access's Tab control (see Figure 5-30) to subdivide the controls on your form into logical groups. To create a Tab control, open your form in Design View, click the Tab Control tool in the Toolbox, and drag out the area for the tabs on your form. To label the tabs, right-click the Tab control, choose Properties, and type text into the Caption property. Right-click the Tab control again to find other commands, such as Insert Page and Page Order.

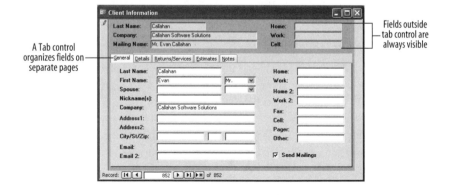

A Tab control organizes fields on separate pages

Fields outside tab control are always visible

Figure 5-30. You can create a form that uses tabs to organize controls into logical groups.

Once your tabs are set up, click the tab where you want to place controls. If you've already placed controls on your original form, you can cut and paste them onto each tab page. (Select each group of controls, click Cut, click the tab you want, and then click Paste.)

Insert page breaks and create buttons that move between pages.

If you don't want to use a Tab control—because, for example, it hides controls so they don't appear when the form is printed—you can still help users find controls that aren't at the top of the form. First, add a Page Break control (available in the Toolbox) at the top of each distinct section of the form. Then place a button in the Form Header section (you may have to choose View→Form Header/Footer first, and then drag open the header). Set the button's Caption to "Page 2," and place the following code in the button's Click event:

```
Private Sub cmdGoToPage2_Click()
    DoCmd.GoToPage 2
End Sub
```

Create additional buttons to take users to each section of the form. In case your users want to jump back to the top of the form at any point, you'll probably also want to add a "Return to Top" button in each section that moves the user back to Page 1.

Move some controls to another form.

You can put less frequently used fields on a separate form, and then create a button on form #1 that opens form #2. You might even want to synchronize the two forms; for information on how to do this, see "Synchronizing Two Forms," earlier in this chapter.

Carry Data Forward to the Next Record

THE ANNOYANCE: I want the default values for fields in a new record to be the values from the previous record. I tried copying the field itself into an expression in the field's Default Value property, but I get #Error?.

THE FIX: Many database systems have a built-in carry forward feature, but not Access. You'll have to create your own. The standard approach is to use each control's Default Value property to carry forward the previous values. However, you can't just set the default value in the properties sheet, because the previous record's value will no longer be available when Access tries to evaluate it. Instead, you need to set the default value in code. Which event procedure you use depends on which records you want to carry the values forward from.

To carry forward fields from the most recently viewed/edited record, add the code to both the Current and After Update events of the form. To carry forward values from the most recently created record, add the code to the

After Insert event instead. The code sets the Default Value property to the current value of the control. (This will override defaults set in the properties sheet, but only until the form is closed.) Because Default Value is a text property, you must put the values that you assign to it in quotation marks. The code is the same for all three events. Here's how you'd use the After Insert event:

```
Private Sub Form_AfterInsert()
    Me!txtCity.DefaultValue = """" & Me!txtCity & """"
    Me!txtState.DefaultValue = """" & Me!txtState & """"
End Sub
```

If you have a lot of controls, you may want to use an approach that iterates through them automatically. Depending on your needs, add the following code to either the form's Current and After Update events or its After Insert event:

```
Private Sub Form_AfterInsert()
    Dim ctl As Control
    Dim strFields As String
    On Error Resume Next
    strFields = ";" & Me!txtAutoFillFields & ";"
    For Each ctl In Me.Controls
        If strFields = "" Or InStr(strFields, ";" & ctl.Name & ";") > 0
Then
            ctl.DefaultValue = """" & ctl.Value & """"
        End If
    Next ctl
End Sub
```

To specify the list of fields you want to fill, create a text box called txtAutoFillFields and set its Visible property to **No**. Set its Default Value property to the list of controls you want to fill, separated by semicolons (for example, you might set Default Value to **"txtSupplierID;txtArrivalDate;txtUnits;txtCost"** to fill just four fields). If you don't create the text box, the code fills every field on the form. You can see that the code uses On Error Resume Next to handle the case where there is no txtAutoFillFields on your form; Visual Basic will recognize an error when it tries to read its value, but the code will just resume at the next line. If that happens, strFields will be empty and the controls loop will process every control.

Reports, Mailing Labels, and Charts

It should go without saying that the information you get *out* of your database is only as useful as the information you put *into* it. However, we've noticed that when people are planning a database, they often fail to budget adequate time for creating reports. While Access's reporting features are powerful, complex issues lurk behind every decision—and it's just plain difficult to make your reports look right, too. If your experience is anything like ours, you will spend more time designing reports (previewing and tweaking and previewing again) than you ever intended. And you will be annoyed.

This chapter starts by dissecting general report annoyances—problems that almost everyone will have encountered by the time they've created a few reports. Since most Access users turn first to the Report Wizard, we'll start there—and once we've covered the basics, we'll move on to parameters, memo fields, and other general annoyances. Then we'll delve into more specialized issues, in the "Page Layout and Printing" and "Sorting, Grouping, and Subreports" sections. Finally, we'll tackle the knotty problems people encounter in two particularly aggravating areas: mailing labels and charts.

GENERAL REPORT ANNOYANCES

Report Wizard Isn't Working Its Magic

THE ANNOYANCE: The Report Wizard asks me a lot of questions I don't know how to answer. Worse, no matter what I do, I can't get it to create the report I want.

THE FIX: The Report Wizard is a fairly flexible tool, but it does ask a lot of questions—and it doesn't always help you make the right choices. Moreover, certain types of reports are beyond the capabilities of the Report Wizard, so you may have to either customize the report it creates in Design View, or start from scratch.

Having said that, in most cases the wizard *will* give you a good head start. To make sure you are getting the most from the Report Wizard, follow these steps:

1. **Choose the right entry point for the wizard.** The simplest way to use the Report Wizard is to create an AutoReport—either Columnar (with records appearing one at a time, with labels to the left of each field) or, more commonly, Tabular (with records appearing in a table, row by row, with field labels at the top of each column). If your report will show data from all the fields in a single table or query, try this first: starting in the Database window, click Reports, and then click New. In the New Report dialog box (Figure 6-1), choose "AutoReport: Columnar" or "AutoReport: Tabular." In the "Choose the table..." drop-down below, select the table or query that contains the data you want to display, and then click OK.

Figure 6-1. The New Report dialog box. You can start the Report Wizard by clicking on "Report Wizard," or selecting one of the "AutoReport" items.

   If you need to include some fields but not others, or if you want to group data, don't use AutoReport. Instead, click "Report Wizard." Consider these tips as you answer the wizard's questions:

   - On the first wizard screen, select the fields you want to appear in your report. You can choose fields from more than one table or query in the Table/Queries drop-down above, as long as you've already specified relationships between them. Be sure to select all the fields you want before clicking the Next button.

   - If you specify grouping levels to organize records in the report, you may want to click the Grouping Options button to group by a date range or by one or more letters at the beginning of a field.

   - If you specify grouping levels, and your data contains numeric fields, the Summary Options button will appear. To display a sum or calculation for each group, click this button and specify the calculations you want the report to perform.

- Be sure to specify one or more fields by which to sort records (last name, then first name, for example). If you specify any group levels, the groups will be sorted automatically; what you must specify is the sort order for the records within each group.

- If your report contains many fields, they may not fit comfortably on a single page. To reduce crowding, you can choose Landscape orientation, or go back and reduce the number of fields you include. To allow fields to spill onto another page, uncheck the "Adjust the field width so all fields fit on a page" box. When you finish answering the wizard's questions, preview your new report and decide on any adjustments you'd like to make.

2. **Apply formatting changes, if desired.** The Report Wizard offers only a few limited style options for your report. AutoReport doesn't even *give* you options; it just uses the style you most recently chose in the Report Wizard. To apply a different format, in report Design View, click Format→AutoFormat. From here, you can select several prefab sets of styles (bold, casual, and so on) that change fonts, borders, and colors.

For still more control, change the formatting manually. Select the desired text boxes or controls, and select a font, size, or alignment from Access's toolbar. (Hint: to select multiple controls, hold down the Shift key while clicking them, or click in the rulers at the top and left side of the window. You can then change the formatting for a group of controls all at once.) Double-clicking in the ruler will bring up the properties sheet; you can also change the formatting of the selected text boxes and/or controls on the properties sheet's Format tab (see Figure 6-2).

3. **Adjust field sizes and locations.** The Report Wizard tries to guess the proper size for each field or label, but it frequently guesses wrong. In report Design View, select controls and drag their handles to resize them; then drag the controls to the desired spots.

Figure 6-2. In report Design View, click the vertical ruler on the left to select multiple controls; then change the formatting using Access's toolbar, or the properties sheet.

4. **Adjust section heights.** When you preview your report, if it has too much vertical space between records, your sections are probably too tall. Drag the bottom of each section to change its height. (See "Too Much Blank Space," later in this chapter, for more information.)

5. **Get help.** For other report ideas, try Access Help. The Report Wizard offers to open Help when the report is complete, but the topic it displays leaves a lot to be desired. Instead, search Help for "report design" (or for a specific topic, such as "report grouping"). For Help on any report or control property, open the properties sheet, click the property, and press F1.

If the wizard gave you a solid head start, continue adjusting your report and consult additional topics in this chapter for solutions to other problems you might encounter. On the other hand, if you can't use what the wizard created, don't despair. In the next Annoyance, "Build a Report from Scratch," we'll show you how to dump the wizard and do just that—build a report from scratch.

Build a Report from Scratch

THE ANNOYANCE: OK, I gave up on the wizard. I selected Insert→Report, clicked "Design View" and selected a table, then clicked OK...and now I'm staring at a blank report. Where do I start? Access doesn't provide a lot of help at this stage.

THE FIX: Report Design View is flexible and powerful. If you want more control than the Report Wizard allows, gather your courage and create a new report from scratch. Here are the steps that will keep you on track:

1. **Get the data source right.** Before you start your report, decide which tables, fields and records you want it to display. You'll specify how you want to group and sort in the report itself, but if you need to join tables, filter records, or include calculated fields, create the right queries before you start. When you create the report, select the name of the underlying table or query in the New Report dialog box, or set the Record Source property after you've started.

2. **Select control defaults.** Before adding fields, decide on the basic format you want for text in your report. To set control defaults, click each of the controls you're likely to use (text box, label, and so on) in the Toolbox, then click View→Properties. From the Format tab, set the Font Name, Font Size, and other properties to your liking. (For more information, see "Define Your Own Defaults for Forms, Reports, and Controls" in Chapter 1.)

3. **Specify report sections.** A blank report includes Page Header and Page Footer sections, where you ordinarily include things like a report's title and page numbers, respectively. You may also want to view the Report Header or Report Footer sections, which appear only once in a given report. To do so, click View→Report Header/Footer. If you decide not to use one of these sections, set its Height property to **0** so it won't use space on the page.

4. **Specify sorting and grouping options.** Click the Sorting and Grouping button on the toolbar, and add fields on which you want to group or sort data (see Figure 6-3). If you want to display headings or summary fields for a given group, set the Group Header and Group Footer properties to **Yes** to display those sections.

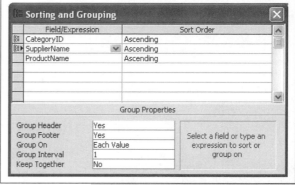

Figure 6-3. In the Sorting and Grouping dialog box, add the fields on which you want to sort or group data, and set the group properties.

5. **Add fields using the Toolbox and Field List.** Click the Field List button to display the fields in the underlying query or table. Click and drag the desired fields from the list to your report.

6. **Add unbound or calculated controls.** Click the Text Box control in the Toolbox, then click the report to create the control. Finally, set the label's Caption property and the text box's Control Source property. For example, you could place a control in the Report Footer section, set the label's Caption to **Total Records**, and set the text box's Control Source to **=Count([ID])**.

7. **Include subreports.** When you want a report to combine data from different sets of records, create separate subreports and add them to the main report. Often, you'll want to include a field on the subreport that links it to the records on the main report. For example, if your main report is based on customer records, you might link to a subreport that displays sales data for each customer. You can also use an unbound main report to combine unrelated subreports, such as subreports for sales totals for the current and previous year.

To add a subreport (once you've created it and saved it separately), simply drag it from the Database window to the desired location on your main report. To synchronize records with the current main report record, set the Link Master Fields and Link Child Fields properties of the subreport control to the name of the field that contains matching values in each record. (If the underlying tables are related, Access sets these properties for you.)

8. **Adjust placement and section height.** To position fields or labels, click them and then use the arrow keys to drag them where you want them; to resize fields or labels, select them and drag their "handles." To change the height of a section, drag the bottom of the section up or down. Remember that the height of each repeating section—especially

the Detail section—has a big impact on how much whitespace appears between records on the report (and how many pages the report takes up).

9. **Set properties as necessary.** Refine your report by setting properties for the overall report, groups, sections, and individual controls. For example, to control how page breaks occur in your report, you can click the Sorting and Grouping button and then set the Keep Together property for sections and groups.

10. **Preview and save frequently.** Switch to Print Preview to see if the changes you're making are having the desired results; if so, return to Design View and click File→Save. If you want to discard changes made since the last time you saved, click File→Revert.

Report Preview Is Too Small

THE ANNOYANCE: Every time I preview a report, I have to reset the window size and zoom in to see what's going on. Even if I save the report at a larger size, Access opens it small (and completely unreadable) the next time. Why can't it open the way *I* want it to?

THE FIX: By default, Access sets every report's Auto Resize property to "Yes," which, perversely, usually opens the report in a tiny window.

To fix the problem, open the report in Design View, click View→Properties, and set Auto Resize to "No." Then set the window size and position to suit yourself, and save the report. From now on, the report will preview at that size (unless the Access window itself is too small, in which case the Print Preview window will be only as large as can fit).

Another solution is to put code in your report's Open event that will maximize it automatically. If you do this, it's important to restore the window's original size (i.e., un-maximize it) when you close the report, because maximizing any window affects all Access windows. Here's how it works. First, create a new macro, add a single line that uses the Maximize action, and save the macro as "Max." Next, create another macro with a single line that uses the Minimize action, and save it as "Min." Then, in each of your reports, call the Max macro from the On Open property (on the Event tab) and the Min macro from the On Close property. To do the same thing with code, place DoCmd.Maximize in the Open event procedure and DoCmd.Minimize in the Close event procedure.

Alas, you can't save a specific zoom level for previewing a report, or change it during event procedures in the report itself. However, if you open the report in preview mode using code, you can set its zoom level like this:

```
DoCmd.OpenReport "Report1", acViewPreview
DoCmd.RunCommand acCmdZoom150
```

Voilà! Your report zooms to 150 percent. To select another RunCommand constant, right-click "acCmdZoom150" in the Visual Basic Editor, and click "List Constants."

Unexpected Parameter Boxes

THE ANNOYANCE: Every time I preview or print my report, the little "Enter Parameter Value" box appears. What did I do to deserve this?

THE FIX: Whenever Access runs a query to display a report, it has to match up all the field names. If there's a name it doesn't recognize, it assumes you've added this field on purpose and *want* Access to display the parameter box so you can enter a value.

To stop this annoying behavior, you must find the offending field name. Make sure that all the field names used in the report's design are spelled correctly and match the actual field names in the underlying tables. Check these areas:

- The Control Source property of all the controls on the report
- The Field/Expression column in the Sorting and Grouping box
- All fields in the report's Record Source

For more information on this common annoyance, see "Enter Parameter Value" in Chapter 1.

Calculated Field Shows #Error?

THE ANNOYANCE: I entered an expression for a calculated field and it looks right. But when I preview or print the report, the field shows #Error?.

THE FIX: When Access can't evaluate an expression, it displays #Error? in the field. If your expression was entered properly, your text box probably has the same name as its underlying field. (This happens frequently, because Access names bound controls after the fields they display.) Using a field name for the control causes a circular reference, because you are referring to the control's name while trying to set its value.

The simplest solution is to rename the control. Double-click the control in Design View to display its properties, and change the value of its Name property on the Other tab. For example, for a text box whose Control Source is =Year([StartDate]), you could change the Name property from StartDate to txtStartYear. This would clear up the confusion and allow Access to evaluate the expression. For more information, see "#Name? and #Error?" in Chapter 1.

Truncated Memo Field

THE ANNOYANCE: I added a text box to my report to display data in a memo field, but the text gets cut off.

THE FIX: Make sure that the text box is big enough to display the data in the memo field. Either resize it manually, or use the properties sheet to set the Can Grow property to "Yes" for both the text box and the report section it's in. Preview your report to see if the entire memo field's contents can now be viewed.

Even when there's room for the memo text, Access will cut it off after 255 characters—under certain conditions. Here's why, and what to do about it:

Format property is set.
> It doesn't make sense to use a format setting with a memo field, but you might have set the property inadvertently. Check the Format property of the text box that displays the memo *and* the Format property of the field in the underlying table. Clear any settings you find.

Grouping in totals query.
> If the underlying query is a totals query, Access truncates fields that are used in grouping data. You might be able to work around the problem by displaying the memo field's value without grouping by that field.
>
> Open the underlying query in Design View by clicking the report's properties sheet, selecting the Data tab, and, in the Record Source property, clicking the Build (...) button. Look in the query design grid—if the memo field has "Group By" in the Total row, change it to "First." This will solve the truncation problem, but the field name will change to FirstOf<MemoFieldName>. Back in report Design View, change the memo field's Control Source to the new name.

Reports with No Data

THE ANNOYANCE: When I open an empty report—one based on a query that returns no records—the report is completely blank, and its calculated fields display #Error? values. Can't Access just say that there are no records in the report?

THE FIX: Yes, but to force Access to do this you will need to create a macro or write some VB code. Reports have a NoData event, so you can perform any action you want when there are no records to display. The simplest fix is to click Insert→Macro and create a macro (see Figure 6-4). Use the MsgBox action to display your message (e.g., "Report wouldn't display any records"). If you want to prevent the report from printing (or previewing) after the user sees the message, include the CancelEvent action. Save the macro with a name such as "NoData." In each report, set the On No Data property (on the Events tab of the report's properties sheet) to the name of the macro.

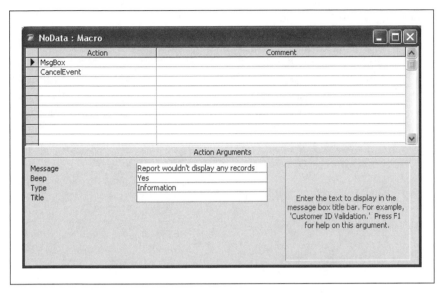

Figure 6-4. You can create a macro that will display a message when a report is empty.

If you'd rather use Visual Basic to add code to the report's NoData event procedure, you can do some fancy stuff. For instance, if you want to prevent the report from printing and have Access issue a clear message, set the Cancel argument to True and add the MsgBox line shown here:

```
Private Sub Report_NoData(Cancel As Integer)
    MsgBox "The report wouldn't display any data.", vbExclamation
    Cancel = True
End Sub
```

If you want to allow users to print or preview a report, even when it has no data (perhaps you need to file a monthly report even when there's no activity), you can display a message in the report itself noting that there are no records. To do this, create a label on the report that will display your message, and set its Visible property to "False" (so it won't ordinarily appear). Then, in the NoData event procedure, use this code to change the property to "True":

```
Private Sub Report_NoData(Cancel As Integer)
    lblNoDataMessage.Visible = True
End Sub
```

If there are any controls on the report that cause problems when there are no records (such as calculated controls), hide them the same way (by setting Visible to "False").

— **NOTE** —

If you use the NoData event procedure to prevent a blank report from printing, you may get an "OpenReport action was canceled" message when you cancel the report. For error-handling tips, see the next Annoyance, "Error 2501: The OpenReport Action Was Canceled."

Error 2501: The OpenReport Action Was Canceled

THE ANNOYANCE: I've set up the NoData event procedure (as you suggested in the previous Annoyance) to cancel printing when there's no data. But now, when I click the command button that opens the report, the code is interrupted with an error: "Error 2501: The OpenReport action was canceled." I canceled the report intentionally; why does this error show up?

THE FIX: Whenever you use DoCmd.OpenReport and then cancel the report as it opens (manually or in code), you'll see this unhelpful error. To prevent it, use error handling in the procedure that opens the report. Here is an example:

```
Private Sub cmdOpenReport_Click()
On Error GoTo Err_cmdOpenReport_Click

    DoCmd.OpenReport "rptEmpty", acPreview

Exit_cmdOpenReport_Click:
    Exit Sub

Err_cmdOpenReport_Click:
    If Err <> 2501 Then
            MsgBox Err.Description
    End If
    Resume Exit_cmdOpenReport_Click

End Sub
```

The On Error GoTo statement sets up an "error trap" that redirects code whenever there is an error. If the DoCmd.OpenReport method fails to open the report for any reason, you'll jump to the bottom section, which displays an error message for unanticipated errors but ignores good old Error 2501.

Filter with Parameters

THE ANNOYANCE: I have a report that I usually want to restrict to specific sets of records—sometimes just one record. For example, I might want the report to show records for just the customer I'm working with. Please don't tell me I have to save separate reports for each customer!

THE FIX: It depends. If you frequently run a report to display the same subset of records, it makes sense to save a separate version of the report with its own query. If you want a flexible report that can display a different subset of records each time you print it, there are various ways to filter records on the fly.

The simplest way to filter a report is to add one or more parameters to its underlying query. Then, every time you run the report, a parameter box will pop up asking you for the value to use for filtering the records. For example, if you want a report to print records for a specific customer, you could add a parameter for the CustomerID field, and you'd get a parameter box like the one in Figure 6-5.

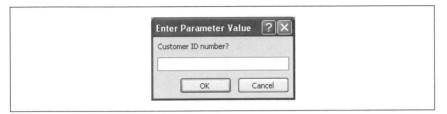

Figure 6-5. Add parameters to your query, and you'll be prompted for a value on which to filter the records.

To add a parameter, open the report's underlying query in Design View. (Open the report's properties sheet, go to the Data tab, and, in the Record Source property, click the Build button.) In the Criteria row under the field you want to filter, enter the message you want to appear in the parameter box, in square brackets (see Figure 6-6). Pick a descriptive phrase for the parameter name, such as **[Customer ID Number?]**. To test your parameter, switch to Datasheet View.

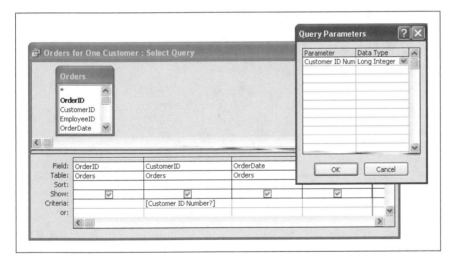

Figure 6-6. A query with a parameter.

To ensure that Access interprets your parameters correctly, it's always a good idea to declare the parameter's data type—especially when the parameter doesn't use the Text data type (for instance, when it's a date or a number). Click Query→Parameters, and enter the name and data type of each parameter in the query. For more ideas on using parameters, see "User-Friendly Parameter Queries" in Chapter 4.

> **NOTE**
>
> *Once your parameters are working properly, you may want to display them in your report. For example, if you filter records to display information for just one specific customer, you might want to use that customer's ID as the title for the report. To do this, just add an unbound text box to the report and set its Control Source to the parameter name. To create an unbound text box, open the report in Design View, click the Text Box button in the Toolbox, then click in the report. An unbound text box will be placed in the report. Right-click it, select "Properties," and go to the Data tab, where Control Source lives.*

Using parameters in your query isn't always the best approach. If you use multiple parameters, you'll get boxes popping up one after another when you run the report. For a friendlier and more flexible interface, consider these options:

Let users select a saved query as a filter.

When you open a report using DoCmd.OpenReport, you can optionally supply the name of a query to use as a filter. The query must include the same tables as the report's underlying query, but it can include additional criteria to filter records in the report. For example, to filter customer records based on State and Country fields, you could save three queries called "In State," "Out of State," and "International." Then, create a form with a list or combo box that users can use to select one of these queries. On the form, add a command button that uses the following code to generate your report (where lbxFilterQuery is the name of the list or combo box containing query names):

```
Private Sub cmdOpenReport_Click()
    DoCmd.OpenReport "rptCustomers", acViewPreview, lbxFilterQuery
End Sub
```

Apply the current filter from a form.

If you filter records in forms—using the Filter by Form or Filter by Selection buttons on the toolbar, for example—you can give users, via a form, a way to open a report based on the current filtered set of records. To do this, create a button on the form and use the following code in its Click event procedure:

```
Private Sub cmdOpenReport_Click()
    If Len(Me.Filter) > 0 And Me.FilterOn Then
        DoCmd.OpenReport "rptCustomers", acViewPreview, , Me.Filter
    Else
        DoCmd.OpenReport "rptCustomers", acViewPreview
    End If
End Sub
```

Build a custom WHERE clause to filter the report.

If you need a user-friendly way for users to select the records they want, you can build custom criteria based on the selections they make in a form (see Figure 6-7). This option requires the most work to set up, but it also provides the most intuitive way for users to filter records.

For example, to filter an Orders report by the OrderDate field, you could create a form with text boxes called txtStartDate and txtEndDate. (Tip: set the Default Value properties of these controls to appropriate defaults, such as **#1/1/2004#** and

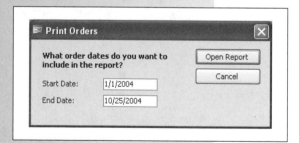

Figure 6-7. This custom form collects the date range for a report.

=**Date()**.) Then, create a button that uses the following code to open your report:

```
Private Sub cmdOpenReport_Click()
    Dim strWhere As String

    If IsNull(Me!txtStartDate) Or IsNull(Me!txtEndDate) Then
        DoCmd.OpenReport "rptOrders", acViewPreview
    Else
        ' Build the WHERE clause.
        strWhere = "[OrderDate] Between #" & Me!txtStartDate & _
            "# And #" & Me!txtEndDate & "#"
        DoCmd.OpenReport "rptOrders", acViewPreview, , strWhere
    End If
End Sub
```

Here's how the code works. If the dates are both filled in (i.e., not null), the code builds a WHERE clause that filters records based on the value of the OrderDate field, disregarding any records where the order date is outside the user-specified range. The WHERE clause then gets passed to the OpenReport method as the fourth (WhereCondition) argument, causing a report to be generated with this filter applied.

As you can see, the code must account for cases where the user does not enter both filter values. Your own filtering code will probably be more complex, requiring several lines of code to build the WHERE clause. Your form might include list boxes, option groups, or other controls where users can specify multiple filter values.

When developing this type of code, make sure you test the value of the strWhere variable with all possible entries in the form; if the WHERE clause syntax is invalid, an error will occur.

> **NOTE**
>
> *Programmers may find it odd that we're suggesting passing the filter string in the WhereCondition argument of OpenReport (the fourth argument), rather than in the FilterName argument (the third argument). It reveals an inconsistency in the way things are named in Access: the FilterName argument must be the name of a saved query, while the WhereCondition argument is a string containing criteria (like the form's Filter property setting).*

TIP

In a WHERE clause, always include quotation marks around string values and # signs around dates (see ""Quotes", #Quotes#, and more #%&@!! """"Quotes""""" in Chapter 7).

Number Records Consecutively

THE ANNOYANCE: I put an ID field on my report because I want records to be numbered. But AutoNumber fields are not always consecutive—numbers get skipped or deleted all the time. Is there a way to number records consecutively on the report?

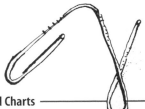

THE FIX: For a report that looks like the one in Figure 6-8, add an unbound text box to the Detail section of the report and place it wherever you want the record numbers to appear. Set its Control Source property to **=1** and its Running Sum property to **Over Group** or **Over All**.

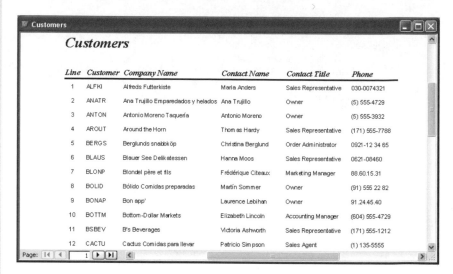

Figure 6-8. You can coerce a report into printing with consecutive line numbers.

Export to Word/RTF

THE ANNOYANCE: I exported my report in Rich Text Format (RTF) format and opened it in Microsoft Word. Most of the data is there, but the formatting isn't the same, some labels and fields are truncated, and lines and charts didn't come across at all. There must be a better—and more complete—way to move reports into Word.

THE FIX: When you export a report to RTF, or use the Publish It to Microsoft Word button, Access puts your data into a document with a similar layout to your report. This can be useful if you want to send a report to someone who doesn't use Access, but it seldom produces an accurate rendition of your Access report. Worse, the document may be missing some data. If the exported report is close enough to what you want, you may be able to work around the shortcomings. For example, if fields or labels are truncated in Word, increase their size in Access and export again. If there are lines or boxes on your report, you can recreate them in Word using Format→ Borders and Shading. Copy any other missing items into Word, and apply the necessary formatting to make the report look right.

If the exported report is *way* off, there are several alternatives, depending on your requirements:

The report must be viewable in Word.

Try Access guru Stephen Lebans's free ReportUtilities suite (*http://www.lebans.com/ReportUtilities.htm*). It will convert your report into a series of Enhanced Metafile (EMF) images embedded in an RTF file, preserving all formatting, layout, and graphics. One downside: the result isn't editable. One plus: if you have any questions, Lebans actively fields queries and bug reports on the Access newsgroups.

The report must be editable/updatable in Word.

The easiest way to create an editable report is to simply pour the Access data into a Word table. First, "draw" the table in Word. Then, in Word, click View→Toolbars→Database and click the Insert Database button. Follow the steps to specify the data source, query, and formatting options. If you want Word to update the data automatically whenever it changes in Access, check the "Insert Data As Field" box in the Insert Data dialog box. For more information, search Word's Help for "Access data."

You simply want to move data into a Word document.

Don't go through all this trouble! Just copy records from your Access datasheet and paste them into Word. You'll get a simple table of records with headings at the top, and you can use Word to format it as you please.

The report must be viewable anywhere.

From Access, export the report as a Portable Document Format (PDF) file. PDF files are the de facto standard for read-only documents requiring wide distribution. They are viewable with Adobe's free and ubiquitous Acrobat Reader.

There's only one catch: Access doesn't export directly to PDF format, so you'll need the full version of Adobe Acrobat (the Standard 7.0 edition that goes for a whopping $299), or one of its competitors. There are more affordable alternatives, such as the $49 PDF4U (*http://www.pdf4free.com*) and the free CutePDF Writer (*http://www.cutepdf.com*). Many PDF writers install as print drivers, so to export your Access report, all you do is "print" it, selecting the PDF writer as the "printer."

Multiple users must export reports in a distributable format.

Installing a PDF writer on every client may not be a viable solution. In this case, Microsoft's Snapshot (SNP) format may be a better way to go. Like PDFs, SNPs preserve report formatting, and the snapshot viewer is included with Microsoft Office. (If you need to distribute copies to non-Office users, the viewer is freely downloadable; see MSKB 175274). When you export to SNP from Access (File→Export→Save as type), you'll be prompted to install the snapshot viewer if it's not already installed.

Give Up and Try Excel Instead

THE ANNOYANCE: I'm an Excel ace but a newbie at Access, and I can't get my Access report to look right. Can you tell me how to get the data into Excel?

THE FIX: If you're accustomed to working in Excel, it might make sense to create and format your reports there. To bring Access data from an existing table or query into Excel, in Excel, click Data→Import External Data→Import Data. (In Excel 2000, select Data→Get External Data→New Database Query.) This brings up the Select Data Source dialog box, where you can choose from a variety of data sources—including MDB. Browse to and select the desired MDB file; you'll then see a series of dialog boxes that let you specify the username and password (if any) for your database and choose which table or query to import. The exact sequence of dialogs you'll see depends on your setup. The last one will be the Import Data dialog, which lets you specify where in your workbook you want the data to go.

These dialogs are mostly self-explanatory, but there's one gotcha: Excel's Select Table dialog (Choose Columns in Excel 2000) won't list any Access query that uses an expression or function (such as MonthName) or any user-defined function that Excel doesn't recognize. If it doesn't recognize yours, you'll have to create a version of the query that doesn't use that function. What a pain in the neck!

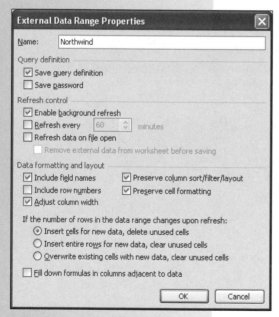

Figure 6-9. The Data Range Properties dialog includes options for data refresh, passwords, formatting, and more.

When you import data into Excel, Excel links to the Access database so it can update your data automatically. You can specify refresh options by simply right-clicking anywhere in the imported data in the Excel worksheet and selecting "Data Range Properties" (see Figure 6-9). Excel will automatically handle your query or table by adding rows over time. The External Data Range Properties dialog also gives you several options for dealing with new or deleted rows. The default, "Insert cells for new data," is generally fine, and formulas and charts that refer to your data range will automatically pick up the new cells as well. You can refresh the data manually by right-clicking anywhere in the imported cells and choosing "Refresh Data," or by clicking the appropriate button on Excel's External Data toolbar. The Data Range Properties dialog also has other useful settings that cover range names, passwords, and data formatting.

If you won't need to update your data after moving it into Excel, or if you have an older version of Excel that doesn't support external data ranges, don't bother linking to Access—just move the data. You can copy a table or query in the Access Database window (or records in a datasheet) and paste the data into Excel. You can also export data directly to an Excel spreadsheet by selecting a table or query and clicking File→Export. If you have trouble, check out the topics in the "Importing, Linking, and Exporting Data" section in Chapter 3.

PAGE LAYOUT AND PRINTING

Too Much Blank Space

THE ANNOYANCE: My report layout has big, blank gaps that cause it to take up too many pages. I tried setting the Can Shrink property, but the blank space is still there.

THE FIX: Adjusting the vertical space between fields and sections is tricky. It's even trickier when you use the Can Shrink and Can Grow properties, because in many situations they don't work as expected.

The most important factor controlling blank space in your report is the height of each section—especially a repeating section, such as the Detail section. If you leave extra space in the Detail section (see Figure 6-10), it will fill your report with blank spaces. To reduce the vertical spacing in your report, move controls (fields and so on) to the top of each section, and drag the bottom of the section up snugly underneath the controls.

> **NOTE**
>
> *You'd think that setting a section's Can Shrink property to "True" would cause any extra blank space in that section to be eliminated. Not so! A section will shrink only to the extent that the controls in it shrink (as described in this section).*

Make sure fields are near the top of the Detail section...

... and drag up the bottom of the section to eliminate extra space

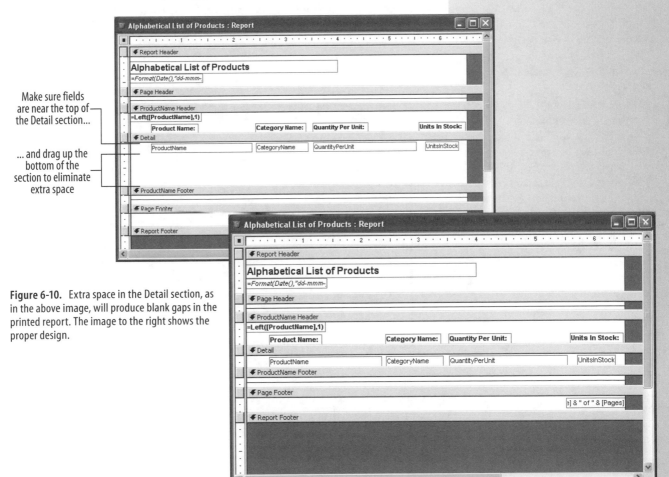

Figure 6-10. Extra space in the Detail section, as in the above image, will produce blank gaps in the printed report. The image to the right shows the proper design.

Can Fields Shrink or Grow Horizontally?

The Can Shrink and Can Grow properties affect only *vertical* space. If you want fields to appear closer together horizontally, or if you want them to widen to fit longer values, you must move and resize them manually. Be aware of the total available width of your report; if you make the report wider, you may need to adjust the margins or page orientation accordingly.

Note, too, that if you reduce field widths, some long values may not fit. In this case, set the Can Grow property to "Yes" (for both the fields and the sections that contain them) so your fields can expand vertically to compensate.

If you want to eliminate the horizontal space between fields—for example, if you want last names to appear right next to first names—use a single calculated field that concatenates the field values. For example, you can replace FirstName and LastName fields with a single text box if you set the Control Source property to:

```
=[FirstName] & " " & [LastName]
```

In addition to section height, consider the sizes of the text box controls themselves. A text box must be large enough to accommodate the largest chunk of data stored in that field. But if the fields on your report are occasionally blank, or the length of the data in a field varies a lot from record to record, you don't want every record to take up enough space to allow its fields to display their largest possible values. Instead, use the Can Shrink and Can Grow properties to adjust the field sizes from record to record. This minimizes blank space. Here are two basic strategies:

Make the field smaller and use Can Grow.

If most values in a field take just one line, but some contain long values that need more space, double-click the field in Design View to open its properties sheet, and set its Can Grow property (on the Format tab) to "Yes." You must also set Can Grow to "Yes" for the report section that contains the field (usually the Detail section). Whenever a field is too small for its data, it will expand vertically, expanding its section along with it.

Make the field larger and use Can Shrink.

If a field is blank, you may not want it to take up any space on the report. In this case, set the Can Shrink property for the field—and its section—to "Yes" (see Figure 6-11). When a line on your report contains only empty fields, blank space will not appear.

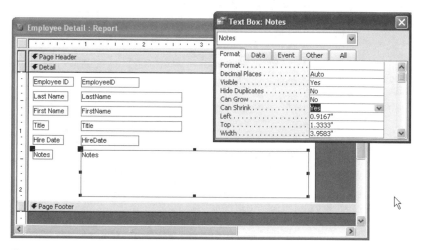

Figure 6-11. Set the Can Shrink property of the Notes memo field to "Yes" so that it will shrink automatically if the full height of the text box is not required.

Shrinking and growing controls can get tricky. For example, if another control—a label, line, or object—is adjacent to the "shrinking" field, the shrinking field won't shrink. The simplest solution, of course, is to move the controls so they don't overlap.

Also, if your field has an attached label, you might expect the label to automatically shrink with the field—but no such luck. You can, however, hide the label whenever the field is empty. First, give the label control a recognizable name that you can refer to, such as "lblNotes." Then, to hide the label, use code such as this in the Format event for the section containing the field:

```
Private Sub Detail_Format(Cancel As Integer, FormatCount As Integer)
    lblNotes.Visible = Not IsNull(Me.Notes)
End Sub
```

Whenever the Notes field is null, this code sets the label's Visible property to "False" (i.e., hides it), allowing the Notes field and label to shrink.

If the fields you want to shrink are adjacent to a tall object or field that *can't* shrink, you can avoid blank lines between them. Create a single text box tall enough to display all the fields together. Then create a VB function in your report module that combines the fields into one string with line breaks. For example, the following function combines four fields—FirstName, LastName, Title, and Office—into a single string with no blank lines:

```
Private Function NameTitleOffice() As String
   NameTitleOffice = ((Me.FirstName & " " & Me.LastName) + _
      vbNewLine) & (Me.Title + vbNewLine) & Me.OfficeLocation
End Function
```

This code avoids blank lines because the + operator, unlike the & operator, evaluates to null if either side is null. To use the function, set the Control Source for the text box to **=NameTitleOffice()**.

Every Other Page Is Blank

THE ANNOYANCE: When I preview or print my report, every other page is blank (or has just a few characters or lines at the left edge). What gives?

THE FIX: Blank or nearly blank pages show up whenever your report's design is wider than the space available on the page. Access makes it very easy to create this problem, but not so easy to fix it. It typically occurs when you move or resize a control, inadvertently pushing the report width outside the boundaries of the printed page (see Figure 6-12). When you preview or print, Access sees that your report (plus its left and right margins) is too wide for the paper, and it assumes that you want the overflow to appear on a second page. Reports created with a wizard are often set to fill the exact width of the page, so even the slightest increase in report width causes this problem.

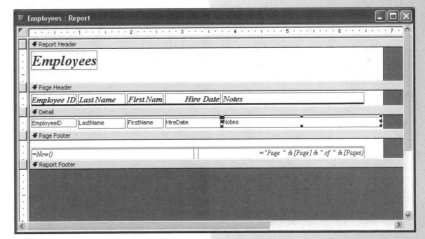

Figure 6-12. When any control moves beyond the right edge of a report—such as the selected Notes field above—the report expands to make room for it.

To avoid the extra pages, use the following simple formula:

Report width + left margin + right margin <= total page width

For example, if your report is 6.5" wide and has 1" left and right margins, it will just fit on a standard 8.5"-wide page.

There are two straightforward fixes for the extra-page problem:

Reduce the width of the report.

Examine the righthand edge of your report in Design View. If any controls extend beyond the others, move them to the left or resize them as necessary. (The Format→Size and Format→Align commands can help here.) Then, drag the righthand edge of any section to the left to resize the report, making it as small as possible.

Increase the page size.

Click File→Page Setup and decrease the left and right margins, or, on the Page tab, switch to Landscape orientation or select a larger paper size.

Blank Page at End of Report

THE ANNOYANCE: A blank page prints at the end of my report. Why? This is driving me crazy.

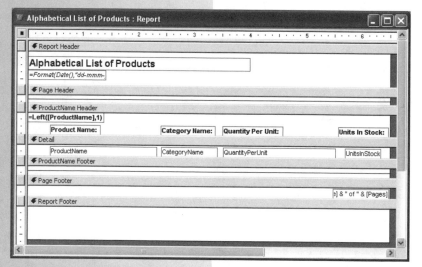

THE FIX: Even if a section is completely blank, it can take up space in your report. A blank page at the end of your report indicates that at least one section—most likely the Report Footer section—has extra space at the bottom (see Figure 6-13).

If the Report Footer section contains no controls, set its Height property to **0**. If any other section has extra space at the end, drag up the bottom of the section to close the gap.

Figure 6-13. The unnecessary space in the footer may cause this report to print a blank page at the end.

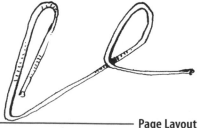

Column Layout Issues

THE ANNOYANCE: My report has only a few fields, so I'm trying to arrange the data in two or three columns (one field to a column) to get more of it on the page. I used File→Page Setup to specify the number of columns and their spacing, but it isn't working.

THE FIX: Columns aren't difficult to set up, but there are a couple of tricks that aren't obvious. For columns to work properly, you must first calculate the amount of space available for each column. In a report with three columns, this formula applies:

> (column width * 3) + (space between columns * 2) + left margin + right margin <= page width

All the stuff on the left must be either less than or equal to the page width. If it is more, the columns won't fit on the page.

For example, to fill a standard 8.5" page, you could have three columns, each 2" wide (6" total), with a .25" space between each column (.5" total) and margins of 1" (2" total). You can specify these settings by clicking File→ Page Setup and, on the Columns tab, filling in the Number of Columns, Column Spacing, and Width properties.

Back in Design View, arrange *just one set of fields* at the left side of the report—not one set of fields for each column. Make sure that the fields don't take up more space than the column width you are shooting for. Reduce the report width to match the column width (by dragging the right side of any section), and you're all set. In the example above, you would reduce the report width to 2," but your report would end up filling the entire 8.5" page because of its column settings.

What if you want your header or footer sections to extend across the page? Leave the report at full width, but make sure all the controls in the Detail section are on the far left side (within the space available for the first column). If you didn't already specify the precise column width, click File→ Page Setup, click the Columns tab, uncheck the "Same as Detail" box, and enter the width under "Column Size" (see Figure 6-14).

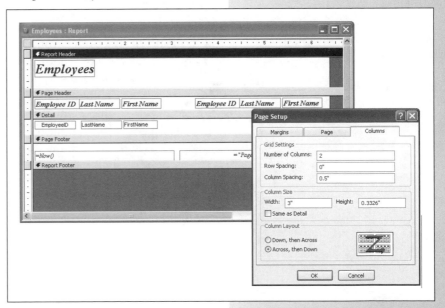

Figure 6-14. A report with two 3" columns and headers extending across the page.

If your report includes column headings in the Page Header section, you may need to duplicate them across the top of the page, even though the fields themselves appear only at the left. Otherwise, the headers will appear only over the first column.

At Least One Printer Required

THE ANNOYANCE: I bought a new computer and copied my database onto its hard drive. Now I can't view my reports in Print Preview! I keep getting a message saying that I have to install a printer. What if I don't *want* to print from this computer?

THE FIX: Access depends on a printer driver to lay out pages in Print Preview. However, you don't need to actually *connect* a printer—just add any printer using the Windows Printers control panel. If there are printers available on your network, installing any network printer will solve this problem.

When you're installing a "ghost" printer (i.e., one that isn't connected) in Windows XP, you'll need to uncheck the "Automatically Detect My Plug and Play Printer" box in order to select a printer from the list. It doesn't matter which printer you choose, but if other computers in your office use a certain printer, that's probably a good choice.

Using the Default Printer

THE ANNOYANCE: When I print my report, Access tries to send it to a printer I don't have access to. I think it was the printer someone in our other office used with the database. Why doesn't Access use my default printer?

THE FIX: Access lets you save a specific printer (in Page Setup) with each form or report. If that printer is no longer connected, you'd think Access would fall back on your system's default printer. Think again. In reality, you'll get an error message every time you try to print the report. To fix the problem, open the report in Design View, click File→Page Setup, click the Page tab, click Default Printer, click OK, and then click File→Save (see Figure 6-15).

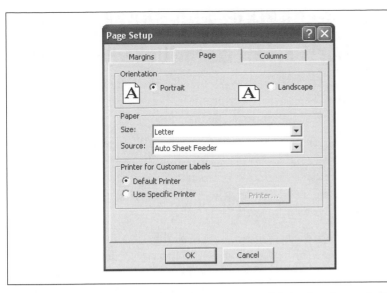

Figure 6-15. Does your report insist on using a mystery printer? Go into Page Setup and tell it to use your PC's default printer.

If you want to reset the printer settings on *all* the reports in a given database so they all use the default printer, use the following code (which works in Access 2002 and later):

```
Sub ClearPrinterSettings()
    Dim rpt As AccessObject

    For Each rpt In CurrentProject.AllReports
        DoCmd.OpenReport rpt.Name, acViewDesign
        If Not Reports(rpt.Name).UseDefaultPrinter Then
            Reports(rpt.Name).UseDefaultPrinter = True
            DoCmd.Save acReport, rpt.Name
        End If
        DoCmd.Close
    Next rpt
End Sub
```

To run this code, enter it into any standard module (Insert→Module), type **ClearPrinterSettings** in the VB Editor's Immediate window, and hit Enter. Repeat this procedure in any other database with unwanted printer settings.

For a good article about checking or changing printer settings in Visual Basic, see *http://msdn.microsoft.com/library/en-us/dnacc2k2/html/ODC_acc10_Printers.asp*.

SORTING, GROUPING, AND SUBREPORTS

Records Aren't Sorted Like the Underlying Query

THE ANNOYANCE: I opened the query that's the record source for my report and added a sort order. The query sorts properly, but records in the report are still in the same screwed-up order as before.

THE FIX: Access has several ways of sorting, and it's often difficult to keep track of them. Setting up sort order or grouping fields via the Sorting and Grouping dialog box overrides any sort instructions in the underlying query. To put records in the desired order, click View→Sorting and Grouping and specify the fields you want to sort.

If you want to change the sort order using Visual Basic—for example, to sort differently each time the report opens—set the SortOrder property of the report's GroupLevel object. The GroupLevel object is a zero-based array containing an entry for each field that your report groups on, so GroupLevel(0) refers to the first group level, GroupLevel(1) to the second, and so on. It's hardly intuitive, but to sort in ascending order you set the SortOrder property to **False**; for descending order, you set it to **True**. For example, the following code changes the sort order of the report's first group level based on a sorting box checked in a form:

```
Private Sub Report_Open(Cancel As Integer)
    If Forms!frmOpenReport!chkDescending Then
            Me.GroupLevel(0).SortOrder = True
    Else
            Me.GroupLevel(0).SortOrder = False
    End If
End Sub
```

To apply an additional sort order *after* any sorting specified in Sorting and Grouping, set the report's Order By and Order By On properties. Set Order By to the name of the field you want to sort, or specify multiple field names (separated by commas), following each field name with **DESC** to sort in descending order; set Order By On to **Yes** (or **True**, in code) to apply the sort. You can set these properties in the report's properties sheet, or use code such as the following:

```
Private Sub Report_Open(Cancel As Integer)
    If Forms!frmOpenReport!chkSortByDate Then
            Me.OrderBy = "[OrderDate] DESC"
            Me.OrderByOn = True
    End If
End Sub
```

Orphaned Group Header

THE ANNOYANCE: My report is designed to group records, but sometimes the group headings appear "orphaned" at the bottom of the page while the records start on the next page (see Figure 6-16). How do I avoid this?

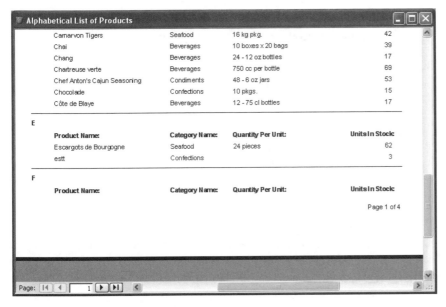

Figure 6-16. Group header appears at bottom of page; records start on next page.

THE FIX: To make a group header move to the next page when there isn't room for any records under it, open the report in Design View, click View→ Sorting and Grouping, click the grouping field in the Field/Expression drop-down list, and then set the Keep Together property to "With First Detail" or "Whole Group."

Beware: if you use "Whole Group," you may end up with partially empty pages, because the header will move to the next page unless *all* records in the group fit on the current page. The "With First Detail" setting is a better choice; with this setting, the header starts on a new page only if *no* records fit underneath.

Subreport Loses Its Headings

THE ANNOYANCE: When I print my subreport on its own, it has a nice header and footer. But when I print the main report, the subreport's header and footer don't appear. How can I bring them back?

THE FIX: As you've discovered, Access ignores a subreport's internal Page Header and Page Footer sections when you print a subreport from within a main report. If you want the subreport's Page Header/Footer controls to appear, move them to the Report Header/Footer or Group Header/Footer sections of the main report.

Total Not Allowed in Page Footer

THE ANNOYANCE: I want to include the count and sum of the orders shown on each page in my report. I placed a text box in the Page Footer section and set its Control Source to calculate the sum, but it displays #Error?.

THE FIX: Access only allows you to calculate aggregate functions per group or per report, not per page. To count and sum the records on each page, you'll need to add a little VB code to three separate event procedures:

1. In the Format event of the Page Header section (in the section's properties sheet, select the Event tab and click the Build button next to the On Format property), add this code:

   ```
   Private Sub PageHeaderSection_Format(Cancel As Integer, _
      FormatCount As Integer)

      curTotal = 0
      intCount = 0
   End Sub
   ```

2. In the Print event of the Detail section, add this code:

   ```
   Private Sub Detail_Print(Cancel As Integer, PrintCount As Integer)
      If PrintCount = 1 Then
         curTotal = curTotal + Me!OrderTotal
         intCount = intCount + 1
      End If
   End Sub
   ```

3. In the Format event of the Page Footer section, add this code:

   ```
   Private Sub PageFooterSection_Format(Cancel As Integer, _
      FormatCount As Integer)

      Me!txtPageTotal = "Page Total: " & Format(curTotal, _
         "$#,##0") & " (" & intCount & " orders)"
   End Sub
   ```

4. Finally, scroll to the top of the code window. At the top of the report module (outside of any event procedure), type the following code to declare the two variables that keep track of the totals between procedures:

   ```
   Dim curTotal As Currency
   Dim intCount As Integer
   ```

The Page Header code resets the totals at the beginning of each page, the Detail section code adds values for the current record, and the Page Footer code sets the value of a text box in the page footer that displays the totals (see Figure 6-17).

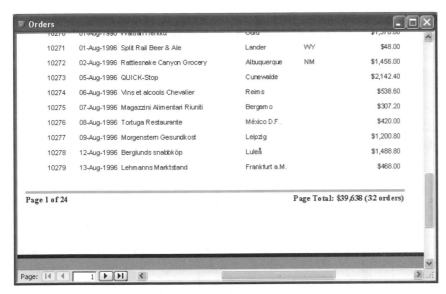

Figure 6-17. With a bit of VB code, you can include page totals in your report's footer.

Crosstab Headings Don't Match

THE ANNOYANCE: I created a report based on a crosstab query. It counts the number of orders by city and splits them into quarterly date ranges. The report worked fine until we moved into a new fiscal year and added records to new date ranges in the query—which meant adding new columns to the crosstab. How can I make sure my report has the same fields as my crosstab query?

THE FIX: A report has a fixed set of fields, even when it's based on a crosstab query. (See the sidebar "Crosstab Traffic" in Chapter 4.) If the underlying data results in new columns in the crosstab, they won't be included in the report. Worse, when a report field no longer has an associated column from the query, you'll get an error when opening the report: "The Microsoft Jet database engine does not recognize <field name>...."

Depending on your requirements, you can choose one of two solutions to this problem.

Fixed Column Headings

If you want the same crosstab columns to appear in your report every time you run it, you can tell your crosstab query to produce those specific fields.

For example, if your crosstab totals values for different product categories, you can list the specific categories you want to show in the report. This will avoid errors on the report, because the fields will always match. However, the report won't include any new columns that are added to the crosstab.

Fixed column headings are especially useful when you expect that some columns might have no data at all. For example, you might include in your report a product category in which you have had no sales. The crosstab query wouldn't ordinarily include that column, but with fixed column headings you can make sure columns will still appear even when they contain no data.

To specify column headings, open the query in Design View. To display the properties sheet, double-click the background in the window above the query design grid, outside a field list. Set the Column Headings property, enclosing each of the column headings in quotes and separating them with commas. The headings you provide must exactly match the names of your crosstab columns (which are values in the field that you've specified as the crosstab's Column Headings field).

For example, suppose you create a report that counts orders for each city. If your crosstab has columns for quarterly order totals, you might set the Column Headings property to **"2003 Q1","2003 Q2","2003 Q3","2003 Q4"** (as in Figure 6-18).

Dynamic Column Headings

If you want your report to adapt to changes in crosstab columns, create a report with all unbound text boxes. Then add code that updates all the labels and text boxes when you open the report. Here are the steps:

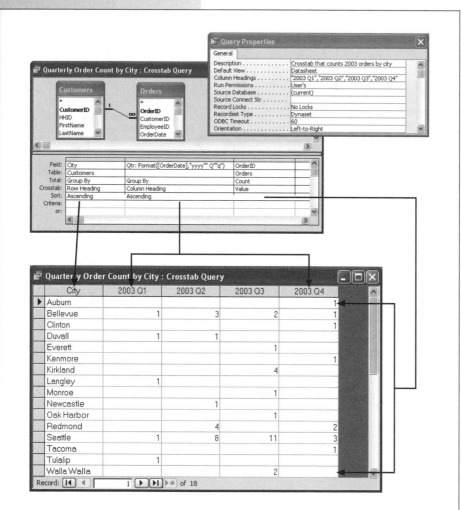

Figure 6-18. This crosstab query uses fixed column headings.

1. Create a crosstab query that produces the rows and columns you want. Don't set the Column Headings property, because you want to use all the current columns each time the query runs.

2. Create a report with unbound text boxes and generic labels, giving them consistent names, such as Label1, Label2, Label3 and Field1, Field2, Field3. Use enough fields to cover the maximum number of columns that you'll need. Your code will hide any that don't get used.

3. Add code in the report's Open event procedure that sets the Caption for each label and the Control Source for each text box. The sample code below assumes that your Detail section consists entirely of text boxes—one for the row header field, and an arbitrary number for the column values. If you have additional controls (such as a line control), subtract those from the intControls value.

```
Private Sub Report_Open(Cancel As Integer)
    Dim rst As DAO.Recordset
    Dim intFields As Integer
    Dim intControls As Integer
    Dim N As Integer

    ' Open a recordset for the crosstab query.
    Set rst = CurrentDb.OpenRecordset(Me.RecordSource)

    ' Find the number of text boxes available in the Detail
    ' section, minus 2 because we don't count the row header
    ' control (City) or the line control.
    intControls = Me.Detail.Controls.Count - 1

    ' Find the number of fields, minus 1, because we don't
    ' count the row header field (City).
    intFields = rst.Fields.Count - 1

    ' We can't use more than intControls number of fields.
    If intFields > intControls Then
        intFields = intControls
    End If

    ' Iterate through report fields to set label captions
    ' and field control sources.
    For N = 1 To intControls
        If N <= intFields Then
            Me.Controls("Label" & N).Caption = _
                rst.Fields(N).Name
            Me.Controls("Field" & N).ControlSource = _
                rst.Fields(N).Name
        Else
            ' Hide extra controls.
            Me.Controls("Label" & N).Visible = False
            Me.Controls("Field" & N).Visible = False
        End If
    Next N
    rst.Close
End Sub
```

Each time the report runs, the current set of fields in the crosstab will appear in the report, while extra fields and labels will be hidden. Figure 6-19 shows the resulting report, in Design View and Print Preview.

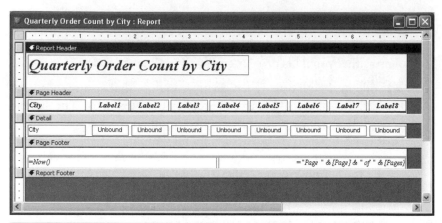

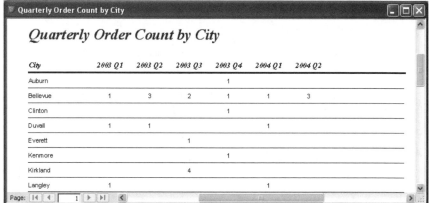

Figure 6-19. The crosstab report in Design View (above) and Print Preview (below). Unbound fields and labels are set dynamically each time the report runs.

MAILING LABELS

Off to See the Wizard

THE ANNOYANCE: In the Database window, I clicked "Create report by using wizard," but I don't see any option for creating mailing labels. Where's this Mailing Label Wizard I've heard about?

THE FIX: Access provides shortcuts to the standard Report Wizard, but for labels or charts, you must go through the New Report dialog box. To create a mailing label report, click Reports in the Database window, click the New button, choose "Label Wizard" from the list box, select the table or query that will provide your data from the drop-down menu, and click OK (see Figure 6-20).

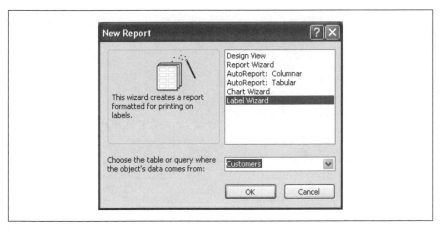

Figure 6-20. Use the New Report dialog box to get to the Label Wizard.

Custom Label Templates

THE ANNOYANCE: I'm setting up my mailing labels using the Label Wizard. I read the entire list of label types, but the one we use isn't on the list. Not that it would help—just as a test I printed out a label type that *is* on the list, and the output still wasn't aligned correctly.

THE FIX: Access won't allow you to download updated label lists (awww...), so if yours isn't listed you may have to create a custom template for it. However, the Label Wizard does include plenty of standard label types, and they aren't always easy to find. When searching the list of label types, make sure you try all the relevant combinations—Unit of Measure (English/Metric), Label Type (Sheet feed/Continuous), and Manufacturer—otherwise, your label may not appear in the list.

If you still can't find your label type, or if you aren't sure of the label manufacturer or number, you can create a custom label template. This will allow you to measure more precisely than Microsoft or Avery did, and account for your printer's margins. Even if your label is in the standard list, the printed labels may not align properly because their built-in specifications aren't correct or don't work with your printer's margins. In these cases, a custom label template might be just the ticket.

Get out your ruler and measure the label's dimensions and spacing. In the first Label Wizard screen, click the Customize button, then the New button. Give your custom label a name and enter all the dimensions carefully. There are text boxes for *nine* different dimensions, including label height and width, label margins, label spacing, and page margins (see Figure 6-21).

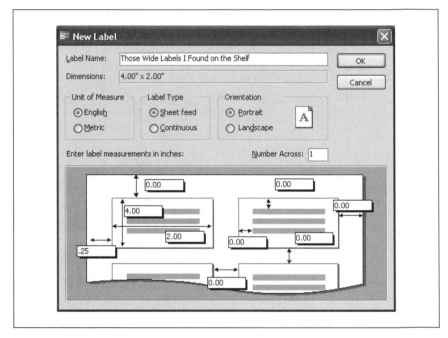

Figure 6-21. If the Label Wizard doesn't include your label type, don't despair—you can create a custom label template with the right dimensions.

It may take some trial and error to get your labels aligned perfectly, but once you do the Label Wizard will be a lot more helpful.

Too Much Label, Not Enough Margin

THE ANNOYANCE: In the Label Wizard, I selected the standard Avery label number to match the labels I bought. When the wizard finished, it said: "Some data may not be displayed. There is not enough horizontal space on the page." Says who? The addresses aren't spilling off the labels!

THE FIX: The error lies not with the Label Wizard, although it *would* be nice if the wizard told you what's wrong. The problem is that your labels are too close to the edge of the page for your printer. Many mailing labels have less than a 1/4" margin, but the minimum margin for your printer may be more than 1/4". (For more information on other margin problems that you may encounter, see "Every Other Page Is Blank" and "Column Layout Issues," earlier in this chapter.)

The best solution, of course, is to buy labels that don't go so close to the edge of the page—but you'd probably prefer to use the labels you have, at least for now. First, simply ignore the error message and print one page of labels. Examine the righthand margin of each row of labels. If your data is not as wide as the entire label and is not being cut off, you can ignore the message and print your labels as they are.

If data is being lost, you'll need to adjust the report settings. Access will have automatically increased the left and right margins to accommodate the minimum margins of your printer, so you'll have to work on the label width and horizontal spacing. Switch to the report's Design View. First, reduce the width of each field just a bit. Then pull in the righthand edge of the report to reduce the width of the label area. This will probably quash the error message, but now your labels won't be properly aligned. To adjust them, click File→ Page Setup, click the Columns tab, and increase the Column Spacing value by a small amount—for example, from 0.125" to 0.175" (see Figure 6-22). Print a page of labels to see the effects of your changes, and readjust as necessary.

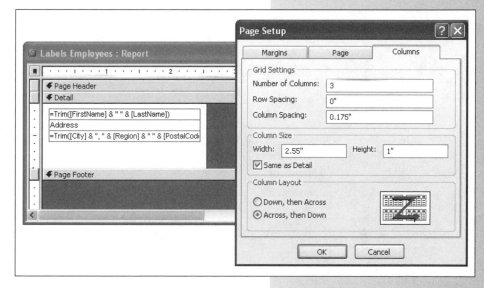

Figure 6-22. Labels too close to the edge of the page? Reduce the width of the field, and then, in Page Setup, increase the column spacing as necessary.

Eliminate Blank Lines, and Other Label Tweaks

THE ANNOYANCE: I created customer mailing labels with two address fields: AddressLine1 and AddressLine2. The problem is, whenever AddressLine2 is blank, Access leaves a blank line in the middle of the label. How can I control exactly what appears on the label?

THE FIX: The most common way to avoid blank lines on a label is to set the offending field's Can Shrink property to "Yes" (see Figure 6-23). As long as there's only one control per line—and they don't overlap at all from top to bottom—the empty control will shrink so it doesn't take up any space. If you still get blank lines with this technique, check whether the control contains any spaces or punctuation marks; if so, it won't shrink. Also, be aware that the space *between* controls never shrinks—only space *inside* them. If there's space between fields on your label, you might want to move them closer together (see "Too Much Blank Space," earlier in this chapter).

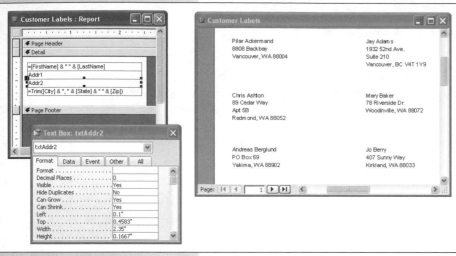

Figure 6-23. With the right property settings (notably, Can Shrink set to "Yes"), text fields on label reports will shrink when empty.

Fortunately, there's a better solution that not only eliminates blank lines, but also addresses other items on many users' label printing "wish lists." The key is to use a single large text box to hold all the address fields, and set the box's Control Source to use an expression that combines all the label fields. Here's how:

1. Type the following utility function into your report module, or into any standard module in your project. (To create a new module, click Insert→Module.) You will then use this function to add line break characters when combining label text.

```
Function sLine(LineOfText As Variant) As String
' Trim text, then add a new line at the end unless zero-length.

    Dim strText As String

    strText = Trim(Nz(LineOfText, ""))
    If Len(strText) > 0 Then
        sLine = strText & vbNewLine
    End If
End Function
```

While you could insert the line breaks directly in your Control Source expression, this function automatically trims blank spaces from around the text you send it, and then adds a line break if there's any text present.

2. Next, type another utility function underneath the first. This function
will combine the city, state, Zip Code, and country:

```
Function csz(City, State, Zip, Optional Country = Null)
    csz = Trim((City + ", ") & (State + " ") & Zip & _
        (" " + Country))
End Function
```

In this function, the + operator evaluates to null if either side is null,
while the & operator disregards null values. In other words, if there is
no city, you get no comma or space following, but you still get the other
fields if they contain values.

Save the module (any name is fine) and switch back to your report.

3. Now you are ready to update your label. On your label report, delete
all but one text box and expand the remaining text box to fill the entire
label.

4. Set the label's Control Source property
to combine all the fields you want on
the label. Use the sLine function to add
line breaks where appropriate (see Figure
6-24). For example, to combine address
fields, you'd enter:

```
=sLine([Name]) & sLine([Addr1]) &
sLine([Addr2]) & csz([City],[State],
[Zip])
```

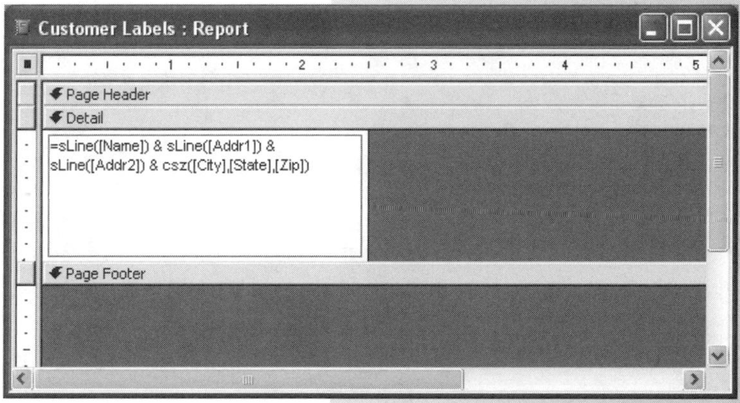

Figure 6-24. To exercise maximum control
over a label's format, use a single text box
to hold all the address info, and then apply
functions to that box.

Once you are using a single text box to contain
the address block for your labels, you'll have
an easier time solving other challenges. For
example, what if you want to include a home
address when no business address is available?
Just rewrite the expression above like this:

```
=sLine([Name]) & IIf(IsNull([Addr1]), sLine([HAddr1]) & sLine([HAddr2])
& csz([HCity],[HState],[HZip]), sLine([Addr1]) & sLine([Addr2]) &
csz([City],[State],[Zip]))
```

In this expression, the IIf function checks whether the Addr1 field is null
and inserts the home address or work address field, as appropriate.

If the conditions you want to handle are complex, your expression can
quickly get out of hand. In that case, create a separate function to combine
fields (similar to the "csz" function above). For example, if you need to
include spouse names and courtesy titles in your name line, write a function to handle all the different possibilities, and then call it from within your
expression to fill in the label.

Prompt for Trim Function

THE ANNOYANCE: I'm trying to print labels, and Access keeps asking me for a "Trim" value. I have no idea what this means.

THE FIX: By default, the Mailing Label Wizard uses the Trim function in every label report; this message indicates that Visual Basic can't find that function. Since Trim is a built-in function, this shouldn't happen—but (sigh) it does. (See MSKB 160870.) Under some conditions, when your database is missing references to required code libraries, VB can't find certain built-in functions. The fix is to clean up your missing references. See "Missing References" in Chapter 1 for more information.

Zip+4 Codes Run Together

THE ANNOYANCE: Why do my Zip+4 Codes run together, with no hyphens, on my mailing labels? When I view them in a table or form they look fine.

THE FIX: This problem occurs because you have an input mask on your Zip Code field that makes the Zip Codes *display* with a hyphen, even though that hyphen isn't actually stored in the field (see "Input Mask Nixes Queries" in Chapter 4). If you place the Zip Code field on its own line, the input mask will work fine and the hyphens will print out properly. However, if you include it on a line with other fields, such as city and state, the input mask won't be applied, because the Label Wizard will combine the fields into a single expression.

To work around this problem, you can fix the label report so that it inserts the hyphen when the Zip Code is nine characters long. Edit the Control Source property for the text box that holds the Zip. Leave the existing expression in place, but replace the field name (such as **[Zip]**) with the following:

```
IIf(Len([Zip]) = 9, Left([Zip], 5) & "-" & Right([Zip], 4), [Zip])
```

This IIf expression tests to see whether Zip has exactly nine characters. If it does, the expression combines the leftmost five characters, a hyphen, and the rightmost four characters; otherwise, it simply returns the Zip value without a hyphen.

More Than One Label for Each Record

THE ANNOYANCE: I'm trying to print multiple copies of a single label. I filtered the records to display only that label (so far, so good). Then I entered the number of copies in the Print dialog box—but Access put the copies on separate pages, so it only printed one label per page!

THE FIX: By default, Access prints one record per label—and there's no easy way to repeat a record multiple times unless your table includes duplicate records. As you've seen, asking for multiple copies will only get you more pages like the first one.

Fortunately, reports have a NextRecord property that gives you precise control over printing. (Don't look for this property in the properties sheet; it's available only in Visual Basic.) By setting this property to **False** during printing, you can cause your report to stay on the same record and print it repeatedly.

To print multiple copies of each label, create a form called frmOpenLabels. On that form, create a text box where users enter the number of label copies they want, and a command button that opens your label report. Then, add the following code to the report's module:

```
Dim intCopy As Integer
Dim intTotalCopies As Integer

Private Sub Report_Open(Cancel As Integer)
    On Error Resume Next

    ' Get the number of copies from the frmOpenLabels form.
    intTotalCopies = Forms!frmOpenLabels!txtLabelCopies
End Sub

Private Sub Detail_Print(Cancel As Integer, PrintCount As Integer)
    intCopy = intCopy + 1
    If intCopy < intTotalCopies Then
            Me.NextRecord = False
    Else
            Me.NextRecord = True
            intCopy = 0
    End If
End Sub
```

The code uses variables to keep track of how many label copies it has printed and the total number of copies you want. In the Print event procedure, it sets the NextRecord property to False to ensure that the record will be repeated until the desired number of copies have been printed. Note that if the user doesn't specify the number of copies to print, it prints normally (one copy per record).

For another solution, check out the free Label Saver module from Peter's Software, at *http://www.peterssoftware.com/ls.htm*.

Printing Partial Sheets of Labels

THE ANNOYANCE: I'm fed up with having to throw away partially used sheets of mailing labels. Can't I start printing in the middle of the page?

THE FIX: Access can only start from the top of the sheet. But if you don't mind writing a bit of code (since these properties are not in the properties sheet), you can skip over labels by setting the report's NextRecord and PrintSection properties.

To skip a specified number of labels, create a form called frmOpenLabels. On that form, create a text box called txtSkipLabels where users enter the number of labels they want to skip, and a command button that opens your label report. Then, add the following code to the report's module:

```
Dim intCurrent As Integer
Dim intSkip As Integer

Private Sub Report_Open(Cancel As Integer)
    On Error Resume Next

    ' Get the number of lables to skip from the frmOpenLabels form.
    intSkip = Forms!frmOpenLabels!txtSkipLabels
End Sub

Private Sub Detail_Print(Cancel As Integer, PrintCount As Integer)
    If intCurrent < intSkip Then
            Me.NextRecord = False
            Me.PrintSection = False
            intCurrent = intCurrent + 1
    End If
End Sub
```

The code uses the `intCurrent` and `intSkip` variables to keep track of which label position is current, and how many labels you want to skip. In the Print event procedure, it sets the NextRecord and PrintSection properties to keep the recordset on the first record while moving through all the label positions you want to skip. Note that if you don't enter a value on the form, it will print normally (without skipping any labels).

For a solution that requires writing far less code, try the free Label Saver module from Peter's Software, at *http://www.peterssoftware.com/ls.htm*.

CHARTS AND GRAPHS

Where's Charting?

THE ANNOYANCE: I know that Access is supposed to support charting, but I've looked everywhere for a chart button and I can't find one. How do I put a chart on my form or report? Also, if I add a chart and it doesn't look right, where are the menus and options to change it?

THE FIX: Charts you create in Microsoft Access are not ordinary Access objects, but embedded objects created by a separate application called Microsoft Graph. Because Graph is not part of Access, its commands and buttons are difficult to find, and its features are buggy (as described below). What's even more annoying is that Access and Graph do not always communicate well. Still, there are times when a chart is a must.

To add a chart to a form or report in Design View, click Insert→Chart, then drag out an area on your form or report where you want the chart to appear. The Chart Wizard (see Figure 6-25) will appear to help you create your chart. Follow the wizard's screens to pick the data source (tables and/or queries) for the chart, the fields, the chart type and name, and so on.

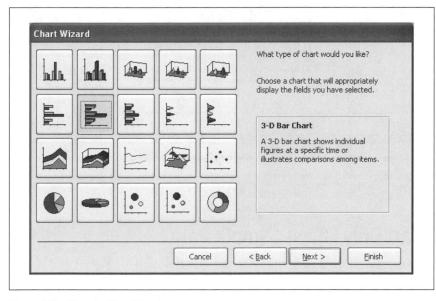

Figure 6-25. Meet the Chart Wizard.

The Chart Wizard rarely gets your chart just right, so you will surely want to make changes. Unfortunately, since charts are embedded objects, this can be tricky. In Design View, click the chart object, and then click the Properties button on the toolbar. Here, you can set properties for the object

> **NOTE**
>
> *When creating a chart on a report, your best bet is to create it on a form first, then copy and paste it onto the report when it is complete. The reason is that charts created on forms reflect underlying data even in Design View, while those created on reports do not. For details, see the next Annoyance, "Chart Only Shows Sample Data."*

control that *contains* your chart. For example, you can specify a border, or change the Row Source that provides data for the chart.

To edit the chart object itself, double-click it (see Figure 6-26). The Access menus and toolbars will be replaced with those for Microsoft Graph, which allow you to change the chart's type, formatting, and options. Double-click an area of the chart, such as the axis, gridlines, title, or legend, to view options for that element. When you are finished editing the chart, click outside the chart control to return to Access.

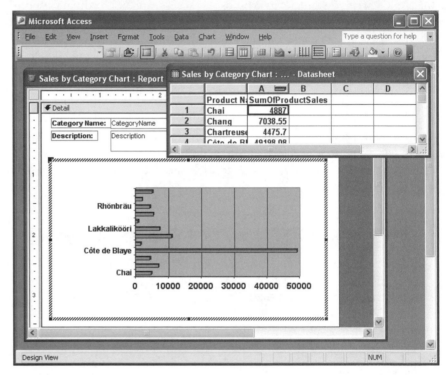

Figure 6-26. Double-click a chart to edit it; double-click an element (such as a label) to edit just that element.

Chart Only Shows Sample Data

THE ANNOYANCE: I created a chart for sales figures, but instead of real data it shows sample data for North, West, and East (see Figure 6-27). I specified the query and fields to use. Why aren't they showing up in the chart?

THE FIX: When you insert a new chart on a form or report, Microsoft Graph displays sample data so that you can get an idea of what the chart will look like. Unfortunately, even when you've provided a valid source of data, your chart will often stubbornly insist on displaying the sample data. This is baffling (to say the least), and it makes it very difficult to format your chart. Here's when you'll see the sample data, and how to banish it:

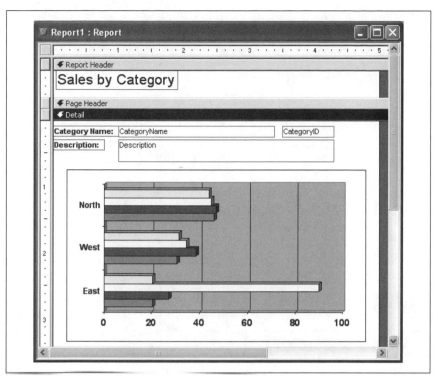

Figure 6-27. Instead of real data, this chart shows "sample" data in Design View.

You created the chart in form Design View and haven't switched views yet.

Switch to Form View or Print Preview to see the real data. When you return to Design View, the chart will continue to display it. (However, the data will not update if the underlying records change. You'll need to switch views again to force it to update.)

You created the chart on a report.

If you created the chart on a report rather than a form, you'll be able to view the real data in Print Preview, but when you return to report Design View the sample data will be back. The fix: create your chart on a form, switching between Design and Form View until you get the chart right. Then, copy the chart and paste it onto your report. The actual data will appear, as it did in form Design View.

If you've already created the chart on your report, copy it to a blank form, switch to Form View and back to Design View, then copy the chart back to your report.

The Locked property of your chart control (i.e., the object frame) is set to "True."

If you are creating the chart on a form, the chart's object frame control will have Locked and Enabled properties (these properties don't exist on a report). When the chart control is locked, Access can't update it before returning to Design View. Set the Locked property to "False" and the Enabled property to "True" (see the sidebar "Enabled Versus Locked" in Chapter 5 for more on these properties).

Your version of Access has problems with Graph.

If these fixes don't work, you may have a buggy version of Access. The initial release of Office XP (and hence, Access 2002/XP), for example, had problems with Graph. (They were fixed in the SP1 release.) Install the latest service pack update for your version of Office before using charts. See "Installation Checklist" in the Appendix for more information.

Chart Changes Are Gone

THE ANNOYANCE: I edited the data labels in my chart. They looked fine in Design View, but when I previewed the report, my changes disappeared! Why weren't my changes saved?

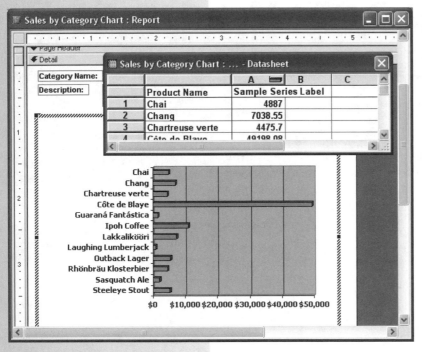

Figure 6-28. Changes you make in Microsoft Graph's datasheet are overridden by underlying data if the chart is bound.

THE FIX: If a chart is bound—that is, if it draws its information from your database—its data and labels come from the chart's underlying data source, not from what you enter in Microsoft Graph. This can be confusing, because Graph has a datasheet where you can enter data to be displayed in your chart. This only works if the chart is unbound. Every time you view a bound chart in Print Preview or Form View, Access gets the current data from the underlying table or query and passes it to Graph, and that data overrides any changes you may have made (see Figure 6-28).

If you want to change the data or labels in a bound chart, you must edit the underlying query so it produces the set of records you want to chart (see Figure 6-29). To change labels that come from field names, such as legend labels, you must provide the field names in the underlying query. For example, if your chart displays data from a totals query, the field name might show up in the chart as "SumOfProductSales." To change the field name, you could precede the field in the query with the name you want, followed by a colon, such as **Total Sales:**.

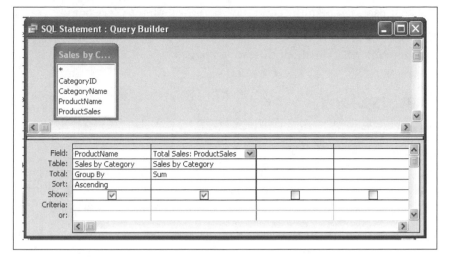

Figure 6-29. Editing the underlying query for a chart.

To change chart data or labels that come from bound data values, you'll have to edit the data in the underlying tables. Alternatively, you may be able to use a calculated field in your query to provide the data values you want. For example, if you wanted to display currency values as "$10K" instead of "$10,000," you would replace the field in your query with a calculated field expression such as **Sales 000s: Sum([ProductSales])\1000**, then set a custom format for your chart's x-axis in Graph, such as **$0k**.

Incorrect Data in Chart

THE ANNOYANCE: My chart is bound to the current record in a report. For some reason, the chart links to the wrong record and displays incorrect data! Is this a bug, or am I going completely crazy?

THE FIX: This is a known bug in Access 97, 2000, and 2002 running under Windows 2000 or XP. Access and Graph are not properly synchronized, and the chart sometimes displays the incorrect record.

To fix the problem for Access 2002 (Office XP), install Service Pack 1 or later. To repair Access 2000 (and 97), insert the following code in the Format event procedure for the section of the report that contains the chart:

```
Me.myChart.Requery
```

If that doesn't do the trick, another option is to insert this code (also in the Format event):

```
Dim i As Integer
For i = 1 To 5
    DoEvents
Next i
```

NOTE

Another time you'll want to edit a chart's underlying query is to change the order of fields or data in the chart. To change the order in which fields appear—in the legend, for example—rearrange the field order in the underlying query (by dragging columns in the design grid). To change the order of data values in the chart, apply a sort order in the query.

In either case, running the code should allow Graph to "get onto the same page" with Access as each record is displayed.

For more information about this Access bug, see MSKB 318096.

Chart Is Blank

THE ANNOYANCE: When I switch to Form View or Print Preview, the chart control is blank. Where'd it go?

THE FIX: A blank chart indicates that the underlying data source for the chart is returning no records. In some cases, you'll see an error message describing the problem; at other times, a blank chart is your only hint.

First, make sure that the chart's data source is correct. In Design View, right-click the chart control and select Properties. Set Row Source Type to "Table/Query," and set Row Source to an existing table or query (or a valid SQL statement). Make sure that the table or query you specify returns records.

If your chart links to each record in your form or report (that is, the chart control's Link Master Fields and Link Child Fields properties are set), you might see a blank chart for some records but not others. For example, if your chart displays sales data for each product category, the chart will appear blank when a category record has no associated products.

When your chart is blank, you might want the chart control itself to be invisible and not take up space. Don't be tempted to use the Can Shrink property—it won't work. Instead, add the code below to the Format event procedure for the section that contains the chart. (For a shortcut to the event procedure, right-click the section header and select "Build Event.") When there are no product records associated with the current supplier record, the code shrinks the chart control completely and adjusts the section height.

```
Private Sub Detail_Format(Cancel As Integer, _
    FormatCount As Integer)

    Dim intRecordsToChart As Integer
    ' Find the number of records that the chart will contain.
    intRecordsToChart = DCount("*", "Products", _
        "SupplierID=" & Nz(Me!SupplierID, 0))
    If intRecordsToChart = 0 Then
        ' Shrink the chart and Detail section.
        Me.Graph1.Height = 0
        Me.Graph1.Width = 0
        Me.Graph1.Visible = False
        Me.Detail.Height = 1080
    Else
```

```
            ' Restore the chart to size and refresh it.
            Me.Detail.Height = 6200
            Me.Graph1.Height = 5220
            Me.Graph1.Width = 6040
            Me.Graph1.Object.Refresh
            Me.Graph1.Visible = True
        End If
End Sub
```

Fixed-Scale Charts

THE ANNOYANCE: I created a chart that appears for each record. The problem is that the scale of the chart varies from record to record, based on the value of the data. For instance, some categories have far fewer sales than others, but in each sales category's chart, bars for product sales fill the available chart area. This makes it very difficult to compare sales values between category records. I tried setting the Maximum value for the axis, but it didn't make any difference.

THE FIX: Unless you provide a specific scale, Graph formats each chart so that the largest value fills the entire chart. Here's how to set up a fixed scale:

1. Double-click the chart to edit it.

2. Double-click the axis you want to keep consistent. (This can be tricky—it's easy to select another part of the chart by mistake. Make sure the dialog box that appears is titled "Format Axis," as in Figure 6-30.)

3. Click the Scale tab, and then type a value in the Maximum box. If you like, you can also set Minimum, Major Unit, and Minor Unit. Make sure the "Auto" box is unchecked for each value you want to apply consistently; otherwise, Graph will adjust the scale again when you view the chart.

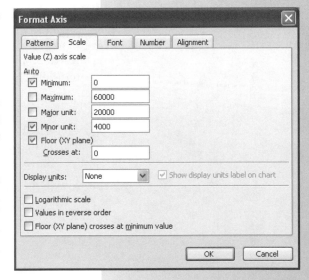

Figure 6-30. Use the Format Axis dialog box to specify a fixed scale for your charts.

Control Charts in Code

THE ANNOYANCE: I want to write code that changes the appearance of my chart, but I can't find the properties or methods to use.

THE FIX: Access includes an object library for Microsoft Graph that includes the Chart object. Using Visual Basic code, you can do just about anything that's possible in the Microsoft Graph interface. However, before using the Chart object in your code, be sure to set a reference to the Microsoft Graph Object Library in the Visual Basic Editor (click Tools→References).

For more information on setting references, see "Missing References" in Chapter 1.

The following code demonstrates how you might take control of a chart on a form. The code sets the chart type, using predefined constants, and (optionally) adds a legend based on the user's selections in two checkboxes. It assumes you've created a chart in a control called myChartControl.

```
Dim theChart As Chart

Set theChart = Me.myChartControl.Object
If Me!chkClustered Then
    theChart.ChartType = xlBarClustered
Else
    theChart.ChartType = xlBarStacked
End If
theChart.HasLegend = Me!chkLegend
```

Link a Chart from Excel

THE ANNOYANCE: I created a chart in Excel and copied it to my Access form. Why doesn't it update automatically?

THE FIX: To place an Excel chart on an Access form and have the chart automatically change when the chart in Excel changes, do the following:

1. In Excel, click the chart and click Edit→Copy.

2. Switch back to your Access form, click Edit→Paste Special, choose "Paste Link," and click OK. Access creates an Unbound Object Frame control to hold the chart object.

3. Set the control's Size Mode property to "Zoom" or "Stretch," so you can resize the chart as needed.

Expressions, Macros, Code Modules, and Custom Controls

7

Using Access without writing your own expressions is like never going beyond paint-by-numbers. Expressions—little snippets of variables and commands—let you customize the way Access works. Working with expressions in Access can be maddening, though, because documentation is often missing, and Access's error messages can be completely unhelpful. We start this chapter by supplying fixes for a variety of expression annoyances, including syntax issues, blank expressions, and common errors. The first section also examines how to work with quoted values, dates, and more.

Then we move on to Visual Basic, a full-blown programming language—this is expressions on steroids! Many Access users hesitate to use Visual Basic because it seems too hard, but the irony is that Access development becomes much easier once you can write a little code. Many of Access's pitfalls and quirks can be sidestepped with a line or two of VB code. We'll show you how to find your way around in Visual Basic (despite the gaps in documentation) and take advantage of the VB Editor, which is actually a pretty nice tool. We'll focus on some of the most common tasks, such as displaying a file chooser dialog box and sending an email from a form. To get a leg up on Access and VB, check out *Access Database Design & Programming*, Third Edition (O'Reilly), *Access Cookbook*, Second Edition (O'Reilly), and *Microsoft Access 2002 Visual Basic for Applications Step by Step* (Microsoft).

EXPRESSIONS

.Dot, !Bang, and [Bracket]

THE ANNOYANCE: I'm writing code, and I need to refer to a subform control's Visible property. Do I use dot or bang? Do I need brackets or not? I'm groping in the dark here!

THE FIX: The syntax VB uses to refer to database objects and their properties is a bit forbidding and certainly nonintuitive—but once you understand it, it's not that big a deal. For analogy's sake, consider the file- and pathnames on your computer. Every file has a short name (such as *Readme.txt*) as well as a full pathname (such as *C:\Cartoons\Dilbert\Readme.txt*). The path specifies exactly where to find that particular file, starting from anywhere on the computer.

Similarly, every database object and property has a short name (such as "txtOrderTotal" or "Visible") and a fully qualified name (such as "Forms! frmOrders!txtOrderTotal" or "Reports!rptOrders.Visible"). In many situations, you can use the short name—for instance, when you're distinguishing one control from another control on the same form. In other situations, such as when you're referring to a control on a form from within a query, you must use the fully qualified name, or Access won't be able to find it.

In the Windows filesystem, path locations are always separated by slashes (\). Access uses two different separators: the bang (!) and the dot (.). Bang is used to refer to user-created objects such as forms, reports, and controls. Dot is used to refer to Access's built-in objects and properties. Consider this example: `Reports!rptOrders.Visible`. The first element, `Reports`, is the name of a built-in collection that contains all the open report objects. The user-defined report, `rptOrders`, is distinguished with the bang notation. The built-in `Visible` property of the orders report is identified using the dot notation.

Why !Bang?

There's a reason why Access has two name separators. The bang notation is shorthand that makes it easier to refer to common types of objects. For example, consider `Forms!frmCustomers`. The Forms object is a built-in collection that contains all open forms. The full way to refer to a form in this collection would be `Forms.Item("frmCustomers")`, because the `Item` method is the way to access the elements contained in a collection. Since `Item` is the "default property" of any collection, you can omit it—it's assumed. You can write `Forms("frmCustomers")`, or

you can use the bang notation, which makes it even more concise: `Forms!frmCustomers`.

Now consider the name `Forms!frmCustomers!txtOrderTotal`, which refers to the orders total text box on the customers form. The full name would be `Forms.Item("frmCustomers"). Controls.Item("txtOrderTotal")`, because controls are contained in a form's `Controls` collection. But, again, since `Controls` is the default property of a form, and `Item` is the default property of a collection, you can replace them with the bang.

In many cases, you'll notice that Access adds brackets around object names (and sometimes property names), like this: [Reports]![rptOrders].[Visible]. These brackets are not normally required, but they do no harm. However, there are two situations in which brackets *are* required. First, if an object name contains spaces or other nonstandard characters, Access needs the brackets in order to handle the name properly. Second, if the name occurs in a context (such as query criteria) where Access might mistake the object name for a text string, the brackets tell Access to treat it as the name of an object. (See "[Brackets] Versus "Quotes"," later in this chapter.)

Finally, we should add that there are two other ways to reference user-defined objects: using quoted names and indexes. A quoted name looks like Reports("rptOrders") and means the same as Reports!rptOrders. Quoted-name syntax permits storing an object name in a variable and then referencing it, like this:

```
Dim strReportName As String
strReportName = "rptOrders"
Reports(strReportName).Visible = False
```

Quoted-name syntax is handy, but just in case this seems too straightforward, know that Access doesn't accept it in queries. Figures!

Index notation, which refers to members of a collection by a numeric index, is most useful in situations where you need to iterate over all the objects in a collection. For example, Reports(0) refers to the first report in the Reports collection, and Reports(Reports.Count - 1) refers to the last. Just remember that collections use a zero-based numbering system.

Expressions That Go Blank

THE ANNOYANCE: My payroll form has a simple expression, =(salary + bonus), that totals salaries and bonuses. I know this expression should never be empty, because salary is a required field—but it's coming up blank.

THE FIX: The most common reason an expression comes up blank is that it's null. Even though part of your expression (the salary field) is not null, what matters is whether the entire expression evaluates to null—and in this case it does, because when you add null to a number you get null. Note that null is not the same as zero!

The fix is to use the Nz function, which converts null values to a default value that you specify. In your case, instead of =(salary + bonus), use =(salary + Nz(bonus,0)). When the bonus field is null, the result is (salary + 0) (because we specified a default of zero). When the bonus field has a value, you get (salary + bonus), as you should.

Nz is not just useful with numeric values. It can also be used with a text field, as in Nz(firstName, ""), to return an empty string if the field is null. You can also have Nz return something other than zero or the empty

NOTE

We don't recommend using the shorthand version of Nz, in which you don't specify any default value—for example, Nz(bonus). In most cases, this will supply an appropriate default (zero for numbers, an empty string for text). However, in some contexts (such as query expressions) it gives an empty string no matter what the data type is. For this reason, we suggest that you always supply an explicit default.

string—for instance, if you use the expression ="Marital status is: " & Nz(maritalStatus, "unknown"), when marital status is null, Nz will return "unknown."

A more obscure reason for unexpected blank values is zero-length strings (i.e., the empty string, ""). Here's how the problem can arise. Suppose you have a query in which you set criteria on the lastName field that dictates it can't be null. You open up the query and see blanks in the lastName field. How is this possible? Well, it's possible if your field is set to allow zero-length strings (check the Allow Zero Length property in table Design View). Zero-length strings are not null, they're just blank. The bad news is that, by default, Access allows them; the good news is that they're not that easy to enter. You can find records containing zero-length strings by setting the Criteria line in the query design grid of the field in your query to "".

Tangled Up in Null

THE ANNOYANCE: I'm trying to apply conditional formatting to the balances on our payments form, using this expression: [balance] <= 0. But the formatting is applied to the wrong records!

THE FIX: This annoyance has nothing to do with conditional formatting—it's about nulls. When expressions give unexpected results, one of the first things to check for is null values. (This isn't a problem specific to Access; nulls are a confusing part of life in the database world at large.) If any part of an expression can be null, you must take that into account. A null value in a field means that no data was entered. Sometimes this means the value is unknown (e.g., DateOfBirth) but it can also mean the data doesn't exist (e.g., SpouseFirstName). You can sometimes avoid nulls by making a field required and defining a default value (such as "None") for cases where no data is entered, but often this is a poor solution. For example, you can't enter "Unknown" in a Date/Time field, and a SpouseFirstName of "None" might mean either no spouse *or* no first name supplied.

Null values are also confusing because they don't behave like ordinary values. Since they represent unknown values, they are treated as values that haven't yet been defined. For example, suppose you're looking for records where [amountPaid] = [rebate]. Records with null values in either field will be excluded from the result, because a null value is not equal to *anything*—not even null. *Null does not equal null.* This is pretty unintuitive, but it does sort of makes sense: just because I don't know Mozart's birthday or Beethoven's birthday doesn't mean they have the same birthday. Similarly, suppose you're looking for all last names other than Smith, using an expression such as this: [lastName] <> "Smith". Null names will not show up in your results, because null values are not *not equal* to anything, either.

In short, *nulls cannot be compared*—to anything. They're not less than anything, they're not greater than anything, they're not equal to, before, or after anything. (And that explains why [balance] <= 0, above, is giving unexpected results—a null balance is not equal to zero.)

To help you cope with nulls, Access provides a number of special functions and expressions:

Nz()

> Used to convert nulls to zeros. Nz([balance],0) <= 0 will treat null balances as equal to zero. By default, Nz() returns zeros, but it can return anything. For more on Nz(), see the previous Annoyance, "Expressions That Go Blank."

Is Null, Is Not Null

> Used in the query design grid to test for nulls (or the lack of nulls). For example, to include null last names in the query mentioned above, in the Criteria line of the lastName field you'd put: **<> "Smith" or Is Null**. You'd use Is Not Null to test for non-null values.

IsNull()

> This is for a null value used to test a Visual Basic function. You can create the equivalent of Nz() by writing IIf(IsNull([balance]), "Balance is unknown", [balance]).

Another instance when nulls cause problems is when you feed them to certain VB functions. For instance, suppose you are using CDbl() to turn integers into double-precision floating-point numbers for the purposes of a calculation. If you feed CDbl() a null value, you'll get a runtime error, "Invalid use of Null." You need to either use Nz() to convert the nulls to some other value—CDbl(Nz([length],0))—or ensure that there are no nulls in the records that get fed into the calculation.

The Group By clause in queries is the one exception to the rule that null does not equal null. You may notice that if you group on a field with null values, all the null records are put into the same group. Although this behavior is inconsistent, it's useful when you need to group on a field that contains null values. If you want to exclude these records, simply put **Is Not Null** in the Criteria line of the grouping field.

Finally, there's one additional twist to working with nulls if you are writing code with ADO (see "DAO Versus ADO" in Chapter 0). When you supply criteria to ADO's Find function, you must test for nulls using the Null keyword, rather than any of the expressions discussed above—for example, [balance] = Null or [balance] <> Null. This is a common practice in VB code, but it's different from the usual tests used in Access SQL.

Debugging Expressions

THE ANNOYANCE: I'm using a complex expression on a form, and it keeps coming up #Name?. I don't know where to begin fixing it.

THE FIX: Trying to guess what's wrong with an expression can be maddening. Start by working through the list of common causes for #Name? and #Error? messages in "#Name? and #Error?" in Chapter 1. There's no way we could list every possibility, but you may get lucky. If not, evaluate the whole expression in the Immediate window (see the upcoming "Rule 3: Examine your data")—this will often produce a more illuminating error message. If *that* doesn't work, take the following systematic approach to debugging your expression. As an example, we'll use this expression, which produces a #Name? error:

```
FormatCurrency(Nz(DLookup(orderTotal, tblOrders, "orderId = """ &
cboOrder)))
```

The following three debugging tips should help you track down the source of the problem.

Rule 1: Simplify, Simplify

The first step in debugging any problematic expression is to start with something small and manageable and gradually build up the expression. In this case, strip away FormatCurrency() and Nz() and start with the DLookup() expression:

```
DLookup(orderTotal, tblOrders, "orderId = """ & cboOrder)
```

What do we get when we evaluate this pared-down expression? We still get a #Name? error. That's good news: we've trapped our bug (at least, one of them) inside a simpler piece of code.

Rule 2: Check the Documentation

DLookup has a complicated syntax that's easy to screw up. Check the Help system to make sure you're using it correctly. Open VB Help (not Access Help) by pressing Ctrl-G to open the VB Editor and then clicking the Help icon on the VBE's toolbar. Search in the Answer Wizard for the function name—in this case, you're looking for DLookup—or just type the keyword name in the Immediate window and press F1. If there's a single help topic for that keyword, it will display immediately; otherwise, you'll see a choice of topics.

There's a lot of useful information in Help—too much, perhaps, if you're not used to reading this kind of documentation. Start by looking at the examples, which are often at the end of the topic. The examples will never exactly match your expression, but in this case, you'll notice that in every DLookup example, the field and table names are enclosed in quotes, like so:

THE FIX: Quoting data in Access can be a little tricky. There are four different data delimiters—five, if you count *no* delimiter as a kind of delimiter (Figure 7-3 shows some examples). That's just too many—and it's only the beginning of the problem. When you have to embed quoted data inside other quotes, it's really easy to make errors. In this fix, we'll clear up some of the confusion about using quotes.

First, the delimiters:

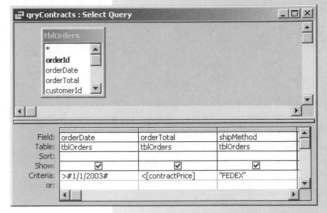

Double quotes (`"This is a test."`)

Double quotes are used to delimit text data. This is essential, since every expression you type looks like text. For instance, in the expression `"Bill & Ted's "` `& "Excellent Adventure"`, the first ampersand is just a text character, but the second is a concatenation operator. The delimiters tell Access which is which.

Figure 7-3. A query showing the use of three different delimiters in its Criteria line. The first column is a date, the second is a field, and the third is a text string.

Pound signs (`#8/2/2004 12:35 AM#`)

The pound sign indicates dates and date/time data. This delimiter is essential, since times and date/times include spaces.

Brackets (`[OrderDate]`)

Brackets delimit object names, such as fields. If, as we strongly recommend, you avoid using spaces in object names, brackets are not usually needed. (See the exceptions below.)

Single quotes (`'This is a test.'`)

Single quotes can often be used instead of double quotes to delimit text. There's no good reason to do this, though, and you're likely to run afoul of apostrophes if you do (see "Apostrophe Errors," later in this chapter).

Now, here's where things get more complicated. There are many situations where you need to construct a text value that itself contains delimiters. For example, as described in the introduction to this annoyance, this problem often arises when you need to create the criteria expression for `DLookup()`. A typical `DLookup` criteria looks like this:

```
DLookup("orderTotal", "tblOrders", "orderId = " & [orderId])
```

Here we've concatenated a number (taken from the orderId field) to a text string (`"orderId = "`), resulting in output such as `orderId = 5`. That works great with numbers, but it'll produce an error with other data types, such as dates and text. For dates, you need something like `orderDate = #10/03/2003#`; for text, you need something like `partName = "Widget-7"`.

Here's how to handle dates:

```
DLookup("orderTotal", "tblOrders", "orderDate = #" & [orderDate] & "#")
```

> **NOTE**
>
> *Numbers are the only type of data that don't require a delimiter.*

This DLookup finds the order total that corresponds to the specific date found in the orderDate field. All we did was treat the pound sign as a text character, concatenating it as part of the other strings. This lets us embed the date delimiters into the text string.

It would be nice if you could do the same thing for quotes around text data, but you can't. You can't embed a quotation mark inside quotes, because Access won't know which quote actually delimits the string. Instead, you must use a *pair* of quotes wherever you need an embedded quotation mark. For example, Access translates the text "Embedded "" Quote" into Embedded " Quote.

Here's how you'd construct DLookup criteria for a text field:

```
DLookup("orderTotal", "tblOrders", "partName = """ & [partName] & """")
```

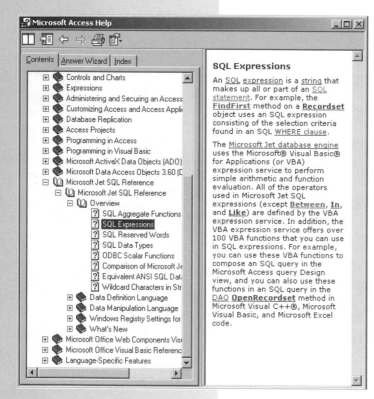

Figure 7-4. If you're willing to dig around in the table of contents, you can find help on these SQL operators.

Like, In, and Between Operators

THE ANNOYANCE: I'm trying to find documentation on the Like operator, but when I ask the Answer Wizard to search for "Like," Access tells me to rephrase my question.

THE FIX: Most operators and functions come from Visual Basic and are documented in VB Help, but three (Like, In, and Between) come from SQL. In addition, because they're named after very common words, the Help search engine considers them too common to even bother searching for. (Actually, it will search for Between—but it won't find the page you're looking for; Access 2003 will find entries for Like, but that's it.)

There *is* documentation for these operators, though. In Access Help's Contents tab, look in Microsoft Jet SQL Reference→Overview→SQL Expressions (see Figure 7-4). Also see "Simple Validation Rules" in Chapter 3 for examples of how these operators are used. You can find additional help for the Like operator by searching for "Like operator" in VB Help.

"Like" Operator Changes to "Alike"

THE ANNOYANCE: I'm trying to create a validation rule using the Like operator, and Access keeps changing it to Alike. Also, it tells me that my data violates the rule, but it doesn't!

THE FIX: If Access changes Like to Alike, that means that your database is set to use SQL-92 syntax. In this case, your wildcards (* and ?) should be % and _ instead. That would explain why your validation rule isn't working as expected. To change back to Access SQL syntax, close all database objects and then choose Tools→Options, click the Tables/Queries tab, and uncheck the "This database" box under "SQL Server Compatible Syntax (ANSI 92)." (This problem occurs only in Access 2002 and later versions.)

Expression-Building Blues

THE ANNOYANCE: I'm using the Expression Builder to construct an expression that will run on our customers form and refer to a control on the orders subform. I found the subform control, but the Expression Builder doesn't list the field I need. How do I make this thing work?

THE FIX: The Expression Builder appears when you click the Build (...) button that you'll see in certain text boxes in a properties sheet. It can be pretty confusing, especially for those who are new to expressions. For one thing, it lets you construct all sorts of invalid expressions; worse, it provides scant guidance on the syntax of functions in general. So is it good for anything? Maybe—as a browser of the objects and functions in your database.

Since expressions are used to manipulate values based on other data, you'll often need to refer to controls, queries, and the like as you create them. For example, if you need to refer to a control on your subform, the Expression Builder can save you from opening the subform and looking up the exact name of that control. Of course, that assumes you can *find* the control you're looking for.

Here's how the builder works. In the bottom-left panel, select an item (see Figure 7-5). Its contents will appear in the middle panel. Click an item in the middle panel, and that item's properties (or contents) will appear in the right panel. Double-click anything in the middle or right panels, and it will show up in the top panel as part of an expression.

If you can't find the control you're looking for, it's probably because you didn't start with that object's parent in the left pane. In your case, you need to double-click the folder icon next to your form name. When the folder opens, you'll see that it contains your orders subform. Click on the subform folder, and *its* contents will appear in the middle panel. Now you'll be able to find the controls on your subform. Locate the control that you want in the middle panel and double-click it. Access will put something like this into the top panel: [sctlOrders]. Form![txtSumOrderTotal]. That's nice—except Access forgets to place an equals sign at the beginning of the expression. You'll have to add it in.

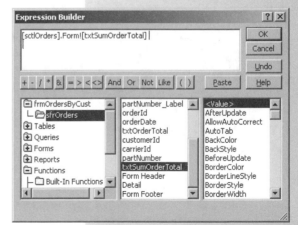

Figure 7-5. Double-click frmOrdersByCust in the left panel, then click sfrOrders to access its contents in the middle panel. Double-click txtSumOrderTotal to insert it into the expression. Note that Access does not supply the required equals sign at the front of the expression.

If you want help building Visual Basic functions, you won't get much in the Expression Builder. For tips on using VB Help, see "Getting Help" in "Tame the Visual Basic Editor," later in this chapter.

Dollar$ Sign$ Functions

THE ANNOYANCE: I looked up the Chr() function because I need to insert line-feed characters in a text string, and I found that VB Help also lists a function called Chr$(). But when I click on Chr$(), I just get the same help page I got for Chr(). Is there a difference?

THE FIX: Help is just so unhelpful sometimes. Beats me why they couldn't put in a link to the (badly named) topic "Returning Strings from Functions"—that's where you get the lowdown on the distinction between Chr$() and Chr(). In VB Help, go to the Contents tab, open the "Visual Basic Conceptual Topics" item, then open "Returning Strings from Functions." (If you can't find *that*, see "Getting Help" in "Tame the Visual Basic Editor," later in this chapter.)

There are about 30 functions that have "dollar sign" versions. As a general rule, you'll be fine sticking with the plain versions—the main difference is that the plain functions return a Variant data type and the dollar sign functions return a String data type. It's easy to remember which is which if you think of the "$" as the "S" in String.

The String data type handles text, and nothing but text; Variant can include text, numbers, dates, and null values. Because of this, plain functions typically handle nulls better than their dollar sign counterparts. For example, suppose you have an expression like Trim(LastName). If LastName is null, Trim() returns null, which is fine. Trim$(), however, can't handle a null value; instead, you get a runtime error—"Invalid use of Null"—that brings everything to a grinding halt. Be aware, though, that not *all* plain functions that have dollar sign counterparts can handle nulls. For example, Chr() will also throw a runtime error if you feed it a null.

Why would you ever use a dollar sign function? If you're concerned about memory use, the dollar sign functions are slightly more RAM-efficient. Also, there are some situations—such as when you're writing directly to files—where your output must be typed as String, not Variant.

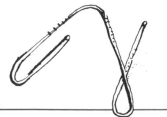

[Brackets] Versus "Quotes"

THE ANNOYANCE: On my orders form, I set the default value of the amount received equal to the order total field, and Access added brackets around it, like this: =[orderTotal]. Then I set the validation rule to 15 percent of the order total, and Access added quotes: > .15 * "orderTotal". Why did Access set orderTotal first with brackets, then with quotes? And why does *every* value I enter violate the validation rule?

THE FIX: Access adds brackets so you can use spaces in field names and object names, such as [Employee Last Name]. (To see why this is a bad idea, read "Bad Field Names" in Chapter 3.) If your names don't have spaces, you probably won't need to use brackets. However (surprise!), Access is not entirely consistent about this, and in certain places brackets are required if you want to refer to a field or object, such as a control. In the Default Value property, for example, brackets are required, and Access adds them for you if you leave them out. In the Validation Rule property, brackets are also required; however, if you omit them, Access adds quotes instead (see Figure 7-6). This schizophrenic behavior means that Access treats your field name as if it is a simple text string. The validation rule > .15 * "orderTotal" is meaningless, since it attempts to compare a numeric field to the string "orderTotal". It will always fail. Replace the quotes with brackets, as in > .15 * [orderTotal], to make it behave.

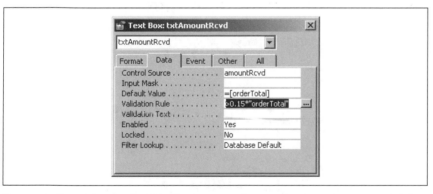

Figure 7-6. This validation rule, which takes 15 percent of a text string, is not what you intended. Use brackets to ensure that Access knows you're referring to a field, not a string.

Another place where Access's penchant for quotes commonly causes trouble is in the Criteria line in the query design grid. As in the examples above, if you want to refer to a field or control name, make sure it's surrounded by brackets, even if you have to put them there yourself.

Last Name, First

THE ANNOYANCE: In Outlook, I can set an option to display person names as "First Last" or "Last, First"—but in Access my mailing list names come out all mushed together, with extra spaces thrown in, too.

THE FIX: It's standard practice in database design to use separate fields for first and last names—but this means that you must recombine them whenever you need to display the full name in a query, form, or report. Fortunately, it's not too hard to do this, but there are a few tricks that make it work better. In a query, for instance, suppose you want a "First Last" display. On the Field line, you could add an expression such as this: **FullName: FirstName & " " & LastName**. The ampersand concatenates strings, so this expression just sticks a space in between the first and last names. That works fine as long as both fields have values, but if any first names are missing (i.e., null), it will tack on a space at the front of the last name, so it won't line up right. A better version is **FullName: (FirstName + " ") & LastName**. This trick relies on the fact that the plus sign is also a concatenation operator for strings. The difference between + and & is that if you "plus" a null value, the entire result is null, whereas if you "ampersand" a null value, it gets ignored. The result is that spaces are added only when first names are *not* null. (You could do the same thing with the IIf (Immediate If) function, but the "plus" gambit is more concise.) Table 7-1 lists some common name expressions with different name orders, for databases with and without spouse names.

Table 7-1. Common name expressions

Expression	Name order
FullName: (FirstName + " ") & LastName	John Adams
LastFirst: LastName & (", " + FirstName)	Adams, John
FullName: (FirstName + " ") & IIf(LastName=SpouseLastName Or IsNull(SpouseLastName), (" & " + SpouseFirstName + " ") & LastName, LastName & (" & " + SpouseFirstName + " " + SpouseLastName))	John & Abigail Adams
LastFirst: LastName & (", " + FirstName) & (" & " + SpouseFirstName) & IIf(LastName<>SpouseLastName, (" " + SpouseLastName))	Adams, John & Abigail

Dates! Dates! Dates!

THE ANNOYANCE: I want to set up an orders query that shows last month's orders. I've looked at the Date functions, and there doesn't seem to be a way to do it.

THE FIX: Although dates show up everywhere in databases, it can be fiendishly hard to craft an expression that delivers just the result you want. The key is understanding how Access represents dates internally. (This approach is complemented by using a calendar table; see "Working with Calendar Dates" in Chapter 4.)

Every date in Access is really a date and a time of day. When you input a date such as **10/21/2004**, what Access stores is *10/21/2004 00:00:00*—which gives both the date and the time in *hours:minutes:seconds* format, using a 24-hour clock (00:00 is the same as 12:00 AM). You don't normally see the time because, by default, Access uses the General Date display format, which omits the time component if it's zero. Despite what's displayed, dates and times are stored internally as just one data type: Date/Time.

Date/Times are represented internally in Access as numbers of type Double (they're double-precision floating points, but the name is Double). The integer part of a Date/Time represents the number of days since the base date (12/30/1899), with negative numbers representing days before that date; the decimal part of a Date/Time number gives the time value as a fraction of 24 hours starting at midnight (see Figure 7-7). For example, 12:00 PM on 12/30/1899 is represented as 0.5, and noon on January 1, 1900 is 2.5. Because of this representation, if you want to combine a pure date value (where the time part equals 0) and a pure time value (where the date part equals 0), you can simply add them—and if you subtract two dates that have the same time, you'll get the number of days in between.

Date/Time:	10/15/2004	6:00:00 PM
Numeric representation:	**38275**	**.75**
	Number of days since 12/30/1899	Fraction of 24 hours

Figure 7-7. Date/Time values are represented in Access as numbers, with the integer part representing the number of days since the base date, and the decimal part representing the time of day.

You can experiment with date numbers by typing **?CDbl(#some date#)** in the Immediate window. You can compare dates using the usual comparison operators (<, >, <=, and so on), and you can specify a date range (endpoints included) using the Between...And operator. If you need to specify a literal date/time value, use the # sign, like this: **#10/21/2004 12:35 AM#**. The # sign does for dates what quotation marks do for text. (See MSKB 210276 for additional useful info about working with dates.)

> **NOTE**
>
> *Tempting as it is, don't use "Date" as the name of a field or expression. "Date" is a reserved word in Access and using it can cause a conflict. Instead, use a specific name such as "OrderDate" or "VisitDate."*

Before we get into specific date problems, take a look at this list of date functions (see also "Visual Basic Functions" in the Appendix):

`Date()`, `Now()`, *and* `Time()`
>   These functions give you the present moment's Date/Time values.

`DateAdd()` *and* `DateDiff()`
>   These two functions let you work with intervals of time (months, days, hours, and so on), adding or subtracting them from dates, or finding the interval between two dates. For example, `DateAdd("m", 2, #2/1/2003#)` adds two months to 2/1/2003, giving 4/1/2003.

`DateSerial()` *and* `TimeSerial()`
>   These functions let you construct dates and times from component values (such as day, month, and year). For example, `DateSerial(2005, 3, 15)` returns the date 3/15/2005.

Other Date/Time functions
>   There are some other VB functions that let you extract particular parts of dates or date names. For example, `Month(#10/21/2004#)` equals 10, and `MonthName(10)` equals October.

Now, let's look at the solutions to some common date problems.

Define a Date Range (Previous Month, Last Two Weeks, and so on)

In your case, to find the previous month's orders, you'll need to add two fields to your query: `orderMonth: Month(orderDate)` and `orderYear: Year(orderDate)`. You'll base your criteria on `DateAdd("m", -1, Date())`, which subtracts one month from today's date. In the Criteria line for orderMonth in the query design grid, put **`Month(DateAdd("m", -1, Date()))`**. For order-Year, put **`Year(DateAdd("m", -1, Date()))`**.

Sometimes it's more convenient to define a range using `Between...And`. To find orders from the past two weeks, for example, add the order date to your query, and in its Criteria line put **`Between DateAdd("d", -14, Date()) And Date()`**.

Find a Specific Date (Last Day of Month, First Day of Previous Month, and so on)

Sometimes you need specific dates, which can be tricky to compute because of the irregularity of the Gregorian calendar. (MSKB 210604 has solutions for many common date expressions. For the date of the previous Monday, see MSKB 210498.) You can often avoid these kinds of computations by using a calendar table.

To find the last day of the month, use this trick with the DateSerial function: the last day of any month is the *0th* day of the *following* month. For example, the last day of August is the 0th day of September, so DateSerial(2004, 9, 0) equals 8/31/2004. To find the number of days in a month (which can be tricky because of leap years), just take the "day" part of the last day of the month. For example, Day(DateSerial(2004, 3, 0)) equals 29.

To find the first day of the previous month, use DateSerial(Year(Date()), Month(Date())-1, 1). Here, we split today's date (Date()) into year and month parts, and subtract one from the month part; then we recombine the whole thing using DateSerial and setting the day to 1. You may wonder what happens if the current date is in January. In that case, Month(Date())-1 equals 0. Fortunately, DateSerial is smart enough to cycle backwards through the months and give you December of the previous year.

Find the Elapsed Time

To find the time in minutes between two date/time values, use DateDiff() with the "n" option. ("n" stands for "minute," since "m" was already taken for "month.") For the time in hours, just divide by 60. For example, DateDiff("n", #10:00 AM#, #4:30 PM#)/60 equals 6.5 hours. Note: this works fine even if your date/time values are not in the same day. (For info about calculating age in months and years, see MSKB 290190.)

Find Overlapping Date Ranges

It's common in the database world to track things like projects and events, which have both start and end dates. Often you need to calculate when different events overlap, but figuring out the exact test to use is a bear. Here's how to do it: two events overlap when EventA.startDate < EventB.endDate AND EventA.endDate > EventB.startDate. Remember, with dates, < means "before" and > means "after," so this is saying that event A overlaps event B *if* event A starts before event B ends, *and* event A ends after event B starts! If these conditions don't give you a headache, they may make a certain amount of intuitive sense. To convince yourself that they are both necessary and sufficient, take a look at Figure 7-8.

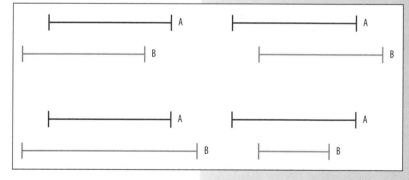

Figure 7-8. When the dates of two events (A and B) overlap, there are four possible relationships between their start and end dates. You can see graphically that in all four cases, Event A's start date comes before Event B's end date, and Event A's end date comes after Event B's start date.

Compare Dates, Ignore Times

THE ANNOYANCE: Our projects table specifies a start and end date for every project. But the dates used for some projects include times as well, and this makes it hard to do date comparisons and to work with date ranges. What's the solution?

THE FIX: First, consider how Access looks at dates. For example, if you set query criteria such as Between #12/01/2003# And #12/15/2003#, you won't include dates such as #12/15/2003 11:00 AM#. That's because #12/15/2003# really means #12/15/2003 00:00:00#, which comes before #12/15/2003 11:00 AM#. (See the previous Annoyance for more on the way Date/Times work.)

There are a few ways around this problem. You can add time specifications in the Between...And operator, like this: Between #12/01/2003# And #12/15/2003 23:59:59#. In this example, we added the latest possible time to 12/15/2003, to include the whole day. But sometimes it's simpler to use comparison operators, bearing in mind time values as well as dates. For example, this is equivalent to the previous expression: >= #12/01/2003# And < #12/16/2003#.

It would be nice if Access provided functions to give you the pure date or pure time parts of a Date/Time value. It doesn't, but you can create these yourself, like this:

Date only
>   CDate(Int(***myDateTimeValue***))

Time only
>   CDate(***myDateTimeValue*** - CDate(Int(***myDateTimeValue***)))

For ***myDateTimeValue***, you can substitute any valid Date/Time field or constant (such as #12/15/2003 3:43AM#).

Working Days Not Working

THE ANNOYANCE: I need to display the number of working days between the start dates and end dates of every job. I tried using DateDiff with the "w" option, but it doesn't work.

THE FIX: It's idiotic, but DateDiff's "w" option—which, by the way, stands for "weekday"—computes the number of weeks between two dates, not the number of weekdays (AKA working days). Another option, "ww", computes the number of calendar weeks, giving you two different ways to count weeks, but no way to find out the number of working days.

There are two different approaches to this problem. First, you can use a custom VB function that counts the weekdays between two dates. This is simple and easy, but it won't take holidays into account. If you need to skip holidays, you'll either need to customize the function to skip them on an ad hoc basis, or use a calendar table (see "Working with Calendar Dates" in Chapter 4). Here's a function for the first approach that accepts two dates and returns the number of weekdays between them. It just loops through every day between the two dates, incrementing a counter if the day is not a Sunday or Saturday:

```
Public Function weekdays(dateStart As Date, dateEnd As Date)
    Dim intNumDays As Integer
    Dim dateNext As Date

    intNumDays = 0
    dateNext = dateStart
    While dateNext <= dateEnd
            If Not (Weekday(dateNext) = vbSunday Or _
                            Weekday(dateNext) = vbSaturday) Then
                    intNumDays = intNumDays + 1
            End If
            dateNext = DateAdd("d", 1, dateNext)
    Wend
    weekdays = intNumDays
End Function
```

To use the calendar table approach, join it to your source table on the date field. Then set criteria on the calendar table fields. For example, you can add the isWorkDay field to your query and set its Criteria line to "True." To exclude holidays, add the isHoliday field and set its Criteria line to "False." To count working days, simply make it a totals query and use a Count expression.

Refer to Subform Properties

THE ANNOYANCE: In order to handle an empty subform, I need to refer to its RecordCount property, but I keep getting a #Name? error.

THE FIX: The syntax for referring to subform and subreport properties is convoluted, but you'll get used to it. This fix discusses subforms, but the same approach applies to subreports.

Here's the short way you'd refer to a subform's Recordset and RecordCount properties from the main form:

```
sctlOrders.Form.Recordset.RecordCount
```

It takes *two* qualifiers to get to the subform:

- The subform control (see the sidebar "Subforms Versus Subform Controls" in Chapter 5), which here is "sctlOrders"

- The Form property of the subform control, which is always "Form"

Likewise, to get to a subreport, you'd reference the subreport control and its Report property.

DateDiff: "w" Versus "ww"

DateDiff provides two different ways to compute the number of weeks between two dates. What's the difference? DateDiff with the "w" option gives the number of complete seven-day intervals between the two dates; it's equivalent to dividing the total number of days by seven and rounding down. By this way of counting, every month will have four weeks.

The "ww" option, on the other hand, gives the number of complete calendar weeks, defined as Monday through Sunday. Any given month, for example, might have only three full calendar weeks.

So what's the reason for this complexity? Access won't let you add one form directly to another form. The only thing you can add to a form is a control. Therefore, Access has a type of control (the subform control) whose purpose is to hold a reference to a subform. Of course, every control has lots of properties (Name, Parent, and so on); the subform control's Form property is where the reference to the subform is actually stored. Note that you never use the name of the subform itself, since the Form property points directly to it.

You'll have to use a longer, fully qualified version of this name in VB code, or when referring to it from database objects that aren't in the main form. For example:

```
Me!sctlOrders.Form.Recordset.RecordCount
Forms!frmCustomers!sctlOrders.Form.Recordset.RecordCount
```

See ".Dot, !Bang, and [Bracket]," earlier in this chapter, for more on fully qualified names.

You may have noticed that you don't need to use the Form property when referring to controls that are on the subform. For example, you can reference a text box on a subform like this: sctlOrders!txtSumOrders. That's because when Access sees a control name, it assumes you mean the subform. Of course, you still need to reference these controls via the subform *control* (i.e., sctlOrders)—not the subform (say, sfrOrders) that it contains.

To put it all together, here's how you might set up a conditional expression, using VB's Immediate If (IIf) function, to avoid referencing a subform control if the subform is empty:

```
=IIf([sctlOrders].[Form].Recordset.RecordCount = 0, 0, [sctlOrders]!
[txtSumOrderTotal])
```

MACROS AND CODE MODULES

Find a Macro Action

THE ANNOYANCE: I'm trying to create a macro that runs a query, but there's no macro recorder like there is in Word. Where do I start?

THE FIX: If you've only used macros in Word, you probably think a macro is a recorded set of keystrokes. Macros in Access are quite different—they're a way for non-programmers to write elementary Visual Basic code. Access provides about 50 predefined "actions" that you use to build macros—kind of like building a house using prefab walls.

The actions range from opening a form to importing a spreadsheet, and you combine them simply by listing them sequentially in your macro. To create a new macro, use Insert→Macro. The only required column is Action. Choose the action you want from the drop-down menu (see Figure 7-9), and then fill in the appropriate arguments in the lower-left pane. For example, the Beep action has no arguments; it just beeps. However, the OpenForm action needs to know *which* form to open, and it accepts optional arguments specifying the form view, Where condition, and so on.

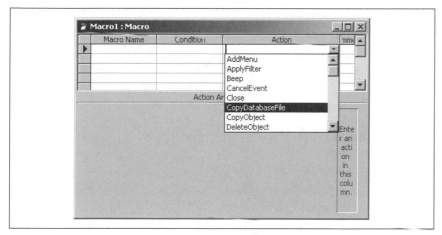

Figure 7-9. There are over 50 choices on the macro Action menu—and no good documentation in recent versions of Access Help. Unbelievable!

Access Help used to provide a useful overview of macro actions, but at some point it got dropped—people must have complained that Microsoft was making it too easy. We've provided an annotated listing of macro actions, grouped by category, in the Appendix.

Tame the Visual Basic Editor

THE ANNOYANCE: I'm looking for a list of the VB Editor's keyboard shortcuts, and I can't find anything in VB Help. They don't even list the VB Editor in Help!

THE FIX: Just when you thought Help couldn't get any worse...if you're like me, you press F1 to open Help, and it's here where Microsoft's designers have thrown you yet another curve ball. Pressing F1 from the Editor only opens up the Visual Basic Language Reference—at least, that's all you'll see on the Contents tab. But if you select Help→Microsoft Visual Basic Help, you'll see topics such as "Visual Basic User Interface Help," "How-to Topics," and so on. Looking for those keyboard shortcuts? Open the "Visual Basic User Interface Help" item, then "Shortcuts."

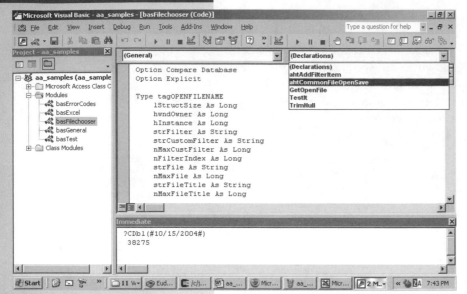

Figure 7-10. The Visual Basic Editor, with some of its windows open. On the left is the Project Explorer—a file tree of all your code modules. In the middle is the code window, and above it, the Object and Procedure menus. On the bottom is the Immediate window.

But there's more than shortcuts to the VB Editor. While we have your attention (don't turn that page!), let's take a whirlwind tour of the VBE (see Figure 7-10), which has some elegant features and some ridiculous quirks.

Navigating Code and Modules

One of the biggest quirks of the VB Editor is that—unlike most code editors—it doesn't treat code files like files. There's no Open command on the File menu, there's no New command, and File→Save tries to save every object in your database. This is *terrible* user interface design. Regardless of how Access stores things (everything does end up in one big MDB file), a code file is still just a text file. As long as you're only putting a line or two of code into an event procedure, this is no big deal, but at some point you'll need to navigate through your code.

To navigate by code module, use the Project Explorer. You can open it from the VB window by choosing View→Project Explorer, typing Ctrl-R, or clicking the Project Explorer button on the toolbar. It shows all your code, both in public modules and in class modules associated with forms and reports. It's a useful way to jump directly to code: just double-click the module name, and it will open in a code window. You can also jump to the form/report object associated with the code by using the View Object button or command. To create a new module, right-click in the Project Explorer and select Insert→Module, or choose Insert→Module from the Database window.

To navigate within a module, use the Object and Procedure drop-down menus sitting atop the code window, which let you jump quickly to a procedure in the current code window. If the Object menu on the left is set to "(General)," the Procedure menu on the right lists all the current procedures. If you're in a class module—say, the code module for a form—the Object menu lists all the objects on the form. If you select one, the Procedure menu will show all available event procedures for that object.

Getting Help

In contrast to Access's Help system, VB Help is actually quite well integrated into the Editor, and it can save you a great deal of time. When you're typing code, you rarely have to look up the exact name of a property or the order of function arguments, since Visual Basic IntelliSense pops open little menus and parameter lists as you type. And you rarely have to type the complete name, since IntelliSense will complete it for you as you type—just press Enter, or a comma or a space, and IntelliSense completes the word (see Figure 7-11).

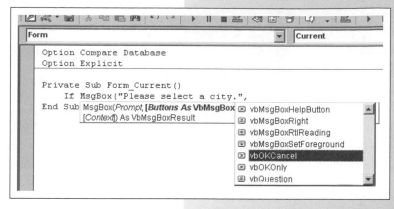

Figure 7-11. VB's IntelliSense works as you type, supplying parameter lists for procedures and drop-down menus for named constants. It's not a substitute for reading the docs, but it does save you the trouble of having to check them every time you want to use a procedure.

If you do need to look up the documentation for a method, object, or property in your code, simply place your cursor on that term and press F1. If there's help available (and there usually is), VB Help will open to the correct page. Of course, this won't work for your own custom procedures, but the Editor does make it easy to jump to procedure definitions from anywhere in your code. Simply place your cursor on the procedure name and press Shift-F2, and the Editor will open the module where the procedure is defined and scroll to the code. To jump back to where you were, hit Ctrl-Shift-F2. To browse all available objects (both custom and built-in) and their methods and properties, use the Object Browser (View→Object Browser). Again, context-sensitive Help via the F1 button is very useful here.

Finally, you'll notice that the Editor checks syntax as you type, looking out for errors such as leaving off a matching parenthesis, omitting an equals sign, and so on. This is great—except when a warning message interrupts you when you've written half a line of code and you then need to go copy something in order to complete it. You can turn off these messages while in the VBE by choosing Tools→Options, clicking the Editor tab, and unchecking the "Auto Syntax Check" box. Your syntax errors will still be highlighted in red.

Debugging

The VB Editor provides the usual complement of debugging tools. Of course, everything that applies to debugging expressions (see "Debugging Expressions," earlier in this chapter) applies to debugging code as well. The Immediate window is particularly useful when you want to check the current value of some property or expression.

For serious debugging, the workhorse of programmers everywhere is the lowly print statement. In Visual Basic it's Debug.Print, which prints to the

Immediate window. For example, to see what's going on in a loop, you could add a print statement such as the following to your code:

```
Debug.Print intCounter; strName
```

The semicolon is used to separate expressions in the same print statement.

You can set breakpoints (see Figure 7-12) by clicking on any code line in the left margin. When you run the code (say, by clicking a button on a form), it will halt at the breakpoint, and the VB Editor will open to that line of code. You can then use the Locals window to view the values of the variables defined in that procedure, as well as the values of relevant objects. To set a conditional breakpoint (for instance, breaking only when a certain expression is true), use the "Add Watch" command available from the right-click menu in the code window.

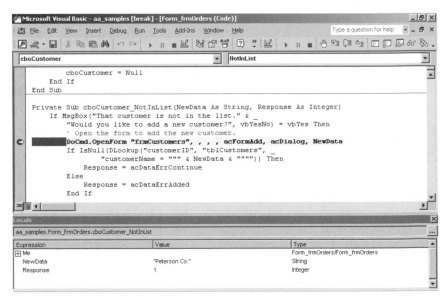

Figure 7-12. A breakpoint was set on the DoCmd.OpenForm line. When the code runs, it stops at the breakpoint and the VB Editor opens to that line. The Locals window shows local variables—in this case, the value of the NewData and Response arguments to the Not in List procedure.

Find a Visual Basic Function

THE ANNOYANCE: I'm trying to find a function that will convert month names into numbers between 1 and 12. VB Help just has a long, alphabetical list of functions.

THE FIX: Obviously, an alphabetical list is only helpful if you already know the name of the function. You'd think Microsoft would provide an overview of functions by topic area—and they do, sort of. The first problem is that you won't find it in the Language Reference under Functions; that would make too much sense. Instead, you must look under Indexes/Lists, which breaks out categories such as math, dates and times, and so on. The second problem is that this list is incomplete, not especially informative, and strangely organized. (For a better overview of functions, we humbly suggest the Appendix in this book.) VB Help also has a Groups section that, despite the meaningless name, has some useful overviews of operators, operator precedence, and data types. It's found in the Visual Basic Language Reference.

That said, unfortunately there is no built-in function that maps month names to integers. However, you could easily use a Switch function for this purpose (Switch(monthName = "January", 1, monthName = "February", 2,), and so on).

Pick the Right Event

THE ANNOYANCE: I want to track which records get viewed, but I can't figure out which form event to use. Forms have so many events—Current, Load, Open, Activate, and so on. How do I choose the right one?

THE FIX: There used to be two Help topics that gave a reasonable overview of events and event orderings: "Events and Event Properties Reference" and "Find out when events occur." In its inscrutable wisdom, Microsoft seems to have taken the first topic out of circulation (although you can still find it on MSDN, and in Access 2000 Help). You can still get info about the order of events by searching for "events" in the Answer Wizard in Access Help, and you'll find an annotated list of events, organized by category, in the Appendix to this book.

To keep track of which records are getting viewed, you'd probably use the Current event, which occurs every time the focus moves to a new record—Load and Open occur only when the form is first opened.

Apostrophe Errors

THE ANNOYANCE: I used the Combo Box Wizard to create a combo box that finds records on our employees form. But we get a syntax error for any employee whose name contains an apostrophe.

THE FIX: When names like O'Brien, O'Malley, O'Reilly, and Children's Hospital cause an error such as "Syntax error (missing operator) in query expression 'lastName = "O'Brien'," it's a sure bet that you've used apostrophes in your string criteria. It's an easy mistake for a beginning programmer to make, but you'd think the Combo Box Wizard would know better!

Here's what's going on. There are many places in code (when running queries, opening forms, applying filters, and so on) where you'll need to construct a criteria string like [lastName] = "O'Brien". Note that the target value of the criteria (here, O'Brien) must be enclosed in quotes. The problem is that these quotes must be embedded in the quoted string criteria, which is tricky to do (see ""Quotes", #Quotes#, and More #%&@!! """"Quotes"""," earlier in this chapter). The correct solution usually looks something like this:

```
Dim strCriteria As String
strCriteria = "[lastName] = """ & Me!cboLastName & """"
```

But since all those quotation marks are confusing to look at, you may be tempted to use single quotes embedded directly in a quoted string:

```
strCriteria = "[lastName] = '" & Me!cboLastName & "'"
```

This is cleaner, and it works because you're allowed to quote the target value in single quotes instead of double quotes (for example, [lastName] = 'Murphy'). However, this trick fails if your target value itself contains a single quote—i.e., an apostrophe—because Access's parser can't tell where your string ends.

The moral of the story: don't use single quotes when you construct string criteria. As for the Combo Box Wizard, you won't run into this problem unless your primary key field is a text field that's allowed to contain apostrophes. If that's the case, you'll have to open up the code (in the combo box's After Update event) and replace each single quote with a pair of double quotes.

Disable Confirmation Dialogs

THE ANNOYANCE: I set up a macro in Access 2002 that deletes old data and imports new data from a text file. But every time it runs, I get a warning message about deleting data (see Figure 7-13). Isn't there some way I can turn that off?

Figure 7-13. By default, Access warns you every time you run an action query.

THE FIX: Those warning messages are great when you need them—and very annoying when you don't. If you really know what you're doing, you can disable them entirely by choosing Tools→Options, clicking the Edit/Find tab (see Figure 7-14), and, in the Confirm section, unchecking the oddly named "Record changes" box (it's really for deletions of individual records), the "Document deletions" box (which is really for deletion of database objects, such as tables or queries), and the "Action queries" box (actually for action queries, such as appends or deletes). Note: this turns off warning messages, but *not* Access error messages.

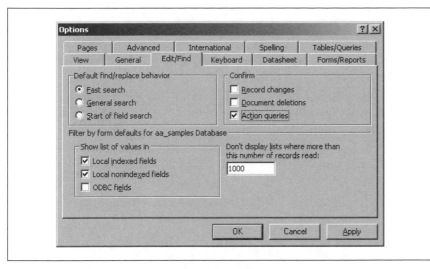

Figure 7-14. In the Confirm section of the Edit/Find tab, the "Record changes" box is for data deletion, and the "Document deletions" box is for deletion of database objects. That make sense?

If you only want to disable confirmations temporarily, just add the SetWarnings action at the beginning of your macro, with its WarningsOn property set to "No." This will disable warnings, but not true error messages. There's no need to turn warnings back on at the end of the macro; Access does this automatically.

If you're writing VB code, you can do the same thing with this line: DoCmd. SetWarnings False. If you turn off warnings in code, however, they will stay disabled until you explicitly enable them again (or until you close Access).

Pause Macro or Code

THE ANNOYANCE: I have a macro that uses the RunApp action to download a text file of Commerce Department financial indicators from a File Transfer Protocol (FTP) site, which is then imported into a database where we run statistics on it. The problem is that Access starts the import before the FTP program finishes the download.

THE FIX: In situations like this, there's no simple way to tell Access to wait for a process to complete. For internal processes, this isn't a problem. For example, a macro that appends data to a table and then opens a query based on that table will automatically wait for the append to complete before opening the query. But when you're running an external application (such as an FTP client) or waiting for user input, Access can jump the gun. We'll discuss fixes for both scenarios, plus a way to create a generic sleep command that pauses execution for a set period of time.

To make Access wait for an external process to finish, you must add some VB code that uses a built-in Windows function called WaitForSingleObject(), which monitors an external process. Don't worry—you don't have to write any code yourself, or even understand how it works. The code is freely available from Access Web (go to *http://www.mvps.org/access/api/api0004.htm*, or search for "Shell and Wait"), thanks to Access guru Terry Kreft. Copy this code into a module. It creates a ShellWait function that's called like this: ShellWait("*fullPathToExternalApp*"), where *fullPathToExternalApp* is the location of the external application. To call the code from a macro, use RunCode instead of RunApp, and invoke the ShellWait function as above. To call this code from your code, of course, you'd use ShellWait directly.

Another common situation is when you want to tell a macro to pause for user input—for example, if you want to open a form, get user input, and then open a second form based on that input. Pausing the macro is not the right solution. When user input is required, a better solution is to allow the user to control the timing of events. For example, you can let the user click a command button on the first form that opens the second form when the user is ready. The Command Button Wizard makes it easy to do this. (See "Wizards" in Chapter 0.)

Occasionally, you may want your running VB code to pause for a fixed amount of time, or to yield to Windows so Windows can process user events such as keypresses or mouse clicks (so, for example, the user can cancel a long-running calculation). To pause for a fixed amount of time, the easiest solution is to use the Windows API Sleep function. To use it in your code, simply declare it in a standard module, like this:

```
Declare Sub Sleep Lib "kernel32" (ByVal lngMilliseconds As Long)
```

Then, call it by placing the number of milliseconds of sleep you want as the argument in parentheses. For example, Sleep(250) gets you 1/4 second of sleep. Place the call wherever you want Access to sleep—the next line of code won't run until Sleep is over. If you're passing a variable to Sleep with the amount of time, you'll want to wrap calls to Sleep in your own procedure and check the validity of the argument before invoking Sleep, since passing invalid arguments to the Windows API can cause your computer to crash.

To yield to Windows so that it can process queued-up events, use the DoEvents function. DoEvents is called without any arguments—it simply yields control to the operating system, and your code pauses until control is returned. Be aware that DoEvents will not return control to your code until the events queue is empty.

Better Error Handling

THE ANNOYANCE: Users get an error on our customers form if they enter a duplicate company name, but the error Access spits out is long and obscure; most users can't figure it out. Can I create my own error messages?

THE FIX: Poorly worded and unhelpful error messages deserve our scorn—but once you learn to write a little code, you can indeed whip up your own error messages (see Figure 7-15). In one case—validation rule violations—it's easy to replace Access's error messages with your own, via the Validation Text property. But for all other error conditions, you'll have to dig a bit deeper.

There are two basic approaches, depending on whether the error arises in Access's code or in your own VB code. Let's take a look at the two cases.

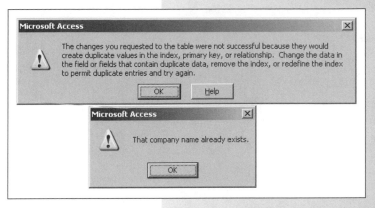

Figure 7-15. Error handling, before and after. The scary default error message is on top; the cuddly custom message is below.

Error Arises in Access

When your users enter a duplicate name and get an error, it's not coming from custom code—there *is* no custom code. It's an Access error, because Access won't let you add redundant data to a field that has been declared unique. Thankfully, every form and report has an Error event that lets you implement custom error handling for just these kinds of errors. Here's an example of the kind of custom error event procedure code you could write:

```
Public Const errNoDuplicates = 3022
Public Const errNoNulls = 3314
...
Private Sub Form_Error(DataErr As Integer, Response As Integer)
    Select Case DataErr
    Case errNoDuplicates
            MsgBox "That company name already exists.", vbExclamation
            Response = acDataErrContinue
    Case errNoNulls

            MsgBox "Company name is a required field.", vbExclamation
            Response = acDataErrContinue
    Case Else
            Response = acDataErrDisplay
    End Select
End Sub
```

As you can see, this procedure is a big Case statement on the DataErr parameter; everything depends on what error triggers the event, and DataErr contains the error number. The Response parameter tells Access what to do once your custom error handler is done running. acDataErrContinue tells Access to suppress its own error messages—we use it because we've already displayed our friendlier message. acDataErrDisplay, on the other hand, tells Access to go ahead and display the default message. We use acDataErrDisplay for the Else case, when an error we didn't anticipate (and don't have a custom message for) occurs. Incidentally, you're not limited to handling data validation errors in the Error event. Any runtime error (such as failed connections, permissions violations, and so on) can be trapped in this event, as long as the form or report is active.

Note, too, that we've defined our own constants for different error numbers. (We recommend defining them outside this procedure in a public module, so they can be referenced from any error procedure.) In order to define them, you must know the error number, but of course Microsoft doesn't make this list readily available. (See the sidebar "Elusive Error Codes" for help.) If you can generate the error—for instance, by entering invalid data in a form—put Debug.Print DataErr into the Error event procedure, and then just look at the output in the Immediate window.

Finally, we should point out that the code in the previous example assumes that duplicate or null errors can arise only in the company name field. That might or might not be a valid assumption. In a more realistic scenario, you'd include tests to determine which field caused the error.

Error Arises in Custom VB Code

The Error event won't trap errors that arise in your own code. For example, if you add invalid data in code, Jet will generate an error—but the Error event won't fire, so the approach the approach described in the previous section won't work. You must trap these errors in your code, and handle them there. Visual Basic supplies a handy mechanism to do just that: the On Error statement.

Here's a typical example:

```
Private Sub cmdAddCompanyName_Click()
    On Error GoTo ErrorHandler
    ... code to add company name
    Exit Sub
    ErrorHandler:
    Select Case Err.Number
    Case errNoDuplicates
        MsgBox "That company name already exists.", vbExclamation
      Case Else
        MsgBox "There was an unexpected error. " & _
                Err.Description, vbExclamation, _
                    "Error Number: " & Err.Number
    End Select
End Sub
```

This code starts with the On Error statement, which tells Visual Basic that if an error arises it should jump to the code that starts with the label "ErrorHandler." (You can, of course, use any label after the On Error GoTo statement.) This code is just like the code we used in the earlier Error event, except it gets the error number from the Err object. The On Error statement tells Visual Basic to suppress its own error messages, and the error-handler code supplies the custom messages. Of course, the handler isn't limited to putting up message boxes—you can also use it to take corrective action, where appropriate. (Note that if your code uses DoCmd statements, Visual Basic may not be able to suppress all of Access's error messages.)

Since the error-handling code is stored right in the procedure, you'll need to make sure that it doesn't execute when there *isn't* an error. That's why error handlers are always preceded by an Exit Sub line, which immediately exits the procedure. If you need to transfer execution back into the body of the sub from the error handler, a Resume statement, such as Resume resumeLabel, can do the job. The label (in our case, "resumeLabel") can be whatever you want.

If you want to define different handlers for different types of errors, you can use the On Error statement multiple times in the same procedure. The On Error statement that was most recently executed is the one that defines the current error handler; only one On Error statement can be in effect at any given time.

Finally, note that the Err object contains only the most recent error. If you're writing DAO or ADO code, especially in a client/server environment, it may be important to trace back through several errors. You can do so by iterating over the DAO or ADO Errors collections.

> **— NOTE —**
>
> *The* On Error *statement has two other forms.* On Error Resume Next *tells Visual Basic to simply skip the line that caused the error and continue at the next line. It's useful in situations where you want to ignore an error.* On Error GoTo 0 *cancels whatever* On Error *statement is currently in effect.*

Elusive Error Codes

It's hard to find error codes in Access. They're not in Help's table of contents, nor in the index; in fact, some versions of Access don't list them at all. Here are some tips for locating them and where you can find some code that will let you generate your own listing.

Jet (DAO) errors

These are the most common data-related errors you'll encounter. To find them, go into Access Help's Contents tab and drill into Microsoft Data Access Objects→DAO Objects Reference. Look up the DAO Error object and its Number property, and follow the link to "Microsoft Jet Trappable Errors."

ADO errors

In VB Help, do an Answer Wizard search for "ADO error codes," or, in Access Help, drill into Microsoft ActiveX Data Objects.

Visual Basic errors

In VB Help, do an Answer Wizard search for "trappable errors."

If you *have* an error code and you need to find its error message, use the AccessError() function. You can use this function to systematically generate all the Jet/VB error codes, by looping and feeding it values from 1 to 3500. MSDN (*http://msdn.microsoft.com*) has code to do this, and it even puts the results in a nice table. To find it, do an MSDN search on "error codes reserved by Microsoft Access." (Don't bother with the companion article on VB error codes; it's buggy and just produces a subset of the full table.) To run the MSDN code, you must refer to the ADOX library. In the VB Editor, select Tools→References and check the "Microsoft ADO Ext. 2.7 for DDL and Security" box. (If your ADO Ext. version is slightly different—say, Ext. 2.8—that's fine.)

Save a Record

THE ANNOYANCE: I need a user data entry form to save the current record before opening a report, to ensure that the report reflects the latest data. There's just one problem: I can't find a command that lets me specify which form record I want to save.

THE FIX: It's quite an oversight that Access forms have Refresh, Requery, and Undo procedures, but no Save Record method. You can resort to calling the Records→Save Record menu command, like this: DoCmd.RunCommand acCmdSaveRecord. But calling the Save Record menu command is an imperfect solution, because it doesn't let you specify which form should receive the Save Record call.

Instead, most developers use an undocumented feature of the form's Dirty property. Access uses the Dirty property to flag whether or not the current record needs to be saved. (A "dirty" record is one that's been changed but not yet saved.) As soon as any edit occurs, Access sets the form's Dirty property to "True." Once the save is completed, the Dirty property is set to "False." However, if a record is dirty and you explicitly set its Dirty property to "False" in code, Access saves the record. Why? I don't know, but it works. In any case, this is the standard idiom for saving a record in a form:

```
If Me.Dirty Then
    Me.Dirty = False
End If
```

Lost Data

THE ANNOYANCE: Users tell me that data they enter in my product description form isn't getting into the database. It's as if they never entered it! I'm not doing anything fancy on this form; how could it lose data?

THE FIX: These symptoms suggest a known bug—and it's a real screamer. Under certain circumstances, Access will silently discard data without any notice. Fortunately, it's not hard to prevent, once you know why it's happening.

When you close a form, Access automatically saves the current record if it's dirty (i.e., if it contains unsaved changes). If the record can't be saved because it has missing or invalid data, Access is supposed to warn you and cancel the close operation (see Figure 7-16). The only problem: this doesn't always happen! You'll get the warning if you close a form using the window's close button, or File→Close, but not if you close it in code with DoCmd.Close (which is the code the Command Button Wizard generates). If Access can't save the record, it simply closes the form without uttering a peep. Microsoft knows about this behavior (see MSKB 207657) but does not consider it a bug!

Figure 7-16. This is the standard error message Access puts up when you try to close a form whose data is invalid. But if you close the same form in VB code, Access gives no warning and simply discards the data.

The fix is to do an explicit save in code before calling DoCmd.Close (see the previous Annoyance, "Save a Record"). It's good practice to do this whenever you're about to move away from a dirty record, even when you know Access won't discard the data. For instance, if you try to move from a dirty record that can't be saved using DoCmd.GoToRecord to another record, your users will get the wonderfully unhelpful message: "You can't go to the specified record." That's sure to cause some gnashing of teeth. Instead, do an explicit save. If the record can't be saved, your users will get a message that explains why, and the opportunity to fix the problem.

Mysterious Syntax Errors, Part Deux

THE ANNOYANCE: I'm trying to use a MsgBox in a Before Update event, and the VB Editor keeps indicating a syntax error—but my syntax follows the example exactly. Am I losing my mind?

THE FIX: This is one of those quirks that makes you want to break something. This line of code is fine:

```
strResult = MsgBox("Hi there!", vbInformation)
```

And so is this one:

```
MsgBox "Hi there!", vbInformation
```

But *this* gives a syntax error:

```
MsgBox("Hi there!", vbInformation)
```

Why? Because Visual Basic has bizarre rules for procedure parentheses. If you're used to programming in any other mainstream language, forget what you know. The easiest solution is to stop using parentheses; they're completely optional anyway. Still, if you want to use them for clarity, here are the rules:

- If you use parentheses for Sub procedures, you must use Call, as in:

  ```
  Call mySub()
  ```

- If you use parentheses for Function procedures, you must either use Call, as in:

      Call myFunction()

  or the return value of the function, as in:

      strResult = myFunction()

  or:

      If myFunction() Then
      ...
      End If

CUSTOM CONTROLS AND EXTERNAL APPLICATIONS

Mysteries of ActiveX Controls

THE ANNOYANCE: I found a button in the Forms Toolbox called "More Controls." It must have several hundred items on it, and I have no idea what any of them are. When I tried to use one, I got an error that said my OLE server was not registered. What is *that* about?

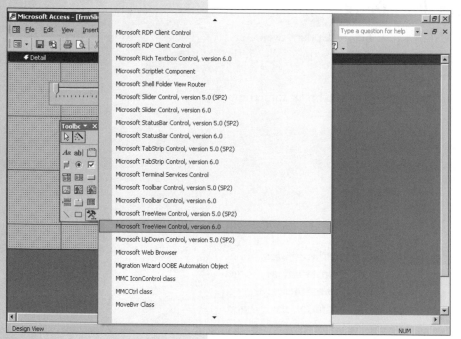

Figure 7-17. You'll see this list of ActiveX controls when you click the More Controls button in the Toolbox.

THE FIX: The "More Controls" button lets you use ActiveX controls (formerly known as OLE controls) in your forms and reports (see Figure 7-17). These controls are similar to Access's built-in controls, except they're *not* built in; they're modular pieces of software that live in their own files (typically OLE Control Extension [OCX] or DLL files). Microsoft Office ships with many ActiveX controls already installed, but the technology is an especially useful way for third-party developers to supply plug-in controls.

You can build many applications without using ActiveX controls, but there are some useful ones that you should know about. For example, a tree-view control presents data in the familiar Windows Explorer–like folder and file view. Some controls, such as the Winsock control for the Windows socket Application Programming Interface (API), don't provide a user interface at all; they provide libraries you can call from Visual Basic. In general, to use any of these controls, you'll have to write a fair amount of custom code.

Before you can use an ActiveX control, you must register it in the Windows Registry. The controls you see in the More Controls list are already registered—that's how Access populates this list. Note that this is a list of all the registered controls on your system; some of these controls may not be appropriate for Access. (See MSKB 208283 for a list of Access-compatible controls.) Furthermore, some of the third-party controls that appear under More Controls may be licensed for use only by end users (not developers). To see the whole list of registered controls and track down their OCX files, select Tools→ActiveX Controls. Click the Register button to register a new control whose file you have acquired (perhaps from a vendor or a shareware site). You can also register controls using *regsvr32.exe* (see "Re-Register Your DLLs" in the Appendix). If you have problems registering a control, see MSKB 249873.

Before you invest a lot of time in learning how to code for an ActiveX control, be aware that the technology has versioning and license problems—many developers turn to these controls only as a last resort. (See "Calendar Controls," later in this chapter, for a typical example.) As you can see from the next few Annoyances in this section, there are often alternatives that use API calls or pure Visual Basic code that avoid the hazards of ActiveX controls.

ActiveX Control Is Missing Events

THE ANNOYANCE: I want to provide a handy way for users to choose values in a fixed range, so I'm trying to use the Microsoft Slider Control that's in the Toolbox under More Controls. But its Updated event doesn't fire when it's moved—and the only other events that are listed for it are focus events. It must have more events than this!

THE FIX: When you use ActiveX controls in Access, the properties sheet that comes up is often incomplete. You can find the complete set of events in the VB Editor (see Figure 7-18). In Design View, open the code module for the form using the ActiveX control by choosing View→Code. The Visual Basic Editor will fire up. Above the module, you'll see two drop-down menus. On the left is a list of the objects in your form; select the slider (Slider0). On the right, you'll see all of its events. In this case, Scroll and Change are probably the ones you want.

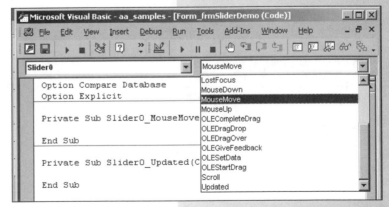

Figure 7-18. Use the Object menu on the left to set the ActiveX control (here, Slider0); the Procedure menu on the right displays all of its events. These events don't all appear in the slider's properties sheet, but you can access them via VB code.

Calendar Controls

THE ANNOYANCE: In Access 2000, we use the ActiveX Calendar control to make it easy for users to pick dates on our events form. It works fine on every machine except the one that's running Windows XP Pro—on that machine, it crashes the database.

THE FIX: Welcome to the ActiveX version of DLL hell. When you use an ActiveX control in an application that's deployed on multiple machines, not only must you ensure that it's installed and registered on every target machine, but you must deal with conflicting versions of the control. The version that's compatible with your application may not be compatible with a user's system. Because of these headaches, many developers avoid using ActiveX controls altogether. In the case of the Calendar control, there are numerous alternatives (see Figure 7-19).

Brendan Kidwell's free Date Picker (*http://www.mvps.org/access/forms/frm0057.htm*) is a simple calendar display built out of standard Access controls. To use it, import his calendar form and module into your database, and call his `InputDateField()` function with this one-liner:

```
InputDateField txtDatefield, "Choose date"
```

The date value automatically shows up in the text box that you specify.

If you need more flexibility (for instance, if you want to display several months at a time) or want a more elegant look and feel, Stephen Lebans has written a free calendar module that avoids versioning and distribution problems by calling the Windows API directly. It's quite a bit more involved to use than DatePicker, but there are good instructions on Stephen's site (*http://www.lebans.com/monthcalendar.htm*).

Because calendar controls are so widely used, there are many other options as well. Tony Toews lists quite a few on *his* site, at *http://www.granite.ab.ca/access/calendars.htm*.

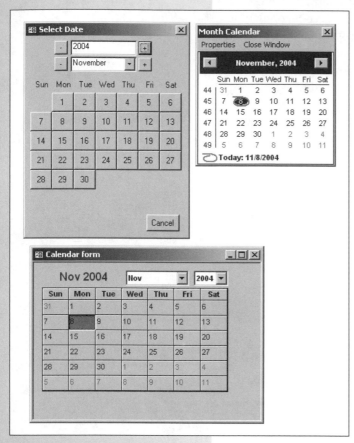

Figure 7-19. Three different calendar controls. At the top left is DatePicker, a pop-up based entirely on native Access controls. A t the top right is another pop-up, called MonthCalendar. At the bottom is Microsoft's ActiveX Calendar Control, embedded in a form.

File Choosers

THE ANNOYANCE: I need to let users browse to and select files from a form, as part of a custom import process. But Access doesn't have a control that does this.

THE FIX: Access *should* have a file chooser control (see Figure 7-20) that's trivial to use...but no such luck. We'll discuss three different solutions: the Windows API, the FileDialog object, and the Common Dialog control. They all require writing a bit of code. Although using the Windows API sounds intimidating, it's really no harder than the others, and it's a rock-solid solution.

Using the Windows API

Writing code that uses the Windows API directly is not for the faint of heart—but fortunately, you don't have to. Access guru Ken Getz has done it for you, and he makes the code freely available on the Access Web (*http://www.mvps.org/access/api/api0001.htm*). The code looks complicated, but it's not hard to use—just copy and paste it into a public module. That gives you a new Visual Basic function

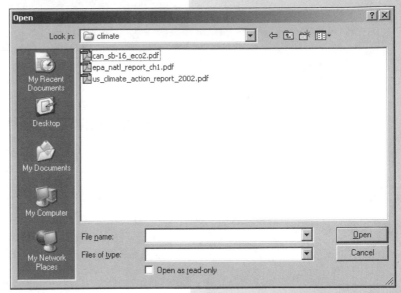

Figure 7-20. Both the Windows API and FileDialog solutions let you give users a native Windows file chooser dialog.

called ahtCommonFileOpenSave(), which is the Windows file chooser function that Access should have come with in the first place. You can call it from Visual Basic or a macro. In addition to ahtCommonFileOpenSave(), you'll see some declarations and helper functions, plus two demo functions: TestIt() and GetOpenFile().

Here's how you'd use this function to open a file chooser with its filter set to text files, and put the resulting choice into a text box on a form. You might use code like this in the Click event of a "Choose File" button. Of course, you won't normally place the resulting filename into a text box control—we've done that just to show you how to get at the filename.

```
Dim strFilter As String
Dim varFilePath As Variant

strFilter = ahtAddFilterItem(strFilter, "Text Files (*.txt)", "*.txt")
strFilter = ahtAddFilterItem(strFilter, "All Files (*.*)", "*.*")
varFilePath = ahtCommonFileOpenSave( _
    Filter:=strFilter, OpenFile:=True, _
    DialogTitle:="Choose the file to be imported")

If Not IsNull(varFilePath) Then
    Me!txtFilePath = varFilePath
End If
```

Note that we're using the named parameter style of VB call (Name:=Value), which makes it easy to keep track of function parameters. Incidentally, there are other parameters in addition to the ones we've used above. For example, if you want to allow multiple file selections, add the Flags parameter, like this: Flags:=ahtOFN_ALLOWMULTISELECT. These parameters are well documented in Ken's module.

Using the Windows API is the most complete and reliable solution. You don't have to add additional libraries, and you don't have to worry about which version of Access or Windows you're running. Because the file chooser API is so integral to Windows, this code will probably work perfectly on Windows 3000.

Using the FileDialog Object

If you're using Access 2002 or 2003, you can use the FileDialog object that comes with Office XP to do this job. First, you'll have to add a reference to the appropriate library. From the VB Editor, click Tools→References and check the "Microsoft Office 10.0 Object Library" box. In addition to being limited to use with recent versions of Access, FileDialog doesn't work with runtime distributions, and it does not support the Save As mode in any Access version (see MSKB 282335).

The following code presents a standard Windows file chooser, and places the resulting choice into a text box on a form. (You can get more info on the different types of FileDialog in VB Help. To handle multiple selections, see MSKB 279508.) Again, you could place code like this in the Click event of a "Choose File" button. Of course, you won't normally place the resulting filename into a text box control—we've done that just to show you how to get at the filename.

```
Dim objFileDialog As Office.FileDialog
Dim varFile As Variant

Set objFileDialog = Application.FileDialog(msoFileDialogFilePicker)
With objFileDialog
    'Multiselect is the default
    .AllowMultiSelect = False
    .Title = "Choose the file to be imported"
    .Filters.Clear
    .Filters.Add "Text files", "*.txt"
    .Filters.Add "All Files", "*.*"

    'If user cancels, Show will be false
    If .Show = True Then
            Me!txtFilePath = .SelectedItems(1)
    End If
End With
```

Using the Common Dialog Control

You can use the Common Dialog control (an ActiveX control available from the More Controls list in the form design Toolbox) to create your file chooser. However, it's notoriously unstable, especially with different versions of Access and Windows. There's no good reason to use it.

Use Excel Functions

THE ANNOYANCE: I need a quartile function for summary statistics for a sales report. If these functions can be built into Excel, why not Access?

THE FIX: Excel's rich menu of functions (see Figure 7-21) puts Access's function list to shame. In every category, Excel's function list is deeper—especially for engineering and statistical analysis. Excel even has a NETWORKDAYS function that actually computes the number of working days between two dates! Imagine that!

The good news is that if you're not afraid of writing a little VB code, it's easy to call Excel functions from Access. The bad news is that you won't be able to use the Excel functions in some of the places you'd probably most like to, such as totals queries, report footers, and other aggregate functions. Nonetheless, being able to call these functions in Access can be useful.

To call an Excel function from Access, you must create a hidden instance of Excel and send it the function call. Be sure that you close

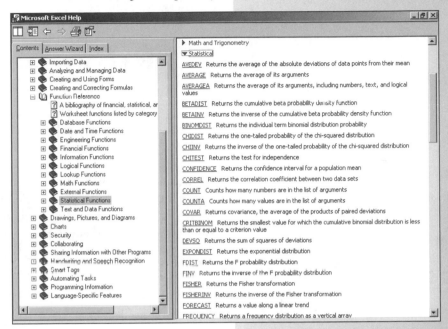

Figure 7-21. Not only does Excel have a far deeper choice of built-in functions than Access, but Excel's Help offers detailed documentation.

Excel when you're done, because loading too many instances of Excel can soak up your memory and bog things down. Open Excel once, reference it in a global variable, and use it for all your function calls. Then close it when you close your database.

If you don't want to hack the VB code, you can either export your data to Excel and do your analysis there, or use a commercial add-in such as the $599 FMS Total Access Statistics (*http://www.fmsinc.com*), which provides a broad array of data analysis features.

Here's a simple example that wraps Excel's CEILING function (which does significant figure rounding) in a function that can be used in Access:

```
Public Function xlCeiling(dblNumber As Double, _
                dblSignificance As Double)
    Dim objExcel As Excel.Application
    Set objExcel = New Excel.Application
    xlCeiling = objExcel.Application.Ceiling(dblNumber, _
                            dblSignificance)

    objExcel.Quit
    Set objExcel = Nothing
End Function
```

Here's a more realistic solution, showing how you'd split this into parts so that you don't have to open and close Excel every time your function is called:

```
Public gObjExcel As Excel.Application

Public Sub initXL()
    Set gObjExcel = New Excel.Application
End Sub

Public Sub killXL()
    gObjExcel.Quit
    Set gObjExcel = Nothing
End Sub

Public Function xlCeiling(dblNumber As Double, _
                  dblSignificance As Double)
    xlCeiling = gObjExcel.Application.Ceiling(dblNumber, _
                                     dblSignificance)
End Function
```

We declare a global variable that refers to our Excel object. Before it can be used, it must be initialized—that's done by calling initXL(). Just call it once before you need to use any Excel functions; then you can define as many different Excel functions as you need. They can all use the same global Excel object. To clean up (before closing your database), be sure to call killXL().

Many Excel functions, such as QUARTILE, accept a range of cells, or an array of values, as an argument. Here's how you'd wrap a function like that:

```
Public Function xlQuartile(ByRef arrNumbers() As Variant, _
                               intQuartile As Integer)
    xlQuartile = objExcel.Application.Quartile(arrNumbers, intQuartile)
End Function
```

OK, that's not so bad. But the real question is how do you get your data into array form in Access? In a database, data is typically stored in rows, not arrays. To get you started, we wrote a version of DLookup() that returns an array rather than a single value. This version is not perfect—for instance, it doesn't handle spaces in names exactly like Dlookup()—but it'll give you an idea of what's possible. For example, if you call it like this:

```
aaDLookup_Array("orderAmount", "tblOrders")
```

it returns an array containing all the values in the orderAmount field of the tblOrders table. To restrict the result set, add criteria like this:

```
aaDLookup_Array("orderAmount", "tblOrders", "orderDate > #2004-10-31#")
```

Here's our version of DLookup():

```
Public Function aaDLookup_Array(strField As String, _
                                strDomain As String, _
            Optional strCriteria As String) As Variant()
```

```
        Dim arrResult() As Variant
        Dim rst As ADODB.Recordset
        Dim strSQL As String

        'Set up SQL WHERE clause, if supplied
        If Not strCriteria = "" Then
                strCriteria = "WHERE " & strCriteria
        End If
        strSQL = "SELECT " & strField & " FROM " & _
                        strDomain & strCriteria

        'Loop through recordset

        Set rst = New ADODB.Recordset
        rst.Open strSQL, CurrentProject.Connection, _
        adOpenStatic, adLockOptimistic

        Dim lngCount As Long
        With rst
                If .RecordCount > 0 Then
                        ReDim arrResult(.RecordCount) As Variant
                        For lngCount = 0 To .RecordCount - 1
                                arrResult(lngCount) = .Fields(strField)
                                .MoveNext
                        Next lngCount
                End If
                .Close
        End With
        Set rst = Nothing
        aaDLookup_Array = arrResult
End Function
```

Create Email Links

THE ANNOYANCE: I'd like to click an email address in my contacts database and have it open my email program, just like a *mailto:* link on a web page. I tried using the Hyperlink data type, but Access thinks my email addresses are web pages.

THE FIX: Behold the Hyperlink data type—a masterpiece of convoluted implementation. When you type an email address into a hyperlink field, Access interprets it like this:

```
phil@yahoo.com#http://phil@yahoo.com#
```

That's because hyperlinks are always stored as multi-part text strings, delimited with the # sign. The first part is the display text, and the second part is the address that Access generates—which by default is a web address. Idiotic! (For more on working with hyperlinks in Access, see "Miscellaneous Export Annoyances" in Chapter 3.) We don't recommend storing email addresses as Hyperlink types, because working with this format is just too awkward. Also, when hyperlinks show up in text boxes on forms, you won't be able to click in the box to edit the data, because Access will follow the hyperlink as soon as you click it. Instead, store your addresses as simple text, and create a Send Email button (or label) on your form by putting one line of code in the button's Click event:

```
Application.FollowHyperlink "mailto:" & Me!txtEmailAddress
```

This code adds *mailto:* in front of the address found in your email text box, and then uses the FollowHyperlink method to pass the address to your email program. It's a simple and effective solution (see Figure 7-22). Make sure you set your default email program in Windows, via the Internet Options control panel. If you need more control over the email (subject lines, CC fields, and so on), see the next Annoyance.

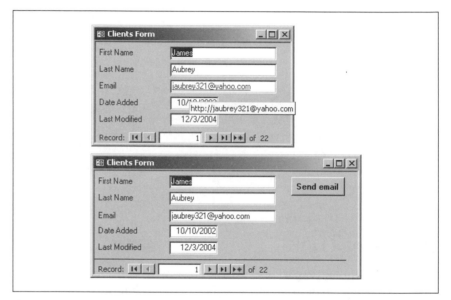

Figure 7-22. Storing email addresses as Hyperlink data sounds reasonable, but it doesn't work well. As you can see from the hover text (top), Access interprets an email address as a web URL. Save yourself the headache, and just store them as text and use a command button (bottom) to hook them up to your email program.

If for some reason you have to use the Hyperlink data type, you can input email addresses into a hyperlink field on a form using Insert→Hyperlink.

To turn a web address into a *mailto:* link, add code such as the following:

```
Private Sub txtEmail_AfterUpdate()
    With Me.txtEmail
        .Value = .Hyperlink.TextToDisplay & "#mailto:" & _
                                .Hyperlink.TextToDisplay & "#"
    End With
End Sub
```

Send Email from Access

THE ANNOYANCE: Twice a week, I need to email reports from our sales database to various departments in our company. Isn't there some way to automate this?

THE FIX: To automate emailing from Access, you'll need to use Visual Basic code that uses the SendObject command (or, alternatively, a macro that uses the SendObject action). In this fix, we'll show you how; at the end, we'll touch on using Outlook automation as an alternative.

SendObject sends email from Access using the default email program on your PC. It lets you specify Subject, Message, To, CC, and BCC fields, as well as a database object (such as a table or report) that will be included as an attachment. You can also specify whether the email is sent immediately, or shows up first in your email program for you to edit. Here's how you might send a report from a form that has an email address on it, using the Click event of a command button:

```
Private Sub cmdSendEmail_Click()
    DoCmd.SendObject ObjectType:=acSendReport, _
                     ObjectName:="rptSales", _
                     OutputFormat:=acFormatHTML, _
                     To:=Me!txtEmailAddress, _
                     Subject:=Me!txtReportName, _
                     MessageText:="Here's this week's report.", _
                     EditMessage:=True
End Sub
```

Note that for clarity, we used the named argument syntax (Name:=Value). All the arguments are optional.

It's common to CC an email to a list of recipients found in a query. Access doesn't make it easy to put these pieces together—you'll have to do it in VB code. Here's how to create a CC string that you could feed to SendObject from a query result set. Place this code before your call to SendObject, and add the line CC:=strCC to that call just after the To argument:

```
Dim rst As ADODB.Recordset
Dim strCC As String
Set rst = New ADODB.Recordset
rst.Open "qryEmailList", CurrentProject.Connection, _
                 adOpenStatic, adLockOptimistic
With rst
    If .RecordCount > 0 Then
        Do Until .EOF
          If Not IsNull(.Fields("emailAddr")) Then
              strCC = strCC & .Fields("emailAddr") & ";"
          End If
          .MoveNext
        Loop
    End If
    .Close
End With
Set rst = Nothing
```

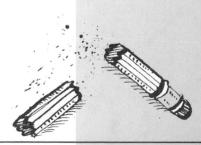

SendObjects is surprisingly flexible and easy to use, but there are some things it won't do: you can't use it to send multiple reports in the same email or to attach files external to Access (such as PDFs), and you can't take advantage of your email program's address book. For such power tricks—assuming you use Outlook—you'll need to write code to automate Outlook from within Access. As a starting point, see MSKB 209948 and 318881. You should also check out Outlook Redemption (*http://www.dimastr.com/redemption*) or Express ClickYes (*http://www.snapfiles.com/get/clickyes.html*), which get around the Outlook security warning that automation provokes in Office 2002 and later.

Appendix

The Devil is in the details—and in the case of Access, it's in the technical appendix. Here you'll find behind-the-scenes particulars about maintaining your Access installation; tips on Access newsgroups that you can turn to for help; dozens of tables detailing Access functions, controls, actions, events; and more.

Installation Checklist

When casual users install Access, they generally run the installer and when it's done, they assume that's that. But Access power users and professional developers know that keeping Access healthy means going beyond what comes out of the box. With some simple preventive maintenance—installing service packs, re-registering DLLs, and so on—you can avoid headaches and mysterious failures too numerous to list. Here are the essentials to keeping Access healthy.

Keep Windows Up-to-Date

Whatever version of Windows you're running, make sure that you have applied the latest security patches and updates. The easiest way to do this is by pointing Internet Explorer at *http://windowsupdate.microsoft. com*.

Keep Office Up-to-Date

Same deal for Microsoft Office. Office updates can be found at *http:// office.microsoft.com/officeupdate*.

Keep Jet 4.0 Up-to-Date

Jet is the database engine under Access's hood, and to minimize bugs, it's essential you apply the latest Jet service packs. (See MSKB 239114 for detailed instructions.) To find out what version of Jet you have, locate the *Msjet40.dll* file; it's usually in the *\Windows\System32* or *\Windows\System* folder. Right-click it, choose Properties, and look on the Version tab. If your version is earlier than 4.0.8618.0, it is *not* up-to-date. Even if you have just purchased and installed the latest version of Access, you can't assume that Jet is up-to-date. (On the other hand, if you have applied the latest service packs, and then upgraded to a new version of Access, you should be fine.)

Install All Access Features

By default, Setup leaves out some Access and Office features you might want later—such as some Wizards or certain Visual Basic Help files. The idea is that you can install them the first time you need them, but that's kind of a pain, having to fetch the install CD over and over. To see what you're missing, run the Add or Remove Programs control panel, click the Microsoft Office entry, then the Change button. This brings up the Maintenance Mode screen. Click the "Add or Remove Features" button, open the Microsoft Access for Windows item, and look for features with a "1" on them. These are features that are installed on "first use." Save yourself time—click each feature's icon and select "Run from My Computer." When you're done, click the Update Now button and you'll install everything you've selected.

Re-Register DLLs

In addition to keeping your software up-to-date, you may occasionally need to re-register DLLs. A DLL file is an external library of functions that Access needs to work properly. DLLs can be shared among different programs, and it's all too easy for one version of a DLL to be inadvertently replaced by another, or for a DLL's listing in the Windows Registry to become corrupted. If this happens, you'll lose the functionality provided by that DLL (for example, importing and exporting text depends on *Mstext40.dll*). Throughout this book we've pointed out how to recognize this situation; here we'll just explain how to fix it.

To re-register a DLL (in this example, *Mstext40.dll*):

1. Find the *regsvr32.exe* utility. It should be on your system, typically in *\Windows\system32*. If not, do a file search for it. If you can't find it, download it from Microsoft (see MSKB 267279 for the details).

2. Click Start→Run, and type something like:

   ```
   C:\Windows\system32\regsvr32.exe C:\Windows\system32\Mstext40.dll
   ```

   and press Enter (see Figure A-1).

Figure A-1. RegSvr32 gives a confirmation message when it runs without error.

Install ODBC Drivers

If you're using Access as a frontend to another database (such as SQL Server, Oracle, or MySQL), you'll need ODBC drivers specific to that database. (If you're connecting to SQL Server, you can also connect via OLEDB.) ODBC drivers for Oracle and SQL Server come standard with Access, but it's a good idea to update those drivers by getting the latest version of MDAC (Microsoft Data Access Components) for your version of Windows. Point your browser to *http://www.microsoft.com/downloads* and search for MDAC. For more info about MDAC, see MSKB 190463. For ODBC drivers for other databases, consult the database vendor.

Access Newsgroups

As you can see in Table A-1, there are quite a few newsgroups devoted to various aspects of Microsoft Access. You'll generally get better results if you search or post questions in the appropriate group. Comp.databases.ms-access is the only general-purpose group, although microsoft.public.access. gettingstarted is also a great place to post newbie or non-specific questions. The most popular groups are those devoted to forms and form coding (i.e., VB code for forms), queries, and reports. To find these newsgroups, go to *http://www.google.com*, click the Groups link, and type the newsgroup name in the box and click the Search Groups button.

Table A-1. Alphabetical list of Access newsgroups

comp.databases.ms-access
microsoft.public.access.3rdpartyusrgrp
microsoft.public.access.activexcontrol
microsoft.public.access.commandbarsui
microsoft.public.access.conversion
microsoft.public.access.developers.toolkitode
microsoft.public.access.devtoolkits
microsoft.public.access.externaldata
microsoft.public.access.forms
microsoft.public.access.formscoding
microsoft.public.access.gettingstarted

Table A-1. Alphabetical list of Access newsgroups (*continued*)

comp.databases.ms-access
microsoft.public.access.internet
microsoft.public.access.interopoledde
microsoft.public.access.macros
microsoft.public.access.modulesdaovba
microsoft.public.access.multiuser
microsoft.public.access.odbcclientsvr
microsoft.public.access.queries
microsoft.public.access.replication
microsoft.public.access.reports
microsoft.public.access.security
microsoft.public.access.setupconfig
microsoft.public.access.tablesdbdesign

Visual Basic Functions

Programmers use functions and statements the way carpenters use hammers and nails. Visual Basic has nearly 150 functions that you can use in expressions or code. It behooves you to become familiar with these off-the-shelf power tools. If you're writing code, you should also familiarize yourself with Visual Basic statements, which are listed in Access Help. (Click the Help button, then the Contents tab, then open Visual Basic Language Reference→Statements.) Statements can't be used in expressions because they don't return a value, but they *do* useful stuff, such as writing to a file or changing the current directory.

In addition to these built-in functions, every menu and toolbar command can be run from VB code using the RunCommand method. For example, you can perform the equivalent of View→Zoom→Zoom 100% by calling RunCommand with the acCmdZoom100 constant, like this: **DoCmd.RunCommand acCmdZoom100**. (To find the constant you need, search for "RunCommand" in VB Help and click the acCommand link or the RunCommand Method Constants item.)

In the following tables (Tables A-2 through A-11) VB functions are grouped by category. The lists are mostly alphabetical, but occasionally we group related functions. Once you find the function you need, look it up in VB Help for details about its arguments and usage. The 10 categories that we use are:

- String manipulation and character functions
- Math functions
- Date and time functions

- Data type conversion and formatting functions

- Files, directories, and environment functions

- Tests and conditional expressions

- Domain aggregate functions (those that operate on sets of records)

- Interactive and process control functions

- Accounting and financial functions

- Other functions for use in Visual Basic code

Table A-2. String manipulation and character functions

Function	Description
Asc	Returns ASCII character code of first character in string, e.g., `Asc("A") = 65`
AscB	Returns first byte of binary data contained in string
AscW	Returns unicode character code of first character in string
Chr	Returns string corresponding to character code of argument, e.g., `Chr(65) = "A"`
ChrB	Returns first byte of binary data corresponding to character code
ChrW	Returns unicode character corresponding to character code of argument
InStr	Finds position of first occurrence of substring within a given string
InStrB	Used with binary data, returns byte position of substring within a given string
InStrRev	Finds position of last occurrence of substring within a given string
Lcase	Returns lowercase version of string
Ucase	Returns uppercase version of string
Len	Returns number of characters in string
LenB	Returns number of bytes in string
Replace	Replaces some or all occurrences of substring in a string with another substring
Left	Returns leftmost character(s) from string
LeftB	Returns leftmost bytes
Mid	Returns middle character(s) from string
MidB	Returns middle bytes
Right	Returns rightmost character(s) from string
RightB	Returns rightmost bytes
Trim	Trims trailing and leading spaces from string
LTrim	Trims leading spaces from string
RTrim	Trims trailing spaces from string
Space	Returns a string consisting of x number of spaces
Split	Splits a string into substrings based on a delimiter. Returns an array.

Table A-2. String manipulation and character functions (*continued*)

Function	Description
StrConv	Performs various case and character set related conversions
StrComp	Compares two strings using alphabetical or other order
String	Returns a string consisting of x number of repeating characters
StrReverse	Reverses the characters in a string

Table A-3. Math functions

Function	Description
Abs	Returns absolute value
Atn	Returns arctangent
Cos	Returns cosine
Exp	Returns inverse of natural logarithm, e.g., Exp(x) = e^x
Fix	Returns integer portion by truncation, e.g., Fix(8.3) = 8, Fix(-8.3) = -8
Int	Returns greatest integer less than or equal to x (a.k.a. floor function), e.g., Int(8.3) = 8, Int(-8.3) = -9
Log	Returns natural logarithm
Partition	Partitions a range into intervals, returning the range label for the interval into which its argument falls
Rnd	Returns a random number between 0 and 1
Round	Rounds a number to specified number of decimal places
Sgn	Returns the sign of the number (negative, positive, zero)
Sin	Returns sine
Sqr	Returns square root
Tan	Returns tangent

Table A-4. Date and time functions

Function	Description
Date	Returns current date
Now	Returns current date and time
Time	Returns current time
DateAdd	Adds or subtracts various intervals of time (days, months, years, etc.) to a given date
DateDiff	Computes the number of time intervals (days, months, years, etc.) between two dates
DatePart	Returns an integer value representing some part of a date, e.g., DatePart("m", #2004-09-30#) = 9
DateSerial	Constructs a date value from year, month, and day values, e.g., DateSerial(2004,9,30)
TimeSerial	Constructs a time value for hour, minute, and second values

Table A-4. Date and time functions (*continued*)

Function	Description
Day	Returns day of the month for a given date, e.g., Day(#2004-09-22#) = 22
Weekday	Returns day of the week for a given date, expressed in range (1-7); default treats Sunday as first day of week, but this can be modified
Month	Returns month of the year for a given date, expressed in range (1-12)
Year	Returns year for a given date, e.g., Year(#2004-09-11#) = 2004
Hour	Returns hour of the day, expressed in range (0-23), e.g., Hour("September 22, 2003 3:11 pm") = 15
Minute	Returns minute of the hour, expressed in range, e.g., (0-59) Minute("September 22, 2003 3:11 pm") = 11
Second	Returns second of the minute, expressed in range (0-59)
MonthName	Returns name of month as string for numeric month, e.g., MonthName(1) = "January"
WeekdayName	Returns name of day of week for numeric value; WeekdayName(1) = "Sunday" by default, but you can set a different first day of week

Table A-5. Data type conversion and formatting functions

Function	Description
CBool	Coerces expression to Boolean data type
CByte	Coerces number (0-255) to Byte data type
CCur	Coerces number to Currency data type
CDate	Coerces date expressions and date strings to Date data type
DateValue	Converts date expressions and date strings to Variant (Date) data type
TimeValue	Converts time expressions and time strings to Variant (Date) data type
CDbl	Coerces numbers to Double data type
CDec	Coerces numbers to Decimal data type
CInt	Coerces numbers to Integer data type, rounding if necessary
CLng	Coerces numbers to Long data type, rounding if necessary
CStr	Converts dates, booleans, numbers, etc. to string
Str	Converts number to numeral string, e.g., Str(7) = "7"
Val	Converts numeral string to number, e.g., Val("7") = 7
FormatCurrency	Formats number or numeric string to currency, with various display options; returns a string
FormatDateTime	Formats date or date string as date, with various display options; returns a string
FormatNumber	Formats number or numeric string as number, with various display options; returns a string

Table A-5. Data type conversion and formatting functions (*continued*)

Function	Description
FormatPercent	Formats number or numeric string as percent, with various display options, e.g., FormatPercent(.15) = 15.00%; returns a string
Hex	Returns a string representing the hex value of a number, e.g., Hex(255) = "FF"
Oct	Returns a variant representing the octal value of a number, e.g., Oct(255) = "377"

Table A-6. Files, directories, and environment functions

Functions	Description
CurDir	Returns full path of current working directory
CurrentUser	Returns username of user currently logged into database (not a VB function...but it's useful, and we refer to it in the text)
Dir	Searches for files or directories matching a given string and attribute set; returns first match
Environ	Returns value of a given environment variable
EOF	Tests file for end of file condition
FileAttr	Returns long value representing mode in which file was opened
FileDateTime	Returns last modified date of file
FileLen	Returns length of file in bytes; use LOF if file is open for editing
LOF	Returns length of file in bytes, for a file that is currently open
FreeFile	Returns integer value representing next file number available for use
GetAttr	Retrieves system attributes of a file or directory
Input	Reads characters from a file; returns a string.
InputB	Reads byte data from a file
Loc	Returns the current read/write position within an open file
Seek	Returns the next read/write position within an open file

Table A-7. Tests and conditional expressions

Functions	Description
Choose	Selects from a list of choices based on value of an index expression that ranges from 1 to the number of choices. For example, Choose(index, "First", "Second", "Third") equals "Second" when index = 2.
IIf	Stands for immediate If; Selects from two choices based on a Boolean expression. If the expression is true, returns the first choice; if the expression is false, returns second choice (e.g., IIf([accountBalance] <= 0, "You're broke", "You've got cash")).

Table A-7. Tests and conditional expressions (*continued*)

Functions	Description
Switch	Selects from a list of choices based on a list of conditions, returning the first choice whose condition is true, e.g., Switch([accountBalance] <= 0, "You're broke", [accountBalance] < $250, "You're poor", [accountBalance] >= $250, "Yippee!").
IsDate	Tests whether an expression can be interpreted as a date.
IsError	Tests whether an expression returns an error.
IsNull	Tests whether an expression has no value.
IsNumeric	Tests whether an expression can be interpreted as a number.

Table A-8. Domain aggregate functions

Functions	Description
DAvg	Returns average of values.
DCount	Returns number of records.
DLookup	Returns value of first record that meets criteria.
DFirst, DLast	Despite the names, not very useful: returns the first (or last) record based on the order in which the records are stored, which is usually meaningless. According to Help, they should be used when you want a "random" record.
DMin, DMax	Returns minimum and maximum values.
DStDev, DStDevP	Returns standard deviation (sample) and estimated standard deviation (population).
DSum	Returns sum of values.
DVar, DVarP	Returns variance (sample) and estimated variance (population).

Table A-9. Interactive and process control

Function	Description
DoEvents	Yields process control, allowing Windows to process events such as key presses or mouse clicks in the middle of a long computation. Does not return until all events in the queue are processed.
InputBox	Displays a prompt that accepts user input in a text box.
MsgBox	Displays a message prompt with various button options (Okay/Cancel, Yes/No/Cancel, etc.).
Shell	Runs an executable program from code.
Timer	Returns elapsed time.

Table A-10. Accounting and financial functions

Function	Description
DDB	Returns depreciation (double-declining balance)
FV	Returns future value of an annuity

What's a Domain Aggregate Function?

Domain aggregate functions let you perform calculations on sets of records in a single expression. For example, suppose you want a calculated expression in a text box that shows the average salary of all employees in the employees table. The DAvg function makes it easy. You could do something like this: DAvg("salary", "tblEmployees"). Domain functions have an optional criteria argument so, for instance, to compute the average salary of employees managed by Bob, you could use DAvg("salary", "tblEmployees", "manager='Bob'").

Note that applying domain functions to large numbers of records can slow Access to a crawl. If that's the case, do the work directly in VB code.

Table A-10. Accounting and financial functions (*continued*)

Function	Description
Ipmt	Returns interest payment of an annuity
IRR	Returns internal rate of return
MIRR	Returns modified internal rate of return
NPer	Returns number of periods for an annuity
Pmt	Returns payment for an annuity
PPmt	Returns principal payment for an annuity
PV	Returns present value of an annuity
Rate	Returns interest rate per period for an annuity
SLN	Returns depreciation (straight-line)
SYD	Returns depreciation (sum-of-year's digits)

Table A-11. Other functions for use in Visual Basic code

Function	Description
Array	Creates an array from a list of values—but returns a Variant type, not a true array
CallByName	Invokes a method on an object using a string name
Command	Command-line arguments
CreateObject	Creates an ActiveX object, based on object class
GetObject	Creates an ActiveX object, based on path to component
CVErr	Returns a custom error number
Error	Returns error message that corresponds to a given error number
Filter	Filters an array of strings based on criteria
GetAllSettings	Returns windows Registry settings for an application
GetSetting	Returns windows Registry setting for a specific key and application
IMEStatus	Current Input Method Editor mode for East Asian languages
IsArray	Tests for array type
IsEmpty	Tests whether a variable has been initialized
IsMissing	Tests whether an optional argument has been supplied to a procedure
IsObject	Tests whether an identifier refers to an object
Join	Concatenates an array of strings
LBound	Finds start value for range of an array index
UBound	Finds end value for range of an array index
MacID	Macintosh constants function
MacScript	Runs an Apple script
QBColor	Converts color codes (0-15) representing standard colors into RGB values
RGB	Constructs RGB value from Red, Green, and Blue values (0-255)

Table A-11. Other functions for use in Visual Basic code (*continued*)

Function	Description
Spc	Returns number of spaces to insert in Print statement
Tab	Specifies tab position for Print statement
TypeName	Returns a string representing the data type of a variable
VarType	Returns an integer constant representing the data type of a variable

Macro Actions

Access has over 50 different actions that can be specified in a macro. (In addition to these built-in actions, every menu and toolbar command can be run from a macro using the RunCommand action.) In the following tables (Tables A-12 through A-17), the actions are grouped by category. The lists are mostly alphabetical, but occasionally we group related actions. Once you find the action you need, look it up in Access Help for details about its arguments and usage. (An easy way to do this is to select the action in the macro design window and press F1.)

The six categories are:

- Work with database objects
- Work with data
- Import, export, and linking
- User interface
- Printing, email, and external applications
- Macro programming

Table A-12. Work with database objects

Action	Description
Close	Closes an open object (query, form, and so on).
DeleteObject	Deletes an object (query, form, and so on).
OpenDataAccessPage	Opens a data access page in page view or design view.
OpenDiagram	Opens a database diagram in design view.
OpenForm	Opens a form in any of various views. You can apply filters, where conditions, data entry, and window modes.
OpenModule	Opens a Visual Basic module to a specific procedure.
OpenQuery	Runs a query, or opens it in design view or print preview.
OpenReport	Opens a report in any of various views. You can apply filters and where conditions.
OpenStoredProcedure	Opens a stored procedure in any of various views.
OpenTable	Opens a table in any of various views. You can set data mode.

Table A-12. Work with database objects (*continued*)

Action	Description
OpenView	Opens a view in any of various views. You can set data mode.
Quit	Quits Microsoft Access.
Rename	Renames a database object. (Note: You can't rename an open object.)
Save	Saves the specified object (form, query, etc.), or the active object if none is specified.
SelectObject	Selects the specified object (form, query, etc.), making it visible and enabling subsequent actions such as Maximize, GoToControl, and so on.

Table A-13. Work with data

Action	Description
ApplyFilter	Applies a filter, a query, or an SQL WHERE clause to a table, form, or report.
FindNext	Finds the next record; used after FindRecord.
FindRecord	Finds a record matching certain criteria.
GoToRecord	Moves to a specific record (by record number) in a set of records, or moves to Previous, Next, First, Last, New or (using offset) jumps back by *N* or jumps forward by *N*.
RepaintObject	Forces pending screen updates on an object (form, datasheet, etc.), e.g., shows values that have been set in a macro but haven't yet appeared.
Requery	Requeries the specified control (or the active object, if no control is specified). This updates the result set, taking into account new, changed, or deleted records.
RunSQL	Runs an SQL statement. You can't run select or crosstab queries this way (use OpenQuery), only action or data definition queries. SQL statement is limited to 256 characters.
ShowAllRecords	Removes any filters from the active table, query, or form.

Table A-14. Import, export, and linking

Action	Description
CopyObject	Copies an object (query, form, and so on) from one MDB to another.
OutputTo	Exports data in table, query, and so on, to specified format (HTML, text, RTF, ASP, DAP, IIS, Excel '98). You can autostart an appropriate application for the output file. Note: Use TransferSpreadsheet for current Excel format; use TransferText to include an import/export specification.
TransferDatabase	Imports, exports, or links database objects between two databases.

Table A-14. Import, export, and linking (*continued*)

Action	Description
TransferSpreadsheet	Imports, exports, or links an Excel or 1-2-3 worksheet.
TransferText	Imports, exports, or links a text file.

Table A-15. User interface

Action	Description
AddMenu	Creates custom/global menus (deprecated).
SetMenuItem	Sets state (enabled/disabled, and so on) of items on menus created with AddMenu (deprecated).
Beep	Returns the system beep
Echo	Turns echo off to hide macro output while it runs (does not hide message boxes or errors).
GoToControl	Moves the cursor (sets focus) to a particular field or control on a datasheet or form.
GoToPage	Moves the cursor to the first control on a specific page, in a form with multiple pages.
Hourglass	Displays hourglass while macro is running.
Maximize	Maximizes the active window.
Minimize	Minimizes the active window.
MoveSize	Moves and/or resizes the active window.
MsgBox	Displays a warning or informational message box.
Restore	Restores a window that has been minimized or maximized. Note: Use the SelectObject action to specify the window.
SetWarnings	Enables or disables system messages (typically used to disable confirmation messages for action queries). Messages are turned back on automatically when macro finishes.
ShowToolbar	Displays or hides a built-in toolbar or a custom toolbar.

Table A-16. Printing, email, and external applications

Action	Description
PrintOut	Prints a report, datasheet, and so on, specifying page range, number of copies, etc.
RunApp	Runs an external application, such as Word or FTP.
SendObject	Sends database object (form, report, and so on) in the body of an email message. You can specify various output formats for objects (XLS, TXT, HTML, RTF), subject line, message, and so on.

Table A-17. Macro programming

Action	Description
CancelEvent	Cancels the event that triggered the macro.
RunCode	Calls a Visual Basic function. Note: You must include parentheses, even if there are no arguments, like this: *myFunction*().

Table A-17. Macro programming (*continued*)

Action	Description
RunCommand	Runs a built-in Microsoft Access command (e.g., from a menu or toolbar).
RunMacro	Runs a macro. You can specify the number of times to repeat, or that it repeats until a condition is satisfied.
SendKeys	Types keystrokes as if input by user (e.g., to fill in a dialog box or send to an external application). Maximum of 256 characters. Timing is unreliable.
SetValue	Sets value of a field, control, or property of a form, report, or control. Note: You must not begin your expression with an equals sign.
StopAllMacros	Stops all macros currently running.
StopMacro	Stops this macro.

Events

Forms include about 45 different event hooks (Open, Close, AfterUpdate, and so on), each of which allows you to run your own code or macro at a certain point in Access's program flow. For example, every time a form is opened, Access sees if any code has been added to the form's Open event, and if it has, it runs it. Writing code in event procedures is a powerful way to customize the way Access behaves.

In the following tables (Tables A-18 through A-22), events are grouped by category. The lists are mostly alphabetical, but occasionally we'll group related events. Note that only forms allow you to use control events; there are no events for controls on reports. The tables also indicate whether an event can be canceled (usually by setting a Cancel parameter equal to True), returning control to the user.

Once you find the event you need, look it up in Access Help for details about its usage. If you need precise information about the order of events, search for "order of events" or look under Programming in Access. The five categories that we use are:

- Window and focus events
- Data events
- Keyboard and mouse events
- Report layout and printing events
- Other events

Table A-18. Window and focus events

Event	Applies to	Description	Cancel?
Open	form, report	Form/report is about to open.	Y
Close	form, report	Form/report is about to close.	
Load	form	Form's record source is about to load.	
Unload	form	Form's record source is about to unload.	Y
Resize	form	Form window is about to resize.	
Activate	form, report	Form/report window is about to become the active window.	
Deactivate	form, report	A different Access window is about to become active. This event doesn't fire if some other application becomes active.	
Enter	controls	Control is about to receive focus from another control on the same form.	
Exit	controls	Control is about to lose focus to another control on the same form.	Y
GotFocus	form, controls	Control is about to receive focus. A form can get focus only if it does not contain any visible, enabled controls.	
LostFocus	form, controls	Control is about to lose focus. A form can lose focus only if it does not contain any visible, enabled controls.	

Table A-19. Data events

Event	Applies to	Description	Cancel?
BeforeInsert	form	New record is about to be created.	Y
AfterInsert	form	New record has just been created.	
BeforeUpdate	form, controls	Data is about to be updated (applies to new/existing records).	Y
AfterUpdate	form, controls	Data has just been updated (applies to new/existing records).	
Change	text box, combo box, tab	User types into a text or combo box, or moves between pages in a tab control.	
Current	form	Some record is about to become the current record. This event fires when a form is first opened, when the user navigates to a different record, or when data is refreshed or requeried.	
Delete	form	A record is about to be deleted. If multiple records are selected for deletion, this event fires once for each record.	Y

Table A-19. Data events (*continued*)

Event	Applies to	Description	Cancel?
Dirty	form, text box, combo box	User is making a change in a bound form or control—typing in a text box, clicking in a combo box, and so on—which would cause the underlying field or record to become "dirty" (edited). (Dirty=unsaved.) Occurs before the change is allowed (and before the Dirty property is set to True). Does not occur for an unbound form or control.	Y
NotInList	combo box	User enters a value that isn't in the list (and LimitToList property is set to Yes). Cannot be canceled, but Response argument determines whether an error message is displayed.	
Undo	form, text box, combo box	User is undoing a change in a bound form or control—clicking Undo or pressing the Escape key. Occurs before the change is undone (and before the Dirty property is set to False). Does not occur for an unbound form or control.	Y

Table A-20. Keyboard and mouse events

Event	Applies to	Description	Cancel?
KeyDown KeyPress KeyUp	form, controls	KeyDown occurs when a key is pressed; KeyUp occurs when it is released; KeyPress occurs when a key is pressed and released. Both KeyDown and KeyPress also occur every time a key repeats due to being held down. When they both occur, KeyPress precedes KeyUp. Keystrokes that are attributed to SendKeys actions or statements also trigger these key events. Key events are received by the control that currently has focus, or (if there's no control available to receive focus) by the form. If the form's KeyPreview property (on the Event tab) is set to Yes, it will receive all key events before they are sent to the control where they originated.	Y

Table A-20. Keyboard and mouse events (*continued*)

Event	Applies to	Description	Cancel?
Click DblClick	form, controls	Click/DblClick occurs when the user clicks/double-clicks the mouse on the control. Forms receive this event if a user clicks/double-clicks the record selector or a blank space in the form that is not within any control or section.	Y
MouseDown MouseMove MouseUp	form, controls	MouseDown occurs when a mouse button is pressed; MouseUp occurs when it is released; MouseMove occurs when the mouse is moved but no button is pressed. Unlike click events, these events tell which button was pressed (1=left and 2=right). The mouse event is received by the control the mouse is over when the mouse button is released, regardless of which control has focus at the time. The form will receive mouse events that occur in the record selector region, and in a region that is outside of any section or control (e.g., around navigation buttons).	Y

Table A-21. Report layout and printing events

Event	Applies to	Description	Cancel?
Format	report sections	A report section is about to be formatted for printing or previewing.	Y
NoData	report	A report that has no data is about to be printed or previewed.	Y
Page	report	A report page has been formatted and is about to be printed or previewed.	
Print	report sections	A report section has been formatted and is about to be printed or previewed.	Y
Retreat	report sections	A report section that cannot be formatted and printed in a single pass is about to get a second pass.	

Table A-22. Other events

Event	Applies to	Description	Cancel?
Timer	form	Fires at regular intervals specified by the form's TimerInterval property (on the Event tab). The interval is specified in milliseconds. If TimerInterval is 0, the event does not fire.	
Error	form, report	Fires when a runtime error occurs. This event includes Access and Jet errors, but not Visual Basic errors.	
BeforeDelConfirm	form	Fires when the delete confirm dialog box is about to be displayed.	Y
AfterDelConfirm	form	Fires when the delete confirm dialog box has just been responded to.	
ApplyFilter	form	Fires when the user applies or removes a filter using Apply Filter, Remove Filter, or Filter By Selection.	Y
Filter	form	Fires when the user begins to create a filter using Filter By Form or Advanced Filter/Sort.	Y

Glossary

ADO

    ActiveX Data Objects. One of two commonly used code libraries for Access programmers writing code that interacts with data. See also the entry for "DAO," and "DAO Versus ADO" in Chapter 0.

automation

    Using Visual Basic code from within one Office application (such as Access) to open a different application (such as Outlook or Excel) and use its features.

backend

    The MDB file (or other database) where the data (i.e., the tables) are stored in a split database design. See also "frontend."

bound

    Tied directly to a data source. See "Bound Versus Unbound Objects" in Chapter 0 for more info.

calculated field

    A field whose value is the result of an expression, such as a field totaling up a customer's purchases.

connection string

    A string used in VB code that tells Access how to connect to a remote database. The string includes the server name and the database name and may contain the username and password.

control

    A design element such as a text box, a combo box, or a label used to build forms and reports. Controls are used both to display data and to accept input.

control source

The place where a control gets its data, and where it stores user input. For example, if a text box has a field in a table as its control source, it automatically displays the value in that field—and when a new value is entered into the text box, it will be stored in that field. Not all controls have control sources.

criteria

See "query criteria."

DAO

Data Access Objects. One of two commonly used code libraries for Access programmers writing code that interacts with data. See also the entry for "ADO," and "DAO Versus ADO" in Chapter 0.

data type

Access handles different kinds of data differently. For example, you can subtract one number from another, but you can't subtract a text string from another text string. Much of the power of databases comes from classifying data and specifying which type of data can go into which fields. Some common data types are Text, Number, and Date.

DBMS

Database Management System. The software that lets you create and use a database. Your customer MDB file is a *database*; Oracle, MySQL, and Access are *DBMSes*.

domain aggregate functions

Domain aggregate functions such as DLookup, DSum, and DAvg allow you to work with sets of records. For example, to compute the average salary of all employees in the employees table, you could employ DAvg as follows: DAvg("salary", "tblEmployees"). For more information, see the entry for "function," and Table A-7 in the Appendix.

DSN

Data Source Name. Provides a sort of Windows shortcut to any ODBC data source (database, spreadsheet, and so on). Once you've defined a DSN (in Control Panel→Administrative Tools→Data Sources (ODBC)), you can just point Access to that DSN and it will know how to get the data out of the remote data source. See also "ODBC."

expression

Any legal combination of symbols that represents a value; for instance, X/Y.

Expression Builder

A tool designed to help you construct expressions. It appears when you click the Build (...) button to the right of any text box where you can type in an expression.

field

For practical purposes, a column in a table—that is, a slot for a particular kind of data. For example, if you want to store cities and states in a table, you'd define one field for the city name and a second field for the state. Then, each row (or record) in the table would consist of one city and one state.

frontend

The MDB file where everything except the data (i.e., queries, forms, reports, and so on) is stored in a split database design. See also "backend."

function

A prewritten procedure or routine that performs a specialized task.

indexing

A technique used to make search (and sort) operations faster; it relies on maintaining a presorted copy of the data.

ISAM

Indexed Sequential Access Method. A kind of data access that allows Access to efficiently process data that's stored in a variety of file types (text files, spreadsheets, and so on).

join

A temporary merging of two tables into a single virtual table.

linked table

A table that is stored not in the current MDB file, but in some remote data source. This could be a second MDB file, or some other data source entirely (a spreadsheet, MySQL database, and so on). A linked table appears in the current MDB simply as a link; the data is viewable and may be modifiable, but the structure of the actual table can be changed only in the data source where it resides.

MDAC

Microsoft Data Access Components. An umbrella term for a collection of related data access technologies including ADO, OLEDB, and ODBC.

MDB file

An Access database file.

ODBC

Open Database Connectivity. A standard that enables different applications, systems, and databases to exchange data. ODBC is oriented toward relational data.

ODBC data source

Any data source for which you have an ODBC driver.

ODBC driver

Software that enables an application to communicate with ODBC data sources.

OLE DB

A Microsoft standard that allows different applications, systems, and databases to exchange data. The successor to ODBC, it works with both relational and nonrelational data.

OLE object

An Access data type that can accept objects or live links to objects, such as pictures, sound files, spreadsheets, or Word documents.

opportunistic locking (oplocks)

A Windows file-sharing protocol that allows multiple clients to share locks on a single file. In a simple locking scenario, once you have a lock on a file, everyone else is locked out until you release it—maybe hours later. Windows is smart enough to contact you if others need access and lets you release the lock temporarily.

parameter

A variable in a query. When the query is run, it prompts the user to supply the value of this variable. Typical examples are start and end dates: run the query, it asks for start and end dates, you supply them, and data is selected based on the values you provide.

query

SQL-based statements that typically retrieve data from tables. They can also be used to modify or delete existing data, add new data, and create new tables.

query criteria

Limitations that narrow down which data you want your query to retrieve. For example, you might *just* want to see sales order totals since March of last year, for the Northeast region. *Since March* and *Northeast region* would be your query criteria.

record

A row in a table or query result. Theorists distinguish between records and rows, but for practical purposes they're the same.

recordset

A set of records that, for programming purposes, can be treated as a single object.

record source

The place where a form or report gets its data (i.e., its records). If you have a customers form that displays the data from the customers table, the customers table is the form's record source.

referential integrity

> If a record in one table refers to a record in another table (see "relationships"), that second record had better exist as long as the first one does. If it doesn't, your data may become meaningless—for example, you could have an order and not know who ordered it. A properly designed database enforces referential integrity, which means that it does everything possible to prevent orphaned records.

relational database

> Contrary to popular rumor, the term "relational" has nothing to do with the table relationships that are used to enforce referential integrity. Instead, it refers to the mathematical construct of a "relation." A relation is any ordered set of objects, such as {"Washington", "George", 1776}. Tables are collections of relations that all have the same structure. There are other kinds of databases that use other mathematical structures as their foundations—for example, hierarchical databases are based on tree structures.

relationships

> When you want a record in one table to refer to a record in another table, you must define a relationship between the two tables. For example, you could create a relationship in which the customerId field in every record in the orders table refers to the customerId field in every record in the customers table. Once you define this relationship explicitly, Access can enforce referential integrity—that is, it will prevent you from deleting one of the related records while leaving the other in place.

sandbox mode

> In sandbox mode, Access won't evaluate expressions that contain functions such as Kill and Shell, which malicious users could employ for nefarious ends. Instead, if it sees such an expression it issues an error message.

SQL

> Structured Query Language. A popular programming language used for querying, creating, and modifying relational databases.

subdatasheet

> A datasheet that is nested inside another datasheet and linked on a specific field. For example, the customers table (in Datasheet View) might have a subdatasheet that shows the selected customer's orders.

subform

> A form that is nested inside another form and linked on a specific field (or fields). For example, the customers form might have a subform that shows that customer's orders.

subreport

> A report that is nested inside another report and linked on a specific field (or fields). For example, the customers report might have a subreport that shows each customer's orders.

unbound

> Not tied directly to a data source. See also "bound."

Visual Basic (VB)

> A programming language (strictly speaking, Visual Basic for Applications, or VBA) that's integrated into Access. You can use VB code to customize the way Access works.

Index

multiple versions of Access, running,
46, 68, 69
MySQL
CASE statements, 183
connection strings, 92
ODBC drivers, 323

N

named parameter style of VB, 313
named ranges, 135
Name AutoCorrect, 14, 60, 190
name expressions, 290
name out of scope, 47
Navigation Buttons property, 197
NETWORKDAYS function (Excel),
315
networking
best practices, 88
network deployment, security failures, 83
network problems, 42
NewData parameter, 209
newsgroups, 29, 323–338
how to ask questions, 30
New Report dialog box, 232, 261
NoData event, 337
NoData event procedure, 239
normalizing data, 98
tutorial, 100
Northwind sample database, 196
NotInList event, 210, 336
Now( ) function, 292, 326
NPer function (VB), 330
nulls
ADO and, 281
setting in a combo box, 217
null names, 280
null values
converting to default values, 279
expressions and, 280
Number data type default values, 17
numeric data, truncated, 129
Nz( ) function, 279, 281
shorthand version, 280

O

objects, 1–3
bound versus unbound, 7–8
object names
spaces in, 289

Oct function (VB), 328
ODBC, 341
data source, 341
drivers, 323, 342
Office Web Components, 133
OLE controls, 310
OLE DB, 342
OLE objects, 342
database bloat and, 58–96
one-to-many relationships, 103
On Error GoTo statement, 240, 306,
307
On Error Resume Next statement, 307
On Error statement, 306
On Load event, 204
OpenArgs parameter, 211
OpenDataAccessPage action (macro),
331
OpenDiagram action (macro), 331
OpenForm action (macro), 52, 63, 64,
196, 198, 210–213, 297, 300,
331
passing filters with, 198
OpenModule action (macro), 331
OpenQuery action (macro), 331
OpenReport action (macro), 198, 243,
331
Error 2501: The OpenReport action
was canceled, 240
passing filters with, 198
WhereCondition argument, 243
OpenStoredProcedure action (macro),
331
OpenTable action (macro), 331
OpenView action (macro), 332
Open Database Connectivity
(ODBC), 41, 89
manual setup, avoiding, 91
Open event, 335
opportunistic locking (oplocks), 42,
89, 342
optimizing performance, 60
optimizing query performance, 152
option groups, 214
Option Group Wizard, 201, 214
Oracle
ODBC drivers, 323
outer joins, 153, 158, 176, 180, 183
Outlook
automating from within Access, 320
running different versions, 70

Outlook Redemption, 320
OutputTo action (macro), 332
OutputTo function, 131

P

pages, 2
Page event, 337
parameters, 162, 342
Parameters command, 241
parameter queries
crosstab queries, 161–183
embedded in expressions, 48
parameter value dialog box, 51
parentheses
Function procedures, 310
procedure parentheses in VB, 309
Partition function (VB), 174, 326
pass-through queries, 65
PDF4U, 245
performance, 59–64
combo box, 220
optimizing, 60
optimizing query performance, 152
permissions, 79
create, 56
delete, 56
write, 56
PivotCharts, 169
PivotTables, 169
Decimal data type problems in, 107
Pmt function (VB), 330
Popup property, 197
pound signs, 285, 291
Power Toys, 18
PPmt function (VB), 330
primary keys, 100
duplicate records, 102
indexing, 15
primary key fields, 207
printer drivers and reports, 252
PrintOut action (macro), 333
Print event, 337
Print Preview, 6, 252
charts and graphs, 271, 272, 274
crosstab reports, 260
report preview too small, 236
procedure parentheses, 309
properties
setting, 6–7

About the Authors

Phil Mitchell has been developing database applications for well over a decade, starting with an embedded database used in a talking electronic map for the blind. He's worked with a smorgasbord of different systems, ranging from the mundane (relational and flat-file databases) to the exotic (native XML and object databases). For the past five years, he's been a lead analyst and programmer at the Harvard University and Harvard Medical School libraries, helping to invent the future of information and knowledge management. Somehow, there always seems to be an Access database involved.

In his other life, Phil is a musician and an active member of Boston's contact improv scene. The most important thing he's doing these days is sustainability activism, as founder of the 2People project.

Evan Callahan has a long history with the BASIC programming language. His first computer program, a "mastermind" logic game, took shape on a RadioShack TRS-80 with 4 K of memory and an external cassette deck for a hard drive. Upgrades ensued, but after 25 years, Evan is still programming in Visual Basic.

Born in Seattle, Evan grew up just a few blocks away from the then-small Microsoft corporate campus. After studying philosophy at the University of Washington, he worked his way into a technical writing job at Microsoft. Evan helped Access take shape in its first four versions—the early Access manuals and Northwind sample database are among his credits.

Evan now splits his time between Access programming, book writing, various nonprofit projects, and a growing family and garden. Evan owns Callahan Software Solutions (*http://www.callahansoftware.com*), a consulting firm specializing in Microsoft Access solutions for small businesses. He is the author of several books on Access and Office, including *Microsoft Access 2002 Visual Basic for Applications Step by Step* (Microsoft Press).

Colophon

The cover fonts are Myriad and Myriad Pro. The text and heading fonts are Linotype Birka and Adobe Myriad Condensed; the sidebar font is Adobe Syntax; and the code font is LucasFont's TheSans Mono Condensed.

Better than e-books

Buy *Fixing Access Annoyances* and access the
digital edition FREE on Safari for 45 days.

Go to www.oreilly.com/go/safarienabled
and type in coupon code WYIK-PTVG-PS3P-HKGY-YT3L

Search
thousands of
top tech books

Download
whole chapters

Cut and Paste
code examples

Find
answers fast

Search Safari! The premier electronic reference
library for programmers and IT professionals.

Related Titles from O'Reilly

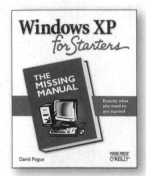

Windows Users

Access Cookbook,
  2nd Edition

Access 2003 Personal Trainer

Access 2003 for Starters:
  The Missing Manual

Access Database Design &
  Programming, *3rd Edition*

Analyzing Business Data
  with Excel

Excel Annoyances

Excel Hacks

Excel Pocket Guide

Excel 2003 Personal Trainer

Excel: The Missing Manual

Excel for Starters:
  The Missing Manual

Excel Scientific and Engineering
  Cookbook

Fixing Access Annoyances

Fixing PowerPoint Annoyances

FrontPage 2003:
  The Missing Manual

Outlook 2000 in a Nutshell

Outlook Pocket Guide

PC Annoyances,
  2nd Edition

PCs: The Missing Manual

Photoshop Elements 4:
  The Missing Manual

PowerPoint 2003 Personal Trainer

QuickBooks 2006:
  The Missing Manual

Quicken 2006 for Starters:
  The Missing Manual

Windows XP Annoyances
  For Geeks

Windows XP Cookbook

Windows XP Hacks,
  2nd Edition

Windows XP Home
  Edition: The Missing Manual,
  2nd Edition

Windows XP in a Nutshell,
  2nd Edition

Windows XP Personal Trainer

Windows XP Pocket Guide

Windows XP Power Hound

Windows XP Pro:
  The Missing Manual,
  2nd Edition

Windows XP for Starters:
  The Missing Manual

Windows XP Unwired

Word Annoyances

Word Hacks

Word Pocket Guide,
  2nd Edition

Word 2003 Personal Trainer

The O'Reilly Advantage

Stay Current and Save Money

Did you know that if you register
your O'Reilly books, you'll get
automatic notification and upgrade
discounts on new editions?

**And that's not all! Once you've registered
your books you can:**

» Win free books, T-shirts and O'Reilly Gear

» Get special offers available only to registered
O'Reilly customers

» Get free catalogs announcing all our new
titles (US and UK Only)

**Registering is easy! Just go to
www.oreilly.com/go/register**